MERCEDES

MW00824180

OWNERS WORKSHOP MANUAL

MODELS COVERED:
MERCEDES TYPE W 123

MODEL	CAPACITY	POWER OUTPUT	DATES OF MANUFACTURE		
200	1988 cc	69kW	1/76	to	6/80
200	1997 cc	80kW	7/80	to	12/84
230	2307 cc	80kW	1/76	to	6/80
230E	2299 cc	100kW	7/80	to	12/84
250	2525 cc	95kW	1/76	to	8/79
250	2525 cc	103kW	9/79	to	12/84
280	2746 cc	115kW	1/76	to	7/81
280E	2746 cc	130kW	1/76	to	3/78
280E	2746 cc	136kW	4/78	to	12/85

Distributed by

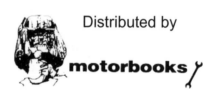

a division of Moport SA (Pty) Ltd.
(Reg No 70/01077/07)
P.O. Box 68801 Bryanston 2021 South Africa

UK distribution
by

Brooklands Books Ltd.,
P.O. Box 146, Cobham, Surrey, KT11 1LG, England.
Telephone: 01932 865051   Fax: 01932 868803
E-mail: info@brooklands-books.com

www.brooklands-books.com

© Copyright 1994 by Delius, Klasing & Co., Bielefeld
Printed in China

CONTENTS

Whilst every car is taken to ensure that the information
in this manual is correct, no liability can be accepted
by the authors or publishers for loss, damage or injury
caused by any errors in, or omissions from, the
information given.

Published by Technibooks

ISBN 0-620-16443-3

All rights reserved. No part of this publication may be
reproduced, stored in a retrieval system or transmitted,
in any form, electronic, mechanical, photocopying,
recording or other means without prior written
permission of Technibooks.

CONTENTS

ENGINE

The Mercedes passenger car, Type W123, is powered by a water-cooled in-line engine, which has 4 or 6 cylinders depending on the displacement.

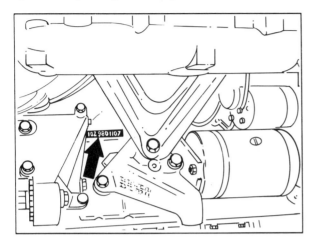

The engine number - arrow - in the MERCEDES engines is engraved on the cylinder block at the front left side under the inlet manifold. It consists of a 6-digit identity number and a 10-digit serial number. Within the identity number the first 3 digits refer to the basic construction of the engine. This means the arrangement of, for example, the camshaft and valves, as well as the construction of the engine block which is the same in all engines in which the first 3 digits correspond with one another. Generally this number is used for the identification of the engine. In the illustration, for example, the engine 102 is represented, besides this the 4 cylinder engines 115 and the 6 cylinder engines 110 as well as 123 are built into the MERCEDES model W123.

The second 3 digit number, in this case 980, indicates that the engine, and in particular the cylinder head is tuned for an injection system.

Often in references to the engine number, the engine end-number is only given, which means the last 6 digits of the serial-number.

The various engines are discussed in separate sections. Chapters which apply to all engines are covered in the section on Engine 102, which is discussed first. Then those few aspects of engines 115 and 123 which differ from Engine 102 are covered.

Engine 102

The identification number 102, which indicates an in-line engine with 4 cylinders, which is fitted either with a carburetor or a fuel injection system. This engine was built into the models 200 and 230 E since July 1980.

The power unit is fitted into the engine compartment longitudinally and can only be lifted out with a suitable crane.

The cylinder bores are embedded in the grey cast iron engine block. In the case of extreme wear or ridging of the cylinder walls, the cylinders can be ground out by a specialist workshop. Subsequently, however, oversized pistons must be installed. The crankshaft is found in the bottom part of the cylinder block, and is supported by 5 crankshaft main bearings. The crankshaft is connected to the connecting rod by means of bearings, which connect to the pistons. The bottom part of the engine is formed by the oil sump in which the engine oil, which is needed for lubrication and assists cooling, collects. The cylinder head is bolted onto the top of the engine block. It is made of aluminium because it has better heat conducting properties and a low specific weight compared to cast iron.

The cylinder head is a cross flow head. This means that the fresh fuel-air mixture flows into one side of the cylinder head and the burned gases flow out of the opposite side. Due to the cross flow arrangement rapid gas-exchange is ensured. The camsahft is found in the top of the cylinder head. It is driven by a timing chain from the crankshaft. A hydraulic timing chain tensioner ensures that the chain always has the correct tension. The camshaft drives the valves by means of rocker arms. The rocker arms rest on adjusting bolts, with which the valve clearance is adjusted during maintenance.

The oil pump takes care of the lubrication of the engine, and is located in the front of the oil sump and is driven by the auxiliary shaft. The auxiliary shaft is situated on the left side of the engine block and is driven by the crankshaft timing chain. The oil is distributed to the bearings of the crankshaft and the camshaft as well as the cylinder bores, by means of bores and pipes.

The water pump is attached to the front of the engine block. The pump is driven by a fanbelt which also drives the alternator. An additional fanbelt drives the power steering pump. It is important that the cooling system is filled with a mixture of antifreeze to give corrosion protection.

The fuel is supplied to the engine through a single Stromberg Flachstrom carburetor which is practically maintenance-free.

The ignition spark is produced by a transistorised ignition system which keeps the ignition point almost constant. The distributor is attached to the left side of the engine block and is gear driven by the auxiliary shaft. In the same way the mechanical fuel pump is driven by a cam on the oil pump shaft, under the distributor.

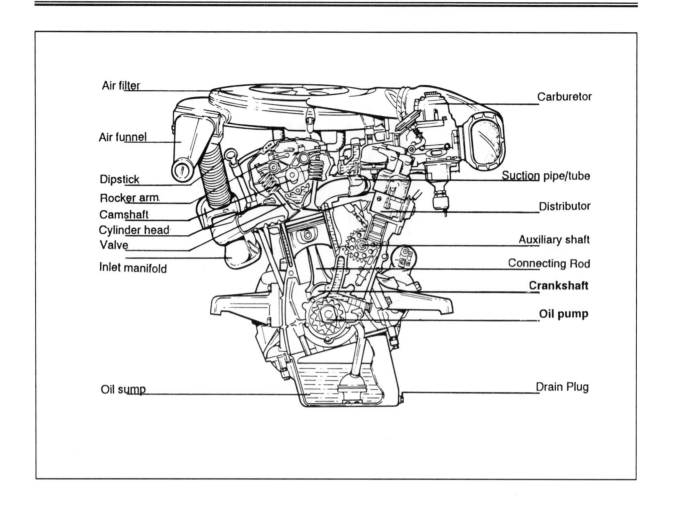

Air filter · Carburetor · Air funnel · Suction pipe/tube · Dipstick · Distributor · Rocker arm · Camshaft · Cylinder head · Valve · Auxiliary shaft · Connecting Rod · Crankshaft · Inlet manifold · Oil pump · Oil sump · Drain Plug

Technical Data

Model	200	200	230	230E	250	250	280	280E	280E
Date	1.76 – 6.80	7.80 – 12.84	1.76 6.80	7.80 – 12.84	1.76 – 8.79	9.79 – 12.84	1.76 – 7.81	1.76 – 3.78	4.78 – 12.84
Type	123.020	123.220	123.023	123.223	123.026		123.030	123.033	
Engine	115.938	102.920	115.954	102.980	123.920	123.921	110.923	110.984	123.984
Displacement cm^3	1988	1997	2307	2299	2525		2746		
Power Kw @ rpm HPc rpm	69/4800 94/4800	80/5200 109/5200	80/4800 109/4800	100/5100 136/5100	95/5500 129/5500	103/5500 140/5500	115/5500 156/5500	130/6000 177/6000	136/5800 185/5800
Torque N.m @ rpm	158/3000	170/3000	186/3000	205/3500	196/3500	200/3500	223/4000	234/4500	240/4500
Bore mm	87,00	89,00	93,75	95,50	86,00				
Stroke mm	83,60	80,25	83,60	80,25	72,45		78,80		
Compr. ratio	9,0:1	9,0:1	9,0:1	9,0:1	8,7:1'	9,0:1	8,7:1	8,7:1	9,0:1
Inlet valve timing *) open after TDC close after BDC	14° 20°	12° 22°	14° 27°	12° 22°	15° 21°	15° 24°	7° 21°		
Exhaust valve timing open before TDC close before BDC	22° 12°	30° 12°	36,5° 18,5°	30° 12°	21° 11°	23° 12°	30° 12°		
Carb/Injector	175-CDTU	175 CDT	175-CDTU	K-Jetronic	4A1	4A1	4A1	K-Jetronic	
Firing order.	1-3-4-2				1-5-3-6-2-4				
Cylinders	4				6				

*): New timing chain with 2mm valve lift.

Engine removal and refitting

The engine complete with gearbox is removed from above. It is recommended to read the chapter on gearbox removal. For the removal of the engine, a crane or engine hoist is needed. Under **no circumstances** may the engine be lowered by means of a trolley jack, as the jack would cause serious damage to the engine.

As several connections also have to be undone working from below the car, four trestles as well as a trolley jack are needed. Before the engine assembly is lifted, the mudguards should be protected by blankets. The bonnet does not need to be removed.

The engine can also be removed without the gearbox. The gearbox must then be supported by a jack and an intermediate layer of wood; connecting bolts must be loosened and the gearbox separated from the engine with a lever.

Caution:

In vehicles with air-conditioning the cooling gas must be released and the system emptied (workshop-job). Only the removal of the 4-cylinder engine will be described, but the procedure is identical for 6-cylinder engines

Removal

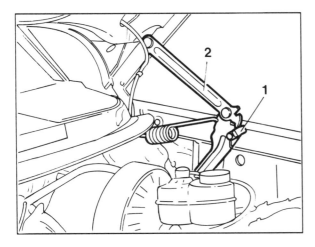

- Open the bonnet into the vertical position. Open the bonnet. Pull the locking lever -1- out of the notch on the left bonnet hinge -2-, lower the bonnet a little to do this so that the locking lever can be loosened. Pull the locking lever out of the notch on the right hinge, and open the bonnet to the vertical position.

Caution

The left locking lever must rest in the top notch of the bonnet hinge.

- Disconnect the earth cable from the battery.

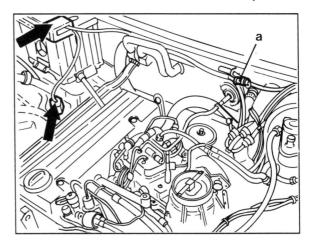

- Disconnect the positive cable, from the battery -arrows- and retainer at the fire wall -a-. Open the cable strap of the fire wall and lay the positive cable over the engine.

- Drain the coolant, see page 79.

- Remove the radiator, see page 74.

- Remove the air filter, see page 98.

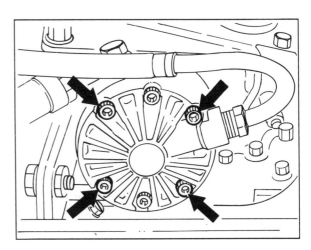

- In vehicles with hydraulic level control: remove the Allenhead bolts -arrows- and put aside the pump with pressure pipes. Undo the retaining cap.

Caution

Do not undo the two inner Allenhead bolts which tighten the lid. These bolts have a continuous thread, visible between the lid and the housing.

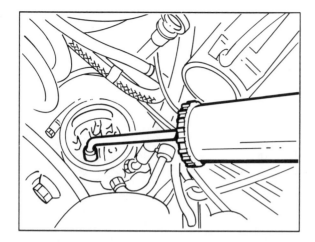

- With an appropriate syringe, suck the hydraulic oil out of the reservoir of the power steering unit or disconnect the pipes from the steering gear and drain the fluid into a suitable container.

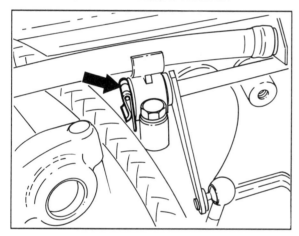

- Remove the axial throttle control shaft. To do this unclip the regulating rods, pull out the safety clip -arrow- , push the shaft to the back and remove.

- Disconnect the coolant pipes at the front coolant flange, at the testing socket and below at the automatic choke. First loosen the hose clamps and push right back.

- Disconnect the bleed tube from the thermostat and waterpump housing.

- Disconnect heating tube from the back of the cylinder head.
- Mark the fuel feed pipe and the fuel pressure pipe with tape and disconnect.

- Pull the grey vacuum lead from the inlet manifold.

- Disconnect the vacuum lead for the brake servo from the inlet manifold and put to one side. Do not lose the washer.

- Mark the following electrical leads, loosen the cable straps and disconnect the leads from their holders: middle cable of distributor cap, green control lead at distributor, earth cable of the testing socket, all the plugs of the testing socket and carburetor, plugs and transmitters for the air mixture gauge, blue plug on the cold starting

valve, black plug on the auxiliary air sliding valve, plug connections on the side airfilter attachments and in front on the inlet manifold. For this press together the serrated surfaces.

- Disconnect the holders for the cable straps in the front of the inlet manifold.

- Disconnect the plug of the alternator. To do this lift out the spring retainer with a small scewdriver and push it aside. Pull out the plug and pull the cables out of the supports.

- Disconnect the electric leads on the starter. If the engine is being removed without the gearbox, remove the starter (except engine 115 and injection engine 102), see page 227.

- Disconnect the cables for the TDC-transmitter at the test socket. To do this remove the two bolts of the socket from the support and pull the grey lead with plug from underneath.

- Put the vehicle on blocks, see page 244.

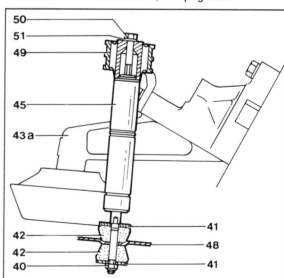

- For vehicles with an engine mounting damper -45-: unbolt the damper at the frame cross-member -48-, by removing the nut -40-. Other illustrated, parts: 41 - washer, 30 mm diameter, 42 - rubber stopper, 43a - engine support, 49 - damper bearing, 50 - bolt M6x45 mm, 51 -spring washer.

- Remove the steering damper.
- Remove the front engine mounting, see page 17.
- Unbolt the exhaust system at the exhaust manifold flange.
- Remove the lower bolt of the starter and undo the support of the speedometer cable.
- Disconnect the chassis earth strap.

Caution:

If the engine is removed with the gearbox, the following jobs are to be undertaken.

- Unbolt the side supports of the exhaust system at the gearbox, undo the clamp bolts of the u-bolt and remove the supports, see page 119.
- Unbolt the propeller shaft at the gearbox, see page 127.
- Disconnect the gear selector rods, see page 132.
- Remove the 2 bolts of the clutch operating cylinder from the gearbox, and lay to one side with pipes connected, see page 129.

Caution:

If the hydraulic pipe is disconnected, the system must be bled after refitting, see page 124.

- Unbolt the pinion shaft of the speedometer drive at the rear gearbox cover and pull it out.
- If the engine and the gearbox are to be separated, remove the engine/gearbox connecting bolts from underneath.
- Put the vehicle on blocks.
- Insert a jack with wooden insert under the gearbox. Jack up the gearbox.

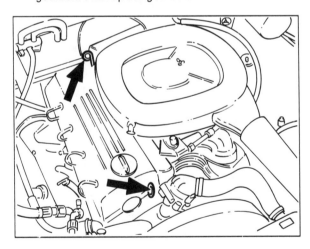

- Lift the engine by hooking a suitable rope or chain to the lifting-eyes -arrow-. Slightly lift the engine with an engine hoist.

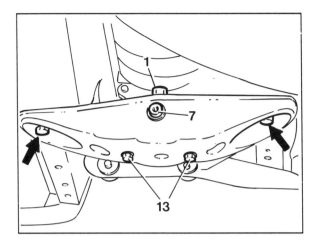

- Remove the rear engine support with the engine mounting, by removing the nut - 1 - and bolts - arrows-.

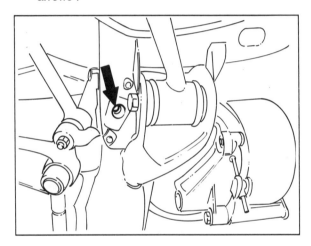

- Remove the bolts, from below, of the engine support on both front engine mountings - arrow - .
- Remove the engine/gearbox connecting bolts from the top.
- Carefully seperate the engine from the gearbox with a lever.

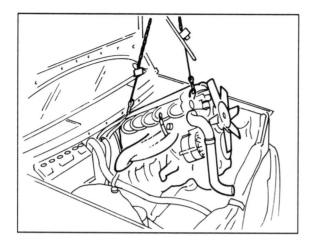 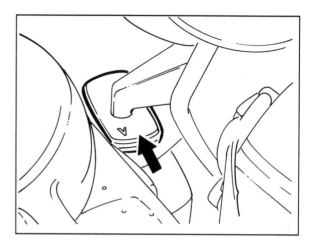

- If the engine is being removed with the gearbox, tilt the unit to an angle of approximately 45 degrees and lift out.

Caution:

The engine must be guided carefully during removal to prevent damage to other components.

Refitting

- Check the engine mounting, coolant, oil, and fuel pipes for porosity or tearing, and replace where necessary.
- Test the engine damper, by holding in position, then pulling apart and pushing together. The damper should move smoothly through the whole stroke. In cases of heavy oil loss, change the damper.
- Test the pilot bearing in the crankshaft, the clutch release bearing and the clutch release lever for ease of movement.
- Check the clutch driven plate for sufficient thickness as well as condition of the friction surface.
- If removed, join the gearbox to the engine and insert into the engine bay together.
- If only the engine was removed, carefully insert the engine into the car. In lowering be careful in guiding the engine, so as not to damage the pinion shaft, gearbox and body.
- Tighten the engine/gearbox connecting bolts.
- Put the vehicle on blocks.
- Insert the bolts for the front engine mounting and tighten slightly

Caution:

Check the position of the tin plate -arrow- at the front right engine mounting.

- Tighten the rear engine support to **70N.m** for the bolt and to **20N.m** for the nut.
- Tighten the bolts for the front engine mounting to **40 N.m.**
- If removed, bolt in the speedometer cable, hook in the gear selector rods and secure with the clips, insert and tighten the clutch operating cylinder. Bolt the shaft and the side supports of the exhaust system to the gearbox.
- Bolt the front exhaust pipe to the exhaust manifold, see page 119.
- Refit the starter, see page 227.
- Insert the engine mounting, tighten and adjust, see page 17.
- If applicable: tighten the engine damper to the frame cross member to 10N.m.
- Refit the radiator, see page 74.
- Insert the triple plug of the cable for the TDC-transmitters into the test socket and bolt the socket onto the support.
- Connect the electrical leads to the starter. Bolt the cables to the support next to the oil filter.
- Lay the leads of the alternator along the front of the engine block and attach. Secure the plug to the alternator with the wire clip.
- Push the plug into the testing socket.
- **Carburetor engine:** Connect plug for the automatic choke, and idle shut-off valve into the carburetor.
- **Injection engine:** Connect blue plug to the cold starting valve and the black plug to the auxiliary air sliding valve.
- Connect the earth strip to the testing socket.
- Attach the green control lead to the distributor, tighten the securing loop.
- Attach the middle lead to the distributor.
- Attach the vacuum pipe of the brake servo to the manifold with the washer and hollow bolt. Attach the thin, grey vacuum pipe to the manifold.
- Attach the inlet and outlet hoses to the carburetor and the fuel pump according to the markings.

- Connect the heater pipe to the back of the cylinder head and secure with a clip.
- Attach the coolant pipes under the automatic choke, to the front coolant flange, to the testing socket and to the lid of the thermostat, secure with clips.
- Insert the axial throttle control shaft and secure with the clip. Push the throttle controls onto the ball-heads.
- Reconnect on the oil-leads.
- Fill up the hydraulic oil for the power-steering, bleed power-steering, see page 154.
- Check the oil level in the engine and the gearbox, fill-up where necessary.
- Check and fill up the cooling system with antifreeze solution, see page 78.
- If removed, refit the suspension oil-pressure pump and torque to 13 N.m.
- Clean the air filter element, replace if necessary, see page 105.
- Refit the air filter, see page 98.
- Attach the positive battery cable to the scuttle dash and connect to the battery terminal.
- Connect the battery earth cable.
- Check ignition timing and adjust if necessary, see page 58.
- Adjust the idling.
- Bring the engine up to operating temperature. Check the cooling system hoses and connections for leaks.
- Check the valve clearance, see page 47.
- Close the bonnet by unhinging the locking lever from the bonnet stays. In lowering, check that both springs are in position.

Front engine mount - removal and refitting/adjusting

The front engine mount is below the engine between the oil sump and the cross member. It must be renewed when the mounting arms are porous or torn, in other words when the hardened plastic plates are perished.

Removal

- Turn the steering totally to the left or to the right.

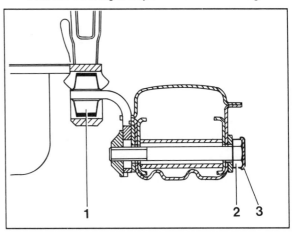

- Lift the locking cap -3- with a screwdriver and push to the side. Unbolt the adjusting bolt -2-.

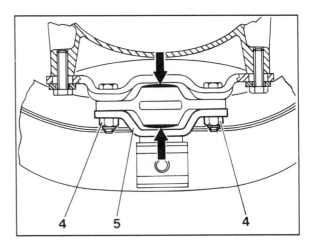

- Remove the nuts -4- and remove the engine mount -1- with the bracket -5-.

Refitting

- Put the engine mount in position and tighten the 2 nuts to 30 N.m

Adjusting

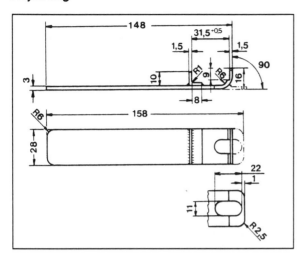

Caution:

A special tool is needed for adjusting, which can be made according to the measurements given in mm.

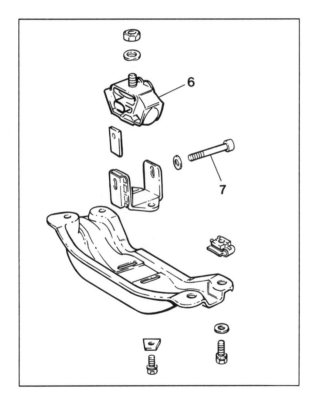

- Completely slacken the adjusting bolt -7- of the rear engine mount -6-.

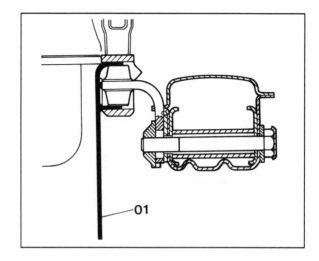

- Attach the adjusting tool -01- to the front engine mount as shown in the illustration.
- Release the tension by rocking the engine in a crosswise direction.
- Tighten the adjusting bolt -7- of the rear engine mount to **30 N.m**.
- Tighten the adjusting bolt -2- of the front engine mount to **130 N.m** and secure with the locking cap -3-.
- Remove the adjusting gauge.

The Crankcase ventilation system

The ventilation of the engine is necessary so that excess pressure cannot build up in the crankcase.

Since the piston rings cannot seal completely, fumes get into the crankcase. Mixed with hot oil and fuel fumes, the resulting excess pressure can damage the crankshaft. To avoid this the fumes are sucked from the engine via a pipe and burned.

The sealed crankcase ventilation system is maintenance-free.

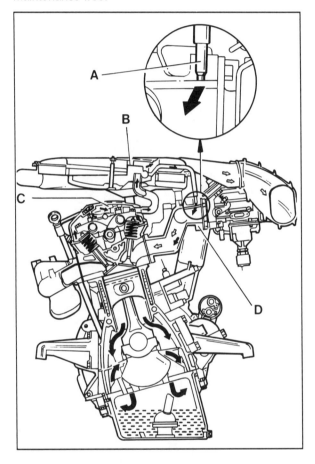

The hot fumes flow through the oil trap -C- in the tappet cover via a pipe to the water trap -B- in the air filter.

The oil is filtered out of the oil trap -C- and flows back to the cylinder head.

From the water trap -B- , the fumes are sucked through a bypass-bore -A- in the manifold -D- and go to the combustion chamber, together with the carburetor air.

The illustration shows the carburetor of a 102 engine.

Welch plug - removal and refitting

The welch plugs are located along the coolant channels and sealed by tin caps. In case of freezing of the coolant due to extreme temperatures, the caps are pushed out, thus preventing damage to the engine block.

Leaking welch plugs must be replaced.

The welch plugs are on the side of the engine block: namely 4 on the right side level with the cylinders as well as one lower down between the third and fourth cylinders. On the left side is another welch plug next to the inner hex head bolt.

- Remove the relevant unit preventing access to the particular welch plug.

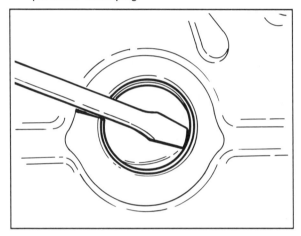

- Place a screwdriver or narrow chisel against one edge of the plug.

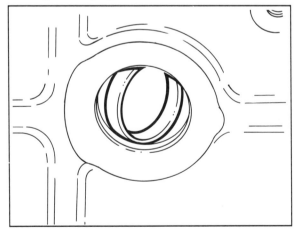

- Hammer the plug carefully on one side until it has turned about 90 degrees.

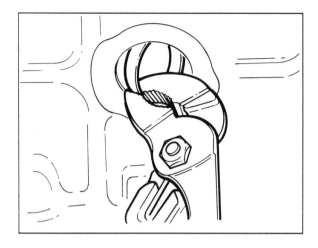

- Pull out the protruding lid with a pair of pipe grips.

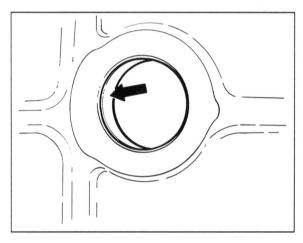

- Clean the welch plug thoroughly. The sealing surfaces -arrow- must be free of grease.
- Brush a sealant onto the sealing surfaces (e.g. Loctite No. 241).

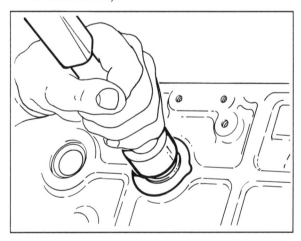

- Hammer the new plug in with a suitable mandrel. Following instructions, allow the sealant to harden.
- Refit the removed units.
- Fill up with coolant, see page 79.
- Warm up the engine and check the level of the coolant as well as the seal of the welch plug.

Timing chain tensioner - removal and refitting/testing

In the case of timing chain noises, which point to a malfunctioning timing chain tensioner, the chain tensioner should be removed and checked.

The timing chain tensioner is bolted to the right side of the crankcase. The spring as well as engine oil pressure, creates the load to tension the timing chain.

Removal

- Remove the fanbelt of the alternator, see page 222.

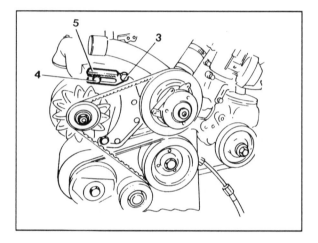

- Swing the alternator clear of the engine, by loosening the tensioning bolt -4- and pushing the support -5- upwards, if necessary loosen the bolt -3-.

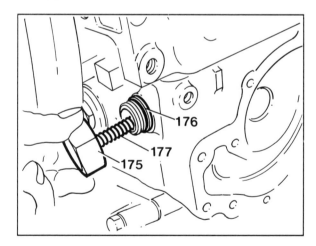

- Remove the nut -175-. **Caution:** The nut is under pressure from the spring -177-.
- Remove the spring and the sealing ring -176-.
- Remove the timing chain housing using an Allenkey (SW 17).

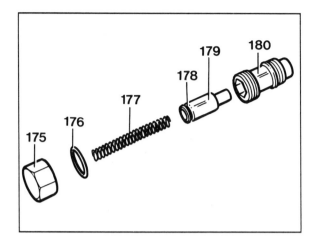

Pull the piston -179- out of the housing -180-.

Testing

- Clean the separate components carefully with fuel and test for re-useability (ridges, wearing). Check the ease of movement of the piston in the housing. Replace damaged parts, or whole timing chain tensioner assembly.

Refitting

- Insert the timing chain casing into the cylinder block and tighten to 10N.m.

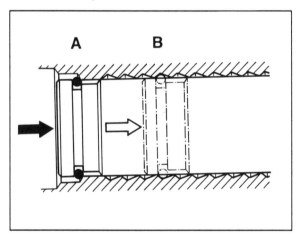

- Push the piston with the circlip -178- up to the notch -A-.
- Fit the new sealing ring, insert the spring and tighten the nut to 70N.m.
- Secure the alternator to the support with the tensioning bolt. Tighten the support to the cylinder head to 45 N.m.
- Refit the fanbelt of the alternator and tension, see page 222.

Timing Chain - removal and refitting

Removal

- Disconnect the earth cable from the battery.
- Remove the green control lead from the transistorised ignition system.
- Remove the air filter, see page 20.
- Remove the rocker cover.
- Remove the spark plugs.
- Remove the timing chain tensioner, see page 20.
- Grind away both pin ends on one link of the timing chain. **Caution:** First place a rag over the cam gear, to prevent any parts from falling into it.

Refitting

- Connect the new timing chain to the old one, while pushing out the opened link.
- Slowly rotate the crankshaft by first putting the car into neutral, tightening the hand brake and attaching a Stillson wrench to the central bolt.

Caution:

The new timing chain must turn the cam shaft sprocket, since the cam timing would otherwise change. One may **not** use the bolt of the cam shaft sprocket, to turn it.

- Disconnect the old timing chain.

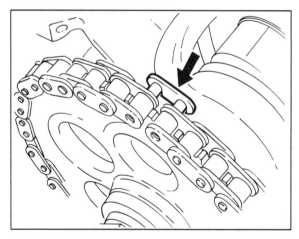

- Connect the new timing chain with the link -arrow-. Hold the ends of the new chain in position with wire. Insert the link from the rear and fit the washers and clips. Remove the wire.
- Adjust the valve timing and check the marking of the cam shaft, see page 24.
- Refit the timing chain tensioner, see page 20.
- Refit the spark plugs.
- Refit the rocker cover.
- Refit the air filter, see page 98.
- Attach the green control lead to the transistorised ignition system.
- Attach the battery earth cable.

Rocker cover - removal and refitting

The rocker cover consists of a magnesium alloy covered on the outside by a layer of black plastic. **Caution:** Contrary to the carburetor engine, the air filter of the injection engine is attached to the rocker head cover only by a rubber stopper. In replacing the cover, the second free threaded tap must be sealed with a plastic stopper to prevent corrosion. Since 10/80, there is a new rocker cover with a new seal to replace the previous version. As a replacement, the new seal can be combined with the cover, but the old seal **cannot** be used with the new cover.

Removal

Caution:

Only remove the rocker cover complete with spark leads and distributor cap.

- Remove the air filter, see page 98.
- Remove the blue plug on the cold starting valve and push the electrical cables on the edge of the cover a little to the side.
- Disconnect all spark plug leads and the distributor cap, see page 60.

- Remove the 5 nuts (SW13) and washers. Remove the rocker cover complete with sparkplug leads.

Caution:

In the case of a stuck rocker cover, do not hit it with a hammer. Try pushing it sideways by hand; if necessary carefully hit the corners with a plastic mallet.

Refitting

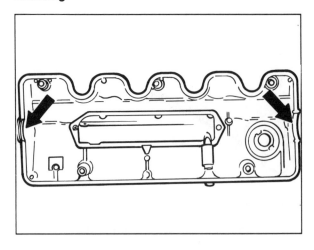

- Test the seals of the rocker cover for damage, and replace if necessary, by first inserting the seal in the front and back -arrows-.

- Place the rocker cover onto the cylinder head.

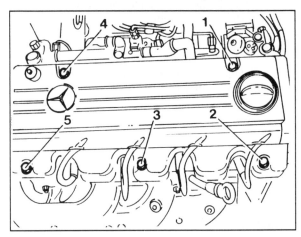

- Tighten the nuts in the shown order from 1 to 5 alternatively. First tighten all nuts to 3 N.m, then all to 6 N.m, then to 12 N.m and finally all nuts in the order from 1 to 5 to 15N.m.
- Refit the spark plug leads and the distributor cap, see page 60.
- Refit the plug to the cold starting valve.
- Refit the air filter, see page 98.
- Run the engine till warm and check the sealing of the rocker cover.

Cylinder head - removal and refitting

Only remove the cylinder head from a cool engine. The exhaust and inlet manifolds remain connected

A defective cylinder head gasket is recognisable by the following signs:

- Loss of performance.
- Loss of coolant. White exhaust clouds from a warm engine.
- Coolant in engine oil; level of oil increases rather than decreases. Oil is grey in colour; bubbles on the dipstick; oil thin.
- Oil in the coolant.
- Strong bubbling in the coolant.
- Low compression in two adjacent cylinders.

Removal

- Open the bonnet vertically, see page 13.
- Pull out the green control lead at the distributor.
- Drain the coolant, see page 79.
- Remove the air filter, see page 98.
- Unclamp the battery earth cable.
- In cars with ride level control: unbolt the oil pressure pump and put to one side, see page 13.

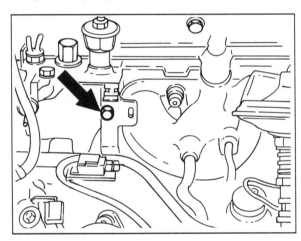

- Remove the mounting bolt -arrow- for the clip of the leakage return line from the engine inlet manifold heater.
- Pull the heater hose away from the cylinder head; open the clip first and push back.
- Mark all the fuel and vacuum hoses on the cylinder head with tape and remove.
- Mark all the electrical cables on the cylinder head with tape and remove.
- Disconnect the return spring of the accelerator linkage.
- Remove the axial throttle regulating shaft, see page 14.

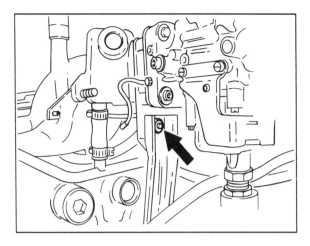

- **Carburetor engine:** Remove the securing nut -arrow-of the bracket of the inlet manifold. **Caution:** Until 6/81 the bracket was attached directly to the inlet manifold.

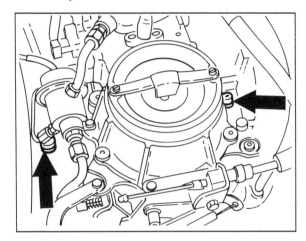

- **Injection engine:** Remove the bolts of the inlet manifold.

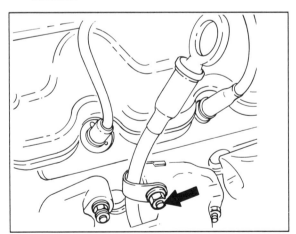

- Loosen the guide tube for the dipstick at the exhaust flange -arrow-. Unclip the pipe, pull out the dipstick and block the guide tube.

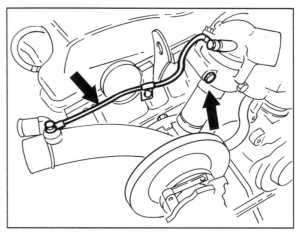

- In vehicles with air-conditioning: remove the bolts to the pipe clips -arrows-.

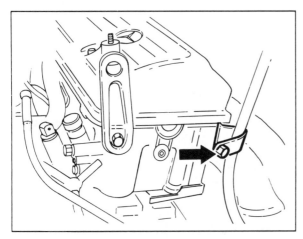

- In vehicles with automatic gearbox: Remove the bolt -arrow- of the dipstick guide tube.
- If present, disconnect the actuating pressure rod and remove the bolt of support for the vacuum lead.
- Disconnect the front exhaust pipe from the exhaust manifold.

- Open the top hose clip of the bypass hose -arrow- and push back.
- Disconnect and remove the bleed lead -left arrow- between the water pump casing and thermostat casing.
- Remove the fanbelt and swing the alternator away the from engine, see page 222.
- Remove the rocker cover, see page 22.
- Set the engine to TDC on the ignition stroke of the first cylinder, by putting the car in neutral, tighten handbrake. Turn the crankshaft by turning the central bolt of the crankshaft pulley with a ratchet wrench and stillson wrench SW 27 in a clockwise direction, i.e. direction of engine rotation, until the following markings are aligned.

Caution:

Do not turn the bolt of the camshaft. **Do not** turn the crankshaft backwards, as the piston of the timing chain tensioner may jump forwards.

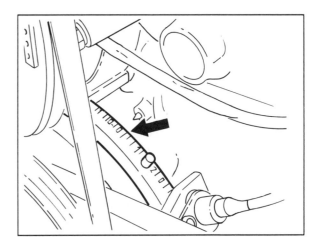

- The TDC mark on crankshaft pulley must be below the pointer -arrow-.

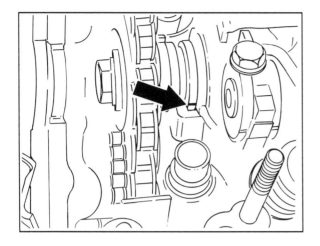

- At the same time the groove in the camshaft must align with the edge of the cylinder head.

Caution:

If the groove on the camshaft cannot be seen while the crankshaft pully is on TDC, turn the camshaft forwards a full cycle. If the markings on the camshaft and crankshaft pulley cannot be brought to alignment turn the engine in such a way, that the marking of the camshaft is flush with the cylinder head and then check the position of the crankshaft to the pointer. If the crankshaft is 6 degrees or more displaced from the pointer, the timing has to be adjusted (workshop job). At a less than 6 degree angle, leave the engine in this position.

- Remove the timing chain tensioner, see page 20.

Caution:

The nut is under pressure. Be careful that the pressure spring does not jump out.

- Mark the position of the camshaft sprocket in relation to the timing chain with paint on both sprocket and chain, so that the chain can be refitted to the same part of the sprocket.
- Remove the bolt -arrow- while holding the camshaft from behind with a flat spanner (SW24).

Caution:

In vehicles with level control, undo the retaining sleeve and camshaft gear with an Allen key. Remove the driving dog bush.

- Remove the camshaft sprocket. Take care that the woodruff key does not fall into the timing case.

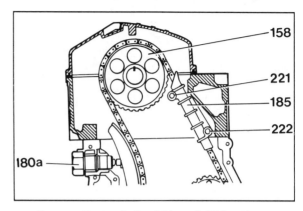

- Remove the two bolts -221- and -222- with an impact wrench and M6 threaded bolt.

If an impact wrench is not available, the bolts can also be removed using a No. 10 nut and M6 bolt (with a length about 3 times the height of the nut). Screw the locknut onto the M6 bolt and place a washer against the locknut. Position the No. 10 nut over the bolt to be removed and screw the M6 bolt into the bolt. Tighten the locknut against the washer. Turn the bolt and locknut together with a socket and open end spanner to remove the bolt.

Caution:

The bolt could be very tight, so only tools in good condition should be used.

- Remove the timing chain guide rail -185-. Other illustrated parts: 158 - camshaft sprocket, 180a -timing chain tensioner.

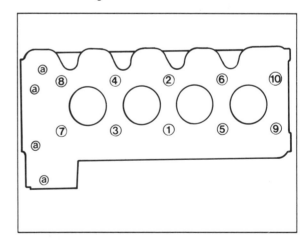

- Remove the cylinder head bolts in reverse order of numbering, i.e. from 10 to 1. For this a special Allen key is needed (e.g. HAZET 990 SLg-12). Do not attempt to use an ordinary Allen key.

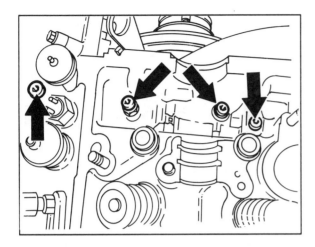

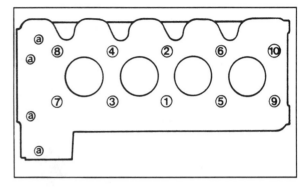

- Tighten the cylinder head bolts in order 1 - 10 in **three stages**.

Caution:

Cylinder head bolts must be tightened very carefully. The torque wrench should be tested for accuracy before starting.

- In tightening the cylinder head bolts in order 1 to 10, first tighten with a torque wrench to **70 N.m**. In the **2nd stage** turn all the bolts **with a special Allen key by 90 degrees**. In the **3rd stage** turn the bolts from 1 to 10 by another **90 degrees with the special Allen key**.
- Tighten the bolts - a - to 25 N.m.

Caution:

In tightening the cylinder head bolts, estimate the turning angles. Insert the special Allen key parallel to the engine and turn until it is at a right angle to engine.

- Refit the guide rail to the cylinder head and refit the bolts.
- Check that the timing chain fits onto the teeth of the crankshaft and intermediary shaft gear.
- Refit the camshaft sprocket to the timing chain so that the markings are aligned.
- If removed, refit the woodruff key into the camshaft.
- Put the camshaft sprocket onto the camshaft, the broader boss goes towards the camshaft. (see illustration page 27).

- Unbolt the 4 special Allenhead bolts -arrows- (e.g. with HAZET key 986 Slg-6)
- Lift the cylinder head. This can also be done with a workshop crane by attaching a suitable rope or chain to the lifting eyes.
- Pull the pressure bolts of the timing chain tensioner forwards (to chain case) out of the timing chain tensioner housing.

Refitting

Before refitting, remove any sealant remains from the cylinder head and cylinder block with a suitable scraper. Take care not to drop any particles into the bores. Cover the bores with a cloth.

- Check the planes of the cylinder head and engine block length and crosswise with a metal ruler for warping or distortion, rectify if necessary (workshop job).
- Check the cylinder head for cracks and ridges.
- Carefully clean oil and other particles from the bores and cylinder head bolts.
- Replace the cylinder head gasket.
- Insert the new gasket without sealant in such a way that no bores are covered.
- Check if the camshaft is in the TDC position before refitting the cylinder head, see "Removal".
- Refit the cylinder head. **Caution:** The cylinder head is located on the cylinder block by dowels. Also insert the supports for the thermostat housing into the coolant short-circuit tube at this point.
- Measure the length of the cylinder head bolts from the bottom of the bolt head. **When new, the length is 119 mm.** Head bolts are to be **replaced** at **122 mm** length.
- Oil the cylinder head bolt threads, refit and tighten by hand.

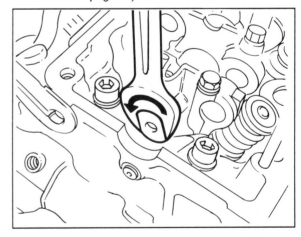

- Tighten the bolt of the camshaft gear to **80 N.m** while holding the other side of the camshaft with a flat spanner.
- In vehicles with level control, first refit the driving dog bush and tighten with an Allen key.

- Refit the timing chain tensioner, see page 20.
- Check the spark-TDC position of the crankshaft and camshaft, see "Removal".

Caution:

To prevent damage to the pistons and/or valves while the engine is turning, the markings must be aligned exactly as at the time of removal.

- Refit the rocker cover, see page 22.
- Refit and tension the fanbelt, see page 222.
- Insert the radiator hose and as with the bypass hose, secure it with hoseclamps. Bolt the bleed tube to the thermostat housing and water pump housing.
- Refit the steering damper and tighten the support for the vacuum lead.
- For vehicles with air conditioning: refit the support for the hoses.
- Refit the guide tube for the dipstick and insert the dipstick.
- Refit the bolt for the inlet manifold support.
- Refit the axial throttle regulating shaft and secure with clips.
- Attach the throttle return spring.
- Attach all coolant, fuel and vacuum hoses and secure with clips.
- Refit the electrical leads according to the markings.
- Refit the front exhaust pipe to the exhaust manifold.
- For vehicles with level control: Tighten the oil pump to 13 N.m.
- Attach the battery earth cable.
- Refit the air filter, see page 98.
- Fill up the coolant, see page 79.
- Check the oil level in the engine and fill up if necessary. If the cylinder head was removed due to a defective cylinder head gasket, it is recommended to do a complete oil change including an oil filter change, since the coolant may have contaminated the engine oil.
- Attach the green control lead to the transistorised ignition system.
- Warm up the engine and check all gaskets.

Note:

It is not necessary to re-tighten the cylinder head bolts or re-adjust valve clearance in a warm engine.

Camshaft - Removal and refitting

Caution:

If the parts of the timing gear are to be re-used, they must be refitted into the same place. To prevent confusion, an appropriate storage board should be used.

The camshaft is located on top of the cylinder head and is removed from above. The rocker housings are integral with the camshaft bearing caps. If a new camshaft is needed, the rocker arms and rocker shafts must also be replaced.

Removal

- Remove the battery earth cable.
- Remove the air filter, see page 98.
- Remove the rocker cover, see page 22.
- Disconnect the green control lead plug from the transistorised ignition system at the distributor.
- Set the engine to TDC on the ignition stroke of the first cylinder, see page 60.
- Remove the timing chain tensioner, see page 20.
- Remove the camshaft sprocket, see page 25.
- Remove the rocker housing, see page 28.
- Remove the camshaft upwards.

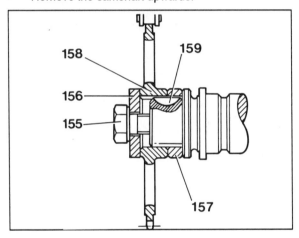

- Remove the Woodruff key -159- and spacing washer -157- from the camshaft. Other illustrated parts: 155 -bolt, 156 - washer, 158 -camshaft-sprocket.

Refitting

Caution:

In case of excessive ridging, the camshaft bearings may be bored out by 0.5 mm in the cylinder head and the rocker bearing blocks (workshop job). Subsequently a camshaft with bigger journals must be installed.

- Thoroughly clean all components with petrol.

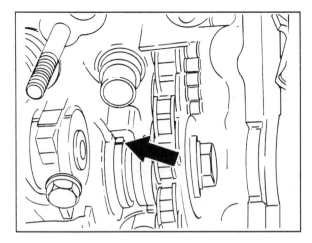

- Oil the camshaft with engine oil and refit so that the groove in the camshaft is in alignment with the edge of the cylinder head -arrow-.

Caution:

If the camshaft is renewed, the rocker arms and rocker shafts must also be renewed. In cases of heavy wear, the camshaft and cylinder head with bearing blocks must be replaced. It is important to change the engine oil and oil filter.

- Refit the rocker housing, see page 29.
- Refit the Woodruff key into the camshaft and fit the spacing washer.
- Refit the camshaft sprocket, see page 26.
- Refit the pressure spring with washer and tighten the timing chain tensioner-nut to 70N.m.
- Check the ignition-TDC position of the engine, see page 60.
- Adjust the valve clearance, see page 47.
- Refit the rocker cover, see page 34.
- Refit the air filter, see page 98.
- Attach the plug to the distributor.
- Attach the battery earth cable.

Rocker Housing/Rocker arm -removal and refitting

Caution:

The rocker housings may not be interchanged for one another.

Removal

- Remove the air filter, see page 98.
- Remove the rocker cover, see page 22
- Remove the green control lead from the transistorised ignition system at the distributor.
- Set the engine to ignition-TDC. The marking on the camshaft must be in alignment with the edge of the cylinder head, see page 25.
- Remove the nut of the timing chain tensioner. **Caution:** The nut is under pressure, do not lose the pressure spring. Remove the pressure spring and washer, see page 20.

Caution:

As long as at least one rocker housing remains fitted, the camshaft sprocket does not need to be removed.

- Remove the camshaft sprocket, see page 25.
- Release the lock nut of the valve-clearance adjusting bolt and backoff the adjusting bolt as much as possible.

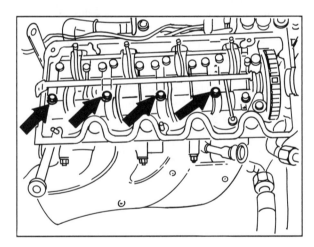

- Remove the oil pipe -arrow-

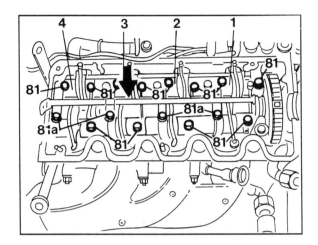

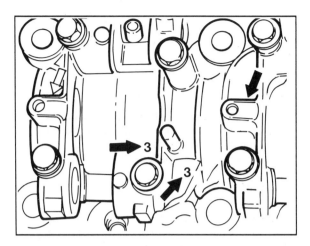

- Remove the bolts -81- and remove the rocker housings -1,2,3,4. Loosen any tight housings with a rubber hammer.
- Remove the housings together with the rocker shaft and rocker arm.

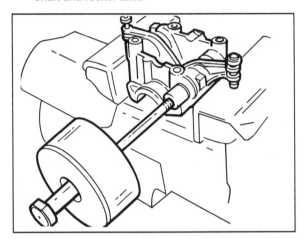

- To remove the rocker arms, the rocker shaft must be pulled out, by bolting an M8 bolt into the rocker shaft and pulling out the shaft.

Refitting

If the camshaft is renewed, the rocker arms and rocker shafts must also be renewed.

If a rocker housing is defective, it can be replaced by a spare-part housing. The spare-part cover bracket has a 0.05 mm larger camshaft cut-away in order to prevent the camshaft from jamming. **Caution:** If two or more housings need replacing, attach one at a time, turning the camshaft requently to test for ease of movement.

Caution:

The rocker housings may not be interchanged, which is why they are marked on the right side with the numbers 1,2,3 and 4. The marking of the housings must coincide with the number cast into the cylinder head -arrow-. If the housings are replaced, the respective numbers must be engraved.

Differences in the rocker housings:
Front housing: Number 1, has two journals.
Middle housings: Numbers 2 and 3, have one journal each.
Back housing: Number 4, has a connecting bore for the oil pipe.

- Oil the camshaft journals with engine oil.
- Refit the rocker housings in such a way that the holes for the 4 oil pipes face to the rear -arrows above-. The numbers on the housings must be on the right side (seen in the direction of driving) and must correspond with those on the cylinder head. The housings are each located by 2 dowels.
- Oil the rocker arm and rocker shafts and refit the housings.
- Refit the oil pipe, bolt in the bolts -81 and 81a as shown in the illustration (top left).

Caution:

Before refitting the bolts for the rocker housingss, turn the rocker shafts so that the cut-aways are aligned with the bores.

- Refit the camshaft sprocket, see page 25.
- Tighten the housing (bearing cap) bolts to **21 N.m.**

Caution:

The bolts may only be tightened when the rocker arms are unloaded. Unloaded rocker arms allow them to be moved up and down and turn the crankshaft further if necessary. Turn the camshaft while tightening the bolts to prevent jamming.

- Refit the pressure spring with it's washer and tighten the nut of the timing chain tensioner to 70N.m.
- Set the engine to ignition TDC and check the position of the camshaft, see pages 60/25.
- Adjust the valve clearance, see page 47.

- Refit the rocker cover, see page 22.
- Refit the air filter, see page 98.
- Refit the plug leads.

Valve stem seal replacement

Excessive oil usage can point to worn valve stem seals. The valve stem seals can also be replaced without removing the cylinder head, although compressed air is then needed.

Removal

Caution:

If the parts of the timing gear are to be reused, they must be refitted into the same place. To avoid confusion it is recommended to use a suitable storing board.

- Remove the air filter, see page 98.
- Remove the rocker cover, see page 22.
- Remove the spark plugs.
- Bring the pistons to the highest position, top dead centre (TDC), see page 48.

Caution:

If the TDC markings of the crankshaft pulley are aligned to the datum point, the pistons in cylinders 1 and 4 are in TDC. If the 180 degree mark of the pulley and the datum point are aligned, the pistons of cylinders 2 and 3 are in TDC.

- Loosen the lock nut of the valve clearance adjusting bolt and backoff the adjusting bolts as far as possible.
- Remove the rocker arm and rocker housing, see page 28.

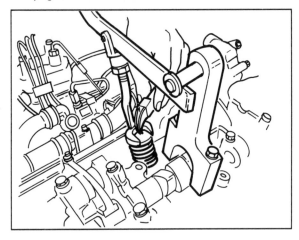

- Bolt in a special valve spring compressor and attach the lever.

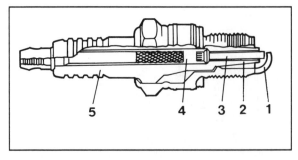

- Remove the earth electrode -1- of an old spark plug. Break the ceramic insulator -2- off with a screwdriver and remove the centre electrode -3- by twisting from side to side. Remove the rest of the centre electrode as well as the glass tube -4- and the bolt -5- with a suitable pin driver (approx 3 mm) by holding the spark plug in a vice. **Caution:** To prevent damage to the threaded bore in the cylinder head, the thread of the spark plug should not be damaged.
- Bolt the spark plug into the respective cylinder and connect it to the compressed air hose.
- Constantly blow at least 6 bars excess pressure into the cylinder.
- Attach the lever to the valve spring compressor and compress the valve spring.
- Remove the valve collets from the valve stem with a magnet.

Caution:

Do not remove the valve spring without compressed air, as damage could occur to the valves and pistons.

- Remove the valve spring retainer and valve spring.
- Remove the valve shaft seals with a screwdriver or pliers. **Caution:** Take care not to damage the valve shaft and valve guide.

- Smooth the slot of the valve shaft -arrow- with fine glass cloth.
- Test the fit of the valve seals on the valve guide for wear. If the seals no longer fit tightly, the valve guide must be renewed (workshop job).

Refitting

- Replace the damaged valve cotters, spring retainer and return springs.
- The damaged valve guides, which have been removed from the securing slot of the valve stem seal, must be replaced (workshop job).

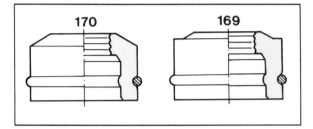

Caution:

Never confuse the exhaust valve seals -170-with the intake valve seals -169-.

- Oil the valve seals and refit by hand.

Caution:

In refitting the intake valve seal, first fit the mounting ferrule, which is found in the repair set. If refitted without the mounting ferrule, the lip of the valve seal will be damaged.

- Refit the valve springs and valve spring retainer and compress.

- Refit the valve collets and loosen the valve springs, compressor

- Refit the rocker arm and rocker cover housings, see page 28.

- Set the valve clearance, see page 47.

- Refit the rocker cover, see page 34.

- Bolt in the spark plugs, connect ignition leads, see page 60.

- Refit the air filter, see page 98.

Valve - removal and refitting

Removal

Caution:

If parts of the timing gear are to be re-used, they must be refitted in the same position. To avoid confusion, it is recommend to put the parts on a suitable board.

- Remove the cylinder head and rest on two wooden blocks, see page 23
- Remove the valve shaft seals, see page 30.

Caution:

To release the valve springs a commercial valve spring compressor can be used. Depending on the tools used the rocker arms, intake or exhaust manifolds may have to be removed.

- Remove the valves to the combustion chamber side.

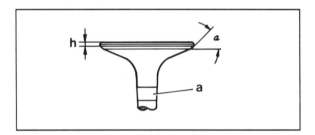

- Clean the valves. Valves are to be replaced if: the valve face is burned, if the valve face is too thin -h- and if the valve stem is worn or has ridges -a-.

Height of valve face -h-:

	New	Worn
Intake valve	1,6mm	1,0mm
Exhaust valve	2,7mm	2,0mm

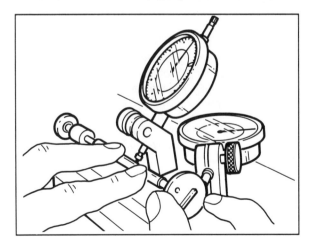

- The workshop can test the valve stem by measuring the axial runout which must not measure more than 0,03mm.

Caution:

Exhaust valves are filled with sodium. They may not be used as a tool or melted down as they can explode!

Refitting

Before refitting the valves, test the valve guide and recondition if necessary, see page 32.

Caution:

If a new valve is needed, the valve seat must also be reconditioned.

- Lightly oil the valve stem and valve guide with engine oil and refit the valve.
- Refit the valve stem seal, see page 30.
- Refit the valve spring, see page 31.
- Refit the next valve, making sure not to confuse the intake and exhaust valves.
- Refit the cylinder head, see page 22.

Valve guide - testing

In reconditioning the cylinder heads with leaking seals, the valve guides must be checked for wear, especially if the engine has a high mileage. If the valve guides are worn, they do not guarantee a concentric valve seat, which leads to excessive oil consumption. If they are badly worn, the valve guides must be replaced (workshop job).

- Remove the valve.

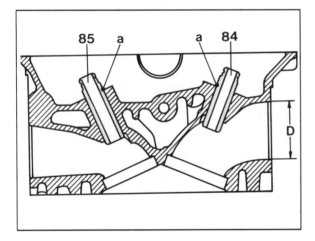

- Clean the valve guide -84,85- with a cylinder brush (approx. 20mm diameter).
- Insert the valve into the valve guide from the side of the combustion chamber and test the clearance by moving the valve from side to side. The valve guide must not show a significant movement. -84- valve guide intake valve, -85- valve guide exhaust valve, -a- circlip.
- Replace the valve guide if necessary (workshop job).

Valve seat in cylinder head - reconditioning

Valve seats which are worn or have combustion marks can be reconditioned provided that the correct face angle and the seat width is maintained. Valve seat inserts can be replaced with normal workshop tools. For the reconditioning, a valve seat cutter is needed and this should be done by a workshop.

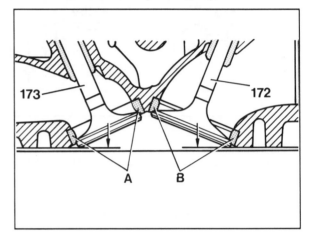

Valve seat insert -A- exhaust valve -173-.
Valve seat insert -B- intake valve -172-.

Fanbelt Tensioning

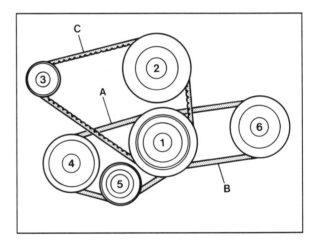

1 - crankshaft
2 - water pump
3 - alternator
4 - air conditioning compressor
5 - idler
6 - power steering pump

- Tighten the fanbelt -A-, 12,5 x 875 mm, at the air conditioning compressor, see page 210.
- Tighten the fanbelt -B-, 12,5 x 750 mm, at the power steering pump, see page 155.
- Tighten the fanbelt -C-, 9,5 x 1005 mm, at the alternator, see page 222.

Engine 115/123

The identification number 115, indicates an in-line engine with 4 cylinders, which was built into the models 200 and 230 between January 1976 and June 1980. The 6 cylinder engine 123 is found in model 250 from January 1976 until December 1984.

The power unit is fitted into the engine bay longitudinally and can only be lifted out with a suitable crane.

The cylinder bores are embedded in the grey cast iron engine block. In the case of extreme wear or ridging of the cylinder walls, the cylinders can be ground out by a specialist workshop. Subsequently, however, oversized pistons must be installed. The crankshaft is found in the bottom part of the cylinder block, and is supported by 5 crankshaft main bearings in engine 115 and by 4 in engine 123. The crankshaft is connected to the connecting rod by means of bearings, which connect to the pistons. The bottom part of the engine is formed by the oil sump in which the engine oil collects, which is needed for lubrication and cooling.

The cylinder head is bolted onto the top of the engine block. It is made of aluminium, because this metal has better conducting properties and a low specific weight compared to cast iron.

The intake and exhaust manifolds are situated on the right hand side of the cylinder head. The camshaft is found in the top of the cylinder head. It is driven by a timing chain from the crankshaft. A hydraulic timing chain tensioner ensures that the chain always has the correct tension. The camshaft drives the valves by means of rocker arms. The rocker arms rest on adjusting bolts, with which the valve clearance is adjusted during maintenance.

The oil pump takes care of the lubrication of the engine, and is attached to the front of the oil sump and is driven by the auxiliary shaft. The auxiliary shaft is situated on the left side of the engine block and is driven by the crankshaft timing chain. The oil that is sucked into the oil pump reaches the bearings of the crankshaft and the camshaft as well as the cylinder bores, by means of bores and pipes.

The water pump is attached to front of the engine block. The pump is driven by a fanbelt which also drives the alternator. An additional fanbelt drives the power steering pump. It is important that the cooling system is filled with a mixture of antifreeze plus water with a low lime content, to give corrosion protection throughout the year.

The fuel is supplied to the engine through a single Stromberg Flachstrom carburettor (115 engine) or a dual Solex Fallstrom carburettor (123 engine).

The ignition spark is produced by points or an electronic ignition system, depending on the model. While the electronic ignition system keeps the ignition point constant over a long period, in the points system. Due to wear, the points must be renewed during maintenance and the points gap adjusted. The distributor is attached to the left side of the engine block and is driven by the auxiliary shaft by means of a gear. In the same way the mechanical fuel pump is driven by a cam on the oil pump shaft, under the distributor.

Engine 115

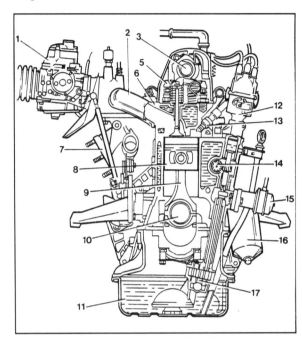

1	-	Carburettor	10	-	Crankshaft
2	-	Inlet manifold	11	-	Oil sump
3	-	Camshaft	12	-	Distributor
4	-	Rocker arm	13	-	Spark plug
5	-	Adjusting bolt	14	-	Auxilliary shaft
6	-	Cylinder head	15	-	Fuel pump
7	-	Exhaust manifold	16	-	Oil filter
8	-	Piston	17	-	Oil pump
9	-	Connecting rod			

The Cylinder head

This illustration shows engine 115.

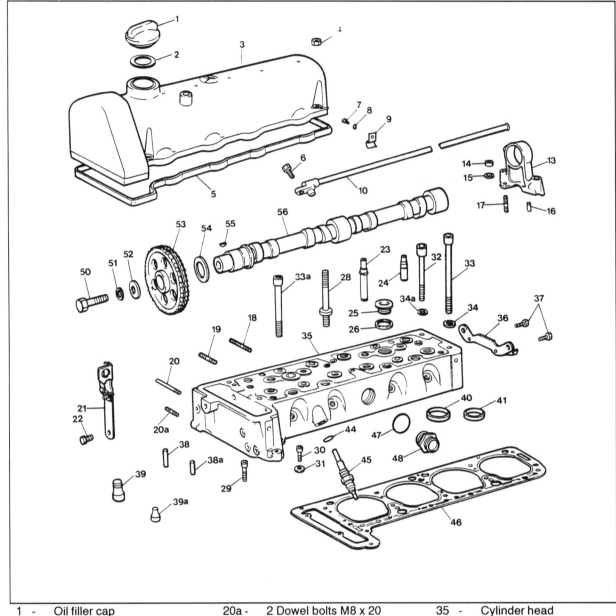

1	-	Oil filler cap	20a	-	2 Dowel bolts M8 x 20	35 -	Cylinder head
2	-	Seal	21	-	Bracket	36 -	Bracket
3	-	Rocker cover	22	-	Bolt	37 -	Bolt M8 x 16
4	-	4 Nuts M8	23	-	4 Valve guides intake	38 -	39a Coolant distributors
5	-	Rocker cover gasket	24	-	4 Valve guides exhaust	40 -	Intake valve seat insert.
6	-	Bolt M6 x 15	25	-	2 Plugs M22 x 1,5	41 -	Exhaust valve seat insert.
7	-	2 Bolts M4 x 10	26	-	2 Washers A22 x 27	44 -	Seal A14 x 18
8	-	2 Spring washers	28	-	4 Dowel bolts	45 -	Temperature sender unit
9	-	2 Pipe clamps	29	-	Bolt M8 x 40	46 -	Cylinder head gasket
10	-	Oil pipe	30	-	2 Bolts M8 x 20	47 -	Seal A32 x 38
13	-	Camshaft bearing	31	-	Washer 8,4 mm dia.	48 -	Heater connector
14	-	3 Nuts M8	32	-	4 cylinder head bolts	50 -	Adjusting bolt
15	-	3 Washers 8,4 mm dia.			M10 x 90		M14 x 1,5 x 40
16	-	6 Dowels	33	-	6 cylinder head bolts	51 -	Spring washer B14
17	-	3 Dowel bolts M8 x 18			M12 x145	52 -	Washer
18	-	5 Dowel bolts M10 x 52	33a		4 head bolts M12 x 34 34 -	53 -	Camshaft sprocket
19		dowel bolt M10 x 30	34		10 washers	54 -	Spacer
20	-	2 Dowel bolts M8 x 75	34a	-	4 Washers	55 -	Woodruff key 4 x 6,5
						56 -	Camshaft

Cylinder head removal and refitting

Removal

- Set the bonnet vertically, see page 13.
- Remove the battery earth cable.
- Remove the air filter, see page 98.
- Drain the coolant, see page 79.
- If air conditioned: remove the compressor with bracket and attached pipes and put to one side.
- Remove all coolant pipes attached to the cylinder head. First open all clips totally and push back.
- Mark all electrical leads, vacuum pipes and fuel pipes on the cylinder head, inlet manifold and carburetor with tape and remove.
- Remove all spark plugs.
- **140-horse power engine:** Unbolt the bracket of the axial throttle control shaft and put aside with shaft and ignition leads.
- Remove the throttle controls
- Automatic gearbox: unbolt the tube for the dipstick at the manifold.
- Remove the rocker cover.
- Disconnect the front exhaust pipe from the manifold and at the mounting on the gearbox housing. Tie back with wire.
- Unbolt the bracket on the exhaust manifold.
- Loosen the top clip of the bypass hose between the thermostat housing and water pump and push back.
- Unbolt the bleed tube between the rocker cover and water pump on the rocker cover **in a 4-cylinder engine** and on the water pump **in a 6-cylinder engine**.
- **6-cylinder engine with automatic gearbox:** unbolt the strut between the engine mounting and cylinder head.
- **140 horse power engine:** Disconnect the heater control valve actuating rod.
- Set the engine to TDC of the first cylinder on the ignition stroke by putting the car into neutral and pulling on the handbrake. Turn the crankshaft pulley bolt with an Allen key in a clockwise direction until the following markings are aligned. **Caution: Do not** turn the bolt of the camshaft gear. Do not turn the crankshaft backwards as the piston of the timing chain tensioner can jump forwards.
- The TDC mark on the crankshaft pulley must be under the pointer on the crankcase.
- At the same time the groove on the distributor rotor must be aligned with the groove on the edge of the distributor case. To do this remove the distributor cap and, if necessary, dust deflector cap. If the markings are not aligned, turn the crankshaft a further full rotation.

- Mark the position of the camshaft sprocket in relation to the timing chain with paint, so that the chain can be re-mounted in the same position on the sprocket.
- **4-cylinder engine:** Remove the inner guide rail, see page 25.
- **4-cylinder engine:** Push back the piston of the timing chain tensioner.
- **6-cylinder engine:** Remove the spring from the timing chain tensioner, see page 44.
- Loosen the bracket of the fuel line and swing aside.
- Remove the bolt of the camshaft, while holding the camshaft sprocket from the back through the bore in the gear with a large screwdriver. The bolt can also be loosened by attaching a key and hitting against the handle of the key by hand.
- Remove the camshaft sprocket. Take care not to drop the woodruff key into the timing case.

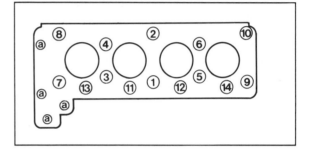

- Remove the bolts M12 in reverse order of numbering, i.e. 14 to 1 (6-cylinder engine, illustration Pg.36). An Allen key is needed for this (e.g. HAZET 986 Lg-10)
- Remove the cylinder head bolts M10 in reverse order of numbering, i.e. from 14 to 1. An Allen key is needed for this (e.g. HAZET 986 Lg-8).
- Remove the bolts -a- (e.g with HAZET Allen key 986 SLg-6)
- Remove the cylinder head using two people. This can also be done with a workshop crane after a suitable rope or chain has been attached to the lifting eyes.

Caution:

While lifting the cylinder head, push the tension rail to middle of engine by pulling on the timing chain. In putting down the cylinder head of the 6-cylinder engine, take care not to damage the guide rail.

- **6-cylinder engine:** Pull out the piston of the chain tensioner to the inside.

Refitting

Before refitting, scrape any sealant remains from the cylinder head and the cylinder block with a suitable scraper. **Take care not to drop any remains into the bores**. Cover the bores with a cloth.

- Check whether the cylinder head and engine block are not warped with the use of a steel ruler, adjust if necessary (workshop job).
- Check the cylinder head for cracks and ridges.
- Thoroughly clean any oil or other dirt from the bores for the cylinder head bolts.
- Always replace the cylinder head gasket.
- Fit the new gasket without sealant, checking that all holes remain uncovered.
- Check that the camshaft is in the TDC position for cylinder 1. The groove on the spacing washer of the camshaft must be in alignment with the groove on the first camshaft bearing. This is normally the case if the camshaft was not removed or turned.
- Refit the cylinder head. **Caution:** The cylinder head is located in the cylinder block by dowels. In refitting make sure that the support of the thermostat housing is inserted into the coolant short-circuit pipe.
- Oil the cylinder head bolts on the thread, refit and tighten by hand

4-cylinder engine

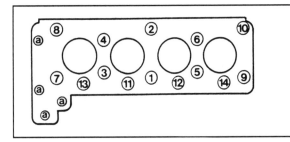

- Tighten the cylinder head bolts in the order 1 to 14 in **three stages**.

Caution:

The cylinder head bolts are to be tightened very carefully. Before tightening the bolts, the torque wrench should be tested for accuracy.

1st stage:
    M12-bolts:40Nm
    M10-bolts:30 Nm
2nd stage:
    M12-bolts:70Nm
    M10-bolts:55Nm

Caution:

At this point take a break of 10 minutes. Do not loosen the bolts before torquing to the final figure.

3rd stage:
    M12 bolts:110Nm
    M10 bolts:55Nm

- Tighten the M8-bolts -a- with an Allen key to 25 N.m
- Refit the guide rail into the cylinder head and drive in the bolt.

6-cylinder engine

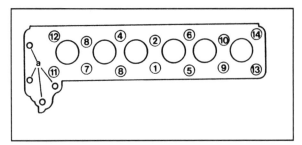

- Tighten the cylinder head bolts in the order 1 to 14 in **three stages**.

Caution:

The tightening of the cylinder head bolts is to be done very carefully. Before tightening the bolts, the torque wrench should be tested for accuracy.

1st stage:	**40Nm**
2nd stage:	**70Nm**

Caution:

At this point, take a break of approximately 10 minutes. Then undo all bolts by 90 degrees and then tighten again to the third stage.

3rd stage: **110Nm**

- Tighten the M8 bolts -a- with an Allen key.
- Check that the timing chain fits perfectly into the teeth of the crankshaft and intermediate shaft gear.
- Refit the camshaft sprocket into the timing chain so that the markings are aligned.
- Insert the bolt of the camshaft and tighten to **80Nm**. Hold the back of the camshaft with a big screwdriver.

Caution:

If the cylinder head face was worked on, the timing must be checked.

- **6-cylinder engine:** Refit the piston and pressure spring of the timing chain tensioner from the outside. Insert the bolt and tighten to **90Nm**.
- Adjust the valve clearance, see page 47.
- Refit the distributor, see page 60.
- Bolt the coolant bleed tube to the cylinder head, i.e. water pump.

- Secure the coolant-bypass hose to the thermostat housing with a bracket. Attach various coolant and heating tubes to the cylinder head and secure with a bracket.
- Bolt on the bracket of the exhaust manifold. Refit the front exhaust pipe to the manifold and tighten the bolts equally. Refit the gearbox bracket and tighten.
- Refit the rocker cover, tighten the nuts to **15Nm**.
- If removed, refit the guide tube of the dipstick and refit the air conditioning compressor. Tension the fanbelt of the air conditioning system, see page 210.
- Refit regulating controls.
- If removed, refit the bracket of the axial throttle control shaft.
- Refit the sparkplug leads in ignition order 1-3-4-2 in a 4-cylinder engine and 1-5-3-6-2-4 in a 6-cylinder engine. The cylinders are counted in sequence from the front to the back - cylinder No.1 is always by the radiator fan. The ignition cable for cylinder 1 is situated on the distributor above the groove on the edge of the distributor housing. To see the groove, the distributor cap and, if present, the dust deflector cap must be removed. The connections of the other ignition cables are counted in the turning direction of the distributor arm in the order of ignition.
- Refit all electrical leads and vacuum pipes according to the markings.
- Refill the coolant, see page 79.
- Check the oil level in the engine, and refill if necessary. If the cylinder head was removed due to a defective cylinder head gasket, it is recommended to do an oil change and oil filter change, as there could be coolant in the engine oil.
- Attach the battery earth lead.
- Refit the air filter, see page 98
- Bring the engine to running temperature and check all seals.
- Test the dwell angle and ignition point gap and adjust if necessary, see page 58.
- Close the bonnet, see page 13.

Engine 110

The identity number 110 indicates an in-line engine with 6 cylinders, which is fitted with a carburetor (model 280) or a fuel injection system, (280E).

The power unit is built into the engine bay longitudinally and can only be lifted out with a suitable crane.

The cylinder bores are embedded in the cast iron engine block. In the case of extreme wear or ridging of the cylinder walls, the cylinders can be ground out by a specialist workshop. Subsequently, however, oversized pistons must be installed. The crankshaft is found in the bottom part of the engine block, and is supported by 7 crankshaft bearings. The crankshaft is connected to the connecting rod by means of bearings, which connect to the pistons. The bottom part of the engine is formed by the oil sump in which the engine oil collects, which is needed for lubrication and cooling. The cylinder head is bolted onto the top of the engine block. It consists of aluminium, because this metal has better heat conducting properties and a low specific weight compared to cast iron.

The cylinder head is a cross flow head. This means that the fresh fuel-air mixture flows into one side of the cylinder head and the burned gases are pushed out of the opposite side. Due to the cross flow arrangement rapid gas-exchange is assured. Both camshafts are found in the camshaft housing at cylinder head. They are driven by a timing chain from the crankshaft. A hydraulic chain tensioner ensures that the chain always has the correct tension. The inlet and outlet valves are driven by the camshaft via rocker arms. Seen in driving direction, the left camshaft is responsible for the driving of the intake valves, and the right camshaft for the exhaust valves.

The oil pump takes care of the lubrication of the engine, it extends into the front of the oil sump and is driven by the auxiliary shaft. The auxiliary shaft is found in the left side of the engine block and is driven by the crankshaft by means of a timing chain. The oil that is sucked into the oil pump reaches the bearings of the crankshaft and the camshaft as well as the cylinder bores, by means of holes and pipes.

The water pump is attached to side of the engine block. The pump is driven by a fanbelt which amongst others also drives the generator. An additional fanbelt drives the power steering pump. It is important that the coolant circulation is filled with a mixture of antifreeze plus water with a low lime for corrosion protection content, throughout the year.

The fuel is fed through a Solex double barrel Fallstrom carburetor which is practically maintenance-free. The ignition spark is produced by a points ignition system or an electronic ignition system, While the electronic ignition system keeps the ignition point constant over a long period, in the points system the points must be renewed during maintenance work and the point gap adjusted. The distributor is attached to the left side of the timing case and is driven by the auxiliary shaft by means of a gear. In the same way the mechanical fuel pump is driven via a cam on the oil pump shaft.

Engine 110

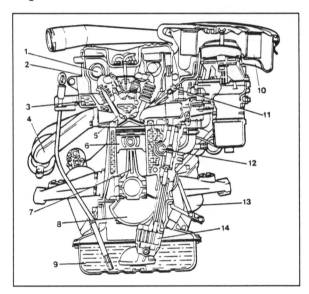

1	-	camshaft	8 -	crankshaft
2	-	camshaft housing	9 -	oil sump
3	-	cylinder head	10 -	air filter
4	-	exhaust manifold	11 -	injector
5	-	exhaust valve	12 -	auxiliary shaft
6	-	piston	13 -	oil filter
7	-	connecting rod	14 -	oil pump

The Cylinder head

Engine 110

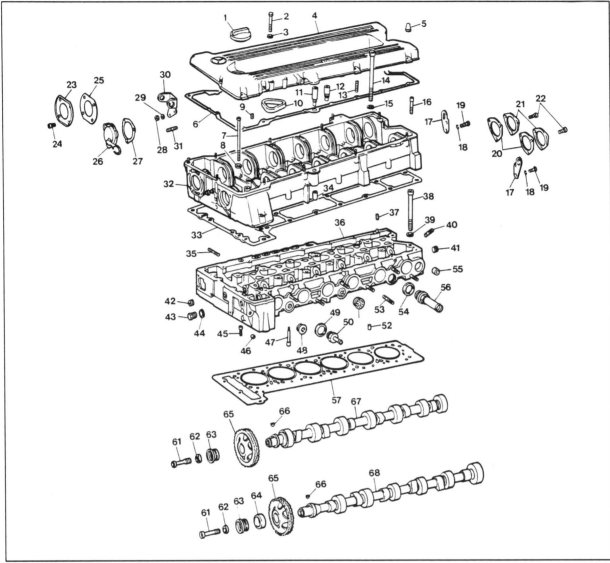

1 -	Oil filler cap	23 -	Cover	45 -	Bolts M8X22
2 -	3 Bolts	24 -	7 Bolts M6X15	46 -	Bolt M10X1
3 -	3 Washers	25 -	Washer shim	47 -	One way oil nozzle
4 -	Rocker cover	26 -	Cover with basket	48 -	OM30X1,5 grubscrews
5 -	Nuts	27 -	Seal	49 -	Sealing ring A30X36
6 -	Rocker cover gasket	28 -	2 Nuts M8	50 -	Connecting tube heater
7 -	2 Bolts M8 x 135	29 -	2 Spring washers	51 -	Connection carb. heater
8 -	Washers 38 x 15	30 -	Front bracket	52 -	2 Dowels 8X16
9 -	Threaded inserts M8x16	31 -	2 Dowel bolts M8X18	53 -	Dowel bolt M8X35
10 -	5 Gaskets for cover	32 -	Camshaft housing	54 -	Sealing ring A30X36
11 -	Bleed valve	33 -	Gasket	55 -	Cover of injection channel
12 -	Bleed nozzle	34 -	Connecting pipe	56 -	Heater connection
13 -	12 Dowel bolts M8 x 18	35 -	Dowel bolt M8X30	57 -	Cylinder head gasket
14 -	9 Rocker cover bolts	36 -	Cylinder head	61 -	2 Stress bolts
15 -	9 Washers	37 -	2 Dowels 8X16		M14X1,5X40
16 -	21 bolts	38 -	5 Cylinder head bolts	62 -	2 Washers
17 -	2 Rear brackets	39 -	5 Washers	63 -	2 Spacing sleeves
18 -	Spring washer	40 -	Dowel bolts M8X20	64 -	Spacing washer
19 -	4 Bolts M8 x 15	41 -	2 Oil channel grubscrews	65 -	2 Camshaft sprockets
20 -	2 Seals	42 -	AM22X1,5 grubscrews	66 -	2 Woodruff keys 4X6,4
21 -	2 Covers	43 -	Bolt M18X1,5	67 -	Camshaft exhaust
22 -	6 Bolts	44 -	Washer A22X27	68 -	Camshaft inlet

Cylinder head removal and refitting

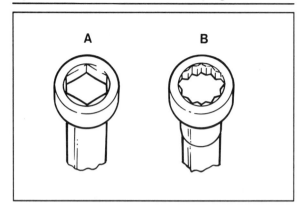

The cylinder head is normally attached to the engine block by an Allenhead bolt -A-. In engines from 2/81 to 9/81 the cylinder head is bolted on by special socket bolts-B-. Special socket bolts are tightened differently to Allen key bolts. special socket bolts also undergo a lasting expansion when tightened. Before re-using these bolts, it is thus necessary to check the length and if the maximum length is exceeded, they need to be replaced.

To prevent the special socketed bolts from sitting at the end of the thread after re-use, the tapped bores are about 5cm longer than in previous cylinder heads. Special socketed bolts may **not** be used in other cylinder heads, as the bottoming of these bolts cannot be noticed while tightening them and the correct loading may thus not be achieved.

Any cylinder heads (new and previous ones) can be fitted with Allen key bolts. In any situation they must, however, be tightened to the torque figure of Allen key bolts. Only one type of bolt may be used in an engine, in other words, do not have a combination of these bolts.

Insertion of the changed cylinder head with the longer thread bores:

Model	Engine	from engine end-number	
		manual	automatic
280	110.923	013591	016780
280E	110.984	017885	051156

Insertion of the special socketed bolts

Model	Engine	from-to engine end-number	
		manual	automatic
280	110.923	016364-016895	019843-020142
280E	110.984	028409-031009	092526-099985

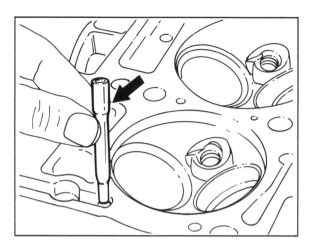

Caution:

In cases of damage to the camshaft due to a lack of oil, the oil nozzle -arrow- in the cylinder head must be cleaned or replaced if necessary.

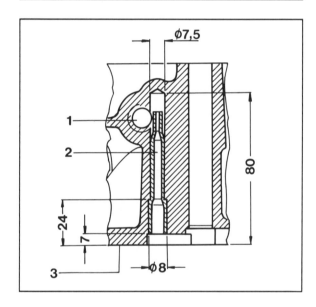

- To remove the oil nozzle -2- unbolt it with a left-handed thread key (6mm diameter). In refitting make sure there is a depth of 7 mm; 2 - oil passage, 3 - cylinder head.

Removal

Caution:

If parts of the timing gear are to be re-used, they must be fitted into the same position. To avoid confusion it is recommended to put them onto a suitable board.

- Set the bonnet vertically, see page 13.
- Remove the battery earth cable.
- Remove the air filter, see page 98.
- Drain the coolant, see page 79.
- If present, unbolt the air conditioning compressor and put to one side with hoses connected.
- If present, unbolt the pressure oil pump of level control and put to one side with hoses connected, see page13.
- Mark the spark plug leads with tape and remove.
- Remove the rocker cover.

- Remove the 2 covers on the front of the camshaft housing.
- Remove all coolant tubes from the rocker cover, inlet manifold or carburetor. First open all clips and push back.
- Mark all electrical leads to the rocker cover with tape and remove.
- Remove the axial throttle control shaft by pulling out the securing split pin and removing the tension spring. Push the shaft to the back and remove.
- Unbolt the oil return tube on the rocker cover.
- Open and push back clips, then remove the coolant tube between the thermostat housing and water pump. Undo the clip of the bypass hose on the water pump.
- Unbolt the guide tube of the dipstick at the rocker arm and bend it slightly to one side.
- Unbolt the front exhaust pipe from the manifold. Unbolt the gearbox bracket, lower the front exhaust a little and secure it with wire. **Carburetor engine:** Unbolt the pre-heating funnel.

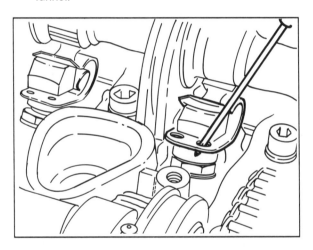

- Carefully prise out all the tension springs of the rocker arm with a screwdriver.
- Remove the rocker arm by turning the engine by hand, until the cam lobe of the rocker arm to be removed points upward. **Caution: do not** turn the engine by the camshafts, but put the gears into neutral and apply the handbrake. Turn the crankshaft with a ratchet wrench and Allen key SW27 by the central bolt of the crankshaft pulley in a clockwise direction.

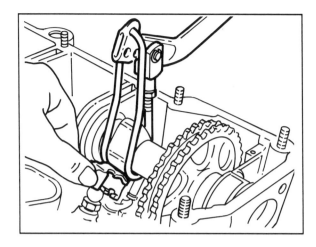

- Press the valve against the strength of the valve spring downwards, lift the rocker arm from the valve clearance adjusting bolt and remove. A workshop will use a special lifting device for this job, but with a little imagination this tool can be made. To do this attach 2 moveable wire hooks (around 3mm diameter) to the front of the lever arm for attachment to the camshaft. The thrust part must also be moveable in the handle and must have a u-shaped surface at the bottom, so that the valve plate can be pushed downwards under the notch of the rocker arm.
- Set the engine to the TDC of the first cylinder, by turning the crankshaft until the following markings are in alignment. **Caution: Do not** turn the bolt of the camshaft sprocket. Do not turn the crankshaft backwards, as the piston of the timing chain tensioner can jump forwards.
- The TDC mark on the crankshaft pulley must be below the pointer on the crank case. **Caution:** In some engines the BDC (bottom dead centre) is marked on the crankshaft pulley with a "00" marking. Check that next to the "00" mark there is a small dowel on the pulley. This dowel is found in the area of the 15 degree mark.
- The marks of the camshaft sprocket and the marks on the front top of the camshaft housing must be in alignment., see page 43.
- Remove both camshaft sprockets by holding a key against one of the cams sticking up.
- Remove the top guide rail in the camshaft housing, see page 25.
- Remove the timing chain tensioner, see page 44.
- Push both camshafts to the back and remove the camshaft sprocket.
- Remove the idler pulley by pulling out the bearing bolt with a M10 bolt in the same way as for the guide rail.
- Remove the guide rail from the cylinder head.

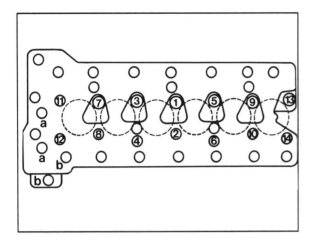

- Remove the cylinder head bolts in reverse order, i.e. from 14 to 1. For this, an Allen key (e.g. HAZET 986 Lg-10) or special socket key (e.g. HAZET 990 SLg 12) is needed.

Caution:

The cylinder head bolts could have a combination of different washers, so while removing, put them down in a way that you can put the same bolt in the same place. If needed, only replace the washers by ones with the same thickness and diameter.

- Remove the 4 Allen key bolts M8 -a/b-. Also remove the 2 bolts in the chain housing with a magnet.
- By pulling up on the timing chain, press the tension rail to the middle of the engine. Tie a rope to the lifting eyes on the cylinder head and lift upwards with a workshop crane.
- Set the cylinder head down onto two wooden blocks, so that the valves which may be protruding cannot be damaged.

Refitting

Before refitting, clean any sealant remains from the cylinder head and cylinder block with a suitable scraper. **Take care not to drop any remains into the bores.** Close up the bores with rags.

Caution:

Since the same part is used for carburetor and injection engines when replacing the cylinder head, the 6 bores for the injection valves must be sealed with plugs if used in a carburetor engine, see also page 19.

- Test the cylinder head for distortion in crosswise and lengthwise directions with the aid of a metal ruler. The cylinder head should not show any distortion. If necessary have the cylinder head skimmed (workshop job).
- Check the cylinder head for cracks, ridges and wear.
- Clean the bores of the cylinder head bolts of oil or other deposits.
- Always use a new cylinder head gasket.
- Fit a new gasket without the sealant so that no bores are covered.
- Make 2 wooden wedges (measurements 15 x 35 x 240). Insert one wedge in front between cylinders 1 and 2 onto the cylinder head gasket. The other is inserted between cylinders 5 and 6.

- Lower the cylinder head onto the wedges and insert the timing chain and tension rail.
- Lift the front of the cylinder head and pull out the front wedge to the side of the exhaust manifold. Lower the head slowly until it locates on the dowel pins.
- Lift the cylinder head slightly at the back and pull the wedge back out to the exhaust side. Lower the head slowly until it locates on the dowel pin.

Caution:

In refitting, ensure that the coolant bypass hose is inserted into the neck of the water pump.

- Oil the thread of the cylinder head bolts, refit with washers and tighten by hand.

Caution:

Since 7/74 a 22 mm diameter washer is used for cylinder head bolt No.14. In earlier camshaft housings a 20 mm diameter washer is used.

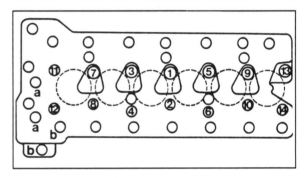

- Tighten the cylinder head bolts in order from 1 to 14 in **three stages.**

Caution:

The cylinder head bolts should be tightened very carefully. Before tightening the bolts, the torque wrench should be tested for accuracy.

Allenhead Cylinder head bolts M12 x 1,5:
1st stage:	40Nm
2nd stage:	70Nm

Caution:

At this point take a break of approx. 10 minutes. Subsequently tighten the bolts further, do not loosen.

3rd stage:	110Nm

Special socket cylinder head bolts M12 x 1,5:

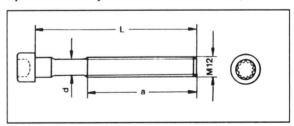

- Measure the length -L- of the cylinder head bolts. If the maximum length is exceeded, the bolts must be replaced. Other illustrated parts: d=roller shaft, a=length of thread, M12=thread diameter 12mm.

Length when new	Maximum length
110mm	113mm
119mm	122mm
144mm	147mm

Tightening Torque:
1st stage: 40Nm
2nd stage: 70Nm

Caution:

At this point, take a break of approx. 10 minutes. Subsequently tighten the bolts without loosening.

3rd stage: turn all the bolts with a spanner by 90 degrees in one go.

4th stage: turn all the bolts with a spanner by 90 degrees in one go.

Caution: To maintain the turning angle, attach the handle of the spanner across the engine and turn in one go until the handle is alongside the engine.

- Tighten the M8 bolts -a/b- with an Allen key to 25Nm.

Caution:

After all the bolts have been tightened, both camshafts must be able to be easily turned by hand.

- Refit the left guide rail into the rocker cover, by pulling up the timing chain, inserting the guide rail with a pair of pliers and tighten the two locating bolts into the rocker cover. Align the guide rail sideways.
- Pull up the timing chain. Insert the idler pulley with one hand and hold it. Refit the oiled locating bolts into the rocker cover with the other hand and tighten.
- Put in the bolt with its washer.

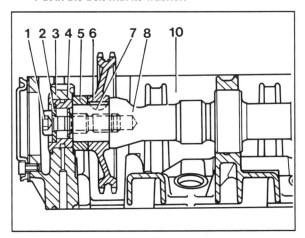

- If removed, refit the woodruff key -7- into the camshaft.
- Refit the camshaft sprocket -6- of the inlet camshaft -8-with spacer -5- onto the camshaft; 10-camshaft housing.
- Oil the spacing sleeve ferrule -3- and insert it into the bearing.
- Refit the stressed bolt -1- with washer -2- and tighten it slightly by hand.

- Check that the timing chain fits properly into the teeth of the crankshaft sprocket intermediary shaft and idler pulley.
- Refit the camshaft sprocket of the exhaust camshaft into the timing chain and push it onto the camshaft housing.
- Oil the spacing sleeve ferule and insert it into the bearing. Refit the stressed bolt with washer and tighten slightly by hand.

Caution:

At the ignition TDC of the first cylinder, the adjusting marks of both camshaft gears must be in alignment with the marks cast on the camshaft housing.

- Refit the guide rail into the camshaft housing and drive in the mechanical pins.
- Insert a metal rod through the timing chain tensioner aperture to depress the guide rail and tension the chain, then re-check that the TDC marks are still aligned.

Caution:

If the cylinder head was skimmed, the timing must be tested (workshop job).

- Tighten the bolts of the camshaft sprockets to **80Nm**, while holding the sprocket stationary using a metal rod through one of the holes.
- Check the oil holes of all the rocker arms, and clean of any obstructions.
- Oil the mating surfaces of the rocker arms and refit, by turning the crankshaft in such a way that the relevant cams point upwards. Push the valve spring slightly down with a lever and insert the rocker arms.
- Press the spring into the ring slots of the valve clearance adjusting bolt, and secure the rocker arm.

Caution:

Because camshafts should be turned as little as possible, the rocker arms should be inserted first where the cams are already pointing upwards.

- Remove the metal rod from the chain tensioner aperture and refit a hydraulic chain tensioner, see page 44.
- Adjust the valve clearance, see page 47.
- Bolt the front exhaust pipe to the manifold, and tighten the bolts evenly cross-wise. Refit the gearbox bracket and tighten. In a carburetor engine, bolt in the pre-heating funnel.
- Refit the guide tube of the dipstick with a bracket and bolt it to the rocker cover. Insert the dipstick.
- Refit the by-pass hose between the thermostat housing and water pump and secure with clips.
- Refit all the removed coolant tubes to the rocker cover, inlet manifold and carburetor and secure with clips.
- Bolt the oil leakage return to the cylinder head.
- Refit the throttle axial regulating shaft and secure it with the clip and split pin.
- Refit 2 lids to front of the camshaft housing.
- If removed, refit the oil pump of the suspension level control. Tighten the bolts to 9Nm, see also page 13.
- Refit the rocker arm cover, tighten the nuts and bolts very slightly to **5Nm.**
- Refit the sparkplug leads in ignition order 1-5-3-6-2-4. The cylinders are counted in order from the front to the back where cylinder No. 1 is always found at the radiator end. The ignition lead of the first cylinder should be located on the ignition distributor above the groove on the edge of the distributor housing. To find the groove, the distributor cap must be removed, and if present the dust deflector cap lifted. The connections of the other ignition cables are counted in the direction of rotation of the distributor rotor.
- Refit all electrical leads and vacuum pipes according to the markings.
- Refill the cooling system, see page 79.
- Check the oil level in the engine and refill if necessary. If the cylinder head was removed due to a defective cylinder head gasket, a major oil change including an oil filter change is recommended, since there could be coolant in the engine oil.
- If removed, refit the air conditioning compressor and tighten the fanbelt, see page 210.
- Refit the battery earth lead.
- Refit the air filter, see page 98.
- Bring the engine to running temperature and check all seals for leakage.
- Check the dwell angle and point gap, adjusting where necessary, see page 58.
- Close the bonnet, see page 13.

Timing Chain tensioner - removal and refitting.

The timing chain tensioner is bolted into the front right hand side of the cylinder head. It tensions the timing chain by a pressure spring as well as the oil pressure in the timing chain tensioner, which depends on the engine oil pressure. **Caution:** Different timing chain tensioners A or B, could be fitted. In jobs on the chain drive, as for example "removal of camshaft gear or tension rail", the timing chain tensioner A must be completely removed, while in the timing chain tensioner B, only the pressure spring need be removed. Which timing chain tensioner has been installed will become apparent when the bolt has been removed. The ball lock ring of timing chain tensioner A has a bore of 3mm diameter which is closed by a ball. The timing chain tensioner B has an oil nozzle with a bore of 1,1mm diameter. This bore can be tested with a 1mm wire to see if it goes straight through.

Timing chain tensioner A

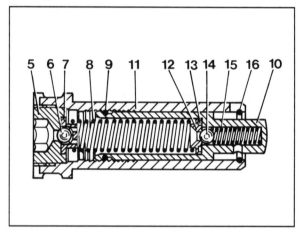

Timing chain tensioner B

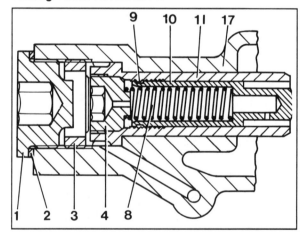

1 -	bolt	10 -	pressure piston
2 -	sealing washer	11 -	housing
3 -	threaded ring	12 -	valve plate
4 -	oil nozzle	13 -	O-ring
5 -	ball seat	14 -	ball
6 -	ball	15 -	pressure spring
7 -	ball cage	16 -	circlip
8 -	pressure spring	17 -	cylinder head
9 -	retaining spring		

Removal

- Undo the bolt - 1- with an Allen key SW17.
- Undo the ball seat -5- with an Allen key SW10 about two rotations. **Caution:** The threaded ring -3- must still be tight. If only the pressure spring -8- is to be removed from chain tensioner B, unbolt the oil nozzle -4- and remove the pressure spring.
- Unbolt the threaded ring -3- with an Allen key SW 19.
- Unbolt the ball seat -5-. **Caution:** The ball seat is under pressure from the pressure spring -8-, so hold pressure against it with the key while removing.
- Remove the ball -6- with the cage -7- and pressure spring -8- .
- !n place of the ball seat, bolt in a bolt M20 x 1,5. Subsequently pull out the bolt and with it also the timing chain tensioner with a pair of pliers.

Dismantling and testing

Caution:

The pressure piston cannot be refitted into the timing chain tensioner while it is assembled. The timing chain tensioner must thus be dismantled before refitting to prevent the timing chain from being stretched too much.

- Remove the valve plate -12-, O-ring -13-, ball -14 and pressure spring -15.
- Press the circlip out with a small screwdriver.
- Pull out the pressure piston -10- to the front (in the direction of the pressure).
- Clean all parts thoroughly with fuel and test for re-useability. Check the ease of movement of the pressure piston in the housing. Replace worn parts, or replace the complete timing chain tensioner where necessary. In this case a B timing chain tensioner can be refitted.

Refitting

- Refit the circlip -16- into the housing -11-. Carefully hold the housing in a vice, so that it is not damaged. The workshop uses 2 soft jaws with semi-circular notches for this purpose.
- Insert the pressure piston -10- with it's retaining spring -9- into the housing from above. See also page 21.
- Complete assembly of the timing chain tensioner as per the illustration.
- Refit the ball seat onto the ball cage, press the pressure spring together and tighten the ball seat about two turns. **Caution:** Do not tighten the ball seat too much, as the pressure piston can then jump forwards and the whole timing chain tensioner will have to be dismantled.
- Place the timing chain tensioner with the ball seat onto an Allen key and insert it into the cylinder head. **Caution:** Do not hit the dowel key in this process, as the pressure piston can jump forwards.
- Refit the threaded ring and tighten to 50Nm.
- Tighten the ball seat to **25Nm**, the pressure piston must jump forwards with an **audible clicking noise** during this process.
- Refit the bolt with the new washer and tighten to 50Nm.

Engine maintenance

Visually checking oil loss

In an oil-smeared engine and in cases of high oil usage, check where the oil is leaking from. Test the following areas:

- Open the oil filler cap and test the gasket for porosity or damage.
- Check if the breather tubes from the rocker cover to the air filter are properly in position.
- The rocker cover gasket
- The cylinder head gasket
- The joint of the distributor flange.
- The oil filter gasket: the oil filter flange at the engine block as well as the oil filter cover at the oil filter housing.
- The connection at the oil filter flange of the oil pressure sender unit.
- The oil bleed bolt (washer)
- The oil sump gasket
- The joint between the engine and gearbox or flywheel inspection plate (the oil seal at the flywheel or gear shaft)

As an oil leak will normally spread over a large part of the engine, the point of exit is not always immediately visible. In the search the following process is thus recommended:

- Clean the engine. Spray the engine with an engine cleaner and rinse the engine with cold water. Cover the distributor and generator with plastic bags first.
- Dust the joints and gaskets of the engine externally with lime or talcum powder.
- Check the oil level and top up if necessary.
- Test-drive the vehicle for about 30km on a highway. Since the oil will become thinner in a heated engine, the oil will flow out of the leak easily.
- Subsequently check the engine with a torch or lamp, localise the leak and repair.

Fanbelt - testing

The fanbelts should be tested for damage every 20 000km.

- Mark the belt in a visible spot with a chalk line.
- If present, remove the green control lead at the transistorised ignition system.
- Check the fanbelt for tears, burned or frayed areas, replacing if necessary.
- Turn the engine bit by bit by the nut on the crankshaft-pulley in the direction of the engine rotation, until the chalk mark again becomes visible. The gearbox should be in neutral and the handbrake applied.

Caution:

Do not turn the engine backwards.

- Test the tension of the fanbelt, tighten if necessary, see page 222.
- If removed, refit the green control lead.

Compression -testing

The compression pressure should be tested every 60 000km.

Testing the compression will draw conclusions on the condition of the engine. In this test it will become clear whether the valves or the pistons (piston rings) are in good condition or worn. The test values also show whether a new engine should be installed or a complete engine overhaul be done. For this test a compression pressure tester is needed, which can be purchased at relatively low cost.

The difference in pressure between the various cylinders can reach a maximum of 1,5 bar. If one or more cylinders have a difference in pressure of more than 1,5 bar compared to the others, this indicates defective valves, worn piston rings or valve guides. If the wear limit is reached, the engine must be overhauled or replaced.

The compression pressure should be between 10 - 12 bar. The wear limit is reached at 8,5 bar.

- To test the compression, the engine should be at running temperature.
- Switch off the ignition.
- In vehicles with a points ignition system, remove the lead from the coil and earth.
- In **280E**, remove the fuel pump relay. The relay is found at the back of the left strut.

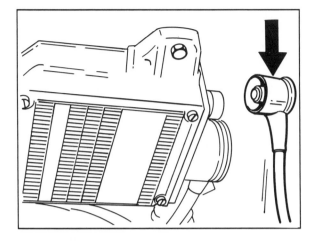

- In vehicles with a transistor ignition, remove the plug with the green lead -arrow- from the test socket of the ignition system. The test socket is on the left side near the wheel arch.
- Remove all sparkplugs. The plug leads should only be pulled by the tin sleeves.
- Blow the sparkplug recesses in the cylinder head with compressed air, and unscrew the plugs with a suitable plug spanner.
- Turn the engine a few times with the starter, so that any particles and soot will be propelled out. **Caution:** Gears in neutral and handbrake on.

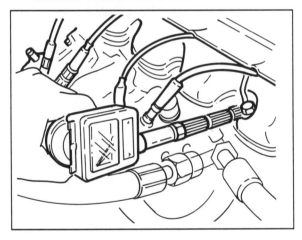

- Push or bolt the compression tester into the sparkplug openings according to the directions.
- Let an assistant push the accelerator pedal right down and hold with a foot during the whole test.
- Let the engine turn approximately 8 turns, until the compression tester no longer shows any pressure increase.
- Test all the cylinders in turn and compare the readings to the specified value.
- Subsequently tighten the sparkplugs to 20Nm and refit the ignition leads.
- Refit the green control lead on the transistorised ignition system, fuel pump relay, or refit the lead to the ignition coil.

Valve clearance testing/adjusting

To compensate for variations in thermal expansion in the valve gear, a certain valve clearance must be maintained.

With a too low clearance, the timing changes, the compression ratio is bad, the engine performance decreases, the running of the engine is irregular. In extreme cases the valves can become distorted or the valve seats can burn.

In an excessive clearance, strong mechanical noises result, the timing changes, the engine gives low performance due to limited cylinder filling of fuel/air mixture and the running of the engine is irregular.

The adjustment of the valves will only have the desired effect if the valves seal properly, they do not have unnecessary clearance in the valve guide and are not seating at the end of the shaft.

The valve clearance should be tested every 20 000km.

The valve clearance can be tested or adjusted in a warm or cold engine.

Testing

- In vehicles with a points ignition system, remove the lead from the coil and earth.
- In vehicles with transistor ignition, remove the green cable from the test socket of the ignition system, see page 47.
- Remove the air filter, see page 98.
- Remove the rocker cover, see page 22
- Put the gears in neutral and pull on the handbrake.
- Turn the engine with an Allen key (27mm) by the central bolt of the crankshaft pulley in the direction of engine rotation. The camshaft will also turn.

Caution:

Do not turn at the bolt of the camshaft. **Do not** turn the crankshaft backwards.

Engine 102

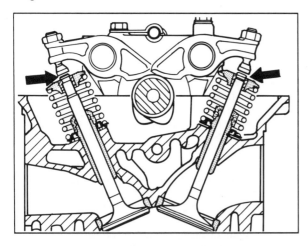

- Set the camshaft in such a way that the tip of the cam points away from the rocker arm of the valve to be tested (the base ring then rests against the rocker arm).
- Measure the valve clearance with a feeler blade between the face of the adjusting bolt and valve shaft end -arrows-.

Valve clearance	cold engine	warm engine
Inlet	0,15mm	0,20mm
Exhaust	0,30mm	0,35mm

The engine is regarded as "cold" at a coolant temperature of less than 50 degrees C. To adjust the valve clearance in a "warm engine", the coolant temperature should be between 60 and 80 degrees C.

- The valve clearance has been adjusted when the feeler blade can just be pulled through.

Caution:

In pulling the guage through take care that it does not jam between the adjusting bolt face and valve end.

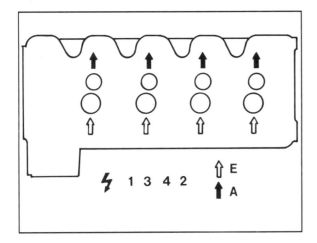

Caution: Do not confuse the intake valve -E- and exhaust valve -A-.

Adjustment

- If the specified value is not reached, adjust the valve clearance at the adjusting bolt. For this, use a ring spanner together with a phillips screwdriver.
- First check if the lock nut of the valve clearance adjusting bolt is cracked or deformed. Replace it if it is damaged.
- Loosen the lock nut of the adjusting bolt with a ring spanner.
- Adjust the valve clearance to the specified value with the adjusting bolt.

Caution:

If the adjusting bolt jams, renew the rocker arm.

- Tighten the lock nut to approximately 20Nm (estimate value), while holding the adjusting bolt with the srewdriver. Re-check the clearance after tightening.

Engine 110/115/123

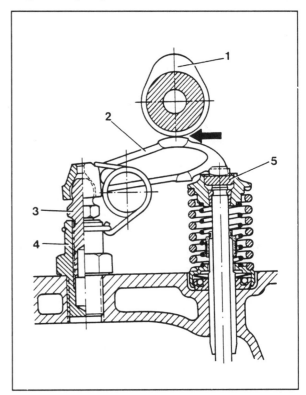

- Set the camshaft in such a way that the cam tip -1- points away from the rocker arm -2- of the valve to be tested.
- Test the valve clearance with a feeler blade between the surface of the rocker and camshaft -arrow-.

Valves	Engine115/123		Engine 110	
	cold	warm	cold	warm
Intake	0,10mm	0,15mm	0,10mm	0,15mm
Exhaust	0,20mm	0,25mm	0,25mm	0,30mm

The engine is regarded as "cold" at a coolant temperature of approx. 20 degrees C. To adjust the valve clearance of a "warm engine", the coolant temperature should be between 45 and 75 degrees C.

- The valve clearance is properly adjusted if the feeler blade can be just pulled through.

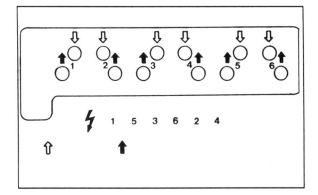

Caution:

Do not confuse the intake and exhaust valves. The illustration shows engine 123. In engine 115, the valves lie behind one another in a row. The order of intake and exhaust valves is the same; firing order: 1-3-4-2. In engine 110, the exhaust valves are on the side where the exhaust manifold is. The intake valves are on the opposite side; firing order: 1-5-3-6-2-4.

Adjustment

- If the specified value is not reached, adjust the valve clearance at the adjusting bolt -3- with an open ended spanner.
- Use the adjusting bolt to set the valve clearance. By tightening, the clearance is increased, by loosening it is decreased.

Caution:

A torque of 20Nm to 40Nm is necessary to turn the valve clearance adjusting bolt. If the torque is below 20 Nm, either the adjusting bolt alone or with the threaded bush -4- must be replaced. The rocker arm must be removed for this. Lubricate the thread of the new bush with a multi purpose lubricant and tighten to 80Nm. Check that there are no metal shavings while fitting the new bush. Refit the rocker arm, see also page 40.

Caution:

If the range of the adjusting bolt is not enough to reach the specified value, a thinner pressure disc will have to be fitted.

- **Engine 110:** Test all pressure springs and rubber washers of the sparkplug recesses for damage or porosity.
- Test the valve clearance once again, then turn the engine.
- In this way test or adjust the clearance of all the other valves.
- Refit the rocker cover, see page 22.

- Refit the air filter, see page 98.
- Refit the green control lead to the transistorised ignition system or attach the lead to the ignition coil.

Jump starting

In jump starting with jumper leads the following should be taken into account:

- For petrol engines with up to 2 500cc, a jumper lead of at least 16mm^2 lead cross section (about 5mm diameter) should be used. For diesel engines or engines bigger than 2 500cc, the lead cross section should be at least 25mm^2. The lead cross section is normally indicated on the pack of the jumper leads. It is advisable to purchase a lead with insulated clamps and a 25mm^2 cross section, as this can be used for all vehicles.
- Both batteries must be 12 volt batteries.
- A flat battery can freeze at -10° C, and this will have to be defrosted before the jumper leads are attached.
- The flat battery must be attached to electric wiring.

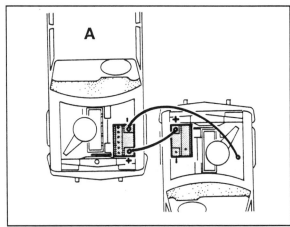

- Position the vehicles far enough apart as to prevent any metallic contact, which could otherwise cause an electric current to flow as soon as the positive cables are connected.
- Apply the handbrake in both vehicles and have the gears in neutral. Switch an automatic gearbox to parking position "P".
- Switch off all electrical items.
- Let the vehicle providing the power -A- idle in neutral.

- Attach the jumper leads in the following order:

1. Attach the red lead to the positive pole of the uncharged battery.
2. Attach the other end of the red cable to the positive pole of the battery which will give the power.
3. Attach the black negative lead to the battery which will provide the power.
4. The other end of the black lead must be attached to a good earth point, for example the engine block of the receiving vehicle. In this way earth losses are avoided. Under unfavorable conditions, the battery could explode when the lead is attached to the negative pole of the receiving vehicle due to spark formation and gas development.

- Check the jumper lead clamps for secureness. Check that the jumper leads cannot be damaged by any parts of the car that they are lying on, eg. radiator.

Caution:

When connected, the clamps of the jump leads must not touch one another or the chassis or frame.

- Start the engine of the receiving vehicle and let it run. Do not use the starter for more than 15 seconds without a break of at least one minute, as the high electrical absorption causes the jumper leads and battery poles to heat up.
- Leave the vehicle which is to provide the power running in neutral. This avoids damage to the generator caused by voltage surges during the starting process. If the idling slows down too much, however, the accelerator pedal may be used.
- **After jump starting** remove the leads in the **opposite** order.

Caution:

If the prescribed method of attachment is not followed, there is a danger of corrosion due to leaking battery acid. Injury and damage could also be caused by an exploding battery. Both vehicles could end up with electrical faults.

Engine fault diagnosis

If the engine does not want to start, systematically narrow down the fault. For the engine to start, two conditions must always be met: the fuel/air mixture must get to the cylinders and the ignition spark must reach the sparkplugs. Thus the first thing to always check is whether fuel is being delivered.

Fault: The engine is hard to start, or doesn't start at all	
Cause:	**Solution:**
Operating fault in starting **Carburetor engine:**	**Cold engine:** Slowly depress accelerator pedal once, and release, depress clutch, switch on ignition, start, do not accelerate. Immediately drive off. Only in extreme cases of frost: allow engine to warm up for 30 seconds.
	Warm engine: Slowly depress accelerator pedal while starting. Release accelerator pedal once engine starts.
	Hot engine: Completely depress accelerator pedal before starting engine, keep foot down without pumping.
Injection engine:	Slightly depress the accelerator pedal and rest in that position. Totally depress clutch pedal.
	Turn ignition key until engine starts. Now release ignition key.
Faulty ignition system, dirty or maladjusted	Test ignition system according to fault table
Faulty fuel system, dirty	Test fuel system according to fault table
Starter turns too slowly	Load battery. Test starter.
Valve clearance wrong	Correct valve clearance
Compression pressure too low	Adjust valve clearance, overhaul engine
Stretching of timing chain	Test timing, replace timing chain
Cylinder head gasket defective	Replace gasket

THE IGNITION SYSTEM

The ignition system provides the spark for each cylinder in the engine at the right time, which ignites the fuel air mixture. The battery voltage is converted from 12 volts to 25 000 to 30 000 volts in the ignition coil.

Depending on the model, it is fitted with either a contact breaker point ignition system, which must be maintained at regular intervals, or a largely maintenance-free transistorised system.

The ignition system consists of:

- the ignition coil
- the sparkplugs
- the distributor with points or transistorised system
- the transistorised testing socket.

The distributor, with the aid of the points, induces the ignition voltage in the ignition coil. A condenser reduces the spark formation at the contact breaker contact, which decreases the burning of the surfaces of contact. The ignition voltage formed in the ignition coil, is sent to the spark plugs via the distributor. The spark then jumps across the sparkplug electrodes and ignites the fuel air mixture.

Function of the transistorised system

The transistor ignition system is an ignition system without contact points. Instead of the contact breaker, the distributer is equipped with a maintenance-free induction transmitter. An ignition condenser is not required. The induction transmitter consists of a durable magnet, a magnet coil and a magnetic sensor connected to the distributor driveshaft.

The induction transmitter drives the transistorised ignition test socket, and determines the point at which the ignition coil power is switched on and off. Thus the induction transmitter determines the point of ignition.

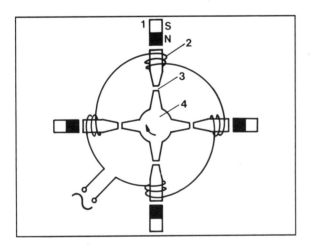

Since the magnetic sensor -4- turns with the distributor shaft, the distance -3- between the sensor and the stator poles changes constantly, which causes alternating impulses in the magnet coil -2-. Depending on the impulse changes, the test socket together with the ignition coil release the ignition spark. The spark always occurs when the poles of the magnetic sensor move away from the stator poles. Other illustrated parts are: -1- permanent magnet, -S- south pole and -N- north pole of the permanent magnet.

To protect the test socket and the ignition coil from over-heating, the test socket switches off the power supply to the ignition coil if the ignition is left on in a stationary vehicle

For safety reasons, the ignition coil has a 5,5mm opening with plug. This allows the leak from the ignition coil to drain in the case of a defect in the transistor ignition test socket.

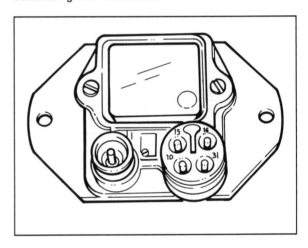

The base plate of the transistor ignition switching device serves as a heat conductor. Before fitting, thoroughly clean the base plate and paint with a heat conducting paste, so that good heat conduction is possible.

Caution:

The heat from operating the device is conducted via the body, which is why the engine may not be running if the switching device is not properly installed.

Safety precautions for the transistor ignition system

In electronic ignition systems, the ignition voltage can be as high as 30 kV. Under unfavorable conditions, for example moisture in the engine block, the voltage may jump the insulation, causing electric-shocks if touched.

To prevent injury to people and/or the damage of the electronic ignition system, the following should be noted when working on a vehicle with electronic ignition system:

- Do not touch or remove the ignition lead while the engine is running or ignition switch is on.
- Only remove the leads of the ignition system when the ignition is switched off. A high voltage shock can be caused by the vibration of the distributor when the ignition is on.
- The attachment and removal of measuring equipment (tachometer/ignition tester) should only be done when the ignition is off.
- No suppressor condenser and test lamp may be attached to 1 (-) terminal.
- Do not attach any measuring equipment or a 12 volt ignition spark lamp to terminal 15 of the ignition coil while the engine is running.
- Terminals 1 and 15 of the ignition coil may not be earthed.
- Tests on, for example, the ignition cables (terminal 4) or the removal of spark plugs, may not be undertaken while the engine is running.
- Do not test the ignition voltage while starting with a removed ignition lead of terminal 4 of the distributor.
- Before operating the engine cranking speed (e.g compression pressure test) or turning the engine over by hand, switch off the ignition and remove the plug from the inlet transmitter of the distributor (green lead).
- The ignition coil may not be replaced by a different type. Under no circumstances may an ignition coil be installed which is meant for a points ignition system.
- If heated to more than 80° C (e.g. when painting, steaming), the engine may not be started immediately after the heating phase.
- The engine should be switched off when cleaning.
- The battery must be completely disconnected for electro and spot welding.
- People with a pace-maker should not carry out work on the electronic ignition system.

Ignition system testing

If the engine does not start, it could also be due to a defect in the ignition system.

- Attach a voltmeter to the battery poles.
- Switch on the ignition; the voltage should be around 12 volts. Load the battery if necessary.
- Remove the ignition lead of terminal 4 from the middle of the distributor and put it against earth. Switch on the ignition and measure the voltage, it should be around 10 volts.

Points ignition system

- Attach a voltmeter to terminal 15 of the ignition coil and earth. Switch on the ignition with the ignition lead still laying against earth. Close the contact breaker by turning the engine in the direction of rotation with a Stillson wrench by the crankshaft pulley. The meter must now show at least 5 volts.
- Switch on the ignition and test the voltage. It should be at least 9.6 volts. **Caution:** First remove the wrench from the crankshaft pulley.
- Test the starter resistor. The starter resistor is situated in a ceramic part above the ignition coil. Remove one lead connection of the resistor and attach an ohmmeter to both contacts of the resistor. At approximately 20° C, it should be around 1,8 Ohms (red securing clip) or 1.4 Ohms (golden securing clip). Higher values are permissible at higher temperatures.

Transistorised ignition system with starter resistance

- Test the input voltage of the starter resistor, by attaching a voltmeter to the black/red cable of the 1,4 Ohm starter resistor and earth. It should be approximately 12 volts. Switch on the ignition - the voltage should now be around 8,5 volts.
- Attach a voltmeter to the ignition coil terminal 15 and earth. It should be approximately 4,5 volts.
- Attach a voltmeter to ignition coil terminal 1 and earth. It should be 0,5 to 2,0 volts. If it is higher, the switching device is defective. If the specified value is reached without the presence of a spark, the transmitter parts in the ignition distributor or the secondary coil must be tested.
- Test the starter resistors with a voltmeter, by taking one lead at a time off and attaching the voltmeter to the various resistors. Specified values: a resistor with a blue anodised clip - approximately 0,4 Ohm, a metallic clip - 0,6 Ohm. **Caution:** These values apply to a temperature of around 20° C, at higher temperatures, the values of the resistors also increase.

Transistor ignition system without starter resistors

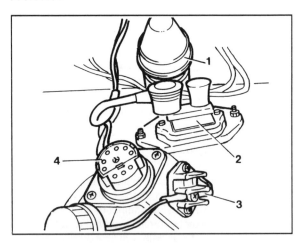

- Remove the cover of the diagnostic socket -4-.
- Attach a voltmeter between terminal 5 and earth, then switch on the ignition. The voltmeter must show a battery voltage (approximately 12 volts), otherwise test according to the wiring diagram.

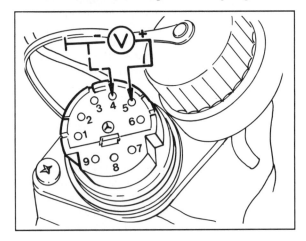

- Test the voltage difference between terminal 5 and 4 of the socket with a voltmeter. Specified value: 0 volt. **Caution:** if the voltage measures more than 0,1 volt, switch the ignition off immediately and replace the trigger box. Also test the ignition coil.
- Test the dwell angle at starter cranking speed. Remove the green lead from the switching device and connect a dwell angle meter to terminal 1 of the diagnostic socket, terminal TD of the switching device and earth.
  Specified value: 7 to 25 degrees.
- If the measured values are higher than 25 degrees, replace the trigger box.
- If the measured values ar different, test the connecting leads according to the wiring diagram.
- Test the resistance of the transmitter coil with an Ohmmeter at the plug of the green control lead. Attach Ohmmeter between the inner and outer contact of the removed plug (terminals 7 and 3), **Specified value: 600 100 Ohms.**

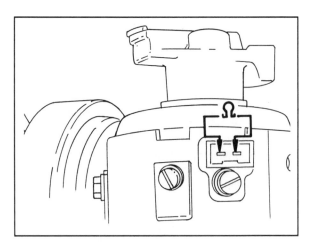

- If the specified value is not reached, remove the control lead from the distributor and attach an Ohmmeter to the contacts of the distributor. If the specified value is now 600 100 Ohms, replace the control lead or distributor.

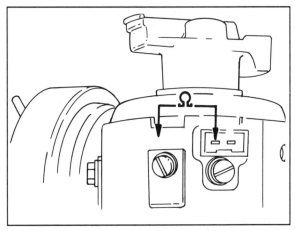

- At the removed plug of the green control lead, connect terminals 3 and 7 to earth via the Ohmmeter. The ohmmeter should show a value of more than 200k Ohms.
- If the specified value is not reached, remove the control lead at the distributor and test the resistance of one of the two contacts against earth. Specified value: 200 k Ohms or more. If the specified value is not reached, replace the control lead or renew the distributor.

Condenser testing

Points ignition

The condenser is found in the distributor. It regulates the ignition spark between the two contact surfaces of the points when opened. In this way premature burning of the contacts is avoided.

A defective condenser causes difficulty in starting, or the engine no longer reaches maximum engine speed. A defective condenser can be recognised by badly burned distributor points and a weak ignition spark. Defective condensers are extremely rare.

Visual testing

- Remove the distributor cap and contacts. If the contacts show blue burn marks, this points to a defective condenser. Grey or black burn-marks are normal.
- Let an assistant start the engine once the distributor cap is removed. Watch the distributor points while starting. If continuously strong sparks occur between the contact points, the condenser is defective. Weak irregular sparks are normal.

Ignition coil testing

The ignition coil can be tested with an Ohmmeter.
- Remove the earth lead from the battery.
- Remove the ignition coil cap, by removing the clip with a broad screwdriver and lifting to the back.
- Remove the connections of the ignition coil.

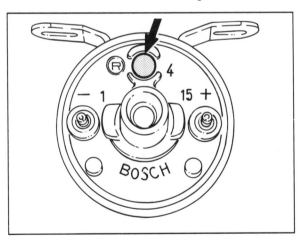

- If the plug -arrow- of the ignition coil is pushed out, replace the coil.
- Test the primary resistance of the ignition coil by attaching an Ohmmeter to terminals 1 and 15.
- Test the secondary resistance by attaching an Ohmmeter to terminals 1 and 4.

Ignition system	Ignition coil resistance	
	primary	secondary
Points	1,2 - 1,6 Ohms	7 - 12 K Ohms
Transistorised ignition with starting resistance	0,33 - 0,46 Ohms	7 - 12 K Ohms
Transistorised ignition without starting resistance	0,5 - 0,9 Ohms	6 - 16 K Ohms

- Remove the electrical leads from the ignition coil.
- Attach the cap at the back, spread and clip forwards. Test that the leads are sitting properly in the cover and clip the cap at the bottom .
- Attach the earth cable to the battery.

Caution:

If the ignition coil is to be replaced, do not mix it with the coil for the contact breaker ignition system. The timing device would be damaged.

Ignition cable testing

Only vehicles with transistorised ignition system
- Remove the earth cable from battery
- Remove the cables from the distributor cap and spark plugs.
  Caution: pull at the plug not the cable.
- Test the resistance of the cable between the distributor cap contacts and the contacts of the spark plugs. Specified value: 1 k Ohm.

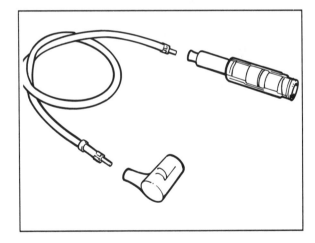

- If the specified value is not reached, remove the sparkplug connector from the cable. The resistance of the connector should be 1 k Ohm. If not, replace the connector, or renew the ignition lead or distributor cap.
- If the resistance is too high, clean the cable connections and re-test, replace the cable if necessary.
- Test the rotor arm.
- Refit the earth cable to the battery.

Rotor arm - testing

For a good ignition spark, the resistance (measured in ohms) should not be too high.

● Remove the distributor cap.

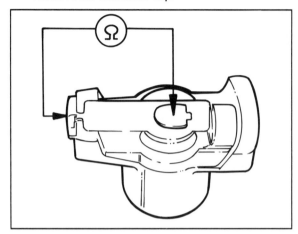

● Attach an ohmmeter to the rotor arm. The specified value should be around 1 k ohm, identification R 1.

Distributor points - replacing

In time, burn marks will develop on the contact breaker points, which are seen as little bumps and craters. The plastic cam follower also gets worn, which decreases the contact distances. The result: A weak spark at the plugs.

Removal
● Remove the earth cable from the battery.
● Remove the distributor cap, by undoing the 2 securing clips. Insert a screwdriver into the slit of the clip and press downwards. Turn to the left about 90°. In this way the clip is removed from the securing bracket on the side of the distributor.
● Remove the rotor arms and, if present, remove the dust deflector cap.

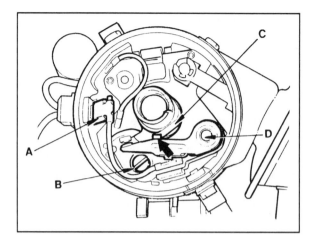

● Remove the low tension cable -A-.
● Unscrew the bolt -B- and remove the points.

Caution:

The bolt -B- should not fall into the distributor, since the distributor would then have to be **removed.**

Refitting

Before refitting, clean the new contact breaker point with a clean rag to remove any grease or moisture.

● Grease the contact pivot -D- and the cam follower -arrow- with high temperature bearing grease. Also grease the cam -c- of the distributor shaft with grease which is normally supplied with the points.

Caution:

Carefully remove any grease which has got onto the contact points, or the engine will not start. Blotting paper is good for this purpose.

● Refit the contact breaker point and screw in the bolt, do not tighten.
● Refit the cables
● Adjust the point gap (dwell angle) Pg 57 and tighten the bolt.
● Where present, refit the dust deflector cap. The nose of the cap must fit into the slot in the distributor housing.
● Refit the rotor arm. By lightly turning the arm from side to side, check that it locates in the distributor shaft.
● Refit distributor cap - the nose of the cap must fit into the slot at edge of distributor. Press the 2 securing clips downwards and secure into brackets on side of distributor by turning.
● Check that clips are securing distributor cap properly on distributor.
● Refit battery earth cable.

Dwell angle - testing/adjusting

To adjust the contact breaker points accurately, the workshops use a dwell angle meter. This meter also has the advantage that even with slightly worn contact surfaces, the dwell angle can still be measured accurately. If using this meter, connect it as per manufacturer's instructions.

Testing with contact point measuring device

- Start the engine and let it idle in neutral, take a reading. Compare the measured value with the specified value.

Engine	Specified value	Adjusting value
115	46-53° 51%-59%	53±1° 59%±1%
123	34-41° 53%-69%	41±1o 69%±1%
110	39-42° 65%-70%	42±1° 70%±1%

Caution:

Depending on the meter used, the measurements will be shown either in Degrees or percent.

- Now let the engine run at approximately 3 000 rpm. The contact point gap should not change from the previously measured value by more than 3° (4 cylinder engine: approximately 3%; 6 cylinder engine: 5%). A larger value variation indicates a worn distributor shaft. In this case the distributor must be replaced.
- If the measured contact gap lies beyond the specified value, replace the contact breaker points.

Adjusting with dwell meter
- Remove the distributor cap and rotor arm.
- Put the gears in neutral and pull on the handbrake. Let an assistant switch on the ignition, and crank the engine.

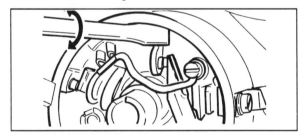

- To adjust the contact breaker point, insert a screwdriver in such a way that it fits into the notch of the contact breaker. Change the points gap at the engine cranking speed by turning the screwdriver back and forth, until the measuring instrument shows ADJUSTING VALUE, see table above.
- After adjusting, tighten the securing bolt of the points.
- Now test the points while the engine is running and idling, repeating adjustment procedure if necessary.

Adjustment with feeler blade

If no dwell meter is available, the point gap may **temporarily** be adjusted with the aid of a feeler blade. Subsequently the dwell angle must be tested with a dwell angle meter.

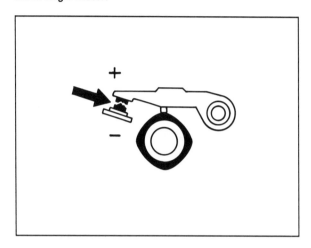

- Turn the crankshaft and thus the distributor shaft by hand until the plastic cam follower rests against the highest part of the distributor cam. Turn the crankshaft, see page 47.

Caution:

Possibly with newly fitted contacts, the cam follower does not touch the cams of the shaft. Loosen the contact breaker points slightly and push into the correct position with a screwdriver. Now tighten the contact breaker point.

- The correct contact gap is around 0,4mm. Push the feeler blade between the two contact surfaces -arrow-.
- If the gap is too large or too small: undo the securing bolt of the contact breaker point slightly. Adjust the bottom part of the contact breaker point with a screwdriver, until the feeler blade slides firmly between the contacts.
- Tighten the securing bolt of the contact breaker point.
- Turn the crankshaft and with it the ignition shaft in the direction of engine rotation until the points open again. Once again check the contact gap and adjust if necessary.
- Refit the rotor arm and distributor cap.
- Adjust the timing.

Timing - testing/adjusting

The timing is adjusted according to the replacement of the contact breaker points in relation to the maintenance intervals. In vehicles with a transistorised ignition system, the timing does not usually change.

To test and adjust the timing use a tachometer and timing light.

- Bring the engine to running temperature; approximately 70° C coolant temperature.

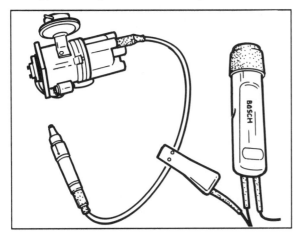

- Attach a tachometer and timing light according to instructions.

Caution:

The vacuum lead to the distributor must either be removed or left in place, depending on the engine version, see "timing specifications" on page 59.

- The air conditioner must be switched off.
- Start the engine and let it run in neutral.

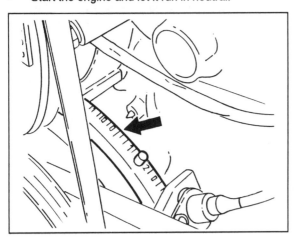

- Aim the timing light at the pointer on the crankcase.

Caution:

There is a danger of injury by the turning fanbelt and pulley. The timing has been correctly adjusted, if the test value seems to stay constant below the point of reference. See the timing table.

- If the timing markings are not aligned, loosen the securing bolt of the distributor slightly, increase the engine speed to 4 500 rpm (280E: 3 000 rpm) and turn the distributor until the point of reference aligns with the adjusting value.
- Tighten the securing bolt.
- Check the idling speed.
- Check the timing again.
- Remove the measuring devices, refit the vacuum hoses, if removed.

● **Timing-specifications**

Caution:

Depending on engine version, the vacuum lead is either left or removed from the distributor while testing the timing.

With fuel with a low octane value (RON less than 98 at sea level or RON less than 93 at altitude), the timing is to be retarded, i.e. 1 - 2 degrees crankshaft rotation per 1 RON. **Caution:** The maximum degrees may not be more than 6 degrees crankshaft rotation.

Caution:

If timing is decreased, high rotational speeds are to be avoided. The fuel consumption would increase and the performance of the engine decrease.

As soon as fuel with the prescribed octane level is again available, readjust to full ignition advance.

Model	Distributor No	Installed value	Test value		Dynamic adjusting value		
		Static timing	Idling speed rpm	Timing BTDC	Engine rpm	Vacuum hoses removed	attached
200 till 6.80		14° BTDC	850 ± 50	15° ± 3 [1]	4500	40° BTDC	54°-60° BTDC
200 7.80		13° BTDC	800 ± 50	13° ± 3 [1]	4500	32° BTDC	40°-44° BTDC
230		14° BTDC	850 ± 50	15° ± 3 [1]	4500	40° BTDC	54°-60° BTDC
230E	0 237003022	13° BTDC	800 ± 50	1° ± 3 [2]	4500	32° BTDC	40°-44° BTDC
	0 237002066	15° BTDC	800 ± 50	15° ± 3 [2]	4500	32° BTDC	40°-44° BTDC
	0 237003025	15° BTDC	800 ± 50	3° ± 3 [2]	4500	32° BTDC	40°-44° BTDC
250		8° BTDC	850 ± 50	0° ± 4 [2]	4500	32° BTDC	45°-49° BTDC
280 1.80		5° BTDC	850 ± 50	3° ± 3 [2]	4500	28° BTDC	36°-40° BTDC
280 2.80		10° BTDC	850 ± 50	0° ± 4 [2]	4500	32° BTDC	40°-44° BTDC
280 9.81		10° BTDC	750 ± 50	10° ± 3 [1]	750	10° BTDC	-
280E		10° BTDC	800 ± 50	0° ± 3 [1]	3000	32° BTDC	40°-44° BTDC
280E 2.80		10° BTDC	800 ± 50	0° ± 3 [1]	3500	30° BTDC	38°-42° BTDC
280E	0 237306045	12° BTDC	750 ± 50	10° ± 3 [1]	3500	30° BTDC	38°-42° BTDC

[1] = Vacuum hose(s) **removed** from distributor
[2] = Vacuum hose(s) **attached** to distributor

Distributor - removal and refitting

Removal

- Disconnect the battery earth lead.
- Remove the plug with the green control lead from the distributor. First unbolt the securing clip.
- Remove the distributor cap, by first undoing the two clips. Insert the screwdriver into the cross slot of the hook, pushing downwards and turning approximately 90° to the left. This unhooks the clip from the distributor.
- Disconnect the vacuum lead.
- Turn the engine with the socket (SW 27) on the crankshaft pulley bolt until the rotor arm is aligned with the mark on the rim of the distributor body. Cylinder No.1 is now at ignition TDC.

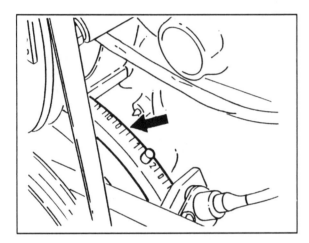

- The mark on the vibration damper should be aligned with the pointer on the crankcase -arrow-. Lift the dust cover slightly if necessary.

Caution:

do not turn the engine backwards

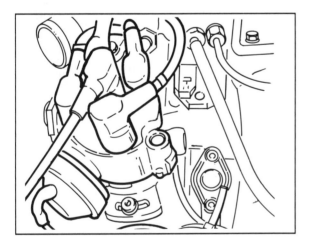

- Remove the securing bolt of the distributor with an Allen key , SW 6, and pull out the distributor.

Caution:

Do not turn the engine any further when the distributor is removed.

Refitting

- Before refitting check that the engine is still at the ignition TDC of cylinder No. 1.
- Turn the distributor shaft in such a way that the marks on the distributor rotor and body are aligned.
- Refit the distributor so that the slot at the base of the distributor is positioned over the bore of the securing bolt.
- Refit the securing bolt, do not tighten.
- Adjust the timing, by attaching a timing light according to the manufacturer's instructions. Switch on the engine and point the light at the mark on the timing case.
- The timing is correct if the correct mark on the crankshaft pulley is constant under the datum point of timing case, see the opposite illustration and ignition timing table.
- If the specified value is not reached, undo the securing bolt of distributor and turn the distributor until the marks are aligned.
- Tighten the securing bolt of the distributor.
- In a point ignition system, adjust the contact points.
- Connect the vacuum lead.
- Check the dust cover to see that the nose of the cover fits into the slot at the rim of the distributor housing.
- Check that the bracket of the distributor housing is secure, tighten the bolt if necessary.
- Refit the distributor cap so that the ignition cables of cylinder No.1 are above the groove on the edge of the distributor. The groove is only visible if the dust cover is lifted slightly. The mark "1" can be found on the distributor cap next to the relevant ignition cable connection.
- Test the fit of the distributor cap by moving it from side to side. The cap should not be able to turn.
- Push the two side clips downwards. Secure into the brackets by turning and release.
- Check that the clips are secured in the correct position and the distributor cap is well secured.
- Connect the green control lead to the distributor and secure with the bracket.
- Connect the battery earth lead.
- Adjust the timing while the engine is running, and check the dwell angle.

THE SPARK PLUGS

The spark plug consists of the centre electrode, the insulator with housing and the earth electrode. The earth electrode is fixed in the insulator. The ignition spark, which ignites the fuel/air mixture, jumps between the centre and earth electrodes. Ease in starting, idling performance, acceleration and maximum speed are all dependent on the spark plugs. Unless there is a very good reason, the recommended spark plugs should be used. A thermal value identification number indicates the degree of heat tolerance of a spark plug in an engine under specific conditions. The lower this identification number of a spark plug is, the higher it's resistance to spontaneous ignition and the lower it's resistance to fouling. The higher the identification number, the lower it's resistance to spontaneous ignition, and the higher it's resistance to fouling.

The thermal value identification number is found in the spark plug code. It is read as follows:

Bosch spark plug

Example

W	R	7	D	C
1	2	3	4	5

1 W = thread M14 x 1,25 with flat sealing seat, SW 21; F = thread M14 x 1,25 with flat sealing seat, SW 16; M = thread M18 x 1,5 with flat sealing seat, SW 25; H = thread M14 x 1,25 with ball sealing seat, SW 21; SW = key width.

2 R = with resistance, for suppression.
The function of the ignition system is not affected by this.

3 Thermal value identification number.
The thermal value scale goes from 06 ("cold") to 13 ("warm").

4 A = thread length 12,7mm, normal; B = thread length 12,7mm extended nose; C = thread length 19mm, normal; D = thread length 19mm, extended nose.

5 Electrode material of centre electrode: Cr-Ni alloy. C = Ni-Cu-alloy centre electrode, S = silver centre electrode, P = platinum centre electrode, O = standard spark plug with reinforced centre electrode. By the copper nucleus (Cu) and even more the silver centre electrode, the heat conducting properties and with them the thermal value is increased.

Beru spark plug

Example

14	K	7	D	U
1	2	3	4	5

1 Thread diameter in mm, in this case M14 x 1,25

2 Construction feature, e.g K = cone seat, R = suppressor resistance.

3 Thermal value identification number (as in Bosch).

4 Thread length (as in Bosch).

5 Electrode material, e.g U = copper nucleus.

The recommended thermal value should only be changed if the working conditions change drastically and problems arise. If the spark plugs are always carbon fouled, due to running over short distances, it is recommended to use a spark plug with the next highest thermal value. If the engine is always driven at high speed, the next lowest spark plug could become necessary.

The correct spark plug for MERCEDES

Engine	Bosch	Beru	Champion	EG*
102	H7D H7DC	14K-7D 14K-7DU	BN-9Y S9YC	0,8 0,8
110/115	W7D W7DC	14-7D 14-7DU	N9Y	0,8 0,8
123 till 8.81	W6D W6DC	14-6D 14-6DU	N8Y	0,8 0,8
123 since 9/81	W5D W5DC	14-5D 14-5DU	N8Y	0,8 0,8

*) EG = electrode gap in mm.

3-THE SPARK PLUGS

Ignition system maintenance

The electronic ignition system is practically maintenance free, although the connections and spark plugs should be checked when servicing.

Distributor cap - testing

- Remove the distributor cap, see page 56.
- The cap should be dry inside.
- Check the connections for wear and corrosion, clean with glass paper if necessary.
- Check the central carbon contact for ease of movement and wear, by compressing with a finger.
- Check inside the distributor cap for tracking marks. These are seen as thin irregular tracks on the surface of the distributor cap.
- Clean the distributor cap with a dry, clean rag. Check for hairline cracks and replace if necessary. Spray the inside of the cap with WD 40 or similar.
- Remove the distributor rotor arm and check for hairline cracks as well as clean contacts, clean if necessary.
- Oil the felt in the distributor shaft with a drop of oil.
- Refit the rotor arm with the nose of the rotor in the slot of the distributor shaft. To test if the distributor rotor arm is secure, turn it slightly from side to side.
- Refit the distributor cap, see page 56.

Electrical connections - testing

- Check that all electrical connections of the ignition coil and the distributor are secure.
- Clean the corroded connections with a steel brush or glass paper, spray with WD 40 if necessary.
- All the contacts must be dry, so clean the contacts and spray with WD 40 if necessary.

Spark plug testing

The spark plugs should be checked every 10 000km and replaced every 20 000km. Platinum spark plugs normally have a longer life. They must be replaced if the centre electrode is no longer recognisable in the insulated base.

- Remove all plug connectors by pulling at the connectors, not the cables. Special pliers, for example HAZET 1849, make this job easier. Blow spark plug recesses with compressed air.
- Unscrew the spark plugs with a suitable plug spanner and check the centre. With a little experience, the condition of the engine can be determined. The following rules apply:

Electrodes and insulation bodies

- Grey-brown = Good carburetor setting and spark plugs in good condition
- Black = Mixture too rich
- Light grey = mixture too lean
- Oil fouling = Malfunction of particular spark plug or worn piston rings
- Clean the spark plugs with a copper brush or sand blaster
- Check the insulation of the spark plugs for thin, irregular tracks on the surface. If they cannot be completely removed, replace the specific plug.
- If necessary, file the centre electrode with a file, thus smoothing out burn marks.

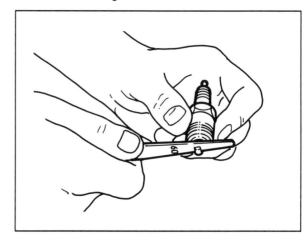

- Check the electrode gap with a feeler blade. specified value: **0,8mm**

- To adjust the contact gap, bend the earth electrode. A simple, practical tool is available for this, or sideways tapping against the earth electrode will do. While bending open, support a small screwdriver on the thread edge of the plug, never on the centre electrode, as it will be damaged.
- Clean the thread of the plugs and cylinder head.
- Screw the spark plug in by hand. **Caution:** Plugs must go in straight.
- Tighten the spark plugs to 20 Nm.

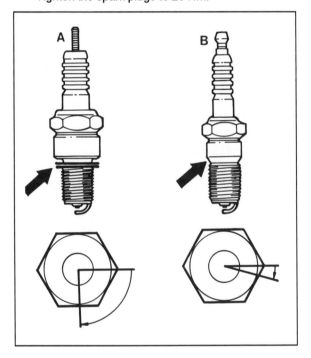

Caution:

If a torque wrench is not available, turn the spark plugs with **a flat sealing seat -A-** with a plug spanner by **approximately 90°.** Turn the spark plugs with **a ball sealing seat -B- by approximately 15°**. This also applies to used spark plugs with a flat sealing seat. If tightened too much, the plugs may crack when removing or damage the thread of the cylinder head. in this case repair the thread with TDC or Heli-coil inserts.

- Refit the spark plugs, checking that they and the ignition cables are secure by moving them from side to side.

Ignition system fault diagnosis

Fault: the engine is hard to start, or does not start at all.	
Cause	**Remedy**
No ignition spark, distributor cap moist/dirty	Clean distributor cap and dry, spray inside with ignition spray
Cracks in distributor cap, burn marks	Replace distributor cap
Worn carbon brush in distributor cap	Replace carbon brush
Defective distributor rotor arm	Replace distributor rotor arm
Resistance of distributor rotor arm too high	Replace distributor rotor arm
Spark plugs connected in wrong order	Connect spark plugs in firing order 1-3-4-2 or 1-5-3-6-2-4
Spark plugs moist due to starting attempts	Remove spark plugs and dry
Spark plugs moist and dirty on outside	Clean and dry spark plugs.
Performance of ignition coil too low	Check that electrical leads of ignition coil are well secured and have good contact
Ignition coil cracked, burn marks	Replace ignition coil
Loose or faulty connections	Check connections
Ignition point badly adjusted	Adjust points
Contact points burned	Replace Contact points
Capacitor loose or defective	Tighten or renew capacitor
Electrode gap of spark plug incorrect	Reset electrode gap

ENGINE LUBRICATION

Despite all attempts of perfecting the MERCEDES by improving the construction and production techniques to increase its life, reliability and degree of economy,the regular lubrication and service according to the MERCEDES service system remains imperative.

Function of the engine oil
Depending on the operating conditions, engine oils undergo a variety of stresses. It is thus very difficult to determine the effects of the various operating conditions on the engine oil. Engines which run at high revolutions or with a full load for long periods, reach high oil temperatures. With the action of high temperatures and oxygen, the oil starts to oxidize. The oxidation products thicken the oil and can be deposited as a varnish-like covering on the upper parts of the pistons, in the piston ring slots and the valve stems. This can lead to a carboning up of the valve heads.

If the cylinders receive a fuel mixture which is too rich, if maximum performance is only required rarely or never from an engine, or if the engine is driven when under cooled (city traffic), an incomplete combustion is the result. Carbon, oil carbon and other products, the unburned fuel even and the condensation of moisture, lead to the formation of sludge, acid and asphalt. The unburned fuel is deposited on the cold cylinder walls and runs into the crankcase, causing the oil film on the cylinders and pistons to be washed off. The result is decreased lubrication of the piston journal and a thinning of oil, which, depending on the fuel content, affects the lubricating properties of the oil.

In extreme cases of oil thinning, a premature oil change should be undertaken. Since the fuel particles in the oil evaporate in a hot engine, the oil level should be checked regularly in winter (many cold starts - high level of fuel in the oil).

Viscosity of engine oil
The viscosity of oil is regarded as its consistency. Depending on the temperature, oil tends to become thinner. With increased warmth, it will become liquid. The adhesive properties of the lubricating film are thus negatively influenced. In the cold, the oil becomes thick and the flow is slowed increasing the inner friction. These properties make it necessary to use an engine oil with a consistency which changes as little as possible in temperature variations. In a cold engine it should be liquid enough to ease the work of the starter and to run to all the lubricating areas quickly from the time of starting. The viscosity or consistency of an oil is synonymous with its inner friction and is marked according to the SAE system (Society of Automotive Engineers), for example SAE 30, SAE 10 etc.

High SAE values point to thick oils, low values to thin oils. The viscosity oil does not explain the lubricating properties of oil.

Multi-grade oil
Multi-grade oils as well as mono-grade oils can be used for the MERCEDES engine. Multi-grade oils have the advantage that they adapt to the temperature variations (winter/summer). Multi-grade oils build onto a thin mono-grade oil(e.g. 15W). The oil is stabilised in a heated state by so-called thickeners, so that the correct lubrication is given to each operating condition. In choosing a multi-grade oil, the modern oils are preferable with a high body range (e.g. 15W-40, 15W-50).The W in the SAE value points to the suitability of the oil for winter use.

Light oils
Light oils are multi-grade oils, to which, amongst other things, friction inhibitors have been added, so that a fuel saving of up to 2 % is apparently possible. Light oils have a low viscosity (e.g 10W-30). They require unconventional primary oils (synthetic oils). In buying a light oil, take care to buy one which has been approved by MERCEDES BENZ.

Areas of application/categories of viscosity

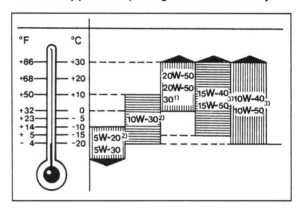

1) In constant exterior temperatures of +30° C, SAE 40 may be used.
2) Use engine oil SAE 5W-20 only at constant exterior temperatures of +10° C, SAE 10W-30 in moderate areas as all-year oil.
3) All-year oil

As the neighbouring oils of the SAE oils overlap, short-term temperature variations can remain unnoticed. It is permissible to mix oils of differing viscosity with one another, when oil has to be added and the exterior temperatures no longer correspond with the oil in the engine.

Additional lubricants - without exception - should not be added to the fuel or the lubricating oil.

Specification of the engine oil

Only heavy duty oils (H.D.oils) are allowed in modern engines. H.D. oils are oils, which have been improved by the addition of various chemical additives. These additives create better corrosion protection, a more favorable relationship against signs of oxidation, a decreased tendency to sludge formation in the crankshaft housing, a better level of viscosity, cleaning and dissolving properties. The cleaning and dissolving additives not only decrease the carbon formation in the engine, but can also dissolve the carbon and can disperse these as well as other impurities, keeping them suspended so that they will drain out during an oil change.

The quality of an H.D. oil is identified by the API system (API: American Petroleum institute). European manufacturers also comply with this system.

The identification is seen as two letters. The first letter indicates the area of application: **S**=Service, suitable **Petrol engines**; **C**=Commercial, suitable for **Diesel engines**.

The second letter indicates the quality in alphabetical order.

The highest quality oil of the API specification for petrol engines is **SG** and for diesel engines is **CD**. **Caution:** CD engine oils, which are designated specifically for diesel engines by the manufacturer, are not suitable for petrol engines. There are oils which are suitable for petrol and diesel engines. In this case both specifications (e.g. SF/CD) are marked on the can.

For MERCEDES engine oils of the API specification **SF** are suitable. Higher value oil of specification SG may also be used. **Always check that the engine oil has been approved by MERCEDES-BENZ.**

Oil consumption

In a combustion engine, oil consumption is seen as the amount of oil used during the combustion process. Oil consumption is not to be confused with oil loss, as it occurs due to leakages at the oil sump, cylinder head etc.

Normal oil consumption occurs through small amounts of oil combusted in the cylinder; by discharging combustion particles and abortion of impurities. Oil also becomes worn out due to high temperatures and pressures to which it is constantly exposed in the engine.

External operating conditions, driving method as well as manufacturing factors also have an influence on oil consumption. Under normal circumstances, this consumption is low, that only an periodic topping up of oil is necessary between oil changes.

Oil must be topped up if the low level mark is reached (maximum amount to be added is 1,5 litres).

Oil Circulation

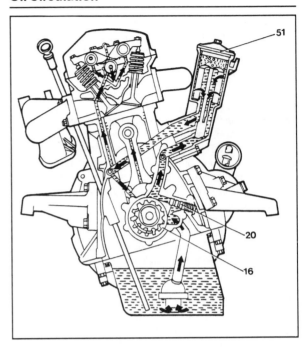

The oil pump -16- sucks the oil out of the oil sump and pushes it into the full-flow filter. Between the pressure and suction side of the oil pump is a pressure valve -20- (oil pressure regulator valve). In cases of excessive oil pressure of above 4 bar, the valve opens and some of the oil can flow back into the suction side of the pump.

Above the bottom channel, past the non-return valve, the oil passes into the oil filter -51-. The non-return valve prevents the oil from flowing back into the oil sump when the engine is turned off.

The filtered oil reaches the main oil channel through the upper channel. If the oil filter is blocked, a bypass valve leads the oil directly and in an unfiltered form into the main channel.

From the main channel, there are channels leading to the lubrication of the crankshaft bearings. The oil is led to the connecting rod bearings by angled bores in the crankshaft, and is led to the piston pins through bores within the connecting rod.

At the same time oil reaches the cylinder head through the oil channel and supplies oil to the camshaft bearings and rocker arms.

Oil pressure relief valve - removal and refitting

Engine 102

The oil pressure relief valve is built into the left side of the timing case cover. If the oil pressure rises above approximately 4 bars, the valve opens and some of the oil can flow back into the suction chamber of the pump.

The valve should be checked if the oil pressure is too low when the oil level is normal.

Removal

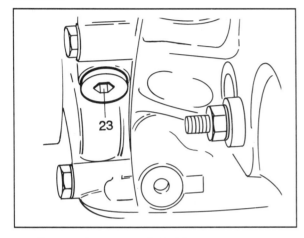

- Remove the securing bolt -23-.

Caution:

The securing bolt is under pressure and can easily shoot off.

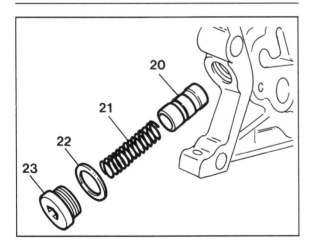

- Remove the pressure spring -21- and the pistons -20-.

Caution:

To remove pistons which are stuck, use circlip pliers.

- Blow out the bores in the timing case cover with compressed air.
- Rock the pistons from side to side a few times. If they are not easy to move, remove the ridge of the piston with an emery cloth.

Refitting

- If the piston is to be replaced, check the new piston for ease of movement in the bore. If necessary, remove the ridge of the piston with an emery cloth.
- Refit the piston with a new pressure spring.
- Refit the securing bolt with a new washer -22- and tighten to 30 Nm.
- Warm up the engine and check the security of the bolt.

Engine 110/115/123

The oil pressure relief valve is found in the front of the main oil channel and opens when the oil pressure exceeds 5 bar (engine 110/115) or 4 bar (engine 123).

Depending on the space in the various engine blocks, different parts will have to be removed.

Removal

- Remove the radiator, see page 74.
- Remove the fan clutch, see page 75.
- Remove the fanbelt and the crankshaft fanbelt, see page 222.
- Remove the securing bolt for the pressure valve.

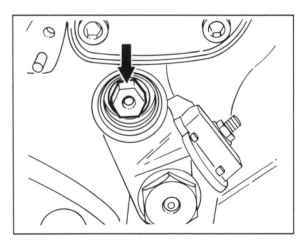

- Unscrew the securing bolt -arrow- of the oil channel with an Allen key SW 8 and remove it. Oil the key so that the bolt sticks to it.
- Remove the flush aluminium washer from the depression of the oil channel. To prevent the washer from falling, first insert a long wire into the oil channel.

Refitting

- Refit the pressure relief valve and tighten to 40 Nm.
- Paint the thread of the securing bolt with a sealing compound,e.g. Loctite, and tighten to 50 Nm.
- Tighten the pulley to 35 Nm.
- Refit the fan clutch, see page 75.
- Fit the fanbelt and tension it, see page 222.
- Refit the radiator, see page 74.
- Fill up with coolant, see page 79.
- Start the engine, check the oil pressure and the seal of the securing bolt.

Oil sump - removal and refitting

Engine 102

Removal

- Drain the oil, see page 69.
- Remove the engine, see page 13.
- Remove the 32 securing bolts of the oil sump and remove the oil sump.
- Thoroughly clean the sealing surface of the oil sump and the crankcase.

Refitting

- Refit the oil sump with a new gasket and tighten the securing bolts evenly to 10 Nm.
- Refit the engine, see page 13.
- Refill the oil, see page 69.
- Heat up the engine and check the seal of the oil sump.

Oil pump - removal and refitting

Engine 115/123

The gear type oil pump is in the oil sump and is driven by the auxiliary shaft.

Removal

- Remove the fuel pump, see page 100.
- Put the vehicle on blocks, see page 244.
- Drain the oil, see page 69.
- Remove the oil sump
- Unscrew the oil pump from the crankcase and the main bearing and remove it.

Refitting

- Refit the oil pump and tighten the bolts to 23 Nm in engine 115 and to 30 Nm in engine 123.

Caution:

Engine 115 is fitted with an oil pump with an integrated pressure valve up to the following engine numbers: manual - 005217; automatic - 003284. If an oil pump without an integrated pressure valve is fitted into these vehicles, a 5 bar pressure valve must also be installed into the main oil channel.

- Refit the oil sump with a **new** gasket, and tighten the bolts evenly to 10 Nm.
- Tighten the fuel pump to 23 Nm.
- Remove the vehicle from the blocks, see page 244.
- Fill up with oil, see page 69.

Maintenance work on the engine lubrication

Oil change

An oil change is necessary every 10 000 km, or if the vehicle is seldom used, once a year. The filter cartridge is to be replaced at the same time.

Under more severe conditions such as short distance travelling, frequent cold starting and dusty roads, the engine oil and oil filter should be changed more regularly. The engine oil can also be removed with a suction pipe.

Caution:

The discarded oil should be handed in at used oil collection points. As a rule, dealers will take the used oil off your hands when you purchase new oil. Information can be obtained from communities and city councils as to where used oil should be discarded. **Never simply pour out the oil or dispose of it with the household rubbish.** Environmental dangers such as ground water pollution would otherwise result.

- Bring the engine up to running temperature (60° - 80° C coolant temperature)

Draining the oil

Caution:

The engine oil may be sucked out through the dipstick tube. In such a case, in engine 102 first unscrew the central bolt of the oil filter cover and pull upwards, so that the oil can flow back into the oil sump from the oil filter without passing the leakage return valve.

For normal oil drainage:
- Put vehicles with engines 110, 115, 123 horizontally onto blocks, see page 244.
- Insert a container to catch the used oil under the oil sump.
- Unscrew the oil drain plug from the side of the oil sump and drain all the used oil. The drain plug is found on the left side of the front section of the oil sump in engine 102, seen in the direction of movement, in the other engines at the back of the oil sump.

Caution:

If a concentration of metal filings and other particles are found in the oil, this indicates a possible seize, for example damage to the crankshaft or connecting rod bearings. To prevent later damaged the oil channels and oil tubes must be thoroughly cleaned after the engine repair. The oil cooler if present must also be replaced.

Oil filter change in engine 102

- Remove the air filter, see page 98.

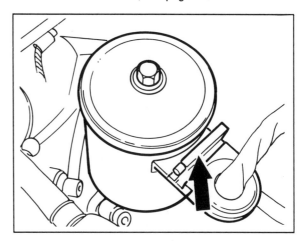

- Remove the central bolt -1-, after which the oil can flow back into the oil sump from the filter housing without passing through the leakage return valve.
- Remove the filter cover with the gasket.
- Flip up the wire hanger to remove the oil filter element. Catch any dripping oil with a cloth.
- Fit a new filter element into the oil filter housing.
- Clean the oil filter cover and refit it with a **new** gasket.
- Check the washer of the central bolt for its condition and replace if necessary.
- Refit the central screw with its washer and tighten to 27 Nm.

Oil filter change in engine 110 and 123 with air conditioning

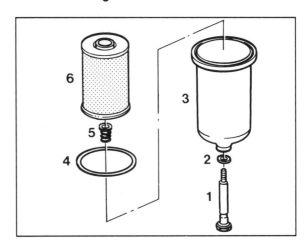

- Remove the securing bolt -1-. Carefully remove the filter case -3- and empty.
- Remove the filter element -6-.

- Remove the pressure spring with the spring plate -5-from the securing bolt and remove the bolt from the filter case.
- Wash the filter case with fuel and then blow out with compressed air.
- Check the washer -2- of the central bolt for its condition and replace if necessary.
- Insert the pressure spring with the spring plate -5- onto the securing bolt.
- Fit a **new** gasket -4- to the filter case and fit a **new** filter element.
- Tighten the filter case to 35 Nm.

Oil filter change in engine 115 and 123 without air conditioning

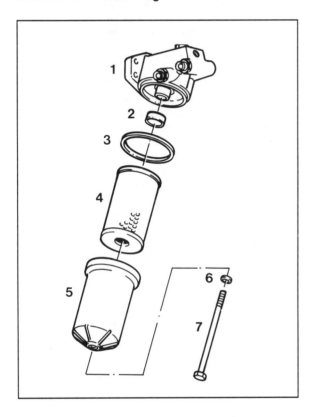

- Unscrew the oil filter case -5-, carefully remove and empty it.
- Check the washer -6- for its condition and replace if necessary.
- Check the gasket -3-. If it is torn, distorted or hardened, replace it.

Caution:

In engine 115, check the two additional washers between the filter element -4- and the filter case -5- for damage, replacing if necessary. In refitting, the rounded side of the larger washer must face the filter element.

- Wash the filter housing with fuel and, if available, blow out with compressed air.
- Reassemble the filter housing and refit with **new** filter element -4- and **new** washer -2-; tighten to 35 Nm.

Caution:

In some models, black coated filter housings are installed. In this case the bolt -7- and the washer -6- are not identical to the same parts in the uncoated aluminium filter housings.

Engine oil refilling

- Refit the drain plug with a **new** washer and tighten to 30 Nm in engine 102 and to 40 Nm in all other engines.
- Pour the new oil into the filler opening in the rocker cover.
- If removed, refit the air filter. If necessary lower the vehicle, see page 244.

Oil change amounts:

Engine		Dipstick identification	
		ruby/pink	yellow-green
102	4,5 l	–	–
115	5,5 l	–	–
123		6,5 l	
110			

Quantity difference between minimum and maximum markings on the dipstick: **1,5 liter.**

- After a test-drive, check the seals of the drain plug and the oil filter, carefully tighten if necessary.
- Switch of the warm engine and check the oil level after approximately 2 minutes, correct if necessary.
- In order to observe the operating conditions easily, it is recommended to use the same type and make of oil during an oil change. It is useful to attach a sign on the engine during an oil change, on which the make and viscosity of the oil are indicated.
- The use of different oil types is not recommended. Engine oils of the same type but different make should not be mixed, if this can be avoided. The same types of oils and the same makes but different viscosity adapting to the times of the year may be used without problem.

Oil circulation fault diagnosis

Fault	Cause	Solution
Low oil pressure after starting the engine.	Oil very hot	Ignore if pressure rises to normal when accelerator applied.
Oil pressure too low at low engine speed	Oil pressure regulating valve stuck in open position due to dirt	Remove valve and check
Low oil pressure over full range of engine speed.	Too little oil in engine.	Fill up with oil
	Suction sieve in suction bell dirty	Remove oil sump, clean suction sieve
	Oil pump worn	Remove oil pump and check, replace if necessary
	Suction pipe loose or broken.	Remove oil sump, check suction pipe
	Bearing damage	Engine overhaul
No oil pressure indication.	No earth connection in indicator	Replace indicator
Oil pressure drops to 2 bar while driving at approximately 80-120 kn/hr, or oil pressure is under 0,3 bar while idling.	Oil filter element is dirty	Replace filter element, change oil
	Oil pressure valve sticking	Remove oil pressure valve, check, replace if necessary
	Defective gauge	Replace gauge on control panel
	Oil return bores in cylinder head blocked	Remove cylinder head cover, pour engine oil into return bores on left side of cylinder head. If oil does not drain, or only very slowly, bore in crankcase is not drilled or carbon has formed in return to oil sump. Workshop job.
	O-ring of oil pump cover defective or not fitted	Check O-ring by removing timing case cover. Workshop job.
Blue smoke in neutral	Air filter blocked with oil	Remove air filter and check and after cleaning, replace if necessary.
	Connecting surfaces of rocker arm bracket damaged	Remove rocker arm brackets and return bores to see if open. Check surfaces for damage.
Needle of indicator remains at 3 bar excess pressure after engine is switched off	Pressure relief valve jammed	Remove oil excess pressure valve check, replace if necessary
	Defective gauge	Replace indicator
Oil pressure drops with rising engine speed.	Incorrect oil level	Check oil level and correct
	Oil sump dented	Replace oil sump
	Equlising rubber piece in suction basket of oil pump defective	Replace deformed or damaged equalising piece
	Oil pump sieve blocked	Clean sieve
	Oil pressure relief valve sticking open.	Remove valve and check, replace if necessary

ENGINE COOLING SYSTEM

The coolant circulation

The coolant circulation is thermostatically controlled. As long as the engine is cold, the coolant only circulates in the cylinder head, the engine block and -if the heater is switched on - in the heat exchanger. With increasing heat, the thermostat opens for the large coolant circuit. The coolant is then led from the coolant pump via the radiator. The coolant flows through the radiator from top to bottom and is cooled by the air which flows past the cooling fins. A fan behind the radiator ensures sufficient air flow.

The radiator fan is mounted differently depending on the model. While in engine 115 the fan is rigidly attached to the shaft of the coolant pump, and turns at the same rotational speed as the pump, the other engines have a fan with coupling. This is normally a magnetic coupling. Only vehicles with air conditioning have visco-coupling.

In vehicles with fan coupling, the fan wheel does not always turn, but is switched on or off as needed. In this way the available engine performance is increased and the fuel consumption reduced.

As soon as the coolant temperature reaches approximately 100° C in **engine 102**, a thermo-switch via the magnetic coupling switches the fan on. The fan then turns at the engine rotational speed at the same rotational speed as the coolant pump. If the coolant temperature sinks to 98° - 93° C, the thermo-switch opens and the fan is disconnected.

In the 6 cylinder engine the magnetic coupling is set up differently. Two separate magnetic discs in the coupling ensure that the fan wheel turns at the same rotational speed as the engine up to a rotational speed of 1700/rpm. Then the coupling "tears" off and if the engine rotational speed further increases, the fan rotational speed can only increase up to approximately 2300/rpm.

The 6-cylinder engine may also be equipped with a visco-coupling. If the visco coupling is switched off, the fan turns according to the engine rotational sped, but not faster than 2100/rpm. If the coolant temperature rises above 90° - 95° C a bi-metal strip of the visco-coupling is switched on, increasing the fan rotational speed up to approximately 3500/rpm.

Coolant circulation of the 4 cylinder engine

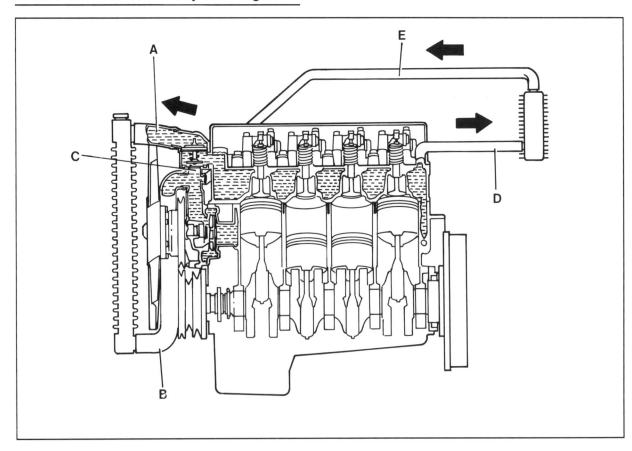

A - from thermostat to radiator
B - from radiator to coolant pump
C - connection thermostat housing/coolant pump
    (small circuit)

D - to heat exchanger (heater)
E - from heat exchanger to coolant pump

Coolant - anti-freeze

The cooling system is filled with a mixture of water and anti-freeze by the manufacturer. This prevents frost and corrosion damage as well as raising the boiling temperature of the water. The cooling system should thus always be filled with an anti-freeze mixture.

Caution:

Only use anti-freeze recommended by MERCEDES-BENZ.

As the corrosion protection factor in the anti-freeze looses its effectiveness after a while, it should be replaced every 3 years.

Anti-freeze mixture relationship

Frost protection to	-30° C		-45° C	
Engine	102	110,115 123	102	110,115 123
Coolant concentrate	3,75 l	4,5 l	4,75 l	5,5 l
Water	4,75 l	5,5 l	3,75 l	4,5 l
Total amount	8,5 l	10 l	8,5 l	10 l

Thermostat - removal and refitting/testing

The thermostat opens the large coolant circuit with the increased heating of the engine. If the thermostat stays closed due to a defect, the engine will over-heat. This can be recognised if the coolant temperature guage remains in the red area, while the radiator stays cold. A defective thermostat can also remain open after the coolant has cooled off. This can be recognised by the engine not reaching its running temperature, in other words the needle of the coolant temperature gauge rises slower than before or the heating performance is decreased in winter.

Caution:

If the engine heats up after a short running time, this could also mean that the radiator has become clogged due to lime deposits.

Removal

- Remove the earth cable from the battery.
- Drain the coolant into a container.

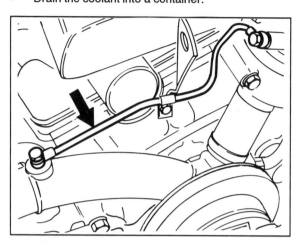

- Unscrew the bleed tube -arrow- and remove; the illustration shows engine 102.
- Remove the securing bolts (depending on the model, 3 or 4), remove the cover of the thermostat housing and put aside.
- Remove the thermostat from the housing.

Testing

- Heat the thermostat in a container of water. The thermostat may not touch the sides of the container. Control the temperature with a suitable thermometer.

At a temperature of approximately 87° C the bi-metal spring of the thermostat will start to open. The maximum expansion is reached at approximately 102° C.

- Check that the thermostat opens and then closes again. If not replace it.

Refitting

- Clean the sealing surfaces of the housing and cover.
- Before refitting, check the ball in the bleed valve of the thermostat for ease of movement.

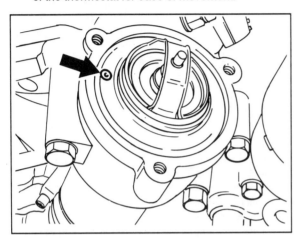

- Refit the thermostat with a new gasket into the housing. **Caution:** Refit the thermostat so that the ball valve -arrow- is at the highest point.
- Refit the bleed tube and secure it with brackets where they are available.
- Fill up with coolant.
- Refit the battery earth cable.
- Warm up the engine until the fan switches on. Check if the radiator heats up from below and that the thermostat housing does not leak.

Radiator removal and refitting

After the vehicle has been driven for a while, the thin tubing in the radiator can become clogged by particles and coolant. The cooling performance will drastically decrease and the engine will become too hot. In this case the radiator must be renewed.

Removal

- Remove the earth cable from the battery.
- Drain the coolant, see page 79.

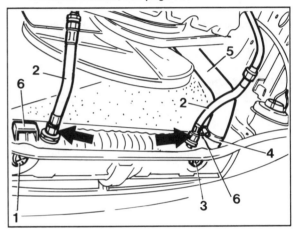

- In automatic vehicles, clamp off the oil leads from and to the gearbox with suitable clamps and unscrew them at the radiator -arrows-. This process should be carried through with the utmost care for cleanliness, clean the connections externally with spirits prior to removing. Subsequently attach small plastic bags to the leads to avoid any dirt from entering.

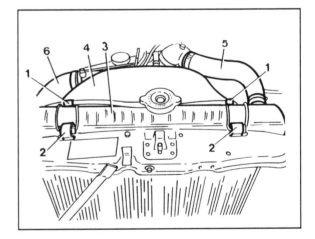

- Remove the upper and lower hoses -5/6- from the radiator, after loosening the clips and pushing them back completely.
- Lift out the securing springs -1- of the radiator cover.
- Lift the radiator cover slightly and lay it onto the radiator.

Caution:

In some vehicles the lower securing bracket is attached to the securing eye of the radiator with a spring, In this case the spring must be pulled out from below.

- Lift out the securing springs -2-.
- Lift out the radiator.

Refitting

- Check all hoses for cuts, tears and other damage, and replace if necessary. Check that the rubber grommets of the radiator casing are in good condition.
- Refit the radiator in such a way that the securing pivots -1- and -3- (illustration page 74) of the radiator fit into the rubber grommets of the cross member.
- Refit the top securing springs of the radiator; set the fan cover in position, press down and at the same time attach the securing clip -6- (illustration page 74) to the radiator.
- Refit the hoses and secure them with the clips.
- If removed, refit the oil cooler pipes with the union nuts and tighten to 20 Nm, remove the clips.
- Check the coolant level, filling up if necessary.

Radiator fan - removal and refitting

Engine 102

Caution:

Depending on the model, the fan connection is secured differently.

Removal

- Remove the battery earth cable.
- Remove the air filter, see page 79.
- Remove the radiator, see page 74.

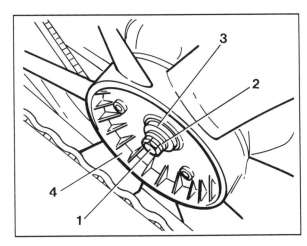

- Unscrew the central bolt -1- and remove it with the washers -2- and -3-. Depending on the model, the fan could be secured by 3 bolts.
- Remove the fan -4-.
- Remove the fanbelt, see page 222.

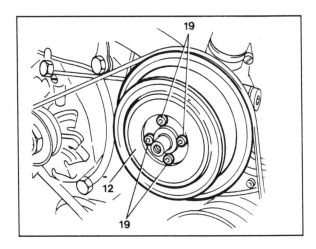

- Unscrew the 4 bolts -19- and remove the fanbelt pulley -12-.

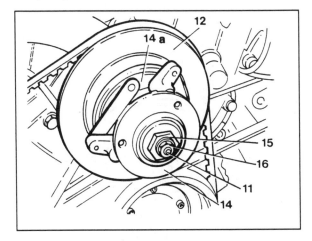

- Remove the fanbelt pulley of the coolant pump. To do this unscrew the securing nut -16- holding from behind with a spanner SW24. Now remove the flange -14- with the flange -14a- and the pulley -12- by hand.

Caution:

If the pulley cannot be removed by hand, unscrew the assembling bolt -11-. If the assembling bolt is stuck (yellow markings on the nut - assembly bolt) remove the armature flange so that the assembly bolt is more accessible. Subsequently screw a bolt M10 x 1 x 45 into the thread of the pulley and thus push the pulley away from the magnetic body. If the pulley does not have a thread (vehicles before 8/81), cut a thread M10 x 1 into it. To avoid the pulley from turning during this process, attach the fanbelt and tension.

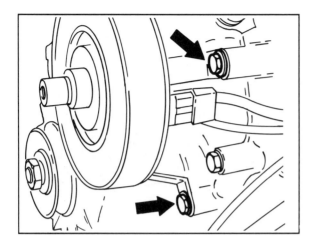

- Remove the electrical lead from the magnetic body.
- Remove the securing bolts -arrows- (3 in all) and remove the magnetic body.

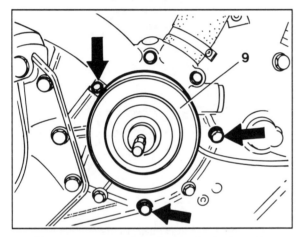

- Unscrew -arrows- the magnetic body -9- and put aside.

Refitting

- Tighten the magnetic body to the coolant pump to 10 Nm. refit the electrical leads.
- Attach the pulley to the flange of the pump shaft and tighten to 10 Nm.
- Smear the studs of the coolant pump shaft with multi-purpose grease. Clean the pulley thoroughly and refit onto the studs of the pump shaft. Fit a **new** washer making sure it is in position properly. Tighten the **new** nut to 35 Nm. If removed, fit a **new** assembling bolt after painting the thread with locking fluid, eg. Loctite 270, and tighten to the pump shaft to 15 Nm. While doing this hold the pivot of the pump shaft with a pair of pipe grips, after first wrapping a cloth or tape around the pivot several times, to avoid it being damaged. If the assembling bolt cannot be turned, carefully recut the M8 thread.

- Refit the fan with the central bolt and washers to the pump shaft and tighten to 25 Nm.
- Refit the fan and tighten to 20 Nm.
- Refit the fanbelt, see page 222.
- Refit the radiator, see page 74.

Coolant pump - removal and refitting

Removal

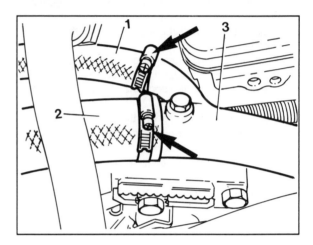

- Remove the heater hose -1- and the coolant pipe -2- from the coolant pump. First completely open the clips -arrows- and push them back.
- Disconnect the hose of the carburetor pre-heating unit from the coolant pump.
- Remove the fan.

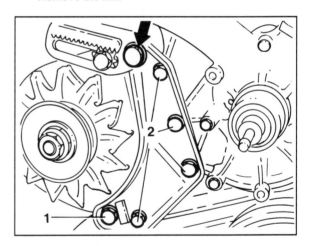

- Remove the alternator with the front bracket and put aside. To do this unscrew bolts -1,2 and arrow-.
- Depending on the model, unscrew the bleed tube from the housing of the coolant pump.

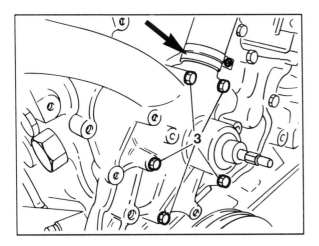

- Remove the hose of the cooling circuit, by opening the clip -arrow- totally and pushing it back.
- Unscrew the coolant pump bolts -3- and remove it.
- Thoroughly clean all sealing surfaces of the pump housing and the timing case cover.

Refitting

- Lightly stick the new gasket to the sealing surface of the timing case cover at two points.

Caution:

If there is no gasket, paint the sealing surfaces of the coolant pump evenly and as thinly as possible with a sealant such as "Loctite 573".

- Refit the coolant pump to the timing case cover and tighten to 10Nm.
- Refit the hose of the cooling circuit and secure it with the clip.
- If removed, refit the drain tube to the housing of the coolant pump.
- Tighten the alternator with the upper bolt to 45 Nm, tighten the fanbelt, see page 222.
- Refit the fan.
- Refit the hose of the carburetor pre-heating to the coolant pump and tighten it to 45 Nm.
- Refit the heating and coolant hoses and secure them with the clips.

Cooling system maintenance

Coolant level - testing

The coolant level should be checked at regular intervals - approximately every 4 weeks -, and especially before a long trip.

Caution:

In a hot engine the radiator cap must be opened very carefully as there is a danger of boiling. Place a cloth over the cover when opening. If possible open the cap at a temperature below 90° C.

- When opening, first turn the cap to the first notch and allow the steam to escape. Then keep turning the cap and remove it.

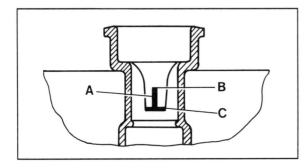

- The coolant should reach position -C- of the filler marking -A- of the radiator in a cool engine. In a warm engine the coolant level should reach position -B-.
- Only fill a **cold engine** with cold **coolant** to prevent engine damage.
- To refill -even during the warm seasons- only use a mixture of anti-freeze and clean water with a low lime content.

Caution:

In order to carry on driving, clean water can also be used in the warm seasons. The radiator frost protector must however be added as soon as possible.

- Visually check for leaks, if the coolant level is often under the minimum marking.

Frost protection - testing

Before the start of winter, the concentration of the anti-freeze should be tested.

- Warm up the engine until the top of the radiator is about luke-warm.
- Carefully open the radiator cap, see under "coolant level-testing".
- Suck some of the coolant with a coolant tester and read off the concentration at the floater.

Evaluating the MERCEDES coolant concentrate

Example: The anti-freeze measurement with the tester indicates frost protection up to -10° C. In this case bleed 3 l coolant and replace it with 3 l of pure anti-freeze.

Measured value in ° C	Amount of difference in liters	
	Engine 102	Engines 110,115,123
0	4,0	5,0
− 5	3,5	4,5
− 10	3,0	4,0
− 15	2,0	3,0
− 20	1,5	2,5
− 25	1,0	1,5

- Close the cap of the radiator and retest the anti-freeze after a test drive.

Visual testing for leaks

- Check the hoses for porosity by compressing and bending them, replace any hardened tubes.
- The tubes must fit fully and properly at the connections.
- Check that the hose clips are securely in place.
- Check the radiator cap seal for damage.
- Warm up the engine and check if the coolant leaks out in the area of the coolant pump.
- If coolant flows out of the warm engine from one of the bores at the bottom of the pump, one of the shaft washers is generally defective. In this case, replace the coolant pump.
- Often it is difficult to determine the location of the leak. In this case it is recommended to have the workshop do a pressure test (special tool needed). The radiator cap can be tested during this test.

Coolant - changing

The coolant should be changed every 3 years.

Caution:

If the coolant is removed during repairs, it should be bled into a container for re-use, since the coolant contains expensive anti-freeze.

Bleeding

- Remove the earth cable from the battery.
- Turn both the heater switches in the interior of the vehicle to maximum. In vehicles with air conditioning, press the "DEF" button.
- Turn the radiator cap to the left until it clicks. Allow the excess pressure to escape from the cooling system. Then carry on turning the cap and remove it.

Caution:

In a hot engine first place a thick cloth over the cover before opening the cover to prevent scalding from the hot coolant or steam. Only remove the cover at coolant temperatures below 90° C.

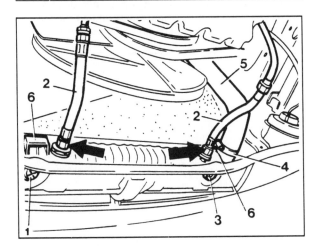

- Put a clean container under the radiator and unscrew the drain plug -1- from the radiator.
- Remove the drain plug from the engine block. The drain tube is on the right hand side around the middle underneath the exhaust manifold.
- Drain all the coolant.
- Refit the drain plug to the engine block with a new washer and tighten to 30 Nm.
- Refit the drain plug to the radiator and tighten to 1,5 to 2 Nm, by placing a coin into the slot of the bolt and tightening by hand.

Refilling

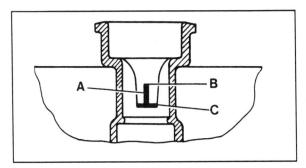

- Pour the coolant into the tank filler opening of the radiator up to the "coolant cold" marking -C-. A - refilling mark, B - "coolant warm". The tank filler opening of the radiator should temporarily remain open.
- Refit the battery earth cable.
- Warm up the engine until the thermostat opens (coolant temperature 90° C - 100° C). Pump the accelerator pedal from time to time.

Caution:

Replace the radiator cap when the coolant temperature reaches 60°C - 70° C.

- Check the seals of the cooling system - hose connections as well as drain plug.

Cooling system fault diagnosis

Fault / Cause	Solution
The coolant temperature is too high, the needle remains in the red section.	Top tank of radiator must be filled to marking. Check for leaks in cooling system
Too little coolant in circulation. Thermostat does not open	Check if hose gets hot. If not, replace thermostat
Fan not working, thermo-switch defective (engine 102)	Remove plug of thermo-switch and place against earth, if fan works with running engine, replace thermo-switch
Fuse No. 10 defective (engine 102)	Check fuse
Magnetic body of fan defective (engine 102)	Remove electrical lead of fan magnetic body and place against earth via test lamp, switch ignition on. If the lamp glows, replace magnetic body, otherwise remove lead circuit breaker
Coolant pump defective	Remove coolant pump and check
Transmitter of coolant temperature gauge defective	Have transmitter tested
Coolant temperature gauge defective	Have gauge tested
Radiator cap defective	Have pressure test done
Fanbelt tension of coolant pump too low	Check tension and adjust
Radiator covered in insects and/or dirt	Blow through radiator with compressed air from engine side
Radiator clogged up inside by lime or rust	Replace radiator
Bleed tube clogged up between coolant pump and cylinder head	Remove tube and check
Visco radiator-coupling defective	Check radiator connection: let engine run at 4 000 - 4 500.rpm. As soon as the coolant temperature reaches 90° - 95° C, the engine speed audibly increases by 1 000/rpm

THE FUEL SYSTEM

The fuel tank, fuel hoses, fuel filter, fuel pump and carburetor or injection system with air filter all make up the fuel system.

The fuel tank is above the rear axle. The fuel quantity is indicated to the driver by a fuel gauge. The tank is aerated via a bleed system.

If filling up from cans, it is advisable to filter the fuel through a clean cloth.

In order to fill up with **unleaded fuel**, the following conditions must be met. 1. Valve seat rings of hardened metal must be present, since the valve seats will otherwise perish faster. It is not worth subsequently fitting this due to the cost involved. 2. Since unleaded super fuel only has an octane of 95 RON (leaded super fuel: 98 RON), depending on the model, the ignition must be retarded to avoid the engine knocking. The result is decreased performance and higher fuel consumption.

It is recommended to ask the MERCEDES dealer if hardened valve seat rings have been installed by reference to the engine number, if the ignition should be adjusted, or whether unleaded fuel should be used alternatively with leaded fuel due to the kilometer performance of the vehicle.

Carburetor/injection system

The models 200 and 230 have a Stromberg Flachstrom carburettor. Carburettor 175 CDTU was fitted until 6/80 and 175 CDT was fitted since 7/80. In describing the carburettor, 175 stands for the diameter of the induction manifold of 1 3/4 inches (45 mm;) CD = constant depression; T = temperature regulated automatic choke.

The 6-cylinder carburettor engines 250 and 280 are fitted with a Solex dual barrel carburettor 4 A, while models 230E and 280 E have a mechanical fuel injection system.

Carburettor adjustment

Every carburettor is tested and adjusted in the factory. This adjustment should not be changed. High fuel consumption and bad engine performance normally have other causes, in which the driving method and traffic conditions play a very large part. Normally careful adjustment of the idling speed will rectify any problems. A correct timing adjustment is much more important than generally believed, since it influences the transition of the engine up to the middle engine speeds.

Caution:

In vehicles with a transistorised ignition system, various safety precautions should be taken, in order to prevent injury to people or the destruction of the transistorised ignition system: see page 53.

Hint: The screws of the carburettor or injection system, with which the mixture can be changed, may be unaccessible. The position and number of adjusting screws depends on the type of carburettor.

The securing caps can partly be removed with a screwdriver or a pair of pliers. With some caps it is useful to screw a tiny bolt with a diameter of about 2 mm into the plastic cap; then pull out the bolt and the cap with a pair of pliers. The securing caps are destroyed in this process. After the adjustment, the adjusting screws must be refitted with new caps (spare part).

If the exhaust emissions do not comply with the legal requirements, or if the securing caps of the carburetor are missing, this could lead to a fine in some countries.

Rules of cleanliness when working on the fuel system

In working on the fuel system, the following rules for cleanliness should be maintained:

- Thoroughly clean all connecting parts and their surroundings before loosening.
- Place the removed parts on a clean surface and cover with foil or paper. Do not use cloths with loose threads.
- Carefully cover any opened disassembled parts, or reassemble them if the repair is not carried through immediately.
- Only fit clean parts.
- Only take replacement parts out of their packet immediately before use.
- Do not use any parts which are not in packets (e.g. in the toolbox)
- Try to avoid working with compressed air while the fuel system is open.
- Avoid moving the vehicle.

75 CDT carburetor

Hint: The letters in the illustration indicate which parts are connected to one another when assembled

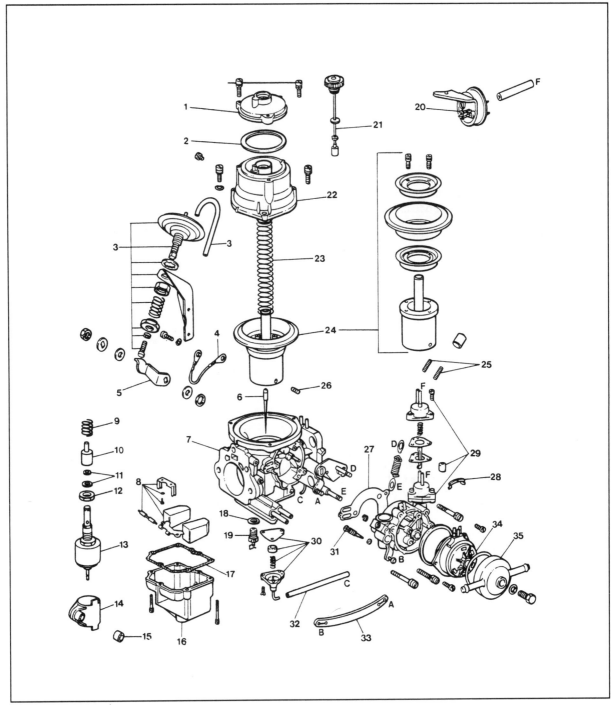

1	-	cover	13	-	idle shut-off valve	25	-	engine speed adjusting screws
2	-	O-ring	14	-	cover	26	-	locking screw
3	-	vacuum govenor	15	-	lock cap	27	-	gasket
4	-	earth cable	16	-	float chamber	28	-	plastic cover
5	-	mounting lever	17	-	gasket	29	-	choke vacuum box
6	-	metering needle	18	-	seal	30	-	fuel return
7	-	carburetor housing	19	-	float needle valve	31	-	fuel enrichment adjusting screw
8	-	Float with pivot	20	-	thermo-valve	32	-	connecting pipe
9	-	spring	21	-	air-piston damper	33	-	fast idle connecting rod
10	-	jet	22	-	carburettor cover	34	-	choke heater (electric)
11	-	O-rings	23	-	spring	35	-	warm water connection
12	-	lock nut	24	-	piston with diaphragm			

Carburetor - removal and refitting

Removal

- Remove the earth cable from the battery.

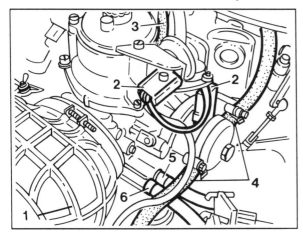

- Remove the connecting tube -1- from the intake, first loosen the clip.
- Remove the vacuum hose -3- from the carburetor.
- Remove the plug -2- of the thermo-delay valve and choke heating element.

Caution:

No open flame or smoking - fire danger!

- Remove the fuel feed and return hoses -5- and -6- and close them with a suitable bolt.

Caution:

If the engine is hot, allow the excess pressure to escape from the cooling system before removing the cooling hoses, see page 78.

- Remove the coolant hoses -4- from the choke cover and hang them up with wire, to prevent the coolant from flowing out. First open the clips totally and push them back.
- Unhook the regulating controls from the throttle control lever, see page 84.

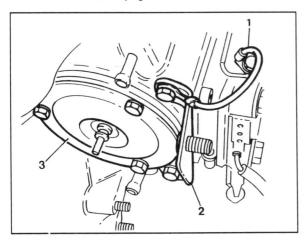

- Unscrew the earth cable from the carburetor.
- Remove the plug of the idle shut-off valve.

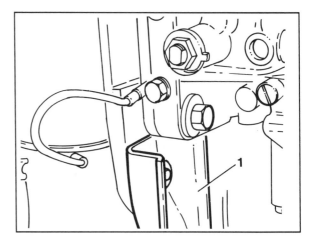

- Unscrew the carburetor from the rubber flange and remove it.
- Remove the gasket and clean the surface of the carburetor.
- Remove the rubber flange of the intake manifold and check for porosity or damage.
- Cover the intake manifold with a clean cloth.

Refitting

- Refit the rubber flange to the intake manifold and tighten to 15 Nm.
- Refit the carburetor to the rubber flange with a new gasket, and tighten to 50 Nm.
- Refit the plugs of the idle regulating valve, thermo-delay valve and starter heating cover.
- Refit the regulating controls and adjust if necessary.

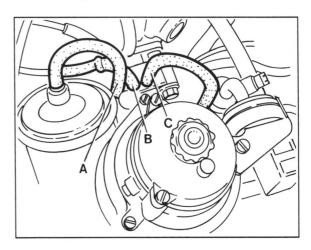

- Refit the vacuum leads to the carburetor. A - for vacuum control (only in vehicles with automatic gearbox or air conditioning), B - for ignition adjustment (red ring), C - for automatic choke.

- Refit the earth cable to the carburetor after having cleaned the points of contact thoroughly.

Caution:

If there is no good earth contact, the regulating valve cannot adjust properly.

- Refit the fuel pipes according to illustration on page 83, and secure with clips.
- Refit the coolant hoses to the choke cover and secure with clips.

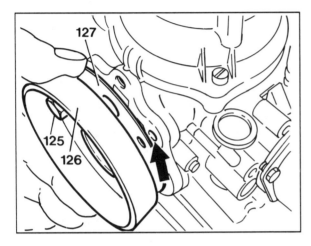

- Check the securing bolts of the adapter -126- to see that they are tightened to 30 Nm.

Caution:

If the gasket -127- is replaced, take care not to cover the bleed bore -arrow-, as this could lead to increased fuel consumption.

- Check the oil level in the air piston damper, fill up if necessary.
- Refit the connecting tube, and secure with clip.
- Refit the battery earth cable.
- Adjust the idling and CO-content in the exhaust.

Accelerator linkage - adjustment

- Check the accelerator linkage for ease of movement and wear. Replace the connecting rods with damaged bearings.

Full throttle stop - adjusting

- **Manual gearbox:** Depress the accelerator pedal completely and keep it in this position by jamming a suitable board between the seat and pedal.
- **Automatic gearbox:** Depress the accelerator to the kickdown position and ask a helper to hold it. Do not use the kickdown switch.

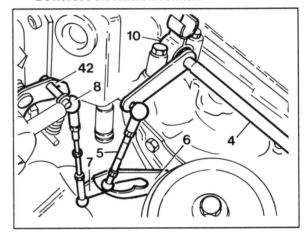

- The throttle control lever -42- is now positioned at the full throttle stop of the carburetor. Other illustrated parts: 4 - axial regulating shaft, 5 - connecting rod, 6 - sliding lever, 8 - plunger rod, 10 - bearing for axial regulating shaft.

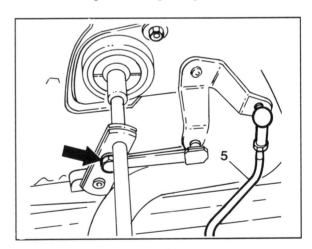

- Alternatively loosen the bolt -arrow-, release the accelerator slightly and tighten the bolt. Now re-check the full throttle stop, correcting if necessary. 5 - plunger rod.

Idle speed and CO-mixture adjustment

- Warm up the engine and switch off, oil temperature 65° - 75° C.
- Switch off the air-conditioning. In automatic vehicles, put the selection lever into the "P" position.
- Switch off all electrical consumers.
- Attach a tachometer and the CO- measuring device according to the instructions; the air-filter remains attached.

Caution:

The tube of the crank case bleeder remains attached.

- Start the engine and let it idle in neutral.
- Check that the throttle control lever rests against the idle stop, by lifting the throttle control lever slightly and increasing the engine speed to approximately 2500/rpm. Now release the throttle control lever, which should return to the idle stop position. If not, grease the accelerator rods and adjust, see page 84.

Until 6/80

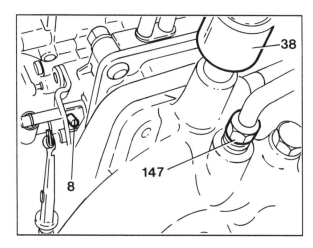

- Adjust the idle engine speed to the specified value by turning the adjusting bolt -147-, see page 95.

Caution:

If the range of the adjusting bolt -147- is not enough to bring the idle engine speed to the specified value, regulate the position of the throttle control with adjusting bolt -8-. To do this undo the starter connecting rod and regulating rod from the throttle control lever, remove the securing cap of the adjusting bolt and turn the bolt -8- slowly to the left, until the throttle control is totally closed. Now turn the bolt -8- about one rotation to the right and fit a new securing cap. Refit the accelerator rods.

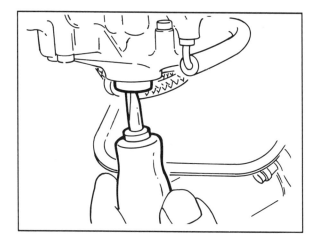

- Remove the securing cap at the bottom of the carburetor with a pair of pliers and adjust the CO-value to the specified value by turning the CO adjusting bolt -152-. After each adjustment push the accelerator briefly. By screwing out the adjusting bolt, the mixture becomes richer. By screwing in, it becomes leaner. Specified value, see page 95.

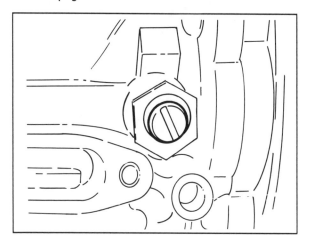

Caution:

The fuel adjusting bolt must remain closed. If necessary, loosen the counter nut, tighten the bolt fully and then tighten the lock nut again.

Since 7/80

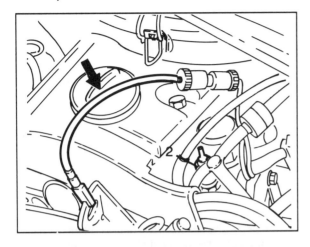

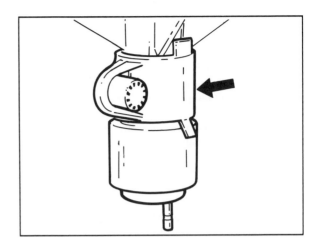

- Remove the plug of the temperature switch -2- and place it against the earth with a self-made test lead. This prevents the coolant temperature from rising above 100° C while adjusting.

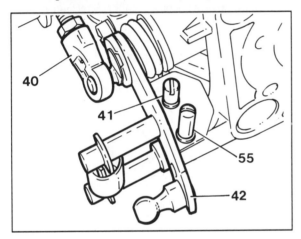

- To adjust the CO-value, remove the locking cap with a pair of pliers, then remove the cover -arrow-from the idle regulating valve.

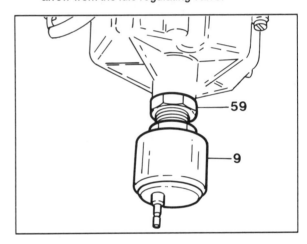

- Adjust the idle engine speed to the specified value by using the adjusting bolt -55- (the longer of the two bolts), see page 95.

Caution:

After each adjustment depress the accelerator briefly.

- Loosen the lock nut -59- and adjust the CO content by turning the idle mixture screw. Depress the accelerator after each adjustment. By screwing out the idle mixture screw, the mixture becomes richer, by screwing in it becomes leaner. Specified value see page 95.
- Tighten the lock nut.
- Reposition the cover and attach a new securing cap.
- Adjust the accelerator rods, see page 84.
- If present, adjust the cruise control, see page 87.
- Refit the plug of the temperature switch.

Caution:

In automatic vehicles or those with air-conditioning, check the adjustment of the vacuum regulator. The plug of the temperature switch remains removed during this process.

Vacuum Regulator -testing

In vehicles with 4-cylinder engines, the vacuum regulator is only fitted with automatic gearboxes and/or air-conditioning, depending on the series, 6-cylinder vehicles are fitted with this.

When the engine is loaded more when idling and the engine speed decreases, for example when engaging drive, or switching on the air-conditioning, the vacuum regulator allows the idling engine speed to increase.

To test the vacuum regulator, the same test conditions apply as for the adjustment of the idle engine speed.

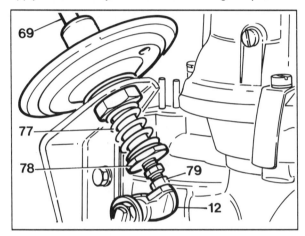

- Remove the vacuum hose -69- and block with a suitable plug.
- Loosen the lock nut of the adjusting bolt -79-, while holding the threaded rod from behind with an open-end spanner SW 6.
- Adjust the engine speed by the adjusting bolt -79-to 1 250/rpm.
- Refit the vacuum hose.Check with a feeler blade that there is a gap of 0,5 mm between the adjusting bolt -79- and the throttle control lever -12-. If necessary adjust the distance with the adjusting nut -78.
- In vehicles with automatic gearbox, pull up the handbrake and put it into drive. If power steering is present, turn the steering wheel from side to side. The engine should still turn over, if necessary regulate the engine speed with the adjusting screw -78
- If present, switch on the air-conditioning. The vacuum regulator should now extend totally and operate the throttle control. The engine must still turn over.
- Refit the plug of the temperature switch.

Damper oil level - testing

- Warm up the engine, oil temperature 70° - 80° C.

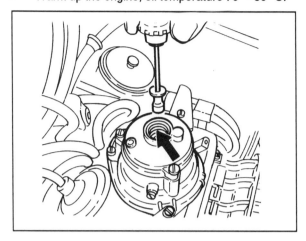

- Unscrew the bolt and remove it with the damper piston.
- The oil should reach the bottom of the lid -arrow-, fill up with automatic transmission fluid.

Cruise control -adjustment

- Let the engine idle.

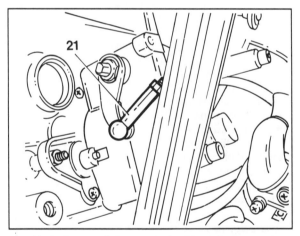

- Undo the regulating controls -21- at the lever of the adjusting link, then press the lever in a clockwise direction into idling position.
- Adjust the regulating control so that the socket is directly above the ball pivot of the lever, by loosening the lock nut and rotating the socket on the regulating control shaft.
- When aligned, tighten the socket by two rotations onto the control shaft and tighten the lock nut.
- Fit the socket onto the ball pivot of the cruise control lever.

Idle shut-off valve-testing

Caution:

Depending on the type of carburetor, two different idle regulating valves have been installed.

Until 6/80

The idle shut-off valve closes the idle circuit when the ignition is switched off, thus preventing the engine from running on. The valve remains closed until voltage is once again present, after the ignition is switched on. If the valve or the voltage supply is defective, the engine will not start. The idle shut-off valve is screwed into the top of the engine inlet manifold, see also -38- in illustration on page 85.

- Switch on the ignition.
- Remove and refit the plug of the shut-off valve several times. The valve should click audibly.
- Alternatively insert a test lamp between the plug and earth. If the test lamp lights up, replace the valve. If the test lamp does not light up, check fuse No.4 or the electrical supply according to the wiring diagram.

Since 7/80

The idle shut-off valve closes the fuel supply to the fuel jet when the ignition is switched off or when a maximum engine rotational speed of 6 100 $\pm$ 50/rpm is reached. The power is regulated through a retardation relay. As long as there is no voltage, the valve is always open. After the ignition is switched off, the relay provides voltage for about 6 - 16 seconds, which closes the valve and thus the fuel supply. The valve then opens again on its own. The CO-content is also adjusted at the regulating valve. If the valve is defective, the engine runs on after the ignition is switched off. If the valve gets stuck in a closed position, the engine will not start. The idle shut-off valves screwed onto the float chamber at the bottom of the carburetor.

The engine does not start:

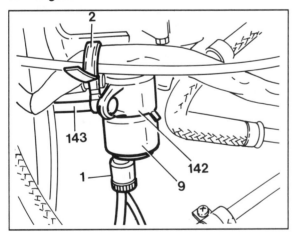

- Remove the plug -1- from the idle shut-off valve-9-.

- Attach the test lamp to the plug and earth.
- Engage the starter. The test lamp should not light up.
- If the test lamp lights up while the starter is engaged or while the ignition is on, check the relay of the idle regulating valve.

Caution:

After the ignition is switched off, the test lamp should be alight for 6 - 16 seconds.

- Attach the test cable to the positive pole of the battery and alternatively connect and disconnect it from the contact pin of the regulating valve. The valve must click, if not, test the earth connection to the carburetor, replacing the valve if necessary.

Caution:

If the valve clicks but the engine does not start, knock hard against the valve and start the engine. Even if the engine then starts, replace the valve as soon as possible.

Engine does not stop immediately after the ignition is switched off:

- The engine is at running temperature, oil temperature 65° - 75° C.
- Start the engine and leave it to idle.
- Remove the plug from the idle regulating valve. Connect the plug connection to the valve and positive pole of the battery via the auxiliary cable. The engine should stop, if not check the earth connection to the carburetor, replacing the shut-off valve if necessary.

Earth connection to the carburetor - testing.

- Attach a test lamp between the carburetor and the positive pole of the battery.
- If the test lamp lights up and the idle shut-off valve does not switch off despite the power supply, replace the valve.

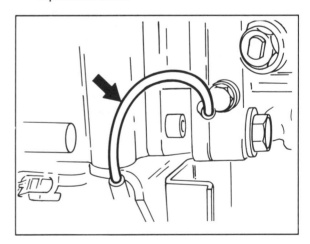

- If the test lamp does not light up, unscrew the earth lead -arrow- from the carburetor, clean the contacts well, refit the earth lead and repeat the test. If necessary trace the interruption in the earth lead and remove it.

Idle shut-off valve relay - testing

Since 7/80

- Start the engine and let it idle.
- Connect a voltmeter between the removed plug of the idle shut-off valve and earth.
- Switch off the ignition. The measuring device should show a battery voltage (approximately 12 Volt) for about 6 - 16 seconds, if not, check the fuses No. 2 and 14.

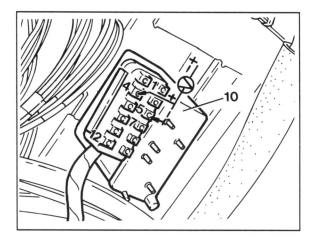

- If the fuses are perfect, remove the plug from the relay -10-. The relay is in the interior behind the lower cover to the left of the steering column.
- Switch on the ignition and attach the voltmeter to earth and terminals 4 and 5 of the relay plug respectively. Subsequently attach the voltmeter to the terminals -12- (earth) and -5-. The meter should in each case show voltage, if not, check the leads according to the wiring diagram.
- Start the engine, the plug of the idle shut-off valve is attached.
- Connect the terminals 1 and 5 of the relay plug with a short test cable. The idle adjusting valve must switch and the engine stop. If not, check the lead of terminal 1 to the idle shut-off valve for interruptions.
- If no fault was detected during these tests, replace the relay of the idle shut-off valve.

Idle shut-off valve - removal and refitting

Caution:

Depending on the type of carburetor, 2 different idle shut-off valves have been fitted. Whereas the shut-off valve in the CDT carburetor since 7/80 is screwed onto the float chamber at the bottom of the carburetor, in the CDTU carburetor until 6/80 it is found at the top of the engine inlet manifold behind the carburetor, see also -38- in diagram on page 85.

To replace the valve, the carburetor need not be removed. Fit only valves from identification number 0.231 into the CDT carburetor.

Removal

- Remove the air filter, see page 98.
- Remove the electrical leads from the shut-off valve.
- Remove the locking cap.
- Loosen the lock nut -59- in illustration on page 86 and remove the valve. **Do not** unscrew the nut.

Refitting

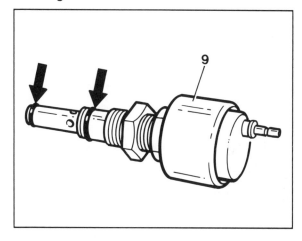

- Replace the damaged O-rings -arrows-.
- Screw in the idle shut-off valve up to the lock nut. If the valve has been replaced, bring the lock nut to the same position as on the old valve.

Caution:

If the lock nut was accidentally unscrewed, remove the float chamber with the nozzle holder and pressure spring. Screw the idle shut-off valve to the float chamber until it reaches 25 ±0,5mm into the float chamber. Press the nozzle holder onto the shut-off valve, refit the pressure spring and refit the float chamber with a new washer. First paint the bolts with the sealant "Curil" and do not tighten too much.

- Refit the electrical leads.
- Adjust the idling and the CO content.
- Tighten the lock nut.
- Refit the air filter, see page 98.

Automatic choke markings - testing

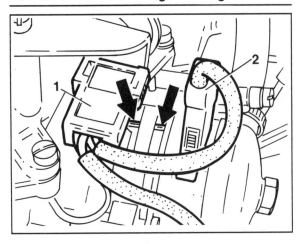

- The markings -arrows- of the automatic choke cover and the carburetor housing must be opposite each other. If not, loosen the bolts and turn the automatic choke cover to the correct position.

Caution:

Since 9/78 an automatic choke cover with the identification number 200 was fitted. In this automatic choke cover, the heater filament has a lower resistance (7 ohm, previously 8 Ohm/ID No. 173 or 10 ohm/ID No. 102), which shortens the shut-off time of the choke. The new automatic choke cover can also be fitted into earlier models.

Choke fast idle speed and heating CO - adjusting

- Attach a tachometer and CO measuring device according to the instructions.
- Heat up the engine, oil temperature 70° - 80° C.
- Remove the electrical leads from the temperature switch and place it against earth, see page 86.

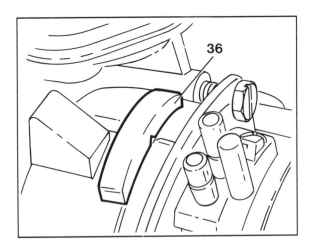

- Unclip the plastic cover -36- and remove it.

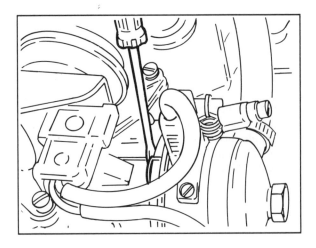

- Let the engine run at 2 500 rpm, by lifting the throttle control lever. Now press the retaining lever -86- towards the engine with a small lever through the adjusting slot until a catch is felt.

Caution:

Do not press on beyond the catch.

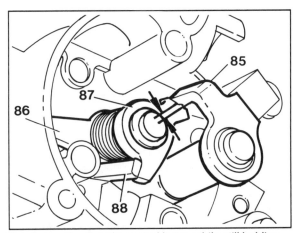

- Let go the throttle control lever, while still holding the retaining lever at the catch.
- The starter lever -85- is now on the second highest notch of the stepped disc, i.e in the pulldown position. -88- dog.
- Take a reading of the choke and CO value. Specified value see page 95.

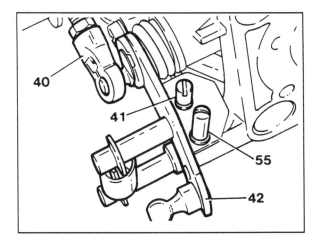

- If the specified value is not reached, adjust the choke fast idle speed at the adjusting bolt -41-. Screwing in = increasing the engine speed, screwing out = decreasing the engine speed.

Caution:

The choke fast idle speed adjusting bolt is the shorter of the two bolts. If there is no adjusting bolt, adjust the choke fast idle speed by shortening (engine speed decreases) or lengthening (engine speed increases) the starter connection rod. A half rotation changes the engine speed by approximately 200/min.

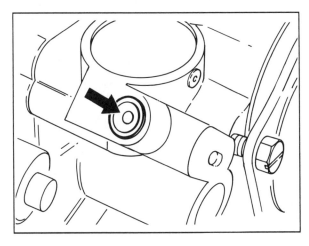

- Adjust the CO value.
- Remove the securing plug -arrow-, by screwing a wooden or tin screw with the appropriate diameter into the plug, then removing the screw and with it the plug with a pair of pliers.
- Adjust the CO value by adjusting the bolt, screwing in = the mixture becomes richer, screwing out = the mixture becomes leaner. Specified value see page 95.
- Fit a new, blue securing plug.
- Let go the retaining lever.
- Check the electrical engine induction manifold heater.
- Check the carburetor air heater.
- Refit the lead of the temperature switch.

Thermal delay valve / pulldown valve testing

Only 175 CDT carburetor

The cold engine receives an enriched fuel/air mixture when starting, so that it starts easily. In a running engine, the pulldown installation closes the start enriching valve by vacuum, to avoid excessive richness of the heated mixture. The thermal delay valve determines the point at which the pulldown equipment switches on after the engine has started. While the pulldown equipment is active immediately in a warm engine, the valve "delays" the point of activation in low temperatures.

- Warm up the engine, oil temperature approximately 70° - 80° C.

Testing the function

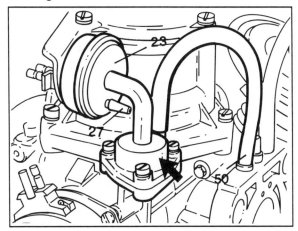

- Remove the vacuum hose -50- from the carburetor. Suck at the vacuum hose with your mouth, it should be blocked. If not, the washer in the thermal delay valve -23- is defective or the bi-metal valve plate is not switching. In this case, replace the valve. 27-vent tube of the thermal delay valve.
- Remove the thermal delay valve. Cool off the valve by holding it under a tap, and at the same time suck at the vacuum hose, the centre connection of the valve. As soon as the temperature of the valve drops below + 20° C, it should switch to open. If not, the bi-metal plate in the valve is defective. Replace the valve.

Electrical heating - testing.

- Refit the thermal delay valve. Attach a test pipe to the middle connection of the valve. Get a helper to start the engine while simultaneously sucking at the test pipe. After a few seconds the valve should click and it should be closed.

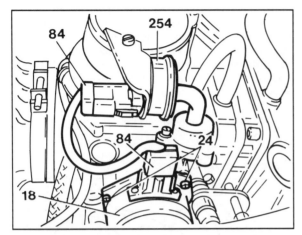

- If the valve does not switch, remove the plug -84- and insert a test lamp between the two contacts while the engine is running. If the test lamp lights up, replace the thermal delay valve, otherwise test the 8 A-fuses in the auxiliary fuse-box and the leads as well as the connections according to the wiring diagram. The auxiliary fuse box is either on or next to the relay plate on the left strut. It has two fuses (2nd fuse: 25 A). Other illustrated parts: 254 - thermal delay valve, 24 - bolts of the choke cover, 18-automatic choke housing.

Delay timing - testing

Testing condition: The temperature of the thermal delay valve is under $+20^\circ$ C, engine is cold.

- Remove the vacuum hose -50- from the carburetor and suck see illustration on page 91. It must be open. At the same time get a helper to start the engine and measure the time until the valve switches with a stop watch, i.e until the vacuum hose closes.

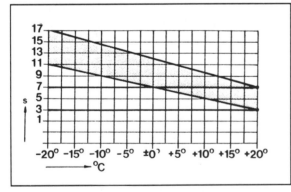

- The measured time is the delay time. Compare this time with the specified time in the diagram. For example: The surrounding temperature is $+15^\circ$ C, the measured time is 6 seconds, i.e. within the allowed region of tolerance. The valve is in order according to the delay time. The region of tolerance at -15° C lies between 10 and 16 seconds.

If the valve does not switch or the delay time lies beyond the region of tolerance, remove the plug from the thermal delay valve while the engine is running, and test the voltage and earth connection with a voltmeter. To do this, attach the voltmeter to the black-red lead of earth, then connecting the voltmeter to the brown lead (-) and to the positive pole of the battery. If a battery voltage (approximately 12 volt) is shown both times, replace the thermal delay valve. If not, check the 8 A-fuse in the auxiliary fuse-box and electrical leads according to the wiring diagram.

Automatic choke - removal and refitting

Removal

- In a warm engine release the pressure in the cooling system, see page 78.

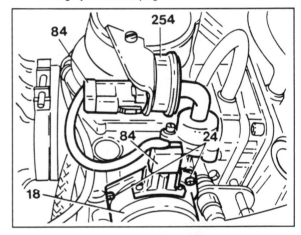

- Close the coolant tubes on the automatic choke -18-with one clip each, totally loosen the tube clips and push back, removing the hose. If no suitable clips are available, hang the hose in an upward position with a piece of wire, so that no coolant can leak out.
- Remove the plug -84-, unscrew the bolts -24- and remove the automatic choke with gasket.
- Remove the vacuum lead at the vacuum box cover -arrow-, see illustration on page 91.

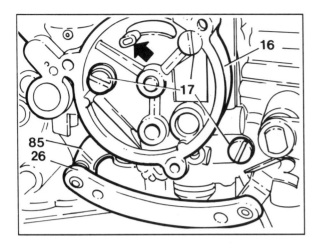

- Unhook the connecting rod -26- at the starter lever -85-.
- Unscrew the 3 securing bolts -17- and remove the housing -16- of the automatic choke.

Refitting

- Refit the housing with a new gasket to the carburetor and tighten.
- Rehook the connecting rod onto the choke lever.
- Refit the automatic choke with a new gasket, while rehooking the bi-metal spring into the retaining lever -arrow- in such a way that the hook of the spring is to the left of the lever. Tighten the clamp bolts of the automatic choke.
- Adjust the automatic choke according to the markings, see page 90.
- Tighten the clamp bolts.
- Refit the electrical leads.
- Refit the coolant hoses and secure them with clips.
- Refit the vacuum lead to the pulldown cover.

Electric inlet manifold heater - testing

Since 7/80

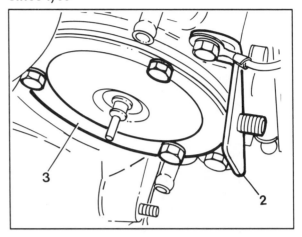

At coolant temperatures below $40 \pm 3°$ C, the pre-heating cover -3- of the engine inlet manifold heater is heated electrically after the engine has been started. At a temperature of $50 \pm 3°$ C the power is interrupted by a temperature switch and the pre-heating cover is no longer heated. **Caution:** In vehicles up to 11/80 the switch-on temperature is $25 \pm 3°$ C and the switch-off temperature at $40 \pm 3°$ C. In this model the insulator is black; since 12/80 blue.

The test can be carried out in a cold engine (coolant temperature below +40° C or +25° C) or in a warm engine (coolant temperature above approximately +50° C or +40° C).

Caution:

Described is testing of a cold engine. When working on a warm engine the following points must be observed:

- Release the pressure from the cooling system, see page 78.
- Remove the temperature switch and cool to below +40° C (+25° C). To do this hold the switch under cold tap water.
- Remove the electrical lead from the pre-heating cover.
- Attach the temperature switch to earth via a test cable. **Caution:** Put the temperature switch down in a place where it cannot heat up - do not place it on the engine.

Testing

Testing conditions: The engine must be cold with coolant temperature below approximately +40° C (+25° C).

- Remove the green control lead from the ignition test socket, see page 47.
- Turn the ignition to start position, then let go.

Caution:

It is not sufficient to simply switch on the ignition.

- Remove the electrical leads from the pre-heating cover. Connect a test lamp between the plug and earth. The test lamp must light up. If not, test the relay drive for the induction manifold pre-heater.

Pre-heating cover - testing

- Refit the plug to the pre-heating cover.

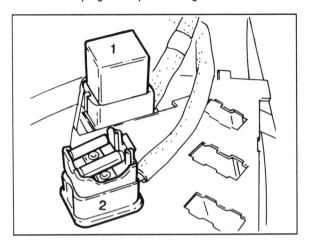

- Remove the relay -1- of the induction manifold pre-heater; 2 - auxiliary fuse box.
- Attach a test lamp to the terminals 3 and 1 of the relay plug. The test lamp must light up. If not, remove the plug of the pre-heating cover and hold it against earth. If the lamp now lights up, replace the pre-heating cover. Alternatively test the red-yellow lead from the pre-heating cover to terminal 1 for disruptions.

Switch-off point - testing

- Switch off the ignition and fit the green control lead to the timing device.
- Heat up the engine until the coolant temperature exceeds +50° C or +40° C.
- Remove the plug from the pre-heating cover. Connect a test light between the plug and earth.

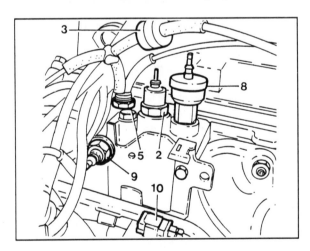

- The test lamp should not light up. If it does, replace the temperature switch -2-. Other illustrated parts: 3 - back pressure valve, 5 - Thermo-valve, 8 - Temperature switch for the fan, 9 - temperature switch for the temperature gauge, 10 - plug connection of the fan clutch.

Procedure for relay -1- testing

Only when there is no voltage at the pre-heating cover.

Testing conditions: The green control lead is removed, key has been turned to starting position for short while and the ignition left on.

- Remove the relay -1-.

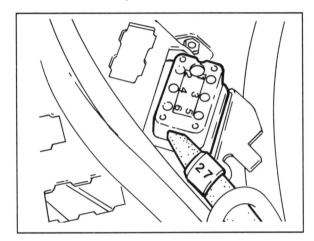

- Connect a test lamp between terminal 1 and the battery positive pole. The lamp must light up. If not, remove the electrical lead of the temperature switch -2- and place it against earth. If the lamp now lights up, replace the temperature switch.
- Attach the test lamp to terminal 3 and earth then terminal 4 and earth. If the lamp does not light up, test the fuses in the auxiliary fuse-box as well as the leads according to the wiring diagram.
- If the test lamp lights up in all three tests, replace the relay.
- Refit the green control lead to the timing device.

Pre-heating cover - removal and refitting

Since 7/80

Removal

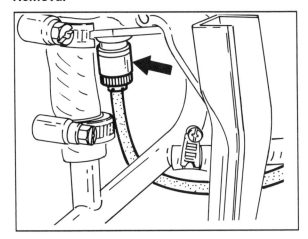

- Remove the electrical lead -arrow-from the pre-heating cover.
- Remove the 3 securing bolts.

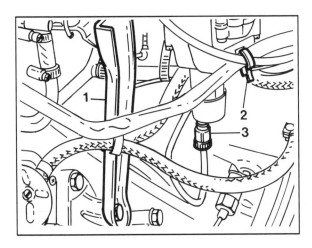

- Unscrew the inlet manifold support -1-.
- Carefully lift off the pre-heating cover.

Caution:

Be careful not to damage the insulation ring.

- Remove the rubber washer from the inlet manifold.

Refitting

- Place a **new** rubber washer onto the pre-heating cover. Fit the insulating ring and refit the pre-heating cover to the inlet manifold.
- Tighten the pre-heating cover screws.
- Tighten the induction manifold support.
- Refit the electrical leads.

Carburettor specifications

Model	175 CDTU	175 CDT
Idle speed rpm	850 ± 50/rpm	850 ± 50/rpm
CO content	1,5 ± 0,5 Vol %	1,5 ± 0,5 Vol %
Vacuum regulator Engine speed Distance -a-	1300 ± 100/rpm ca. 0,5 mm	1250 ± 50/rpm ca. 0,5 mm
Idle regulating Valve Delay time	–	6 16 seconds
Starter cover ID Choke fast idle speed Engine speed CO content	200 1900 ± 100 5,5 ± 0,5 Vol. %	200 1700 ± 100rpm 7 ± 1 Vol. %
Jet needle	MB	CC
Fuel jet	100	100
Float needle valve Washer, thickness Float position ball compressed	2,25 1,5mm 16 - 17mm	2,25 1,5mm 18 - 19mm
Float weight	11.00, ± 0,6g	12.1, ± 0,6g

Solex 4A1-carburetor

The Solex carburetor is a four barrel carburetor, which consists of 4 main components bolted together: carburetor cover, carburetor body, throttle control and starting device. The "4" in the carburetor description refers to the 4 barrels of the carburetor, whereas "A" and "1" point to the principle of construction and the model. Since it is a dual carburetor system, 2 carburetors are practically built into one housing, with each of the two carburetors having 2 venturi (stage I and II). The engine receives the fuel/air at idle and up to the middle engine speeds via the two first stages of the carburetor, and the two second stages are opened during full-throttle when the automatic choke is off. The carburetor is attached to the intake manifold by 4 nuts tightened to 7 ± 1 N.m.

Operating instructions are practically identical to the Stromberg carburetor and are described there.

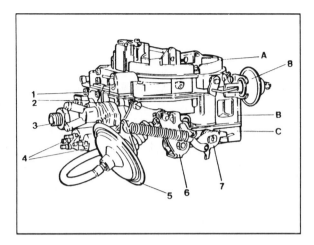

1 - Accelerator pump
2 - TS starter (TS=thermo shunt)
3 - Fuel inlet
4 - Idle regulating valve
5 - Vacuum regulator
6 - Throttle control lever (stage I)
7 - Throttle control lever (stage 2)
A - Carburetor cover
B - Carburetor body
C - Throttle control body

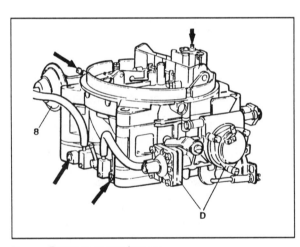

8 - Damper second stage
D - Automatic choke

Caution:

The bolts marked with an -arrow- are adjusted by the manufacturer. They may **not** be adjusted, since even a workshop cannot adjust them.

Idle engine speed and CO content - adjustment

- Warm up the engine and switch it off, oil temperature 75°-85° C.
- Switch off the air conditioning and in automatic vehicles set the selector lever in the "P" position.
- Switch off all electrical consumers.
- Attach the tachometer and CO measuring device according to instructions; leave the air filter attached.

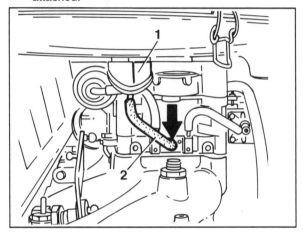

- Remove and block the pipe of the crankcase air vent -arrow- as well as the vacuum hose of the accelerator pump (to the right of it).
- Start the engine and allow it to idle.
- Check the seals of the vacuum by painting all seals with a brush and fuel. If the engine speed increases periodically, the engine is sucking in air. Locate the leaking areas and repair.

Caution:

Do not breathe in the fuel fumes - poisonous! Do not spill fuel onto hot parts or the ignition system. Fire danger!

- Check whether the throttle control lever is against the idle stop by lifting the throttle control lever slightly and increasing the engine speed to approximately 2500/min. Let go the throttle control lever, which should go back to the idle stop on its own. If not, lubricate the accelerator rod and adjust it.
- If fitted check the cruise control adjustment. First model with bowden cable: The cable must be tension free and lie against the regulating lever, if not - turn the adjusting nut accordingly. Second model: Unhook the connecting rod and press downwards to the stop. Rotate the socket on the rod until it is directly above the ball head. Now unscrew the socket by two turns and secure with a lock nut. Rehook the connecting rod.

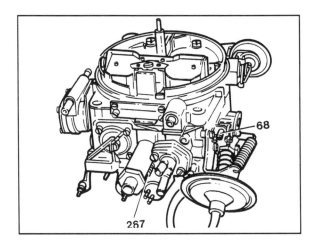

- Adjust the engine speed to the specified value by the adjusting screw -68-.

Until 8/79

- Remove the securing cap of the carburetor with a pair of pliers and adjust the CO content to the specified value by turning the CO adjusting screw -267-Accelerate briefly after each adjustment. By unscrewing the screw, the mixture becomes richer, by screwing in, leaner. Specified value, see page 98.

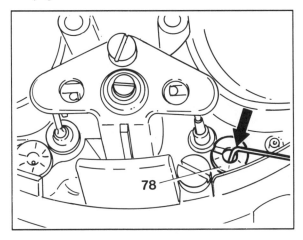

- Check the synchronisation by bending the front of a test wire of 5mm diameter and in turn inserting it into both idle air jets -78-. The test wire should push in to a maximum of 10mm. The CO level must be the same on both sides. In variations of above 1,0%, have the carburetor synchronised (workshop job). **Caution:** Uneven adjustment of the idle system affects the main jet systems, which leads to difficulties in starting, and jerking in the medium engine speeds.

Since 9/79

- Remove the screw of the exhaust pipe at the front of the exhaust manifold (cylinders1-3) and attach a CO measuring device.
- Check the CO value and record it. Replace the screw.
- Now remove the screw of the rear exhaust pipe (cylinders 4-6) and attach the CO measuring device.
- Check the CO content and compare the measured value with the previously measured value (cylinders 1-3). Both values should be about equal and lie within the specified value tolerance, see page 98. Replace the screw.

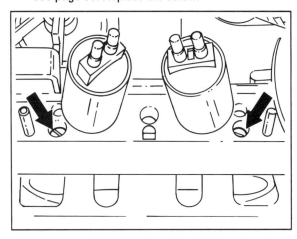

- If not, regulate CO values by the two CO adjusting screws -arrows-. The arrow on the right in the illustrations shows the screw for cylinders 1-3, while the left arrow points to the screw for cylinders 4-6. By unscrewing, the mixture becomes richer, by screwing in, leaner.
- Adjust the regulating rod so that when accelerating, the transfer of the movement at the gate lever occurs without play.
- Adjust the vacuum regulator, see page 87.
- Specified values for the adjustment of the vacuum regulator, see page 98.

Idle regulating valve -adjustment

The 2 idle regulating valves close the idle channels when the ignition is switched off and thus prevent the engine from running on. The valves remain closed until volatage is restored after the ignition is switched on again. If the valve or the volatage supply are defective, the engine will not easily start and will vibrate when idling. If there is not volatage at both valves when the ignition is on, the engine will not start. The idle regulating valves are screwed from the side into the throttle control part of the carburettor.

- Switch on the ignition.

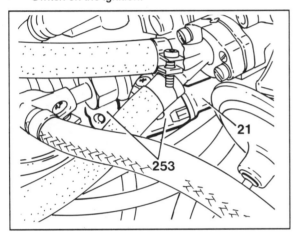

- Remove and replace the plugs -253- from the regulating valve -21- several times. The valve must click audibly.
- Alternately switch a test lamp between the plug and earth. If the test lamp lights up, replace the valve. If it does not light up, test fuse 14 or the electrical leads according to the wiring diagram.
- Start the engine and let it idle. Remove the plugs of both valves simultaneously, the engine must stop immediately without running on. Start the engine again and remove the plug from the left valve. The engine speed should decrease noticeably or the engine should shake. Now refit the plug of the left valve and remove the plug of the right valve, the speed should again decrease. If not, replace the relevant valve.

Caution:

In carburetors without a central CO adjusting screw between the idle regulating valves, the valves can be replaced with the carburetor still fitted.

Carburetor data II

Engine	110		123	+
Carburetor type	4A1		4A1	+
Engine idle speed CO content	850 ± 50 rpm 0,7 ± 0,5 Vol. %		850 ± 50 rpm 0,7 ± 0,5 Vol. %	
Vacuum regulator Starting engine speed	2000/rpm		2000/rpm	
Distance -a- Engine speed loaded	ca 1,0 mm 650 ± 50 rpm		ca 1,0 mm 650 ± 50 rpm	
Starter cover ID	80		80	
carburetor stage	I	II	I	II
Jet needle	–	B2	–	B4
Main jet	X95	–	X95	–
Idle fuel jet	–	–	45 [1]	–
Idle air jet	110	–	110	–

[1] = can be replaced

Air filter -removal and refitting

Removal

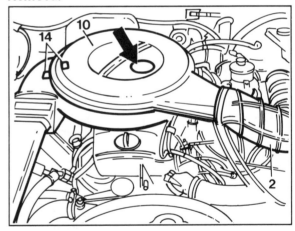

- Remove the rubber piece -2- from the intake sleeve of the carburetor. First completely open the hose clip.
- Remove the 3 securing nuts of the air filter cover -10-.
- Remove the vacuum pipe from the intake manifold.
- **Engine 115:** Mark the vacuum leads at the temperature regulator in the intake manifold of the air filter with tape and remove.
- Loosen the 7 retaining clips and remove the air filter cover.

- Remove the filter insert.
- Unscrew the air filter housing with the three nuts from the rubber-metal supports.
- Slightly lift the air filter housing and pull it out of the warm air pipe. Remove the engine ventilation hose at the bottom of the air filter housing from the cylinder head cover.

Refitting

- Refit the air filter housing by pushing the engine ventilation hose onto the cylinder head cover and checking that the warm air pipe is secure.
- Tighten the air filter housing.
- Refit the filter insert so that the marking "top" is to the top.
- Refit the crankcase ventilation hose.
- Refit the air filter cover, push the rubber piece back onto the carburetor and tighten the hose clip.
- Tighten the air filter cover, tension the clips and refit the vacuum hose to the intake manifold.
- If removed, refit the vacuum leads to the temperature regulator according to the attached markings.

Carburettor air heater - testing

Engine 102

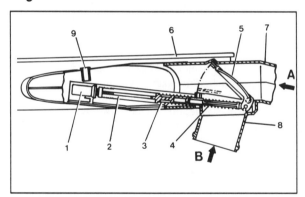

The carburettor air heater is fed depending on the temperature via a regulating element (thermostat) -1- in the intake tube -7- of the air filter -6-. The arrow -A- indicates the direction of the "fresh air", the arrow -B- that of the "warm air".

At intake air temperatures below +13° C the flap -5- is held in the "warm air" position by the spring -3-. From a intake air temperature of approximately +13° C to approximately +25° C, the flap is gradually lowered by the thermostat, so that the ratio of "fresh air" increases according to the temperature. If the intake air temperature lies at +25° C or above, the regulating process is ended, the flap is in the "fresh air" position, the warm air channel is totally closed.

Other illustrated parts: 2 - regulating rod, 4 - pressure spring, 8 - connecting sleeve for the warm air tube, 9 - compensation bore for the air lead tube.

Testing

- Look into the intake sleeve -7- of a cold engine and a external temperature of below +13° C.
- The flap must stand upright and totally block the cold air supply.
- At external temperatures between +13° C and +25° C, the flap is slightly raised and allows the cold air to pass through according to the temperature.
- If the external temperature is above +25° C the flap must be right at the bottom. The cold air supply moves through freely and at the same time the warm air supply is closed off totally from below.

Engine 110, 115, 123

The carburetor air heater is regulated according to the temperature and load. This means that the position of the air flap is regulated by the intake manifold vacuum of the engine. The intake manifold vacuum is a measure of the current load of the engine.

Testing

- Remove the warm air tube. Start the engine and let it idle.
- Below +30° C the air flap must totally close the fresh air channel, i.e it must be pulled totally up.
- Above 40° C the air flap must totally close the warm air channel.
- Accelerate by applying the throttle control lever. If the intake air temperature lies below approximately +25° C, the air flap must stay up with the fresh air channel closed. From +25° C to +40° C the air flap must open the fresh air channel when accelerating and close again when the accelerator is released. The position of the air flap must change depending on the amount of acceleration.

Thermostat - removal and refitting

Engine 102

The thermostat regulates the position of the air flap for the carburetor air heater according to the temperature of the inlet air.

Removal

● Unscrew the inlet sleeve from the air filter housing.

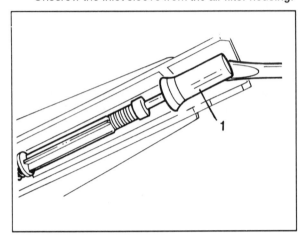

● Press the thermostat -1- out of the case with a screwdriver.

Refitting

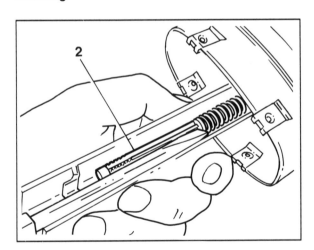

● Push back the regulating rod -2- so that the thermostat can be refitted into the case without any pressure.
● Refit the air filter inlet pipe.

Fuel pump - removal and refitting

The fuel pump is on the side of the cylinder head next to the distributor.

Caution:

Only pumps with an etched manufacturing identification number from 1.132 should be fitted into engine 102.

Removal

Caution:

No naked flame - fire danger!

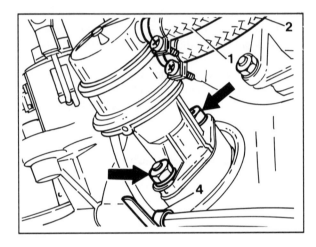

● Close off the inlet and outlet pipes -1 & 2- with a clamp each. If no suitable clamp is available, put a bolt with the relevant diameter into the pipes after removal, so that no fuel can flow out.
● Remove the fuel pipes from the pump after loosening the clips.
● Loosen the cable ties -4- from the insulation flange of the pump and put the cables to one side.
● Depending on the type of fuel pump, unscrew the 2 nuts -arrows- or 2 bolts and remove them with the insulation flange.

Refitting

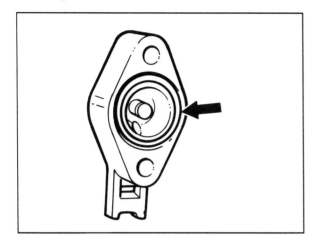

- Check the rubber seal -arrow- of the insulation flange for damage, replacing the insulation flange if necessary. The seals are not separately available.
- Fit the actuating tappet into the insulation flange so that the circlip points to the fuel pump. Check the tappet for ease of movement by moving it from side to side.
- Refit the fuel pump with the insulation flange and tighten. **Caution:** If the pump is tightened with bolts, first paint with sealant (e.g. Locktite).
- Clip on the cable ties.
- Refit the fuel pipes and secure with the clips. Pipe -1- comes from the tank, pipe -2- goes to the carburetor.

Carburettor fault diagnosis

When interruptions to the fuel supply occur, the system should be tested in the following order:

- Check that there is fuel in the tank.
- Remove the fuel pipe between the fuel pump and the carburetor and hold it into a suitable container. Briefly switch on the starter. Fuel should pulsate out of the pipe. **Caution:** Fire danger - no open flame!
- If no fuel comes out, remove the lead to the fuel pump.
- If no fuel pours out here, check the pump seals or the strainer for dirt. To do this unscrew the cover of the fuel pump and clean the strainer with fuel. **Caution:** In newer fuel pumps the cover can no longer be removed, and so the strainer cannot be cleaned.
- If no fuel flows out, remove the fuel pipe to the tank and blow through it.
- Check that the air goes straight through to the tank, cleaning if necessary.
- Remove the filter in the fuel tank and clean it.

Fault		Possible cause	Solution
1.The cold engine will not start	1.	Idle adjusting valve does not open	Test the adjusting valve
	2.	Automatic choke is not switching	
	a)	Starter cover not on mark	Adjust the mark
	b)	Bimetal spring in starter housing broken	Replace bimetal spring
	c)	Starter idle jammed	Remove starter cover, engage start slide via retaining lever, possibly remove start slide and clean with glass cloth
	d)	Starter enriching valve jammed	Push pulldown rod upward with small screwdriver, engage enriching valve, if jammed, replace starter housing
	e)	Thermal delay valve hangs in closed position. Vacuum pipe blocked	Test thermal delay valve, replace if necessary
	3.	Throttle valve is not in starting position	Test warm-up engine speed, adjust

Fault		Possible cause	Solution
2.The engine stalls after cold starting	1.	Throttle valve not in starting position	Test choke idle speed, adjust
	2.	Thermal delay valve hanging in open position	Test thermal delay valve, temporary solution: attach bleed tube to valve, release bleed tube
	3.	Air piston does not completely return	Loosen air piston, replace air piston muffler
	4.	Insufficient fuel in the float chamber due to vaporisation	Start, depressing accelerator several times, start while pedal is depressed
	5.	Intake manifold heating defective	Test
	6.	Intake air pre-heater defective	Test

Fault		Possible cause	Solution
3.The engine stalls before running temperature is reached	1.	Throttle control is not in starting position	Test choke idle speed, adjust
	2.	Incorrect idle adjustment	Adjust CO content and engine speed
	3.	Automatic choke not switching:	
	a)	Starter cover not on mark	Set to mark
	b)	No heating	Restore contact, replace starter cover if necessary.
	c)	Bimetal spring defective or unhooked	Replace starter cover or hook in spring
	d)	Pulldown diaphragm torn	Check seals of pulldown box
	e)	Thermal delay valve is not being heated	Test thermal delay valve
	4.	Intake manifold heater defective	Test

Fault	Possible cause	Solution
4. Starting difficulties when hot	Too rich due to overheating and vaporisation from heat build-up	Start at full throttle (hold accelerator)

Fault	Possible cause	Solution
5. Irregular idling - engine stalls (engine hot)	1. Idle adjustment	
	a) Engine speed too low	Adjust
	b) CO value too low/too high	Adjust
	2. Idle jet hole too small	
	a) Jet blocked	Clean
	b) Jet damaged	Replace
	c) Jet needle bent	Replace
	3. Air piston damper too low	Check damper oil level, fill up, if necessary, replace air piston damper
	4. Leakages at intake manifold or carburettor	Paint seals with brush and fuel while engine is running, if leaking, engine speed increases. Replace gaskets.
	5. As in 3.3 and 3.4	

Fault	Possible cause	Solution
6. Intermediate interruptions when accelerating	1. Throttle control jammed	Loosen
	2. Accelerator rod hooked	Loosen or replace
	3. Bearing of throttle control shaft damaged	Replace carburetor

Fault	Possible cause	Solution
7. Maximum performance not achieved	1. Jet blocked	Clean
	2. Jet needle bent	Replace
	3. Full throttle position not reached	Adjust accelerator rod
	4. Air filter element dirty	Replace

Fault	Possible cause	Solution
8. Engine runs on	Idle adjusting valve or relay of adjusting valve defective	Test valve and relay, replace if necessary

Fault	Possible cause	Solution
9. Consumption too high. Fuel consumption is influenced by traffic density, operating conditions and driving style. Without any fault in vehicle, consumption can double	1. Idle mixture too rich CO adjustment incorrect	Adjust
	2. Jet needle bent	Replace
	3. Air filter dirty, oil clogged	Replace
	4. As in 3.3 and 3.4	

Carburettor maintenance

Carburetor testing

Engine 102

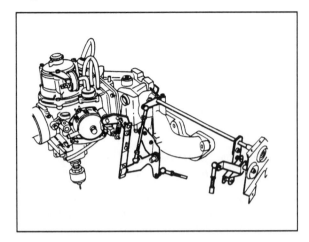

Engine 110

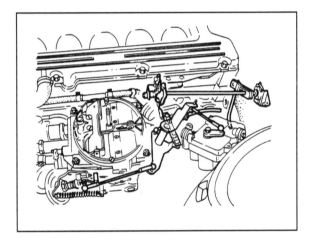

- Test the accelerator linkages for ease of movement, bending and play in the bearings.
- Lubricate all the bearings of the accelerator linkages, throttle arm and joints with engine oil.
- Check the function of the carburetor air heater, see page 99.
- Check the oil level of the air piston damper.
- Check the engine idle speed and CO content.

Air filter - replacing

The air filter should be changed every 60 000km. In very dusty conditions, replace the filter insert more often.

- Remove the air filter cover, see page 98.
- Remove the air filter.
- Thoroughly wipe the filter housing.

Caution:

Do not clean the filter with fuel, or clog it up with oil.

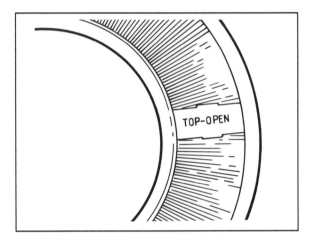

- Refit the new filter so that the marking "top" points upwards.
- Refit the cover, tighten and secure it with the wire clips.

THE FUEL INJECTION SYSTEM

Schematic Diagram of the K-Jetronic

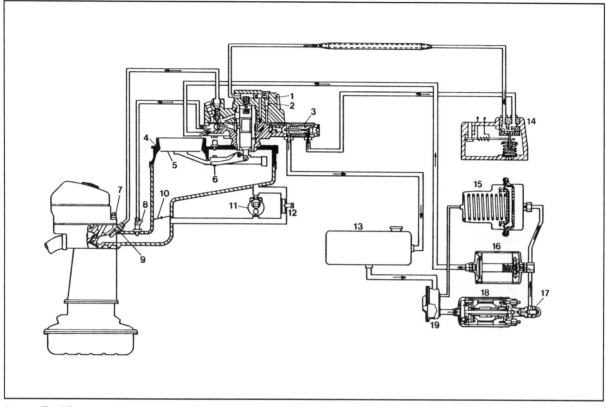

1	-	Fuel flow regulator	8	-	Cold starting valve	15	-	Fuel accumulator
2	-	Pressure equalising valve	9	-	Injection valve (nozzle)	16	-	Fuel filter
3	-	System pressure regulator	10	-	Throttle control	17	-	Back pressure valve
4	-	Air flow sensor	11	-	Auxiliary air valve	18	-	Electrical fuel pump
5	-	Sensor plate	12	-	Idle speed adjusting screw	19	-	Diaphragm damper
6	-	Idle mixture (CO) adjusting screw	13	-	Fuel tank			

The K-Jetronic is a mechanical fuel injection which continuously injects fuel into the inlet manifold in front of the inlet valves.

The fuel is sucked from the fuel tank by the electrical fuel pump and is transmitted to the fuel distributor via fuel accumulator and filters. The air sucked in by the engine via the induction manifold is measured by the airflow sensor. The fuel flow regulator distributes the amount of fuel to the cylinders via the relevant injection valve according to the measured air. Sensors and transmitters regulate the correct fuel amounts for all temperatures and driving situations.

- The fuel accumulator keeps the fuel under pressure for a certain time even after the engine is switched off.

- The fuel pump has a delivery capacity of approximately 130 liters per hour.
- The fuel pump relay supplies the fuel pump and the cold start valve with power when starting and running the engine. The relay blocks the fuel supply when the ignition is switched off and when there are no spark impulses (engine stalled, ignition switched on). It also switches off the pump when the maximum engine speed is reached.
- The cold start valve injects extra fuel into the collective inlet manifold while starting, so that the engine starts more easily.
- The thermal time switch regulates the injection time of the cold start valve.
- The system pressure regulator regulates the system pressure to approximately 5,5 bar.

- The electrically heated auxiliary air valve stabilises the engine speed during the warming up phase.
- The heating-up regulator enriches the mixture during the heating-up phase.

Since 9/81 the injection system has been fitted with an idle overrun switch to lower the fuel consumption. This causes the fuel supply to the injection valves to be cut off automatically when the driver releases the accelerator. The switching on of the idle overrun switch is dependent on the engine speed and the car speed. A micro-switch on the accelerator rod ensures that the fuel supply cuts in even at the lightest application of the accelerator. This ensures that the vehicle accelerates smoothly.

- The idle overrun switch opens when the micro-switch is off and supplies the engine with fresh air avoiding the air flow sensor. This causes the sensor plate to go back into the zero position, blocking the fuel supply to the injection valves.

Caution:

Extreme cleanliness is important when working on the injection system. All relevant parts are to be cleaned with fuel before removing. **The system is under pressure. Before removing any parts, release the pressure by slowly loosening the fuel lead at the cold start valve. Put a cloth around the fuel connection as it can splatter.** Catch any exuding fuel with a cloth.

Cleanliness while working on the injection system

- Thoroughly clean all connection points and their surroundings with fuel before loosening.
- Put the removed parts down on a clean surface and cover. Use foil or paper. Do not use frayed cloths!
- Cover any opened parts carefully while not working on them.
- Refit only clean parts. New parts should be taken out of their wrappings only immediately before use.
- While the system is open: avoid working with compressed air and moving the vehicle.

Injection system - testing of seals

If there are problems with starting a hot engine, the seals of the injection system should be tested. Visual testing is described here, but the fuel pressure must also be tested (workshop job).

- Remove the air filter.
- The fuel connections in the regulator should not be damp; carefully tighten the connections if necessary.
- Remove the fuel pump relay and join terminals 7 and 8 with a test lead for a short while to build up pressure in the fuel system.

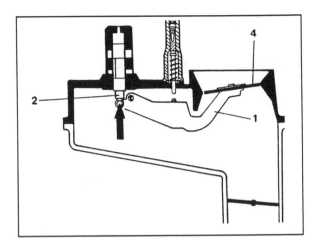

- Test the seals of the control piston -2- by pushing the sensor plate -4- totally down and holding it in this position.
- In this position only a very small amount of fuel should become visible in the air duct, or the washer for the control pistons must be renewed. The fuel regulator must be removed for this (workshop job).
- Refit the fuel pump relay and air filter.

Engine ildle speed/CO content - testing

- Switch off the air conditioning.
- In Automatic vehicles put the selector lever into the "P" position.
- Connect the tachometer and CO testing device according to the instructions.
- Warm up the engine, the oil temperature should be around 75° - 85° C.

Caution:

Do not adjust the idling in a very hot engine.

- Test the ignition dwell, see page 58.
- Check the seals of the intake section by starting the engine and letting it idle. Paint all the seals of the intake section with a brush and fuel. If the engine speed increases, the engine is sucking in excess air at the point just painted. Replace the relevant seal.

Caution:

Do not spill any fuel onto hot parts or the ignition system, fire danger! Do not breathe in fuel fumes, poisonous!

- Check the adjustment of the accelerator rods.
- Start the engine and let it idle.

Engine 102

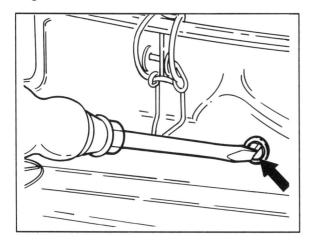

- Adjust the idle engine speed with the engine idle speed adjusting screw -arrow- to 800 ± 50/rpm.

Engine 110

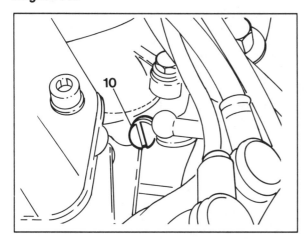

- Adjust the engine idle speed with the engine idle speed adjusting screw -10- to 750 ± 50 rpm.
- Test the CO content, specified value Engine 102: 1,0 ± 0,5 Vol.%; Engine 110: 1,5 ± 0,5 Vol. %.

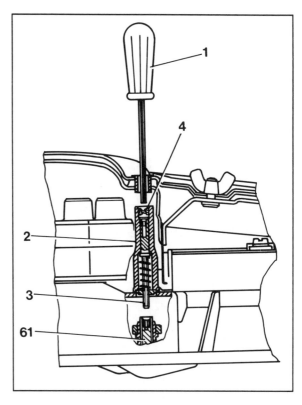

- Remove the securing plug -4- through the slot at the top of the air filter. If the special tool is not available, screw a suitable wooden or tin bolt into the securing plug and pull this out with the securing plug.
- Press the adjusting device -2- down and turn it slightly against the strength of the spring with a narrow screwdriver -1-, until the hexagon -3-fits into the CO adjusting bolt -61-. Turn the screwdriver to the left - the mixture becomes leaner; turn it to the right - the mixture becomes richer.
- Release the screwdriver so that the adjusting device comes out of the CO adjusting bolt.
- Accelerate slightly, then test the CO value, adjusting again if necessary.
- Refit a blue securing plug of 6,5mm diameter after the adjustment.
- Apply the hand brake and put the selector lever into a driving gear, switch on the air conditioner, pull the power steering totally to one side. The engine should run perfectly, if not, adjust the engine speed.
- Remove the CO measuring device.

Accelerator linkage - adjustment

- Check the accelerator linkages for ease of movement, wear and bending.
- Lubricate all joints of the accelerator linkage with oil.

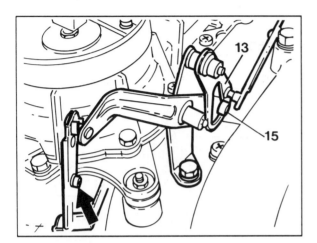

- Unhook the connecting rod -arrow- at the return lever. Push the throttle arm into idling position and check that the connecting rod can be hooked in without tension. The roller -15- of the gate lever -13- must lie at the end notch. If not, adjust the length of the connecting rod accordingly. If the connecting rod is replaced, adjust the length (middle of the socket to middle of the socket) to 96mm.
- If fitted, adjust the traction bar of the cruise control, see page 87.

Full throttle stop-adjustment

- Manual gearbox: Totally compress the accelerator and hold it there by jamming a suitable board between the pedal and the seat.

- **Automatic gearbox:** Compress the accelerator to the kickdown-stop and keep it there (helper). Do not engage the kickdown switch.

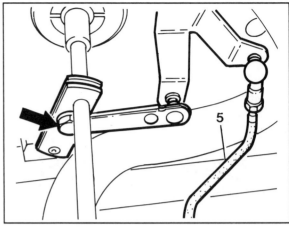

- The throttle control lever must now rest against the full-throttle stop. If not, loosen the bolt -arrow-, pull the accelerator back a little and tighten the bolt. Now test the full throttle stop again, correcting if necessary.

Caution:

If the full throttle stop cannot be adjusted in this way, disconnect the rod -5- and adjust it to a length of 200mm (middle of socket to middle of auxiliary ring). Re-connect the pressure rod.

Cruise control adjustment

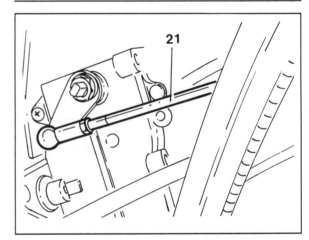

- Check that the lever of the adjusting joint rests against the idle stop of the cruise control by disconnecting the bar -21- and pressing the lever in a clockwise direction against the idle stop.
- Re-connect the bar; the lever of the adjusting joint must be lifted by about 1mm from the idle stop to do this.
- Alteratively adjust the bar. Prise off the socket, loosen the lock nut, screw the socket in or out and tighten the lock nut.

Cold start valve - testing

When starting with a cold engine, the cold start valve injects additional fuel into the inlet manifold.

A defective cold start valve causes starting difficulties (cold and warm), intermediate interruptions and high fuel consumption.

The thermal time switch limits the injection time of the cold start valve in accordance with the engine temperature. The switching temperature of the valve lies at +15° C or since 9/82 at +5° C.

A defective thermal time switch causes starting problems.

- Remove the green control lead from the Transistorised ignition system, see page 47.
- Remove the air filter, see page 98.

Voltage supply testing

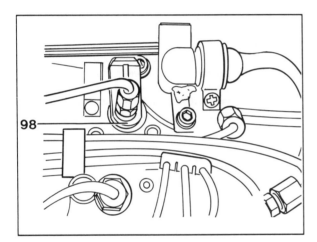

- Remove the plug from the cold start valve -98-. Attach a voltmeter to the plug by putting the positive connection of the voltmeter to the pink/blue lead.

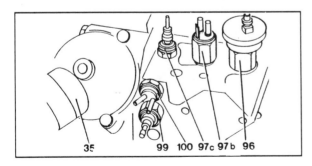

- Remove the connection from the thermal time switch 97b. Other illustrated parts: A - sensor housing on cylinder head, 35 - thermostat housing, 96 - temperature switch fan air coupling, 97c. - Temperature sender unit, (if not used a screw), 99 - temperature gauge sender unit, 100 - thermovalve (carburettor models only)

- Put the brown/blue lead of terminal W of the thermal time switch with an auxiliary cable to earth. This simulates a temperature of below +5° C.

Caution:

Do not put the pink/blue lead next to earth, danger of short circuit!

- Apply the starter. The voltmeter should show about 10 volt. If this is the case, remove the cold start valve and test it. Alternately test the leads according to the wiring diagram for interruptions.

Cold start valve testing

- Release excess pressure from the fuel system, see page 78.
- The brown/blue lead of the thermal time switch remains at earth.

Caution:

No naked flame, fire danger!

- Remove the fuel pipe from the cold start valve.
- Remove the cold start valve, refit the fuel pipe and hold the valve into a measuring cup.
- Remove needle from cold start valve.
- Briefly apply the starter. The cold start valve must spurt out in a regular flow.
- Dry the jet of the cold start valve.
- No drops are allowed to fall from the cold start valve for one minute. The valve may also not become damp on the outside.
- Refit the plug to the thermal time switch
- Refit the cold start valve with a new gasket, tighten the fuel line to about 10 Nm.

Thermal time switch testing

Coolant temperature below +15° C (since 9/82 below +5° C). Alternately remove the thermal time switch and cool it off in the fridge.

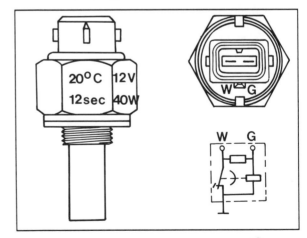

- The switching time (e.g 12 seconds at 20°C) is etched into the hexagon of the switch.
- Remove the plug of the cold start valve and attach a test lamp.

Caution:

Hold the removed thermal time switch against earth during the test. Refit the electrical lead.

- Apply the starter for about 15 seconds. The test lamp must light up for 1 to 12 seconds. If this is not the case, replace the thermal time switch.

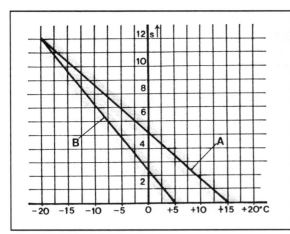

Hint: The injection time must co-incide with the switching-on time of the thermal time switch. For example: at a coolant temperature of 0° C, switching-on duration 4,5 seconds or 2,5 seconds. Line -A- of the thermal time switch with a switching temperature of +15° C, line -B- of the thermal time switch with a switching temperature of +5° C since 9/82.

- Test the thermal time switch with an ohmmeter. **Switch "A" +15° C:** attach the ohmmeter first between contacts G and earth, then W and earth. If the temperature of the thermal time switch lies below +15° C, the measuring device must show about 48 ohm then 0 ohm, above +15° C about 62 ohm then 270 ohm. **Switch "B" +5° C:** attach the ohmmeter between contacts W and G. At a temperature below +5° C a value of about 93 ohm must show up, above +5° C, open circuit.
- If removed, refit the thermal time switch.
- Refit the plugs of the cold start valve and thermal time switch.
- Refit the green control lead to the transistorised ignition system.
- Refit the air filter, see page 98.

Auxiliary air valve - testing

During the warming up phase a larger amount of fuel air mixture is supplied to the engine than corresponds with the throttle control position. This is obtained by bypassing the throttle control via an auxiliary air valve. At running temperature, the auxiliary cross section must be closed.

A defective auxiliary air valve causes the engine to stall or irregular running during the warming-up phase, excessively high idle engine speed in a warm engine, or non-adjustable engine speed. The auxiliary air valve is between the cylinder head and oil filter under the heating tube.

- Remove the green control lead from the transistorised ignition system, see page 47.
- The engine must be cold for this test.

Voltage supply testing

- Remove the plug of the auxiliary air valve and connect a test lamp.
- Apply the starter. The test lamp must light up, alternatively ascertain the power interruption according to the circuit diagram and remove it.
- Connect an ohmmeter between the contacts of the auxiliary air valve. Specified value: approximately 40 ohm. If the measuring device shows infinite ohms, the heating filament is defective; in this case replace the auxiliary air valve.
- Refit the plug of the auxiliary air valve.
- Refit the green control lead.

Testing the operation

- Start the engine and let it idle.

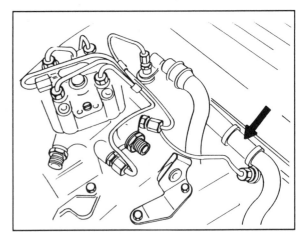

- Clamp the connecting tube -arrow-. The engine speed must drop, otherwise the auxiliary air valve is jamming and must be replaced.
- Retest in a warm engine. The engine speed when the tube is clamped should not change or the auxiliary air valve must be replaced.

Sensor plate - testing/adjusting

The sensor plate in the air regulator is lowered in accordance with the amount of air that is sucked in. If the resting position of the plate is too high, the engine will not start. A wrongly adjusted resting position can also lead to warm starting problems and intermittent interruptions.

- Remove the air filter
- Remove the fuel pump relay and connect terminals 1 and 2 (or since 9/81, terminals 7 and 8) to the relay socket with a test lead. The fuel pump will start operating and building up pressure. Now remove the connecting lead and refit the relay.

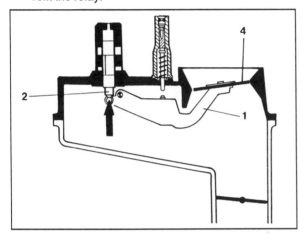

- Press the sensor plate -4- downwards by hand. An even resistance must be felt all the way.
- Quickly move the sensor plate upwards. No resistance should be felt, since the slow following control piston -2- lifts up from the adjusting lever -1-. In a slow upward movement, the control piston must follow.
- If the adjusting lever or the control piston move with difficulty, replace the fuel distributor.

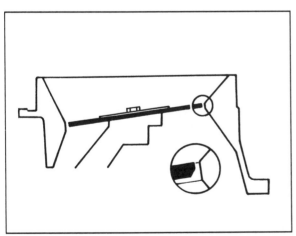

- The surface of the sensor plate must align with the top surface of the beginning of the bevel -arrow- at the air intake. The sensor plate may be up to 0,5mm higher.

- In this position there must be a play of 1 - 2mm between the adjusting lever and control piston. To check this, press the sensor plate down slightly until a light resistance is felt.

Adjusting

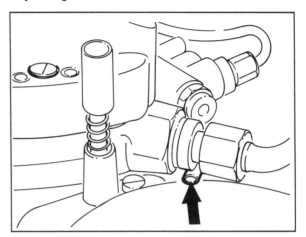

- **If the level is too high:** Hit the guide pin -arrow- with a punch in slightly deeper. If necessary, unscrew the fuel feed sleeve.

Caution:
Do not hit the guide pin in too deeply.

- **If the level is too low:** Remove the mixture regulator and hit the pin out a little from below.

Caution:
Avoid frequent adjustment of the pin in both directions.

- Refit the air filter.
- Adjust the idling.

Fuel pump relay - testing

The fuel pump relay is in a relay clip to the left of the wheel arch. It supplies power to the fuel pump and the auxiliary air valve during starting and while the engine is running. The relay blocks the power supply to the pump when the ignition is switched off and when the maximum engine speed is reached until the engine speed drops again and no ignition impulses occur (engine stalled, ignition switched off).

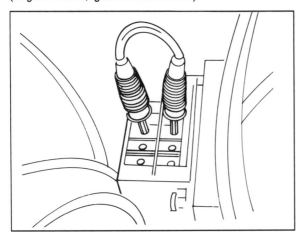

If the fuel pump should run while testing the injection system, without the engine running, remove the relay and connect terminals 7 and 8 (until 8/81: terminals 1 and 2) with a short test lead.

Caution:

To test the fuel pump relay the battery must be charged.

- Remove the relay.

Until 8/81

- Connect a voltmeter to terminals 2 of the relay switch and earth (engine block). Specified value: approximately 12 volt. Alternatively check the red lead to the cable connector for interruptions, replacing if necessary.
- Switch on the ignition. Attach the voltmeter to terminal 3 and earth. Specified value: approximately 12 volt. Alternatively check the red/black lead for interruptions, replacing if necessary.
- Attach the voltmeter to terminal 3 (+) and 5 (-) of the relay socket. Specified value: approximately 12 volt. Alternatively check the brown lead up to the earth point for interruptions.
- Attach a tachometer to terminal 3 and 4 and apply the starter. Specified value: approximately 200rpm. If the tachometer shows 0rpm, check the green/yellow lead to the transistorised ignition system for interruptions. If the lead and contacts are in order, replace the switch device.
- Attach a voltmeter with positive connection to terminal 1 so that the relay can be clamped on. If necessary make up a help cable. Lay the negative connection of the voltmeter against earth (e.g. engine block).

- As soon as the starter is applied, the voltmeter must show 12 volt, and the engine must start. If the engine does not start, and no voltage is indicated, replace the fuel pump relay.
- Check the engine speed limit in a warm engine by fully opening the throttle and bringing the engine to the maximum engine speed for a short while. From 6200 50rpm (engine 110: 6650 ± 50rpm), the engine speed should not rise any further, otherwise replace the relay. **Caution:** this test is only to be carried out in a warm engine.

Since 9/81

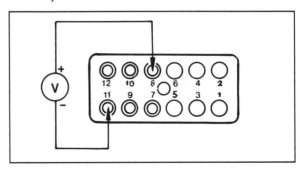

- Attach a voltmeter to terminals 8(+) and 11(-) of the relay place. Specified value: approximately 12 volt.
- Alternatively switch the voltmeter between terminal 8 and earth. If the voltmeter now shows approximately 12 volt, test the brown lead according to the wiring diagram for interruptions. Otherwise test the red lead according to the wiring diagram, replacing if necessary.
- Switch on the ignition, attach the voltmeter to terminal 9(+) and earth. Specified value approximately 12 volt. Alternatively test the black/red lead to the fuse box for interruptions, replacing if necessary.
- **Engine 102:** Attach a dwellmeter to terminal 10 and earth. Apply the starter. The device must show a dwell angle of 7° - 34°. Otherwise check that the green/yellow lead to the transistorised ignition system is intact. If so, replace the timing device of the ignition system.
- **Engine 110:** Attach a tachometer to terminals 10 and 11(-). Apply the starter. Specified value: approximately 200rpm. If the tachometer shows 0rpm, check the green/yellow lead to the transistorised ignition system for interruptions. If the leads and contacts are in order, replace the switch device.
- Connect terminals 7 and 8 with a short test lead. If the pump now starts, replace the fuel pump relay.
- Alternatively check that the black/red/white lead to the fuel pump is not broken, replacing the lead if necessary.
- If it is connected, replace the fuel pump.

Fuel pump - removal and refitting

The fuel pump is on the left side in front of the rear axle on the chassis floor.

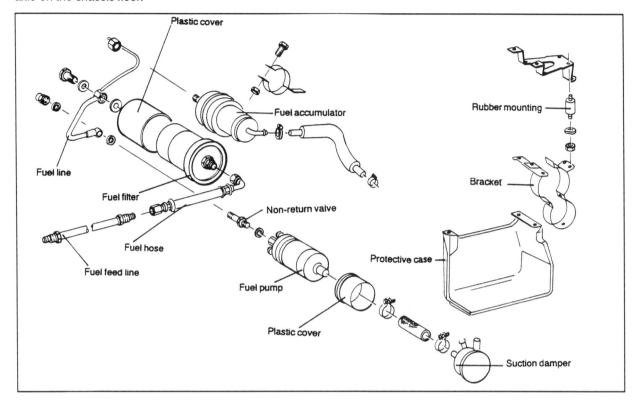

Plastic cover

Fuel accumulator

Rubber mounting

Fuel line

Bracket

Fuel filter

Non-return valve

Protective case

Fuel hose

Fuel feed line

Fuel pump

Plastic cover

Suction damper

Removal

- Put the rear of the vehicle onto blocks.
- Remove the battery-earth lead.

Caution:

No naked flame, fire danger!

- Briefly open then close the fuel tank cap to release the excess pressure in the fuel tank.
- Unscrew the protection case.
- Clamp up the fuel suction tube before the suction damper.
- Unscrew the fuel pipe from the fuel tank to the pump and filter.
- Remove the fuel pipe from the fuel pump, after loosening the clip.
- Remove the electrical leads.
- Loosen the 2 screws of the bracket and pull out the fuel pump.

Refitting

- Refit the fuel pump with the plastic cover.
- Refit the fuel pipe to the fuel tank, pump and filter with a new washer.
- Tighten the screws of the bracket.

Caution:

The plastic cover must stick out on both sides of the bracket. The bracket may not come into direct contact with the fuel pump.

- Refit the fuel pipe to the pump and secure it with a clip.
- Refit the electrical cables. The connecting pins must stand in a vertical position.
- Remove the screw clamp.
- Refit the battery earth cable.
- Start the engine and check the seals of the fuel connections.
- Refit the protective case.
- Lower the vehicle.

Air filter removal and refitting

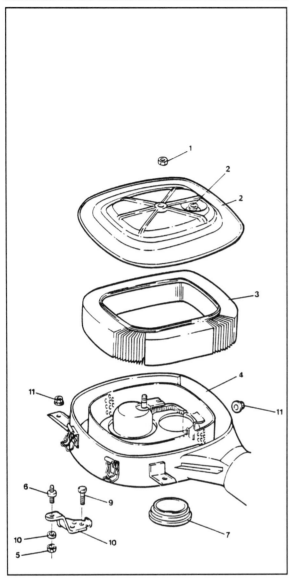

1 - Nut
2 - Air filter cover
2a - Connection for thrust switch
3 - Filter element
4 - Filter housing
5 - Nut
6 - Rubber-metal mounting
7 - Rubber seal
9 - Bolt
10 - Bracket
11 - Nut
13 - Washer

Removal

- Remove one nut on the side of the air filter cover as well as two nuts from the rubber mountings -6-.
- Slightly pull the air filter upwards. Remove the crankcase ventilation hose from the cylinder head cover by the air filter base.
- Remove the air filter.

Refitting

- Remove the air filter cover, so that the correct positioning of the seal -7- of the air regulator can be controlled when refitting the air filter. To do this undo the clips and remove the nut -1-.
- Place the air filter over the fuel regulator. Refit the crankcase ventilation hose to the cylinder head cover.
- Refit the air filter, checking that the seal -7-is properly in position.
- Refit the air filter cover, tighten with the clamps and nuts.

Fuel pump - testing

Testing

- Remove the fuel pump relay.
- Attach a voltmeter to the fuel pump.
- Connect terminals 7 and 8 (**until 8/81:** 1 and 2) to the relay. The fuel pump should start, and the voltage of the pump must be at least 11,5 volt. If not, test the battery or electrical leads according to the wiring diagram.
- Remove the test lead.

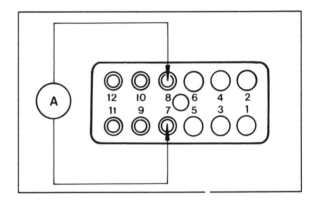

- Attach an ammeter to terminals 7 and 8 (1 and 2). The current to the fuel pump should be approximately 7,5 (11,2) amperes. If the value lies above 10 A (15 A), replace the fuel pump.

Caution:

No naked flames, fire danger!

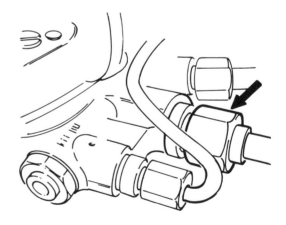

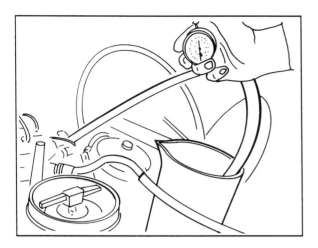

- Remove the fuel pressure return pipe from the fuel regulator.
- Refit an additional fuel pressure pipe and hold it into a measuring cup. For this you need a 50cm long piece of fuel pipe, a short tube with a sealing bevel, a pipe clamp as well as a union nut M14 x 1,5.
- Connect terminals 7 and 8 (1 and 2) with a test lead at the fuel pump relay for a maximum of 40 seconds (engine 110: 30 seconds).
- The pump output during this time should be approximately 1 liter. If not, do the following tests:
- Remove the union nut from the feed sleeve of the fuel regulator, remove the sieve, blow through it, and replace if necessary.
- Check the fuel lines for kinks, replacing if necessary.
- Clamp the fuel pressure return pipe between the fuel tank and suction damper with a screw clamp and once again test the pump capacity. If the correct capacity is now reached, replace the fuel damper.
- Replace the fuel filter and again check the output. If the amount is still too low, replace the fuel pump.
- Tighten the fuel line to about 10 Nm at the regulator.
- Refit the fuel pump relay.

Injection system maintenance

Air filter - replacing

The air filter insert should be replaced every 20 000km. **Caution:** In very dusty conditions replace it earlier. Do not clean the insert with fuel or clog it with oil.

- Remove the air filter cover, by unscrewing the securing nut and opening the clips.

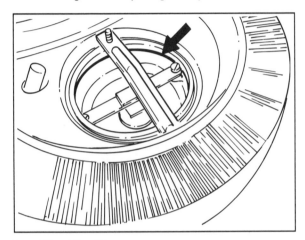

- Lift out the filter.
- Wipe the filter housing and air filter cover with a clean cloth.
- Check the seal at the air filter cover for damage.
- Insert a new filter, making sure the gasket is secure.
- Refit the cover, secure the clips and screw in the securing nut.

Fuel filter - removal and refitting

The fuel filter should be replaced every 60 000km. A damper is also integrated into the fuel filter to reduce noise.

Removal

- Put the back of the vehicle onto blocks.
- Remove the earth cable from the battery.

Caution:

No naked flame, fire danger!

- Totally open the fuel cap, then reseal to release the excess pressure from the fuel tank.
- Unscrew the protection case of the fuel pump system, see illustration on page 113.

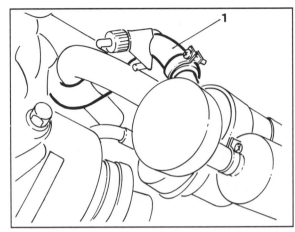

- Clamp the fuel suction pipe with a screw clamp -1- from the suction damper.
- Unscrew the fuel lead and fuel pipe at the fuel filter.

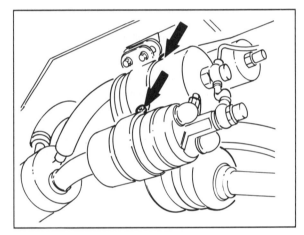

- Unscrew the two securing screws -arrows- of the bracket, then pull out the fuel filter.

Refitting

- Fit a new fuel filter with the plastic sleeve.

Caution:

The plastic sleeve must project on both sides of the bracket. The bracket may never be mounted directly onto the fuel filter, as this will cause contact corrosion.

- Attach the fuel pipe and fuel lead to the filter with a new gasket.
- Remove the screw clamp.
- Refit the battery earth cable.
- Start the engine and check the seals of the fuel connections.
- Refit the protection case.
- Lower the vehicle.

Injection system fault diagnosis K-Jetronic

Before tracing the fault using the fault table, the following tests must have been completed: starting satisfaction: for a warm or cold engine - slightly depress the accelerator and hold it there while starting; for a hot engine fully depress the accelerator before starting and hold it theretill the engine starts.

Fuel in the tank. Engine mechanically sound. Battery connected. Starter turns engine at correct speed. Ignition adjustment and system satisfactory. No leaks in the fuel system. No blockage of the fuel system. Crankcase ventilation operating. Electrical earth connections (engine - gearbox - body) satisfactory. **Caution:** if the fuel leads are to be loosened, they must first be cleaned with fuel.

Fault: The engine will not start	
Cause	Solution
Electric-fuel pump will not start when the starter is applied (no running sound audible)	Lightly knock against pump housing to loosen the pump if jammed. Check for voltage in the pump by removing both cables and switching test lamp in between, test electrical contacts for good contact.
Incorrect resting position of the sensor plate	Test the resting position of the sensor plate
Fuel pump relay defective	Test the relay
Temperature sensor defective	Test the temperature sensor
Incorrect fuel pressure	Have the fuel pressure tested

Fault: Difficulty in starting the cold engine, runs unevenly	
Cold start valve defective	Test the cold start valve
Temperature sensor defective	Test the temperature sensor
Auxiliary air valve defective	Test the auxiliary air valve
Warming up regulator defective	Test the warm-up regulator.
Incorrect fuel pressures	Have the fuel pressure tested

Fault: The hot engine will not start	
Cold start valve leaking	Test the cold start valve
Air intake system leaking	Test the seals and connections of the intake system
Incorrect resting position of the sensor plate	Test the resting position of the sensor plate
Thermal time switch does not switch off	Test the switches

Fault: The engine stalls	
Electrical connections to the fuel pump interrupted at intervals	Test plug connections of electrical leads at the fuel pump, air regulator and fuel pump relay for tight, resistance-free connections. Test securing and contact points of fuel pump relay. Clean or replace contacts.
Vapor lock formation	Replace fuel intake lead, test fuel pump
Fuel filter defective	Replace fuel filter
Fuel pump defective	Test fuel pump
Fuel regulator defective	Test fuel regulator
Injection valve defective	Test injection valves

Fault: Excessive fuel consumption	
Temperature sensor defective	Test the temperature sensor
CO content/idle engine speed incorrect	Check idle mixture and idle speed
Fuel pressures incorrect	Have fuel pressure tested

Fuel gauge tank unit - removal and refitting/testing

When the fuel level drops, the float of the tank transmitter sinks. Due to an abrasive contact on the float the electrical resistance of the transmitter increases. This causes the voltage of the indicator to drop and the fuel indicator moves to the "empty" position.

As the float continues to sink, the warning contact is made and the reserve warning light goes on on the dashboard. **Caution:** Since 9/82 the reserve warning light flashes when the ignition is switched on and goes off if there is enough fuel while the engine is running.

Removal

- Remove the battery earth cable

Caution:

No naked flame, fire danger!

- Remove the emergency kit. Unscrew the 2 bolts from the bracket of the joining case and remove it.

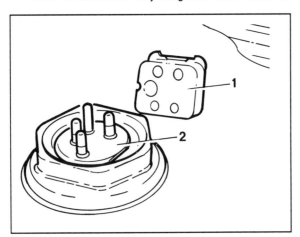

- Remove the plug -1- from the tank transmitter. **Caution:** hook up the cable with wire, so that it cannot slip down.
- Unscrew the tank transmitter with a spanner SW 46.
- Lift out the tank transmitter. Put a cloth underneath it to catch any escaping fuel.

Testing

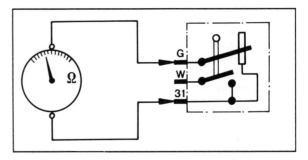

- Attach an ohmmeter to terminals G and 31
- Hold the tank transmitter in refitting position, the float is at the bottom, and the indicator in the vehicle would show "empty". Specified value: about 57 ± 2 ohm, in the T-model: about 52 ± 2 ohm
- Turn the tank transmitter by 180° (upside down), the float is on top, and the indicator in the vehicle should show "full". Specified value: about 1,6 ± 0,7 ohm, in the T-model: about 3,2 ± 0,8 ohm
- Test the reserve warning contact: attach the ohmmeter to terminals W and 31 and measure the resistance. Specified value: in refitting position about 0 ohm; turned at 180°: infinite ohms.

Refitting

- Before fitting a new tank transmitter, remove the securing pin of the float.
- Fit the tank transmitter with a new washer and tighten to 40 Nm
- Refit the electrical plug
- Refit the bracket of the joining case and tighten.
- Refit the battery earth cable
- Check the function of the fuel indicator at the dashboard.

THE EXHAUST SYSTEM

The exhaust system consists of the front exhaust pipe with a silencer, the central silencer and the rear exhaust pipe with a silencer.

The front exhaust pipe is bolted to the exhaust manifold which is attached to the cylinder head. All the parts are bolted to one another and can be separately replaced. Self-securing nuts and gaskets are to be replaced after removal. Check the supporting rings and rubber stoppers for porosity, replacing if necessary.

In refitting a new exhaust system, it is recommended that all the securing parts are replaced.

Hint: If the engine performance is bad from 3000rpm, combined with strong roaring, an inner part could have come loose in one of the two front double walled exhaust pipes. In this case remove the front exhaust pipes and shine a torch into the pipes. If the bore is narrowed, replace the front exhaust system.

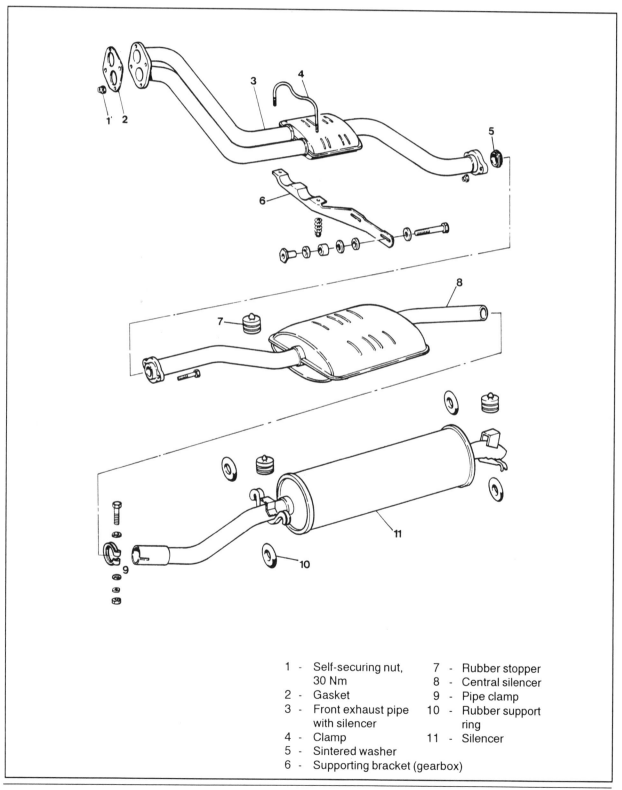

1	-	Self-securing nut, 30 Nm	7	- Rubber stopper
2	-	Gasket	8	- Central silencer
3	-	Front exhaust pipe with silencer	9	- Pipe clamp
4	-	Clamp	10	- Rubber support ring
5	-	Sintered washer	11	- Silencer
6	-	Supporting bracket (gearbox)		

Exhaust system - removal and refitting

Removal

- Put the vehicle on blocks
- Spray all the bolts and nuts of the exhaust system with a rust removing solution, letting it soak for a while.

- Unscrew the front exhaust pipe at the exhaust manifold from below.
- Support the exhaust system by wooden supports.
- Remove the exhaust side supports.

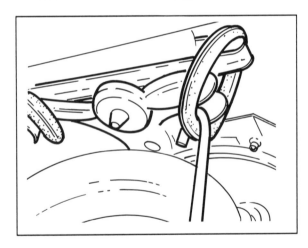

- Unhook the rubber rings using a home-made hook.
- Lower the exhaust system.

Refitting

Before mounting the exhaust system, check whether the flange is distorted, replace if necessary.

- Refit the front exhaust system to the manifold with a **new** gasket and tighten the **new** nuts evenly.
- Connect the central and rear silencers tightening the clamp slightly. Fit the rear exhaust system and hook it into the rear axle bracket with new rubber support rings.

Caution:

Before assembling the exhaust system to the flange, place the front exhaust pipes onto the gearbox bracket, to avoid the tubes being strained by the weight of the exhaust system when refitting the exhaust system. So first refit the gearbox bracket, see illustration pg.121.

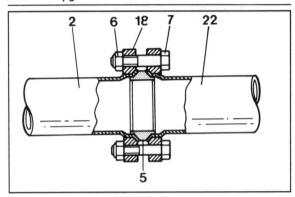

- If necessary clean the conical connection parts of the pipes -2- and -22- with a glass cloth before assembling.
- Check that the washer -5- is securely in place when reassembling the pipes. Always replace the self-locking nuts.

Caution:

To be able to loosen the nuts and bolts of the exhaust system more easily at a later stage, paint these with a high temperature paste or anti-sieze compound, for example Liqui Moly LM-508-ASC.

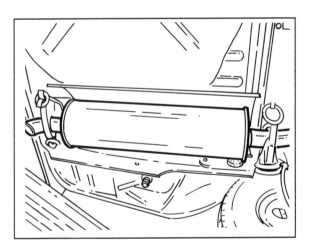

- By turning and pushing the exhaust system sideways, adjust it so that there is sufficient distance between it and the body of the vehicle as well as all the brackets have an even load, if necessary slightly loosen the bolts of the brackets.
- Tighten the bolts to the brackets to 20 Nm.
- Tighten **new** self-securing nuts to the flange connection of the exhaust manifold in stages, crosswise to 30 Nm.
- **Carburetor engine:** Refit the side brackets without tension. Tighten the bolts to the gearbox to 20 Nm.

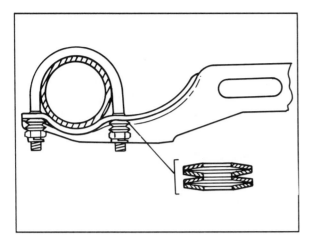

- Attach the new nuts of the U-clamp with 4 new washers each - as shown in the illustration - , and tighten to 7 Nm.
- Start the engine and check the seals of the exhaust system.
- Lower the vehicle.

Silencer replacing

- Remove the exhaust system.

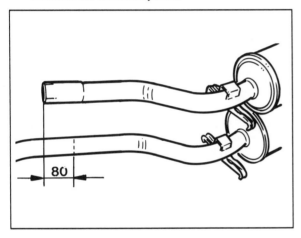

- Place the new silencer on top of the old one and mark the pipe length on the removed exhaust system.
- Make another mark about 80mm from the first in the direction of the silencer.
- Saw off the exhaust pipe at the second mark.
  Caution: The overlapping depth should be 70 - 80mm.
- Clean the old exhaust pipe with a glass cloth, first place the pipe clamp over the exhaust pipe.
- Refit the bolt with the washers, do not tighten.
- Refit the exhaust system.
- Tighten the bolt.

THE CLUTCH

The clutch consists of the clutch pressure plate, the clutch disc and the hydraulic control system. The pressure plate and clutch disc are mounted on the flywheel of the engine.

The clutch fork is in the gearbox bell housing. It carries the maintenance-free clutch release bearing, which is pressed against the clutch pressure plate when declutching. The piston of the clutch operating cylinder of the hydraulic system lies against the clutch fork. The hydraulic system of the clutch operates with brake fluid and is supplied with brake fluid by the combined brake and clutch reservoir

When engaged, the clutch disc of the pressure plate is pressed against the flywheel by the pressure plate, which produces the adhesion between the crankshaft and gearbox drive shaft.

When compressing the clutch pedal, pressure is applied via the master cylinder and is transmitted to the clutch operating cylinder via a hydraulic hose. The piston of the operating cylinder presses the clutch bearing against the diaphragm of the pressure plate via the clutch fork, which lifts it slightly. This frees the clutch disc from the flywheel and pressure plate and the connections between the engine and gearbox is thus broken.

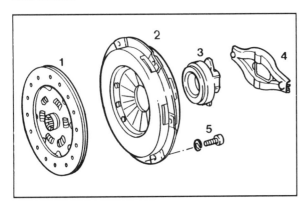

1 - Clutch disc
2 - Pressure plate
3 - Clutch release bearing
4 - Clutch fork
5 - Pressure plate bolt, 25 Nm

Clutch removal and refitting/testing

Removal

- Remove the gearbox, see page 127.
- Mark the relative position of the pressure plate and flywheel to ensure identical positioning on refitting
- Loosen the bolts of the clutch pressure plate by 1 turn each, until the pressure plate is slack.

Caution:

If the bolts are individually loosened totally the diaphragm spring could be damaged.

- To stop the flywheel from turning while the bolts are loosened, hold it with a screwdriver.
- Now remove the bolts totally.
- Remove the pressure plate and clutch disc noting which way round the clutch disc is fitted.
  Caution: Do not drop the pressure plate and clutch disc when removing.
- Blow the inside of the flywheel housing, or wipe it with a fuel soaked cloth.

Testing

- Check the clutch pressure plate for burn marks and ridges.

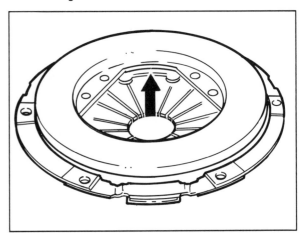

- Check the diaphragm spring for cracks -arrow-

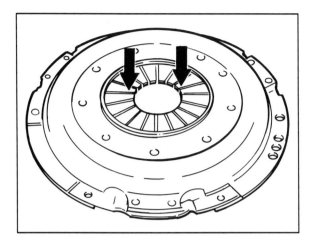

- Check the tongues of the diaphragm spring -arrows- for wear and equal height, adjusting carefully with a pair of pliers if necessary.
  Caution: The maximum wear is 0,3mm.
- Check the flywheel for burn marks and ridges.
- Put a rough glass cloth over the clutch pressure plate and flywheel.

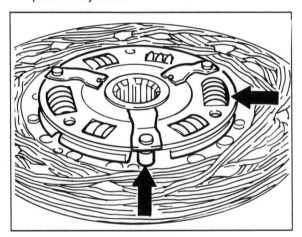

- Replace any oil clogged, greasy or mechanically damaged clutch discs.
- Measure the face thickness of the clutch disc, which is 3,8 - 4,0mm when new. If there are cracks or a thickness of 1,8mm is reached, replace the clutch disc.
- Check the stop bolts, spring windows, torsion spring and hub for wear and tracking -arrows.
- Remove and test the thrust bearing of the bearing pipe at the front gearbox cover, see page 124.
- In the workshop, the clutch disc can be flex tested. The side flex may reach a maximum of 0,5mm. **Caution:** This test is only necessary if the old clutch disc is to be refitted and the clutch previously did not declutch properly.

Refitting

Caution:

Since 6/78, a self-centering thrust bearing together with a clutch pressure plate without a thrust ring has been fitted; it was previously a pressure plate with thrust ring. The thrust ring is at the ends of the diaphragm springs pointing to the centre -arrows in the left illustration -. The Illustration at the bottom of this page shows a pressure plate with thrust ring. The previous thrust bearing may **not** be combined with a pressure plate without thrust ring; if necessary replace the thrust bearing. If a self-centering thrust bearing is to be fitted with a pressure plate with a thrust ring, the thrust ring must first be removed.

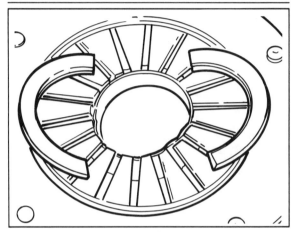

- If necessary, remove the thrust ring by placing the pressure plate onto a surface of 80mm height and 60mm diameter. Open the thrust ring in 2 places with a pin driver and remove it. Bend open the tin ring with a pair of pliers and remove it. Now check the diaphragm spring for wear and equal height, adjusting carefully if necessary.

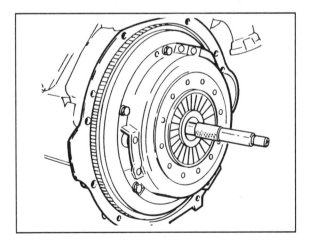

- Refit the clutch disc and clutch pressure plate into the flywheel. The clutch disc must be centered with a suitable mandrel (e.g. HAZET) or an old gearbox-driveshaft.

- Tighten the bolts of the clutch pressure plate by 1 to 1,5 rotations each, until the pressure plate is tight. Now remove the mandrel. **Caution:** Make sure that the pressure plate moves into the flywheel evenly when tightening.
- Refit the gearbox, see page 127.

Thrust bearing - removal and refitting

Bearing noises when declutched, i.e when the clutch pedal is compressed, indicate a faulty thrust bearing.

Removal

- Remove the gearbox, see page 127.

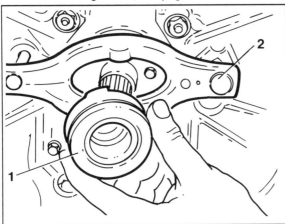

- Remove the thrust bearing -1- from the bearing pipe of the front gearbox cover.

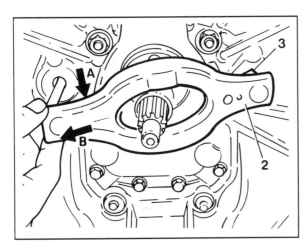

- Move the clutch fork -2- in the direction of the arrow -A- and then into direction -B-. Pull it from the ball pin -3- of the clutch housing and remove it.
- Check the ease of movement of the thrust bearing by hand.

Refitting

- Wipe all the bearing and contact surfaces with a clean rag and lubricate with Moly Bdenum sulphide grease.
- Press the clutch fork -2- onto the ball pin -3- against the direction of the arrow -B-, until the spring bracket of the fork clicks into place. Now move the fork against the arrow direction -A-, until the pressure rod of the clutch operating cylinder lies against the slot of the clutch fork.
- Lubricate the thrust bearing inside and the two side wings at the rear sleeve.
- Place the thrust bearing over the bearing carrier and turn it until the side wings snap into the fork.
- Refit the gearbox, see page 127.

Clutch - bleeding

The clutch must be bled when the clutch pedal does not return, or only slowly comes back, or if the hydraulic system was opened. Since the hydraulic system of the clutch uses brake fluid, the relevant chapter on "the brake system" should also be read.

- Put the front of the vehicle onto blocks.
- Check the brake fluid in the common reservoir, filling it up to the max. mark if necessary.
- Remove the dust caps from the bleed screw of the clutch operating cylinder and front right brake calliper.
- Carefully loosen the bleed screws.
- Place the clear tube over the screw on the calliper.
- Fill the tube with brake fluid by opening the bleed screw of the brake calliper. Slowly compress the brake pedal (helper) and hold it in this position. Close the bleed screw and reiease the brake pedal. Now re-open the bleed screw and compress the brake pedal. Repeat this procedure until the tube is full of brake fluid. Place a finger over the tube, so that no brake fluid can escape. **Caution:** The fluid level in the reservoir may not drop too much, if necessary fill up with **new** brake fluid.
- Attach the free end of the tube onto the bleed screw of the clutch operating cylinder, opening both bleed bolts.
- Apply the brake pedal, close the bleed bolt at the brake caliper and release brake pedal. Repeat this until no more air bubbles come out of the fluid reaching the reservoir. Top up brake fluid during this procedure
- Close the bleed screws at the brake caliper and the clutch operating cylinder. Remove the tube and refit the dust caps.
- Lower the vehicle
- Fill up with brake fluid to the Max. mark
- Check the brake and clutch system.

Clutch fault diagnosis

Fault		
Clutch snatches	Engine idle speed too low	Adjust engine speed
	Engine bearing defective	Test, replace if necessary
	Gearbox not secure in suspension	Tighten bolts
	Clutch pressure plate loaded unevenly	Replace pressure plate
Clutch slips	Clutch plate worn	Test thickness of clutch plate, replace if necessary
	Clutch pedal stop defective	Test stop in footwell
	Clutch operating cylinder jammed	Replace clutch operating cylinder
	Tension of diaphrgm spring too low	Replace pressure plate
	Clutch operating cylinder leaks	Do a sight test
	Clutch lining hardened or oil soaked	Replace clutch plate, remove cause of oil leakage
Clutch does not disengage properly	Clutch pedal does not reach the stop	Test if stop is reached, if necessary cut foot stopmat
	Master cylinder leaks	Observe while clutch pedal is compressed, whether fluid builds up in brake fluid storage container
	Coating of clutch plate clogged with abrasion particles	Replace clutch plate
	Clutch plate sticking on gearbox drive shaft	Clean spline and lubricate, if necessary remove rust
	Clutch plate has shimmy	Have clutch plate tested, replace
	Clutch fork defective	Test clutch fork for deformation
Increasing noise when applying and decreasing noise when releasing clutch	Thrust bearing defective	Test thrust bearing, replace the thrust bearing
	Clutch plate knocks against pressure plate	Replace clutch plate
	Torsion muffler of clutch plate jamming	Replace clutch plate

Clutch maintenance

Clutch plate -thickness testing

The clutch is self-adjusting and maintenance-free. The wear of the clutch plate is thus not recognisable in the play of the clutch pedal. The thickness of the clutch plate is measured by a specially fitted control gauge. The gauge can be home-made.

The thickness of the clutch plate should be tested during maintenance every 20 000km.

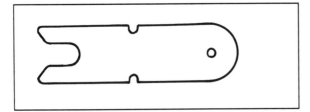

- Make a control gauge measuring 1:1 according to the diagram from 0,8mm plate.
- Put the vehicle on blocks.

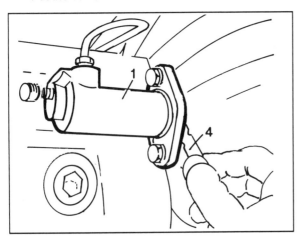

- Push the gauge -4- up to the notch in the slot of the plastic adjusting shim at the clutch operating cylinder.

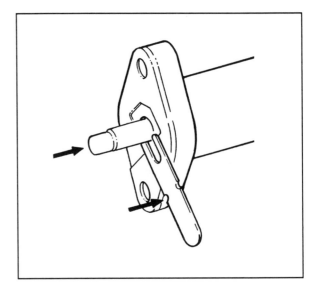

- If the notches of the gauge -arrow- disappear behind the flange of the clutch operating cylinder, the clutch plate is still thick enough.

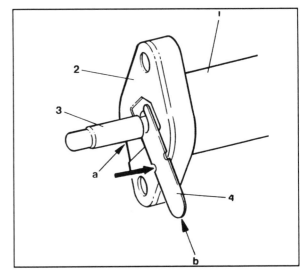

- If the notches stay visible even though the gauge is pushed up to the stop, the clutch plate is worn and must be replaced.
- Lower the vehicle.

THE GEARBOX

The gearbox can be removed without the removal of the engine. It is however only necessary to remove it if the whole gearbox has to be replaced or overhauled, or if the clutch must be replaced. Since it is not recommended to repair the gearbox with home tools, reference is made here to the workshop and only the removal of the gearbox is described.

Gearbox - removal and refitting

The sections in brackets only refer to diesel engines 615 and 616 since 10/80, as well as for the petrol engines 102.

Removal

Caution:

To facilitate the refitting, put into gear before removal.

- Remove the earth cable from the battery.

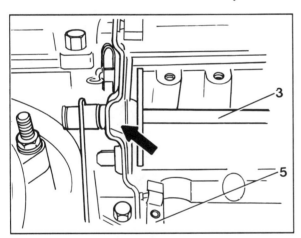

- (Unhook -arrow- the throttle rod -3- of the above mentioned engines and engine 110).
- **Engine 110:** Totally remove the exhaust system, see page 119.
- Put the vehicle onto blocks, slightly lift the gearbox with a jack with wooden blocks.

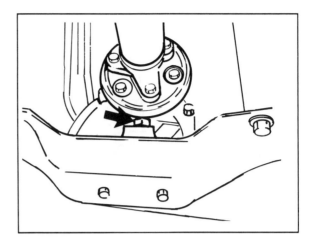

- Unscrew the engine mounting nut -arrow- at the rear gearbox cover.
- Unbolt the cross member from the underbody.

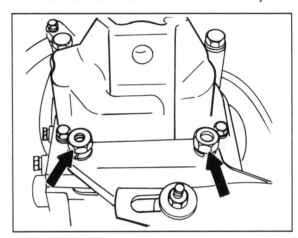

- Unscrew the support bracket of the exhaust system at the gearbox -arrows-. (First mark the position of the washers with a pen, so that they can be refitted in the same position).

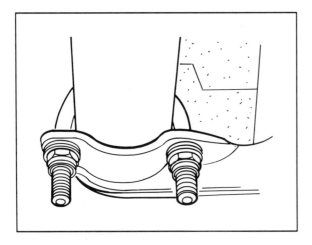

- Unscrew the nuts of the clamp and remove the bracket.

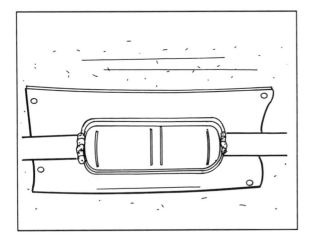

- (Unscrew the heat shield of the propeller shaft intermediate bearing.)

- Loosen the nut of the propeller shaft.
- Loosen the bolts of the propeller shaft intermediate bearing, **do not** remove.

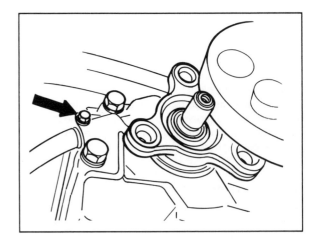

- Remove the propeller shaft from the gearbox. The flexible coupling must remain on the propeller shaft.
- Push the propeller shaft back as far as the intermediate bearing and clip will allow.
- Unscrew the drive shaft of the speedometer at the rear gearbox cover by the bolt -arrow-. Pull out the speedometer cable.
- Unscrew the bracket of the speedometer cable below at the gearbox (or clip it out of the bracket).

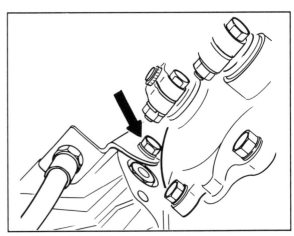

- Unscrew the bracket at the clutch housing -arrow-. **Caution:** Since 9/78 the clutch lead no longer has a bolt connection.

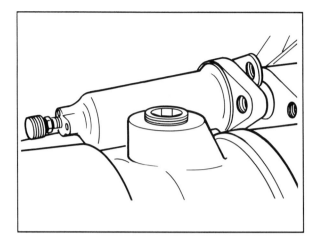

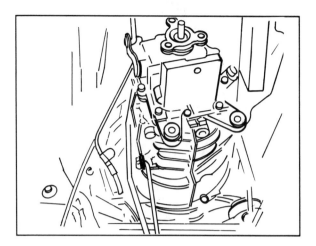

- Remove the clutch operating cylinder and pull it back with the hose until the pressure rod is freed from the clutch housing. Hang the clutch operating cylinder up on the body. **Caution:** If the hose is opened, the system must be bled when refitting.
- Remove the gear shift rods from the intermediate levers of the gear shift lever bracket by prising off the clips

Caution:

Do not engage the reverse gear when the gear rods are unhooked, as this will damage the reversing light switch.

- Unscrew the bolts from the starter flange. Remove the starter and hang it up with wire.

- Unscrew all the bolts securing the gearbox to the engine. Remove the two top bolts last.

- Pull the gearbox horizontally to the back from the dowels and pull it out of the clutch with a helper.
- Lower the gearbox.

Caution:

Only lower the gearbox once the drive shaft is securely pulled out of the clutch plate, to avoid the clutch plate from being damaged.

Refitting

- Before refitting, test the clutch, see page 112.
- Test the clutch thrust bearing for ease of movement. Lubricate the bearing, e.g. with Liqui Moly M-320. If running noises of the thrust bearing when declutching were noticed before removal, replace the bearing, see page 124.
- Clean the spline of the drive shaft and centering nipple, lubricating lightly with Moly spray.
- Put in to gear if not already in gear.

Caution:

Before fitting the gearbox, place the clutch operating cylinder over the gearbox.

- Lift the gearbox and place it horizontally into the clutch. If the gearbox drive shaft does not click into place on the clutch plate, turn the driveshaft from behind at the flange by hand.
- Tighten the gearbox securing bolts at the engine, attaching the earth cable below left and, if necessary, the bracket of the speedometer cable to the gearbox.
- Tighten the starter with 2 bolts.
- Refit the clutch operating cylinder and pressure rod into the clutch housing and tighten. Make sure the plastic adjusting shim is in place.
- Secure the hydraulic lead with bracket to the clutch housing. If necessary bleed the hydraulic system, see page 124.

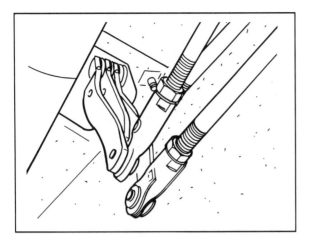

- Rehook the gear rods to the intermediate levers and secure with the clips by pressing open the spring clip, pushing the long hole into the slot of the gear rod. The clips must click in when refitting, to guarantee proper support.
- Refit the drive shaft of the speedometer into the rear gearbox cover and tighten. (Clip the speedometer cable into the gear bracket).
- Pull the sliding section of the propeller shaft forward as much as possible and attach the flange to the gearbox. To do this slightly lift the engine and gearbox with a jack and wooden blocks.
- Tighten the rear engine mounting bracket to the gearbox.
- Bolt the cross member to the underbody.
- Tighten the propeller shaft intermediate bearing without pressure.
- Tighten the nut to 35 Nm.
- Tighten the heat shield of the propeller shaft intermediate bearing.
- If removed, refit the exhaust system, see page 119.
- (Rehook the throttle rod and secure with the clip.)
- Tighten the bracket of the exhaust pipe to the gearbox (making sure the washers are replaced to the marks made when removing).
- Refit the brackets and tighten the nuts to 7 Nm. Make sure the Bellville springs are in the correct position, see page 121.
- Check the adjustment of the gears, see page 132.
- Lower the vehicle.
- Refit the battery earth cable.

GEAR CHANGE

GEARBOX MAINTENANCE

Sight testing for leaks

Leaks are possible at the following points:
- The joint between the engine block and the gearbox (flywheel gasket/shaft seal -gearbox).
- The oil plug / oil drain plug.
- Flange of propeller shaft at the gearbox.

In searching for the leak, proceed as follows:
- Clean the gearbox housing
- Check the oil level, filling up if necessary.
- Dust possible leaks with lime or talcum powder.
- If possible test drive the vehicle on a highway for about 30km, so that the oil becomes hot and thin.
- Now put the vehicle on blocks and check the gearbox with a torch for leaks.
- Repair the leaks immediately.

Checking the oil level in the gearbox

The gearbox oil need not be changed, but the oil level should be checked at 20 000km intervals.

- The gearbox should be lukewarm before checking.
- Jack the vehicle up horizontally, see page 244.

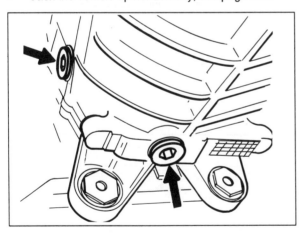

- Unscrew the filler plug -left arrow- from the gearbox, using an allen key SW 14.
- If a little oil flows out when undoing the bolt, the oil level is correct. Alternatively check with a finger that the oil level reaches the bottom rim of the filler hole. Fill up if necessary.

Caution:
An oil syringe or pump is needed for this. Insert a dish under the vehicle while filling to catch excess oil. Fill the oil slowly.

Gearbox oil specification: ATF (automatic transmission fluid), use only a gearbox oil approved by the manufacturer (this is indicated on the can).

Fluid capacity

Engine	4 speed gearbox	5 speed gearbox
110,115,123,617 615,616 till 9/80	1,6 liter	1,6 liter
102 615,616 since 10/80	1,3 liter	1,6 liter

- Tighten the filler plug with a new washer to 60 Nm.
- Lower the vehicle.

Testing the flexible coupling at the propellar shaft

The flexible coupling should be checked at 20 000km intervals.
- Put the vehicle onto blocks.

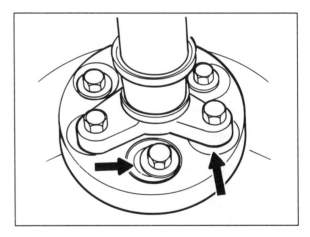

- Check the front and the back of the flexible couplings with a torch for wear, damage and distortions.
- Check the stays in the region of the pins -arrows- for cracks.
- Replace the flexible coupling if necessary. Loosen the flexible couplings in cases of distortion; if it remains distorted, replace it.
- Lower the vehicle, see page 244.

THE GEAR CHANGE

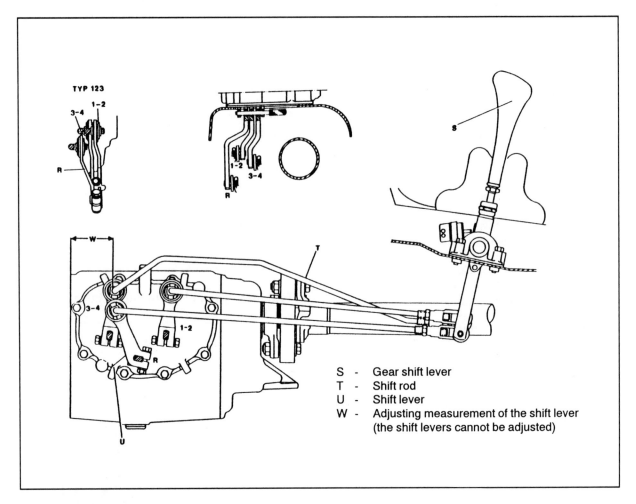

S - Gear shift lever
T - Shift rod
U - Shift lever
W - Adjusting measurement of the shift lever
(the shift levers cannot be adjusted)

Gear linkage adjustment

- Put the gearbox into neutral.

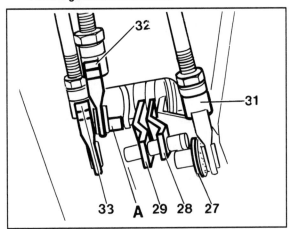

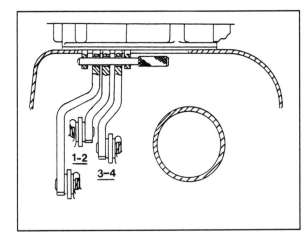

- Remove the securing clips, then unhook the gear rods at the gearshift levers. -27-, -28-, -29- are levers for reverse gear, 1st/2nd gear, 3rd/4th gear; -31-, -32-, -33-, = shift rods for reverse gear, 1st/2nd gear, 3rd/4th gear.

- Insert the fixing bolt -A- into the bores at the bottom of the gear shift lug, thus fixing the 3 gear intermediate levers.

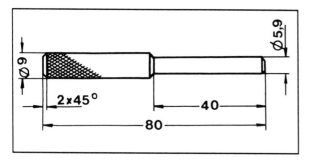

- If necessary, make a fixing bolt with the above measurements.

Caution:

In a gearbox with forged shift levers -U-, check the measurements -W- of the 3 shift rods. Adjust if necessary by unscrewing the bolts and repositioning the levers on the splines. Dimensions for measurement -W-: 1st/2nd gear - 142mm, 3rd/4th gear - 58mm, reverse gear - 111mm. Tighten bolt once adjusted. The drawing on the opposite page shows a gearbox with stamped shift levers. In this gearbox, the position of the intermediate levers has been fixed, and cannot be adjusted. The shift levers in models 200, 230E, 200D, 240D since 10/84 also cannot be adjusted.

- The gear rods can now easily be pressed onto the bolts of the intermediate levers. If not, loosen the lock nut of the gear rods and adjust the relevant rod to the appropriate length. Tighten the lock nut.

- Secure the gear rods with clips.

- Remove the fixing bolt.

- Check the function of the gears while the engine is running. The gears must engage without sticking.

AUTOMATIC GEARBOX

The Mercedes can be supplied with a fully automatic gearbox. The automatic gearbox has four forward gears which are changed automatically.

To accelerate harder, for example when overtaking, the automatic has a kick-down switch, which switches on when the accelerator is totally depressed. The kick-down effect causes the gearbox to either remain in a lower gear for longer, or to changedown from a higher gear to a lower gear.

To check the function of the automatic gearbox and the detection of faults, a good knowledge of automatic gearboxes and their operation is necessary. As this experience can only be gained through years of experience, only small test jobs are described in this chapter.

Towing an automatic vehicle

- Selector lever position "N".

Maximum towing speed: 50km/h!

Maximum towing distance: 120 kilometers!

- For longer distances, the vehicle must be lifted at the back, or the axle must be disconnected at the rear axle. The reason: in a stationary vehicle the gear oil pump does not work and the gearbox is thus not sufficiently lubricated at higher road speeds and long running times.

- Switch on the ignition, so that the steering is not locked and the indicator lamps, horn and windscreen wipers are functional.

- Since the brake servo and power steering only work in a running engine, the brake pedal and steering need to be applied with more strength if the engine is not running.

Checking the automatic gearbox oil level

The prescribed oil level is extremely important for the function of the automatic gearbox. The test should be carried out meticulously at 10 000km intervals.

The automatic gearbox dipstick is in the engine compartment. The ATF (automatic transmission fluid) is also filled up through the dipstick tube.

Caution:

The test can be carried out in a warm or cold gearbox. It is however easier to determine the oil level in a cold gearbox (gear oil temperature 20° to 30° C) than in a warm gearbox (gear oil temperature around 80° C), since an oil temperature of 80° C can only be reached after a fairly long drive and even then only be estimated.

- Have the unloaded vehicle on a flat surface.

- Let the engine idle about 1 to 2 minutes.

- Put the selector lever into the "P" position, apply the hand brake.

- The engine must idle during the test.

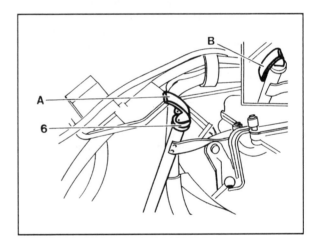

- Open the sealing lever -position A-, pull out the dipstick and wipe it with a clean, non-fluffy cloth. Now insert the dipstick totally, pull it out again and read off the oil level.

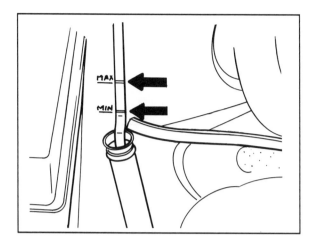

- If the gearbox oil is hot (about 80° C), the level fluid level should be around the Max. mark of the dipstick. At an oil temperature of 20° to 30° C the oil level should lie around the measurement -X- under the Min. mark.

Model	Measurement - X -
200 till 5/83 230 230 E till 4/83 250 till 8/81 280 280 E till 8/81 200 D till 6/83 220 D 240 D till 6/83 300 D till 6/83 300 TD turbo diesel till 8/81	30mm
200 since 6/83 230 E since 5/83 200 D since 7/83 240 D since 7/83 300 D since 7/83	12mm
250 since 9/81 280 E since 9/81 300 TD turbo diesel since 9/81	10mm

Caution:

If the oil level is too low, air is audibly sucked in by the oil pump. The oil bubbles due to this and the test can show incorrect results. In this case, switch off the engine, add a little oil after about 2 minutes, then check the oil level again with the engine running.

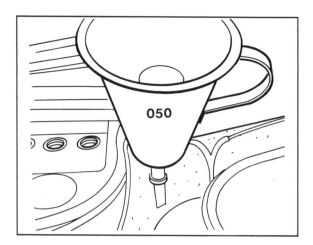

- If ATF must be refilled, use a clean funnel and a fine sieve. The filling amount between Min. and Max. marks on the dipstick is around 0,3 litre.

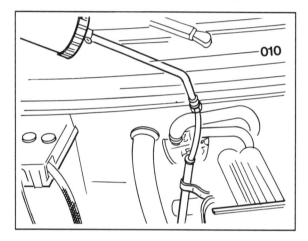

Caution:

Do not add too much oil as this can cause blockages in the automatic gearbox. If too much oil was added, this must be bled or sucked off with a syringe.

- Check the old oil on the dipstick for its appearance and smell at the same time. Burned friction deposits cause a burned smell. Problems in the gearbox shifting can be caused by foul oil.

Caution:

Only ATF oils recommended by the manufacturer should be used.

All the suitable ATF oils can be mixed with one another. Do not use any supplementary lubrication.

The engine must not run nor can the vehicle be towed without ATF in the torque converter or the automatic gearbox.

- After the test or filling up of oil, refit the dipstick and close the securing lever -position B-.

- Apply the brake and slowly go through all the selector lever positions. Then again check the oil level.

THE FRONT SUSPENSION

The front suspension is of idependent coil spring type incorporating upper and lower control arms, support arms and telescopic shock absorbers. A stabiliser bar is attached to the upper control arms, and all suspension mounting points are of rubber.

The steering knuckle is attached to the control arms by sealed balljoints. The adjustable front wheel bearings are of taper-roller type.

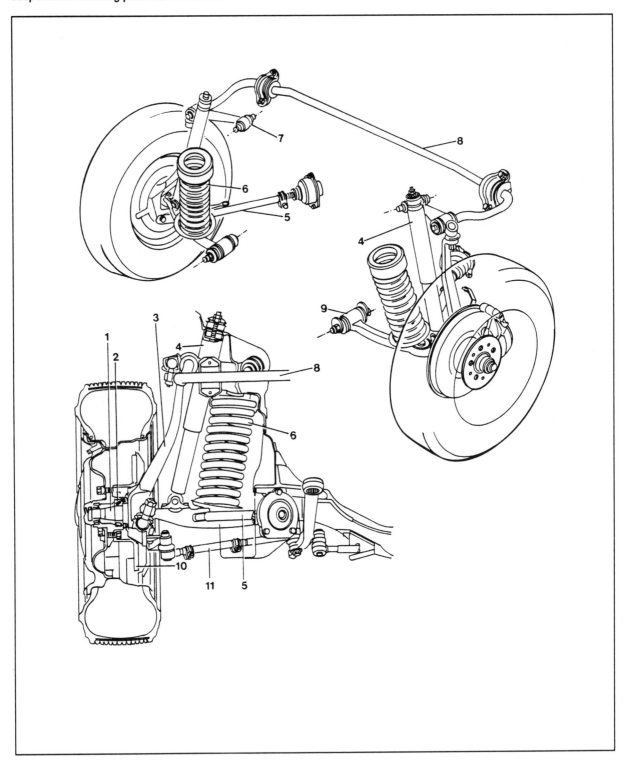

1 -	Wheel hub	7 - Upper control arm
2 -	Wheel bearing	8 - Stabiliser
3 -	Steering knuckle	9 - Lower control arm
4 -	Shock absorber	10 - Brake disc
5 -	Support arm	11 - Tie rod
6 -	Coil spring	

Shock absorber - removal and refitting

Shock absorbers can be individually replaced, irrespective of the make. The type of shock absorber (marked by a coloured stripe) must however co-incide.

Caution:

The shock absorbers are filled with oil and gas and are under pressure, so old shock absorbers should not be discarded with the household refuse.

Removal

Caution:

While loosening the upper shock absorber bolt, the vehicle must be on the floor, as the shock absorber also acts as a spring stop for the front wheels.

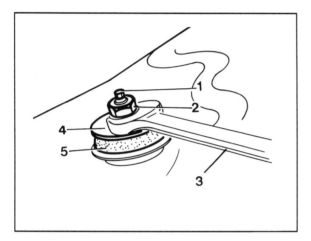

- Remove the upper nut -2-, while holding the lower nut with a spanner -3-.
- Remove the lower nut while holding the piston rod -1- with a spanner. **Caution: the piston rod must remain stationary. Danger of accident!**
- Remove the metal -4- and rubber -5- washers.
- Loosen the wheel bolts and put the vehicle on blocks, see page 244.
- Remove the wheel bolts and remove the front wheel.

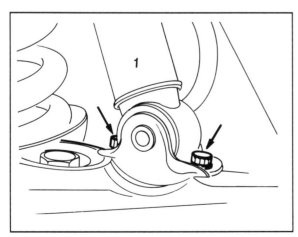

- Remove the securing bolts -arrows- of the shock absorber -1- at the lower control arm and remove the shock absorber.

Components of the front shock absorber with separating pistons

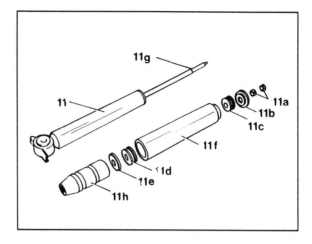

Components of the front shock absorber without separating piston.

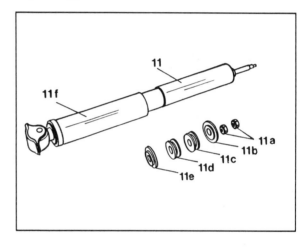

11	- Shock absorber body
11a	- Lock nuts
11b	- Top washer
11c	- Top rubber washer
11d	- Bottom rubber washer
11e	- Bottom Washer
11f -	- Protective sleeve
11g	- Circlip
11h	- Supplementary spring buffer

- Remove the shock absorber mounts and check them for damage.

Refitting

Before refitting, check the shock absorbers. Only fit shock absorbers with the same colour markings.

- Clean the contact surface of the lower control arm.

The bottom mount of the shock absorber must be secure in the rubber bush. If a new shock absorber is fitted, the angle of the mount must be the same as in the old shock absorber, or the bolts will not fit.

Shock absorber with separating piston

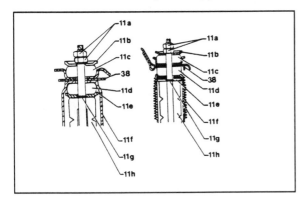

Caution:

Do not confuse the bottom plate -11e- with the top plate -11b-. The plate could otherwise work itself over the circlip -11g- while driving.

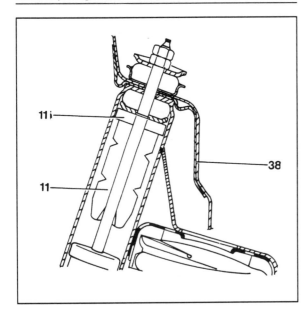

Caution:

On vehicles which have shock absorbers with separating pistons and 15 inch wheels, or stronger springs, an additional 9mm adjusting shim -11i-is built in between the buffer and the bottom plate.

Shock absorbers without separating pistons

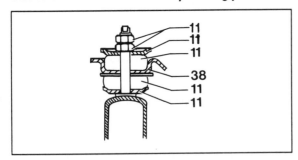

- Reassemble the shock absorbers according to the illustrations.
- Refit the shock absorbers and tighten to the control arm to 20 Nm.
- Pull the piston rod upwards and insert it into the body -38-.

- Tighten the front wheel bolts and lower the vehicle, see page 244.
- Fit the upper securing parts of the shock absorber.
- Tighten the lower nut to the end of the thread, while holding the piston rod with a spanner. Now tighten the upper nut while holding the lower nut.
- Tighten the wheel bolts crosswise to 110 Nm.

Shock absorber testing

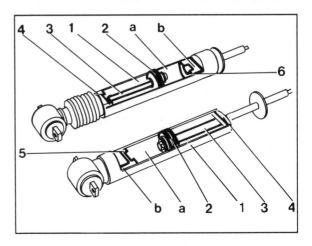

1 - Cylinder
2 - Working piston
3 - Piston rod
4 - Sealing piece with washer
5 - Separating piston
6 - Shock absorber disc
a - Oil chamber
b - Gas chamber

Caution:

Gas pressure shock absorbers with or without separating pistons could be fitted. In shock absorbers with separating pistons between the gas and oil chamber, the piston rod is built into the top, whereas shock absorbers without separating pistons, are built in with the piston rod at the bottom.

Knocking sounds from the rear shock absorbers could have the following causes:

- The top mount is not correctly mounted.
- The rubber bearing in the lower mounting is loose.
- If the oil consumption is high, the separating piston could knock against the piston rod.
- The working piston is loose. Compress the piston rod, let it go then compress again. If a knocking is heard in the switch from pressure and pull, replace the shock absorber.

Hissing noises of the rear shock absorbers

- If the release piston is not totally sealed, gas can escape into the oil system and form foam, which is heard as hissing while driving. In this case replace the shock absorber, even if it is still functioning well.

Testing removed shock absorbers (front and rear)

- Remove shock absorbers.
- Thoroughly check the piston rod for surface damage.
- Check if the piston rod is bent. Place the shock absorbers onto a wooden surface in refitting position. Insert the piston rod. If it is bent, the piston rod will jam in the guide bush.

Caution:

A slight oil film on the piston rod is present at manufacture.

- Hold the shock absorbers in the refitting position, pull it apart then compress it. The shock absorber should move evenly and without sticking during this process.
- Replace the shock absorbers if they are losing oil.

Checking the oil reserve

To check the oil reserve, the gap -a- of the piston rod is measured. If there is oil loss, the piston rod gap in shock absorbers with separating pistons increases, while in absorbers without separating pistons, it decreases.
During this test, the temperature of the shock absorber should be around 20° C.

Caution:

A slight oil film is present at manufacture, and does not indicate oil loss.

- Pull out the piston rod and place it on a surface upside down.

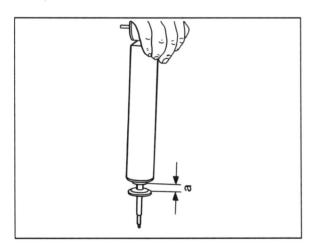

- **Shock absorber with release piston:** Compress the piston rod up to the stop on the working piston of the separating piston. Measure the gap - a - and compare it to the specified value.

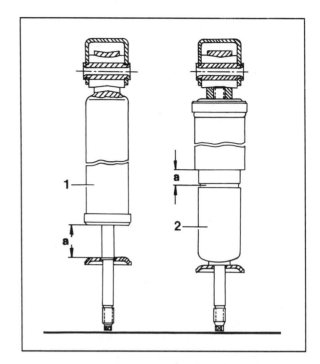

- **Shock absorbers without separating pistons:** Compress the shock absorber until a distinct resistance is felt. The piston is now on the oil pillar. In this position, measure the gap -a- and compare it to the specified value.

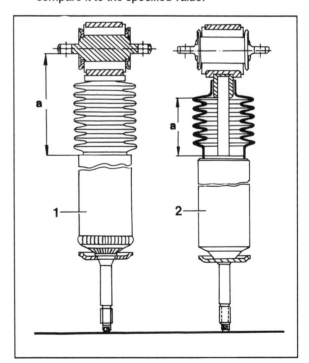

- This illustration shows 2 rear shock absorbers. Shock absorber -1- of "Fichtel & Sachs" has one or two white crosswise lines. Shock absorber - 2 - of "Boge" is marked with a white slanting line.

Caution:

Hissing sounds which occur when the shock absorbers are compressed have no significance.

Piston rod gap value -a-:

Shock absorber with separating piston	New	Allowed Max. value
Front and rear	0+2mm	32mm
Shock absorber without separating piston		
Front	20 ± 2mm	0 mm
Rear		
F&S	105 ± 2mm	82 mm
Boge	147 ± 2mm	137 mm

Caution:

Replace the shock absorbers if the maximum value in shock absorbers **with** separating pistons is **exceeded** or in shock absorbers **without** separating piston if the value **falls short** of the maximum value.

- Further tests of the shock absorber can only be carried out in the workshop, since special test equipment is needed.

Front coil spring - removal and refitting

Caution:

Depending on the vehicle, different coil springs with the appropriate rubber mountings have been fitted. To identify the spring, a red or blue line is painted on the last curve of the spring with an etched part number. In replacing, only use a spring with the same identification.

Removal

- Unscrew the shock absorber upper mounting with the vehicle standing on the ground, see page 137.
- Loosen the wheel bolts, put the front of the vehicle on blocks and remove the front wheel.

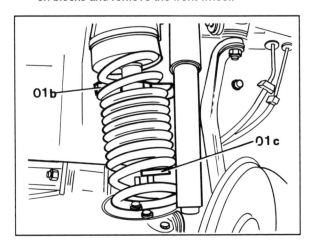

- Fit a spring compressor to the coil spring so that it covers 9 turns of the spring. If a spring compressor with tension plates -01b/01c- is used, displace the plates by 90° before fitting, checking that the coil spring is securely locked. A lot of strength is needed to compress the coil spring. **Never** tension the spring from one side only as this is dangerous.

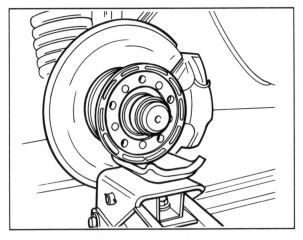

- Lift the bottom control arm carefully with a jack to make the compressing of the spring easier.

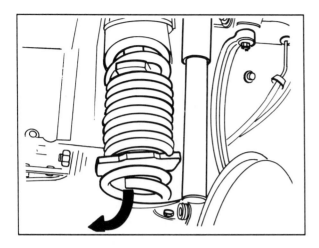

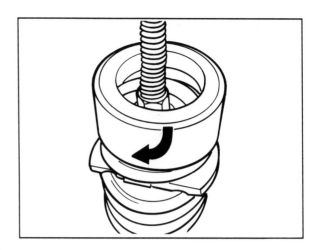

- Lower the control arm slightly and remove the compressed coil spring with the rubber mounting towards the front.

- Turn the rubber mounting to the left and remove.

- Put the spring crosswise between vice jaws and slowly release it.

Refitting

Before refitting, check the rubber mounting for porosity or damage, replacing if necessary. Before refitting the spring, clean the contact surface of the control arm.

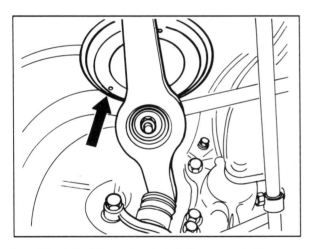

- Check that the water drain hole -arrow- in the spring plate is open, cleaning if necessary.

- Attach the spring compressor and slowly compress the spring.

- Fit the rubber mounting to the spring by turning it once to the right -arrow-.

- Refit the coil spring so that the end of the bottom loop sits in the recess of the spring plate.

- Slightly lift the control arm with a jack, insert the shock absorber and tighten it.

- Slowly release the coil spring, checking that the rubber mounting is correctly positioned in the frame base and the control arm.

- Refit the front wheel, lower the vehicle and tighten the wheel bolts crosswise to 110Nm.

- Check the front of the car sits level.

- Check headlamp alignment.

Front wheel bearing removal and refitting/testing

Caution:

If noises are heard from the outer wheel when driving around a curve or sharp bend, this indicates defective wheel bearings.

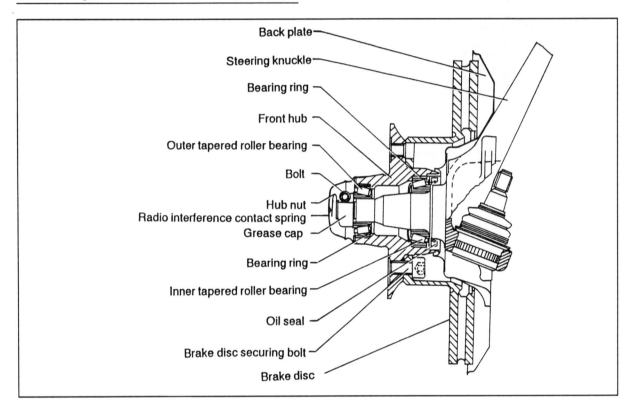

Back plate
Steering knuckle
Bearing ring
Front hub
Outer tapered roller bearing
Bolt
Hub nut
Radio interference contact spring
Grease cap
Bearing ring
Inner tapered roller bearing
Oil seal
Brake disc securing bolt
Brake disc

Removal

Caution:
Position the roller cages and outer races of the wheel bearing in a way that they are not mixed up in case of refitting.

- Remove the brake caliper and hang it up, see page 162.

- Remove the grease cap with a screwdriver, remove the radio interference suppression, contact spring, loosen the bolt and unscrew the nut of the stub axle, see also page 143.

- Remove the front wheel hub with the brake disc from the stub axle. **Caution:** Make sure the outer wheel bearing does not fall off.

- Remove the brake disc, see page 162.

- Hit the outer bearing ring out evenly and carefully with an appropriate brass or aluminium mandrel. **Caution:** The mandrel must be made of a soft material and be in perfect condition to prevent the ring and its seat from being damaged.

- Remove the inner bearing ring with an allen key insert. If this is not available, carefully use a mandrel. **Caution:** Do not damage the ring.

Testing

- Check the surface of the stub axle, particularly in the running surface of the oil seal, replacing the stub axle if necessary.

- Thoroughly clean the inside of the tapered roller bearing (wheel bearing) and the wheel hub. Use a special cleaning solution.

- Check the condition of the bearing seats in the hub.

- Check the bearing rings in the hub for scratches. The bearing rings are fine if they show a smooth, grey track of the roller bearing.

- If the bearing rings show indentations of the roller bearings or are light brown to blue from heat discolouration, replace the wheel bearing.

- Check the condition and the ease of movement of the roller bearings. If rust has formed on the bearing this usually indicates a defective oil seal. In this case replace the wheel bearing.

Refitting

Caution:

Always replace both bearings of a hub. In refitting the existing bearings, do not confuse the roller cages and outer races.

- Refit the bearing rings carefully and evenly.
- Fill the hub and bearing with 45g high temperature roller bearing grease. Fill the roller cages so that the hollow areas between the rollers are filled with grease.
- Fit the roller cages into the hub and grease the frontal area of the rollers.
- Fill the **new** oil seal between the rubber lips with grease and brush the outer edges with sealing compound such as Curil. Now press the seal into the wheel hub, putting a wooden cube or a short tube with the same diameter as the seal onto it and hitting it in a circular motion.
- Fill the front wheel hub with the remaining grease. **Caution:** If too much grease is used, it heats up while driving and can so lose its lubricating properties. If there is too little grease, lubrication of the wheel bearings is not guaranteed.
- Refit the brake disc and brake caliper, see page 162.

Front wheel bearing play adjustment

- Loosen the wheel bolts.
- Put the vehicle onto blocks, remove the wheel.
- With a screwdriver carefully press the disc pads away from the brake disc.

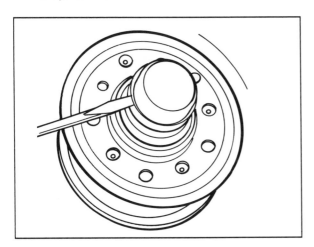

- Attach a broad screwdriver to the grease cap and prise it off.

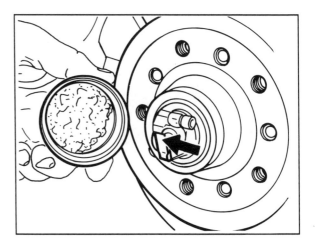

- Remove the radio interference suppression contact spring -arrow- .

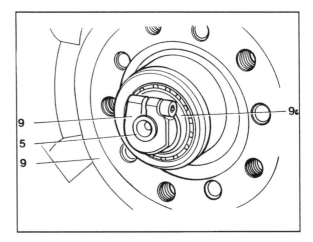

- Loosen the bolt of the clamp nut -9d-.
- Tighten the nut and hub simultaneously -9- until the hub can hardly be turned any further. Now turn the nut back by about 60°, and release the tension by hitting the stub axle -5a-once with a rubber mallet. The illustration also shows the outer wheel bearing -9c-.

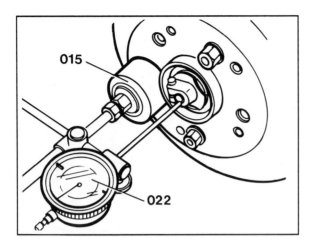

- A workshop measures the end play with a dial gauge and a relevant support. The specified value: 0,01 - 0,02mm.

- Adjust the dial gauge to 2mm load. The gauge thus shows a measurement of 2mm before the test.

- Test the play by strongly pulling and pressing at the disc. Before each measurement turn the wheel hub over a few times.

Caution:

During the measurement the wheel hub may not turn. If the special tool is not available, adjust the wheel bearing play so that no more play is noticeable. Then have the play tested by a workshop.

- Tighten the bolt of the clamp nut to 14 Nm and again check the wheel bearing play.

- Refit the radio interference suppression contact spring.

- Fill the grease cap with about 15 grams of high temperature roller bearing grease, see also illustration on previous page. In vehicles until 11/82, remove the old grease and fill the grease cap with new grease.

- Refit the grease cap by positioning the cap and lightly hammering it with a rubber mallet.

- Refit the front wheel. Lower the vehicle and tighten the wheel bolts crosswise to 110 Nm.

Front axle maintenance

Visual checking the front axle

Visual checking should be carried out every 20 000km.

- Loosen the wheel bolts, put the front of the vehicle on blocks and remove the front wheels.

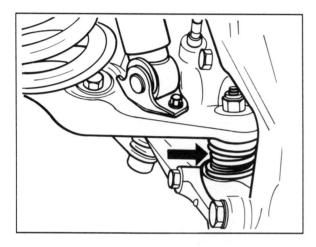

- With a lamp check the dust cap rubbers -arrow- of the joints for damage. Look for oil marks on the cap and its area.

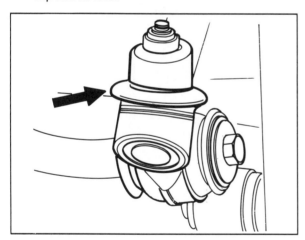

- Check the dust cap rubbers -arrow- of the ball joints for damage.

Caution:

If the dust cap rubber is damaged, replace the ball joint, since dust destroys the joint in a very short space of time.

- Check the shock absorber for traces of oil. A slight oil film on the piston rod is normal. If necessary remove the shock absorber and check it, see page 138.
- Refit the front wheels, lower the vehicle and tighten the wheel bolts crosswise to 110 Nm.

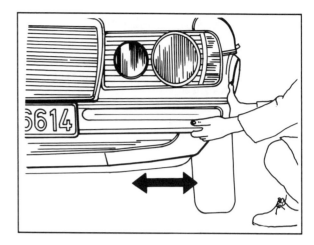

- Carefully check the ball joints for their play, by pushing the vehicle hard sideways at the bumper (helper).

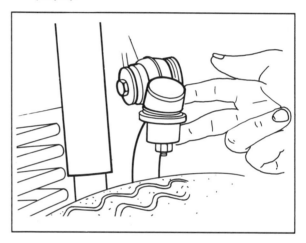

- Simultaneously feel the ball joint and the steering knuckle, to see if there is play in the ball joint. If there is play, replace the upper control arm.

THE REAR SUSPENSION

The rear suspension is of independent type incorporating semi-trailing arms, coil springs and telescopic shock absorbers.

Some models are equipped with a hydropneumatic self-levelling system operating on the rear suspension only.

All suspension points are of rubber, and the rear wheel bearings are of adjustable taper-roller type. A stabiliser bar is fitted.

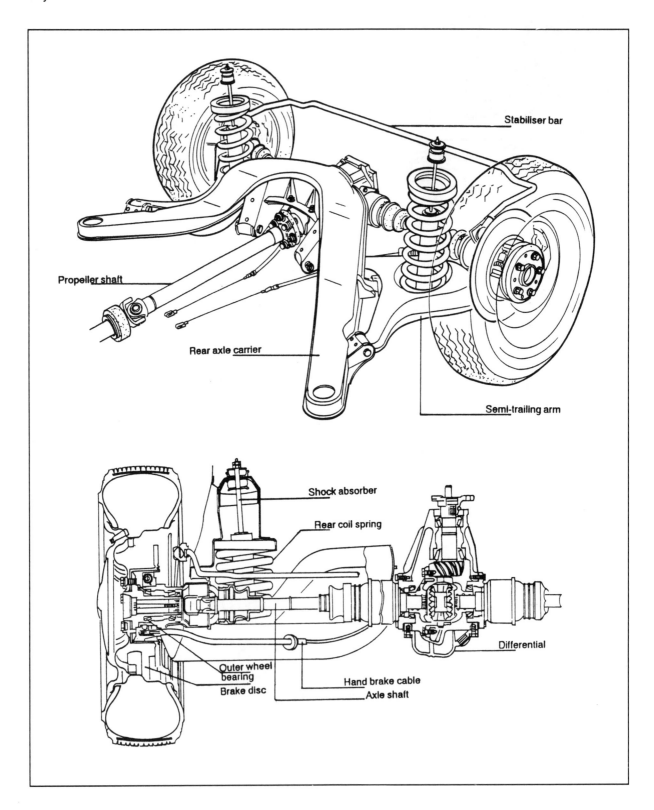

Stabiliser bar

Propeller shaft

Rear axle carrier

Semi-trailing arm

Shock absorber

Rear coil spring

Differential

Outer wheel bearing

Brake disc

Hand brake cable

Axle shaft

Rear coil spring removal and refitting

Caution:

Depending on the model, different coil springs with the appropriate rubber bearings have been fitted. To identify the spring, a red or blue line is painted on the last turn of the spring with an etched part number. In replacing, only use a spring with the same identification.

Removal

- Remove the rear shock absorber. First loosen the shock absorber at the top, see page 148.

- Compress the coil spring with an appropriate spring compressor. The spring compressor should incorporate 5 coils.

- Remove the rear coil spring with the rubber mounting.

- Compress the spring lengthwise in a vice, remove the rubber mounting by turning it to the left and slowly release the spring.

Refitting

Before refitting, check the rubber mounting for porosity and damage, replacing if necessary. Clean the contact area of the semi-trailing arm, the water drain hole must be free of dirt.

- Attach the spring compressor, and slowly compress the spring.

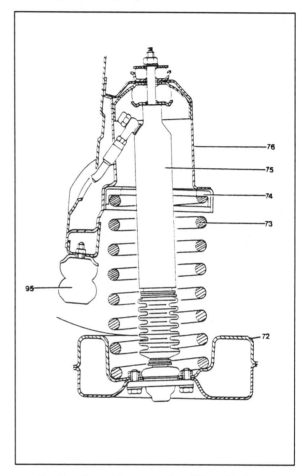

- Position the rubber mounting -74- and refit the coil spring -73- so that the end of the bottom coil sits in the hollow of the semi-trailing arm -72-.

- Release the spring checking that it and the rubber mounting is correctly positioned in the body floor and the semi-trailing arm.

- Remove the spring compressor.

- Refit the shock absorber, by first attaching it to the semi-trailing arm then to the shock absorber housing -76-.

- Check the bump stop -95- for damage, replacing if necessary. **Caution:** In vehicles which have been fitted for heavier loads or have stronger springs, an 8,5mm spacer disc is fitted between the bump stop and the body floor. In this case the bump stop is attached by a longer bolt.

Rear shock absorber removal and refitting

Irrespective of the make, shock absorbers can be individually replaced. The type of shock absorber (coloured line identification) must however co-incide.

Caution:

Shock absorbers are filled with gas and oil and are under extreme pressure. Defective shock absorbers should therefore not be discarded with the normal household refuse.

Removal

Caution:

In loosening the top mounting, the shock absorber tube must not turn, since this could loosen the working piston.

- Remove the back seat and rest, see page 199.
- Remove the round cover plate from the back wall.

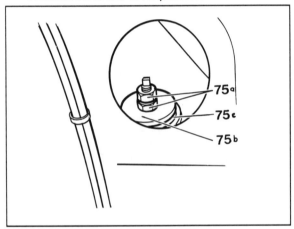

- Unscrew the nuts -75a-. If the shock absorber tube turns as well, hold it steady by hand. When loosening the lock nut, hold the bottom nut with a spanner. Remove the washer -75b- and the rubber washer -75c-.
- Put the vehicle on blocks, to provide enough room for the shock absorbers to be removed downwards.

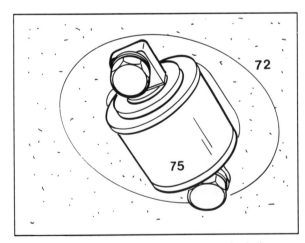

- Working from below the car, remove the bolts from the trailing arm -72- and remove the shock absorber to the bottom.

Refitting

- Before refitting check the shock absorber, see page 138.
- Check the rubber parts for porosity, replacing if necessary.

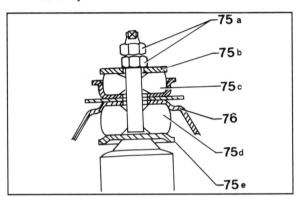

75a — Hexagonal nuts
75b — Washer
75c — Top rubber washer
75d — Bottom rubber washer
75e — Washer
76 — Shock absorber housing

- Reassemble the shock absorber according to the illustration, refit it and tighten, by screwing the bottom nut to the thread end and locking it with the top nut.

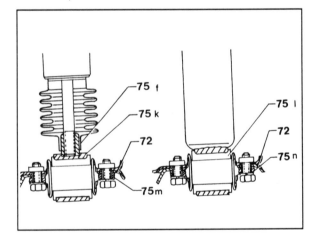

Shock absorber with separating piston/without separating piston

72 Trailing arm
75f - Dust cover
75k Mounting eye
75l - Rubber bush
75m Mount

- Tighten the shock absorbers to the trailing arm to 45 Nm.
- Lower the vehicle, see page 244.
- Refit the cover plate into the back wall, refit back seat and back rest, see page 199.

Rear axle maintenance

Oil level testing of the differential

The oil in the differential of the rear axle does not need to be changed.

The level of the oil should be checked every 20 000 km.

- Go for a short test drive for the oil in the differential to reach operating temperature.
- Put the car on blocks.

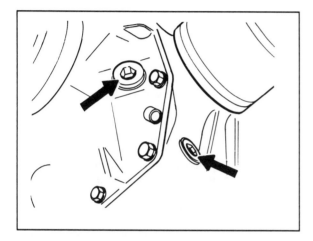

- Unscrew the oil filler cap -left arrow- with an allen key SW 14. The illustration shows a differential gear from 2/81; the right arrow shows the drain plug.
- If the oil escapes slowly, the oil level is fine. Alternatively test with your finger that the oil reaches the bottom edge of the opening.
- If not, add oil with a pump or syringe.

Caution:

If the oil loss is excessive, locate the cause and repair the fault.

Oil specification: Hypoid-Gear oil SAE 90. Only use oil recommended by Mercedes (indicated on the oil can).

Caution:

Gear oil has a thick consistency, so fill up a little at a time, pausing from time to time. Put a container underneath to catch any oil which overflows.

- Tighten the oil filler screw to 50 Nm.

Drive shaft boot testing

- Put the vehicle on blocks.
- Look for visible grease marks at the boots and their immediate area.
- Check that the clips are secure.
- Check the rubber of the boot with a lamp for leaks and cracks. Replace cracked boots.
- If the boot has been pulled into the joint by vacuum or is defective, it should be replaced.

Level control oil level checking

On vehicles with self-leveling suspension, the oil level should be checked every 20 000km while the engine is switched off.

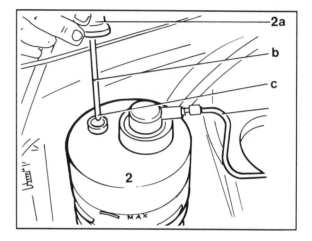

- Remove the dipstick -2a-, clean it with a clean rag and insert it again.
- Pull the dipstick out again and read the oil level.
- If the vehicle is full of fuel, and is loaded normally, the oil level should be between the maximum and minimum mark -b/c-.
- If the vehicle is loaded, the oil level lies at the minimum mark.
- If necessary, top up the oil with a funnel and a fine sieve. Only use an oil approved by Mercedes.
- The filling amount between the minimum and maximum marks is about 0,6 liters. The total capacity of the hydraulic system is around 3,5 liters.

THE STEERING ASSEMBLY

The steering assembly consists of the steering wheel, the steering shaft, the steering gear and the steering damper. The steering wheel is screwed onto the steering shaft which transmits the steering movement to the steering gear.

The more the steering wheel is turned, the less direct the steering becomes. The steering wheel is then easier to turn, for example when parking.

As soon as the steering wheel is approximately in the central position, the steering ratio is more direct ensuring increased steering precision, in particular at higher speeds.

Depending on the model, the steering is assisted by hydraulic power. The hydraulic power steering ensures that the effort in steering is kept to a minimum. The power steering consists of the oil pump, the tank and the oil pressure leads. The oil pump is driven by a fanbelt. The pump draws the hydraulic oil from the tank and transmits it to the steering gear at high pressure. Here a control unit together with the working piston ensure the necessary steering assistance.

Steering wheel removal and refitting

Removal up to 8/79

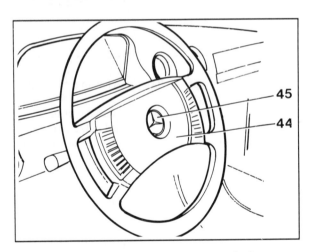

- Remove the cushion plate -44- upwards, by starting at the bottom left or right corner near the steering wheel spoke.

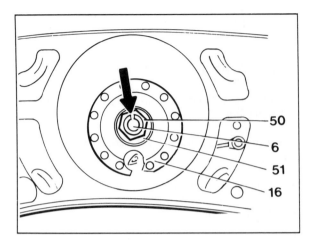

- Position the steering, so that the notch -arrow- points upwards.
- Unscrew the hexagonal nut -50-. This can be difficult to remove.
- Remove the steering wheel -16- from the steering shaft -6-.

Refitting

- Position the steering wheel onto the splines of the shaft so that the straight spoke lies horizontal. The curved spoke must be at the bottom. Check that the notch of the steering shaft is at the top, adjust if necessary.
- Tighten the steering wheel with the hexagonal nut to **80Nm.**
- Refit the padded cover to the steering wheel starting at the top left or right corner.

Removal since 9/79

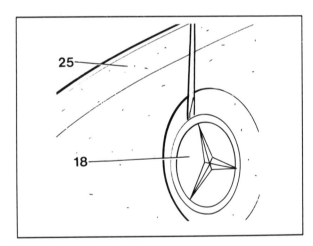

- Remove the cap -18- from the padded cover -25- with a small screwdriver.

Caution:
Do not remove the padded cover -25-.

- Turn the steering wheel until the steering lock engages.

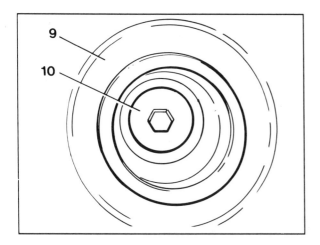

- Remove the screw -10- with an allen key SW10.
- Remove the steering wheel from the steering shaft.

Refitting

- Check that the notch on the steering shaft points directly upwards, turning the steering shaft if necessary.
- Fit the steering wheel onto the splines of the shaft. The curved spoke must be at the bottom and the upper spoke must be horizontal.
- Turn the steering wheel and engage the steering lock.
- Fit a **new self-securing** screw and tighten it to **80Nm**.
- Press the cap -18- into the padded cover.
- Test drive the vehicle checking the position of the steering wheel when driving straight ahead. The upper spoke of the steering wheel must be horizontal.
- If the steering wheel is not aligned it can be adjusted on the splines by a maximum of 2 teeth.

Caution:

If this adjustment to the steering wheel is not enough, check the alignment of the front wheels, see page 156.

- Check that the horn is working.
- Check the automatic indicator cancelling.

Hint: A dirty or sticky steering wheel can be cleaned with an all purpose household cleaner and luke warm water. Do not use a scourer.

Tie rod end removal and refitting

Removal

- Loosen the wheel bolts.
- Put the front of the vehicle on blocks, remove the wheel.

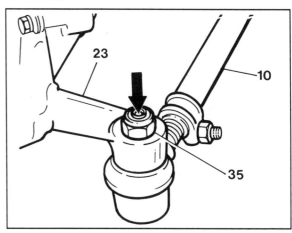

- Unscrew the securing nut -35- from the tie rod end -10-. Hold the tie rod end -arrow- with an allen key. 23- steering arm.

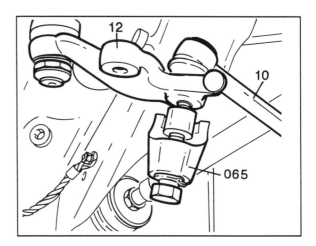

- Press the tie rod ends from the steering arms with a tie rod puller.

Caution:

Do not damage the rubber boot.

Testing

- Move the tie rod joints backwards and forwards. If there is play or they move too easily, replace the tie rod end.
- Check the dust boots for leaks and damage (grease exuding). If the boot is damaged, replace the tie rod end.

Note:

If the boot was only damaged during removal, replacing of the boot alone will suffice.

Refitting

- If necessary, clean any grease from the cone of the rod joints as well as the seats of the steering arms.

- Press the ball joint securely into the cone of the steering arm.

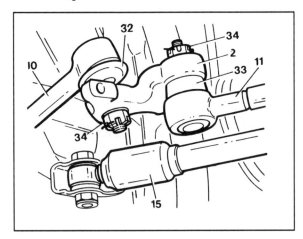

- Tighten the slotted nuts -34- to **35 N.m,** insert the split pin and bend it. **Caution:** if necessary tighten the slotted nut a little more until the split pin can be inserted. Other illustrated parts: 2 - steering arm lever, 10 - tie rod, 11 - steering rod, 15 - steering damper, 32 - dust cap, 33 - plastic cover.

- Fit **new** self-tightening nuts, while holding the joint with an Allen key and tightening the nuts to **35 N.m.**

- Refit the wheel.

- Lower the vehicle.

- Tighten the wheel bolts crosswise to 110 N.m.

- Have the wheel alignment tested.

Tie rod and steering rod joint dust collar - removal and refitting

Note:
To facilitate the refitting of the rings, 2 mounting covers can be made.

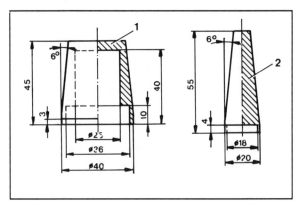

To mount the wire circlip

To mount the plastic ring

Removal

- Remove the track-, steering rod.

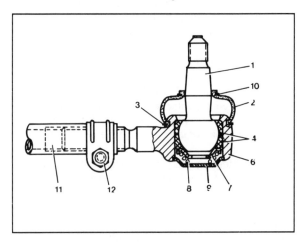

- Prise off the wire circlip -3- with a screwdriver.

- Remove the boot -2- with the plastic ring -10- upwards. Other illustrated parts:
  1   tapered joint,
  4   plastic bearing shells,
  6   steering rod joint,
  7   pressure plate,
  8   pressure spring,
  9   cover,
  11 tie rod,
  12 clamp bolt.

Refitting

- Fill the ball joint with multi purpose grease, for example SHELL Retinax A.

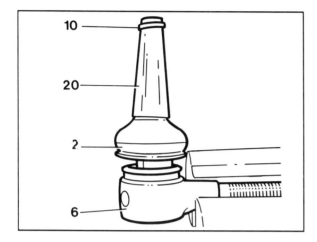

- Refit the rubber boot -2- over the tapered joint.

- Fit the mounting cover -20- and insert the plastic ring -10- into the rubber boot over the mounting cover.

- Remove the mounting cover.

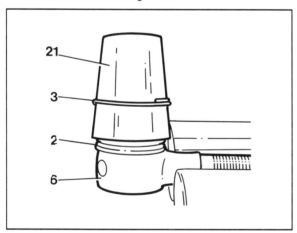

- Fit the mounting cover -21- over the rubber boot and insert the wire circlip -3- into the rubber boot.

- Refit the track-, steering rod.

Tie rod joint removal and refitting

Caution:

Depending on the type of tie rod joint, it is secured to the tie rod by one or two clips and on the other side by one clamped cone ring and a lock nut. The joints are secured to the steering arm or drag lever by slotted nuts and split pins or by self securing hexagonal nuts. When removing the tie rod joint, take note of the right handed or left handed thread.

Removal

- Remove the tie rod.

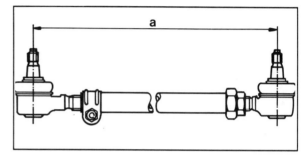

- Unscrew the clamp and the outer tie rod joint and remove from the tie rod.

Hint: To facilitate refitting, make a note of the number of turns when removing the joint.

- Loosen the lock nut and then unscrew the adjusting nut from the tie rod joint.

- Unscrew the inner tie rod joint out of the tie rod.

Refitting

- Refit the tie rod joint by the number of noted rotations. Both joints must be screwed in about equally.

- Check the measurement -a- of the tie rod, specified value 345 ± 2mm. If necessary alternately screw or unscrew the tie rod heads.

- Tighten the outer joint with the clamp to 20 N.m.

- Tighten the adjusting nut on the other side of the tie rod to 59 N.m and secure it with a lock nut.

- Refit the tie rod.

Steering assembly maintenance

Dust caps of the tie rod/steering rod joints - testing

- Put the front of the vehicle on blocks.
- Check the dust cap with a light for damage as well as grease marks on and around the boots.
- If the dust cap is damaged, replace the relevant joint. Dirt which has entered will have damaged the joint.
- Check that the securing nut of the joint is secure, but do not turn the nut. Replace loose nuts.

Steering play - testing

- Centre the steering wheel.
- Move the steering wheel from side to side through an open window. There may be a maximum play of 25mm without the wheels moving.
- If the play is more, the steering rods, idler arm, steering gear and bearing play of the front axle must be tested.

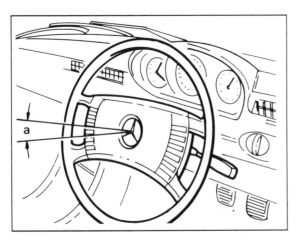

- Move the tie rods -10- as well as the steering rod -11- from side to side by hand. The ball joints must not show any play, if so replace the joints or steering rod. Other illustrated parts:
  2 - steering lever, 12 - steering idler arm, 15 - steering damper, 23 - drop lever
- Check that the tie rods are not bent.

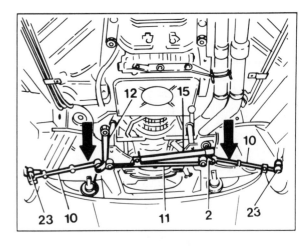

Mechanical steering oil level checking

Unscrew the screw out of the steering gear. In the central position of the steering, the **oil level** should reach the **bottom part** of the threaded hole for the screw. If necessary fill up with steering gear oil (ATF) according to Mercedes specifications.

Power steering oil level checking.

The oil level of the power steering should be checked every 20 000km.

- The oil level can be tested cold (room temperature) or working temperature oil about 80° C
- Remove the screw and the lid of the pump housing. **Caution:** In place of a screw, a wing nut may have been fitted.
- In warm oil (about 80° C) the oil level should reach the mark in the container, or 20 mm below the edge of the container.
- In cold oil the oil level should be 6 to 8 mm below the mark in the container.
- If necessary, fill up with ATF (automatic transmission fluid). Always fill up with **new oil** since the smallest particle of dirt can lead to blockages in the hydraulic system.
- The total capacity is around 1,4 liters.
- Check the lid gasket for leaks or damage.
- Replace the lid of the pump housing and secure it with the screw or wing nut.
- Now move the steering wheel from lock to lock several times with the engine running, to remove air from the system.

Securing bolts of the steering - tightening

The bolts of the steering system are to be tightened to the correct torque every 20 000km.

- Put the vehicle on blocks, see page 244.
- The securing screws of the steering gear at the side member of the chassis floor: **70 to 80 N.m.**
- Hexagonal screws at the steering coupling: **25 N.m.**
- Self securing nut of the idler arm: **120 N.m.**
- Self securing nut on the steering shaft: **140 - 180 N.m** (steering shaft of 30 mm diameter); **160 -200 N.m** (steering shaft of 32 mm diameter and power steering).
- Self securing nut of the steering damper on the steering rod: **45 N.m.**
- Slotted nuts or self securing nuts on the steering and track rods: **35 N.m.**
- Hexagonal bolt on the clamp of the track rod: **20 N.m.**
- Check that the counter nut on the conical ring of the track rod is secure. Tightening torque: **50 N.m.**
- Lower the vehicle.
- Securing nut or sunken screw of the steering wheel: **80 N.m.**
- Securing nut for the steering column tube of the cross member: **25 N.m;** steering column tube at the bottom bracket: **10 N.m.**

Power steering hydraulic pump fanbelt-replacing/tensioning

Remove the fanbelts which are mounted on the crankshaft pulley in front of the fanbelt of the power steering.

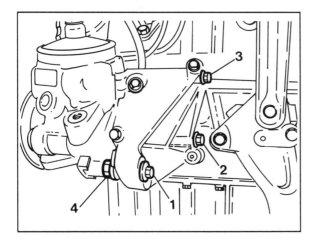

- Loosen the securing bolts -1,2,3-.
- Turn the tensioner -4- thus slackening the fanbelt, which can now be removed.

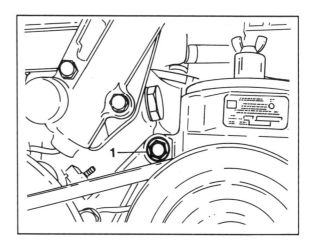

- In **engine 110** loosen the screw -1- on the front side of the hydraulic pump.

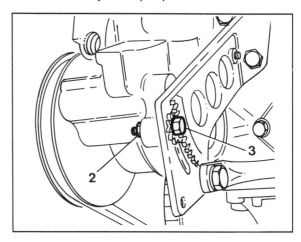

- Loosen the nut -2-. Turn the adjusting screw -3- to the left, slackening the fanbelt which can then be removed.
- Fit a new fanbelt and tension it with the adjusting wheel. The belt should be compressible by about 5mm, in the middle between the two fanbelt pulleys.
- Tighten the securing bolts or nuts.
- Refit the remaining fanbelts and check them.

Caution:

The workshop is able to test and adjust the fanbelt tension accurately with a special measuring device. The specified value of a new fanbelt is 50, a used fanbelt is 40 to 45. These values refer to the special tool, see also page 224.

THE WHEEL ALIGNMENT

Favorable driving characteristics and minimal tyre wear are only achieved if the wheel alignment is correct. In cases of abnormal tread wear, as well as bad road holding - if the directional stability when driving straight as well as steering characteristics when turning are bad - one should take the vehicle to a workshop, to have the alignment optically checked.

Without the appropriate measuring equipment, the alignment cannot be checked, so only the basic concepts will be described here.

The Track

The track is regarded as the lateral distance between the wheels. As a rule the front wheels must have wheel toe-in, as they - due to rolling resistance - run outward a little when driving straight, since there is play in the wheel bearings, wheel suspension and tie rod joints. The wheel toe-in compensates for the tendency of the front wheels to splay outward. For the wheel toe-in the wheels are adjusted so that they - measured at the height of the wheel centre - are a little closer in the front than the back.

Toe-out means that the front wheels, measured at the height of the wheel centre, are a little wider in the front than the back.

In the Mercedes both the front and rear wheels can be adjusted to set wheel toe-in.

Camber and Toe-in-in

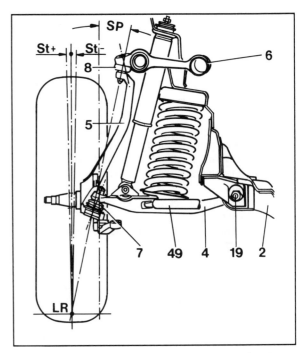

Front axle: St - camber, Sp - steering axis inclination, LR - swivelling radius, 2 - cross member, 4 - lower control arm, 5 - steering knuckle, 6 - upper control arm, 7 - lower ball joint, 8 - upper ball joint, 19 - eccentric bolt for camber adjustment, 49 - support tube.

Camber and toe-in dampen the transmission of road bumps to the steering and in turning, minimise the friction.

Camber is the angle by which the wheel plane deviates from the vertical position. The front wheels thus stand closer together at the bottom than at the top in positive camber. The camber of the Mercedes is adjusted to neutral ($0°$).

Toe-in/out is the angle between the spindle of the stub axle and the vertical point of contact, seen longitudinally.

Due to the camber and toe-in, the contact points of the wheels with the road are brought closer to the spindle of the stub axle. This keeps the swivelling radius down to a minimum. The smaller the swivelling radius, the easier the steering is. The road bumps also have less effect on the steering. In the Mercedes, the swivelling radius is zero.

Castor

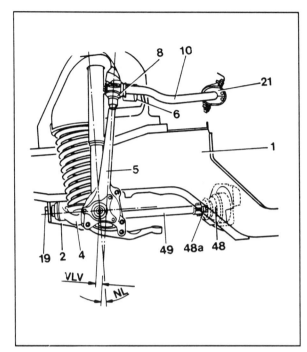

Front axle: NL - castor, VLV - backward rake deviation, 1 - side member, 2 - cross member, 4 - lower control arm, 5 - steering knuckle, 6 - upper control arm, 8 - upper ball joint, 10 - stabiliser, 19 - eccentric bolt for camber adjustment, 21 - rubber bush of stabiliser, 48 - supporting joint, 48a - ball pin of castor adjustment, 49 - support tube.

Castor is the angle between the spindle of the stub axle and the vertical of the wheel connection point seen transversally to the vehicle. The castor is adjusted with the camber by 2 eccentric bolts.

The castor influences the straight line running of the front wheels. Too little castor causes deviations from the driving direction on bad roads and windy conditions, as well as not allowing the steering to return to the central position after turning.

Adjustment

To measure the vehicle, a measuring pit or floor jack is needed. The following conditions must be met before measuring:

- Prescribed wheel pressure

- Vehicle empty in driving condition: full fuel tank, spare wheel, toolbox

- Steering correctly adjusted

- No excessive play in the steering rods

- No excessive play in the wheel suspension

Adjustment values for track, camber and castor

The following values apply to all models when empty.

Front axle	
Camber of the front wheels	$0°{}^{+10}_{-20}{}'$ [2]
Measurement in straight position	8° 45' ± 30'
Castor Measurement with wheel turned fully	8° 15' ± 30'
Permissible difference between left and right	0° 30'
Wheel toein (front wheels pressed apart by 90 - 110N)	0° 25' ± 10' or 3 ± 1mm [2],
Track angle difference at 20° turning of curve inner wheel	-1° 10' ± 40' [3]
Maximum turning angle	43° or 44° 20'

[1] Effective castor value, measurement with mechanical castor measurement device
[2] Attempted specified value when adjusting
[3] Value without wheel toe. Subtract the measured wheel toe value when determining the actual track angle difference (without wheel toe)

Camber adjustment of the front wheels	
Eccentric adjustment to the bearing of the lower control arm	
Camber adjustment range of the eccentric bolt (theoretical) at the specified castor value	from -1° to +0°45'
Influence of the camber adjustment on the castor	
Camber adjustment at the eccentric bolt: results in castor changes:	
0°10' $\dfrac{\text{in positive direction}}{\text{In negative direction}}$ about 0°10' $\dfrac{\text{in positive direction}}{\text{in negative direction}}$	

Castor adjustment	
Castor adjustment at the bearing of the brake support to the chassis floor by changing the distance of the lower control arm - supporting joint	
Castor adjustment range of the ball pin in supporting joint to supporting tube at specified camber value	from 6°30' to 11°

Influence of the castor adjustment on the front wheel camber
Castor adjustment at ball pin of supporting joint: results in camber changes:
0°30' $\dfrac{\text{in positive direction}}{\text{in negative direction}}$ about 0°10' $\dfrac{\text{in negative direction}}{\text{in positive direction}}$

THE BRAKING SYSTEM

The hydraulic foot brake consists of the master cylinder, the brake servo and disc brakes for both the front and rear wheels. Operating in two circuits. One brake circuit acts on the front, the other on the rear wheels. If one brake circuit malfunctions,for example due to leakage, the other circuit will still function. The pressure for both circuits is built up in the tandem master cylinder via the brake pedal.

The brake fluid reservoir is above the master cylinder and supplies brake fluid to the entire brake assembly. The brake servo stores part of the inlet vacuum produced by the engine (the diesel engine has a special vacuum pump). Via appropriate valves, the pedal pressure is increased if necessary.

The front and rear disc brakes are fitted with a locking brake caliper. This means that the brake pad in each brake caliper is pushed against the brake disc by 2 pistons when braking.

The hand brake is operated via wire cables and works on the rear brakes. Since the disc brake is not suitable as a parking brake, the rear wheels have 2 additional drum brakes integrated into the disc brakes. The drum brakes are operated solely by the hand brake.

The brake linings are tuned to the particular vehicle model. It is thus recommended to only use only Mercedes approved brake linings.

Work on the braking system requires utmost cleanliness and precision. If you do not have the necessary experience, it is recommended that a workshop be used to carry out these jobs.

Hint: When driving on very wet roads, the brakes should be applied from time to time to free the discs of particles.

Although the water is spun from the brake discs by the centrifugal force, a thin film of silicones, rubber shavings, grease and dirt can remain, decreasing the effectiveness of the brakes. If new brake linings are fitted, they have to be worn in. Unnecessary heavy application of the brakes should be avoided for the first 200 km.

Caution:

If a different pedal free-play is noticed, particularly after turning, the brake disc must be tested for shimmying on the outer diameter. The wheel bearing play should be tested at the same time and adjusted if necessary. If the brake disc shimmies too much, adjust the wheel hub. If there is no marked improvement, replace the brake disc.

Front and rear disc brake pads - removal and refitting

Caution:

Brake calipers of the manufacturers BENDIX, GIRLING and TEVES could be installed. They vary slightly in the attachment of the brake pads.

Removal:

- Loosen the wheel bolts.

- Put the vehicle on blocks, see page 244.

- Remove the wheels from the front or rear axle.

Caution:

Changing the pads from the outside to the inside or from the right to the left wheel is not allowed. The change could lead to irregular braking action. Always replace all disc brake pads of one brake axle at the same time.

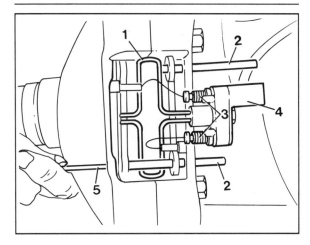

- Remove the plug -3- of the brake lining wear indicator(if fitted) from the plug connection -4-. The illustration shows the BENDIX/GIRLING brake caliper.

- Remove the securing pin from the dowel -2-, hammering the dowels out with a punch -5-.

- Remove the pad securing springs -1-.

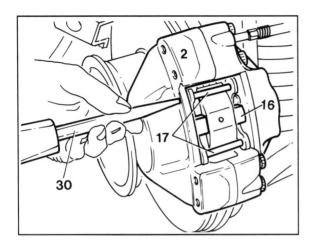

- Prise out the dowels -17- with a punch -30- from the caliper. The illustration shows the TEVES brake caliper.
- Remove the cross spring -16-.

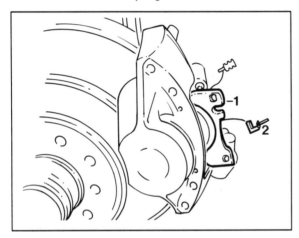

- Remove the brake-wear sensor -2- (if fitted) from the brake pad. **Caution:** If the insulation of the contact pin is worn through, or the sensor or lead insulation is damaged, replace the sensor.
- Pull the brake lining -1- out with pliers or a screwdriver. If the brake lining is rusted tight a special puller is required.
- Push one disc pad, forcing the pistons into their bores, to ease removal. Repeat for the other pad.

Refitting

Caution:

Do not press the brake pedal when the brake pad removed. This will force the pistons out of their bores.

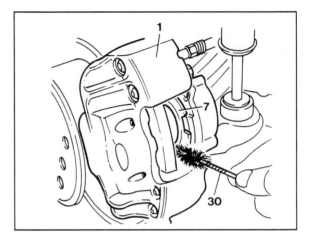

- Clean the seating faces of the pads in the caliper with a soft metal brush and vacuum cleaner, or wipe them with a cloth and spirits. Do not use any solvents with a mineral oil base or sharp-edged tools.
- Before refitting the pads, check by hand that there are no ridges on the brake disc. Replace damaged brake discs. Clean brake discs which have a grey or blue discolouration before refitting new brake linings.
- Measure the brake disc thickness, see page 172.
- Check the dust cover for cracks. Replace damaged dust covers as dirt that has entered quickly leads to leaks in the brake caliper. The caliper must be removed and disassembled (workshop job).

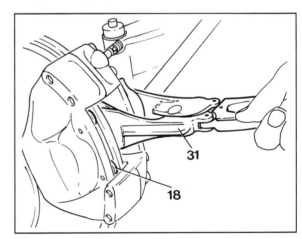

- Press back both pistons with piston ring pliers -31-. A hardwood lever may also be used (hammer handle), but care must be taken not to damage the piston or dust cover.

Caution:

If a piston is pushed back, fit a brake pad -18- on the other side, since the opposite piston would otherwise be pushed forwards. If necessary use an old brake pad for this.

Caution:

When pushing back the pistons, brake fluid is pushed out of the brake cylinders into the reservoir. Observe the fluid level in the reservoir, sucking off some brake fluid with a syphon.

Use a syphon used only for brake fluid. **Brake fluid is poisonous and may under no circumstances be sucked orally through a tube. Use only a syphon or syringe. Even after changing the pad, the maximum mark of the brake fluid container may not be exceeded, as the liquid expands when heated. Leaking brake fluid runs down the master cylinder, destroys the paintwork and leads to corrosion.**

Hint: Test the ease of movement of the pistons if there is excessive brake pad wear. If the pistons jam, repair the caliper (workshop job).

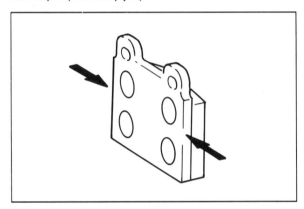

- To prevent the disc brakes from squeaking, paint the back of the braking pads as well as the side panels of the backing plates -arrows- with grease (e.g. Plastilube, Tunap VC 582/S, Chevron SRJ/2, Liqui Moly LM-36 or LM-508-ASC). Only paint the backing plate, **The paste must not be on the actual brake pad.** If necessary, immediately wipe it and clean it with spirits.
- Refit the brake pads into the brake caliper.
- Refit the pad securing springs, taking care not to damage the dust cover. Do not press the securing spring between the dust cover and brake caliper.
- Drive the dowels from the inside out, positioning them so that they can be pushed through the disc pads. Make sure the dowels do not turn while driving them in.
- Push the dowels into the bores of the caliper. Check that the pad springs are secure.
- Position the cross spring and refit the dowel securing pins.

Caution:

Always replace the swivel spring or pad spring and the supporting dowels.

- Refit the sensor of the brake pad wear indicator (if fitted) into the brake pad, and the plug connection onto the brake caliper.
- Refit the wheel, lower the vehicle and tighten the wheel bolts crosswise to 110 N.m.

Caution:

Compress the brake pedal several times while the engine is off, until definite resistance is felt.

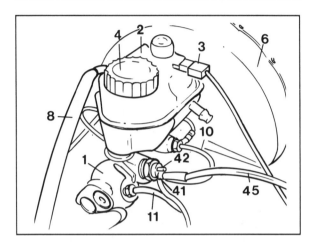

- Check the brake fluid in the reservoir -2-, filling up to the Maximum mark if necessary.

Caution:

In vehicles with a pressure difference warning indicator (PDW), the PDW warning lamp could light up after the pad has been changed. In this case press in the dowel -42- at the switch -41- after the pad change. Other illustrated parts: 1 - brake master cylinder, 3 - plug of brake fluid level warning indicator, 4 - cap, 6 - brake servo, 8 - vacuum lead, 10/11 - brake pipes, 45 - Pressure lead of PDW switch, arrow - brake fluid level warning indicator switch.

- Carefully wear in the new brake pads, by slowly braking from about 80km/h to 40km/h several times. Allow the brake to cool down in between.

Caution:

The brake should not be used hard until about 200km have been driven, except in an emergency.

Front brake disc - removal and refitting

Removal

- Loosen the wheel bolts.
- Put the front of the vehicle on blocks.
- Remove the front wheel.

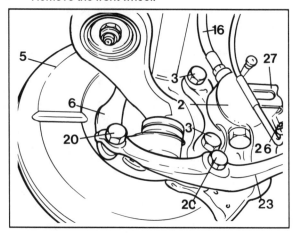

- Unscrew the securing screws -3- and remove the caliper -2- from the stub axle -6-. Other illustrated parts: 5 - cover, 16 - brake hose, 20 - self locking bolts, 23 - drop lever, 26 -plug connection, 27 - cable support.

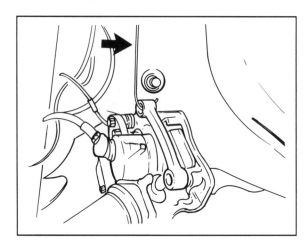

- Hang up the caliper with a wire hook -arrow- in such a way that the brake hose as well as the cable of the brake pad wear indicator are not twisted or tensioned.

Caution:

Do not loosen the brake hose, or the brake system will have to be bled.

- Remove the wheel hub, see page 142.
- Screw three hexagonal headed bolts M12x1,5 into the front wheel hub (wheel assembly surface).

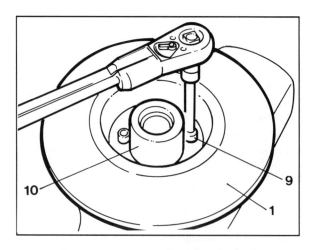

- Hold the front wheel hub -10- into a vice so that the jaws of the vice grip the hexagonal headed bolts.
- Unscrew the securing bolts -9- from the wheel hub -10- with an allen key and remove the brake disc -1-.

Refitting

To ensure that both sides brake equally, both brake discs must show equal surfaces regarding grind and hollow roughness. So **always** replace **both** brake discs.

- If present, remove any rust from the flange of the brake disc and the front wheel hub.
- Clean new brake discs with solvent to remove the protecting varnish.
- Secure the brake discs to the wheel hub with **new** self locking hexagonal bolts to **115 N.m.**
- Press the front wheel hub with the brake disc onto the stub axle, refit the outer wheel bearing and tighten the nut.
- Adjust the wheel bearing play, see page 143.
- Tighten the brake caliper with **new** self securing bolts to the stub axle to **115 N.m.**

Caution:

Take care not to twist the brake hose or to tension it.

- Refit the contact spring of the radio interference suppression, see page 143.
- Remount the wheel, lower the vehicle and tighten the wheel bolts crosswise to 110 N.m.

Caution:

With the engine off, push the brake pedal several times, to allow the play between the brake disc and brake pad to adjust itself.

- Check the brake fluid level in the resevoir, see page 171.

Rear brake disc - removal and refitting

Removal

- Loosen the wheel bolts.
- Put the rear of the vehicle on blocks.
- Remove the rear wheel.

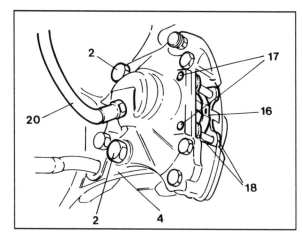

- Unscrew the securing bolts -2- and remove the caliper from the semi-trailing arm -4-. Other illustrated parts: 16 - retaining spring, 17 - dowels, 18 - disc pads, 20 - brake hose.

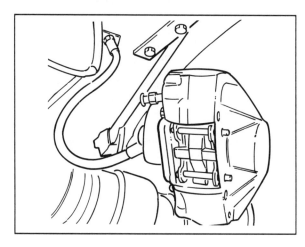

- Hook the caliper to the stabiliser in such a way that the brake hose is not entangled or tensioned.

Caution:

Do not loosen the brake hose, or the brake assembly will have to be bled.

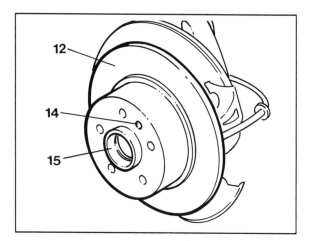

- Remove the brake disc -12- from the rear axle shaft flange -15-. -14- dowel pin.

Caution:

The parking brake must be free. Loosen a jammed brake disc by hitting softly with a rubber mallet.

Refitting

To ensure that both sides brake equally, both brake discs must show equal surfaces regarding grind and hollow roughness, so both brake discs should be replaced at the same time.

- If present remove any rust from the flange of the brake disc and rear axle shaft.

Caution:

To facilitate the removal of the brake disc later, paint the dowel seat of the rear axle shaft flange with a high temperature paste (e.g. Molykote-U or -G-Rapid, Liqui-Moly LM-36 or LM-508-SC)

- Clean the new brake disc with a solvent to remove the protective varnish.
- Refit the brake disc onto the rear axle shaft flange so that the dowel pin locates the brake disc.
- Position the caliper on the semi-trailing arm, while checking the ease of movement of the brake hose.
- Tighten **new** self securing screws to **90 N.m.**

Caution:

If the screws are hard to tighten, clean the thread of the semi-trailing arm with a tap M12x1,5.

- Refit the wheel, lower the vehicle and tighten the wheel bolts crosswise to 110 N.m.

Caution:

With the engine off, push the brake pedal down hard several times, to allow the play between the brake disc and disc pads to adjust itself.

- Check the brake fluid level in the resevoir, see page 171.

The brake fluid

In working with brake fluid take note of the following:

- Brake fluid is poisonous. Never suck brake fluid orally through a tube. Only fill brake fluid into containers which cannot accidentally be consumed.
- Brake fluid is corrosive and may thus not come into contact with the vehicle paintwork. In this case wash it off immediately, rinsing with a lot of water.
- Brake fluid is hydroscopic, i.e. it absorbs moisture from the air, and must thus be stored in an air-tight container.
- Brake fluid may not be re-used. Even when bleeding the brake system, only use new brake fluid.
- Specification: **DOT 4**.
- Brake fluid may not come into contact with mineral oil, since even small traces of this render the brake fluid useless, or lead to the failure of the brake system.

Bleeding the brake system

After any repair to the brakes, during which the assembly is opened, air can get into the system. Thus the brake system must be bled. There is also air in the system if the brake pedal feels soft when compressing it. In this case the leak must be rectified, and the brake system bled.

The brake system is bled by pumping the brake pedal, for which a second person is necessary.

If the entire brake system must be bled, bleed each caliper separately. This is the case when air has got into each separate caliper. If only one caliper was renewed or repaired, it is normally enough to bleed the specific caliper only.

The order of bleeding: 1. caliper left rear, 2. caliper rear right, 3. caliper front left, 4. caliper front right.

- Remove the dust cover from the bleed valve of the brake cylinder. Clean the bleed valve, push a clean tube onto it, with the other end in a half-filled container of brake fluid.
- Let the helper compress the brake pedal (pump) until pressure is built up in the brake system. This is felt with increasing resistance when the brake pedal is compressed.
- If there is sufficient pressure, totally compress the brake pedal and hold it in this position.
- Open the bleed valve about a half rotation with a ring spanner. Collect any overflowing liquid in the container. Make sure that the tube end in the container remains below the fluid level.

- As soon as the fluid pressure decreases, close the bleed valve.
- Repeat the pump procedure until the pressure is built up again. Compress the brake pedal, holding this position. Open the bleed valve until the pressure is released, then close the bleed screw.
- Repeat the bleed process on one brake cylinder until no more bubbles form in the brake fluid flowing into the bleed container.
- After bleeding, remove the hose from the bleed valve and refit the dust cover to the valve.
- Bleed the other brake cylinders in the same way.

Caution:

While bleeding, look at the reservoir every now and then. The fluid level must not sink too much, or air will be sucked into the system. **Only fill up with new brake fluid!**

- After bleeding, the reservoir should be filled to the "max" mark.

Brake lines and brake hoses

Steel tubes are used for the brake line system, which makes up the connection from the master brake cylinder to the flexible brake hoses at the wheels.

The tube ends are swaged in front and then have a cone shaped connection for the cone shaped thread opening in the brake cylinders or distribution blocks. Before the tubes are swaged, a tube nut is pushed over the tube, which later pushes the cone shaped connection to the cone shaped thread opening thus securely sealing it.

The brake hoses make up the flexible connections between the rigid and moveable vehicle parts.

Brake line/brake hose replacing

- Put the vehicle on blocks, see page 244.

- Loosen the brake lines at the union nut and remove.

- Block the line connection in the direction of the master cylinder with a suitable plug.

- Try to put the new line in the same position.

- When connecting the brake line, put a little brake fluid on the bevel shaped contact surface, and tighten the nut to 10 N.m.

- Fit the new brake hose so that it hangs through without twisting, tightening it to 10 N.m.

- Only fit approved brake hoses.

- After fitting, test with an unloaded wheel (vehicle lifted), whether the hose follows all the wheel movements without brushing against anything.

Caution:

Brake hoses must not come into contact with oil or petroleum. Do not varnish them.

- Bleed the brake system.

- Lower the vehicle.

The hand brake

Brake servo testing

The brake servo is to be tested if unusually high pressure on the brake pedal is needed.

- While the engine is off, compress the brake pedal totally at least 5 times, then start the engine with the brake pedal down. The brake pedal should give way underfoot.

- If not, unscrew the vacuum hose of the brake servo, starting the engine. By putting a finger on the end of the hose, check that a vacuum is created.

- If there is no vacuum: check the hose for leaks or damage, replacing if necessary. Tighten all clips.

- If there is a vacuum: have the vacuum measured and replace the brake servo if necessary (workshop job).

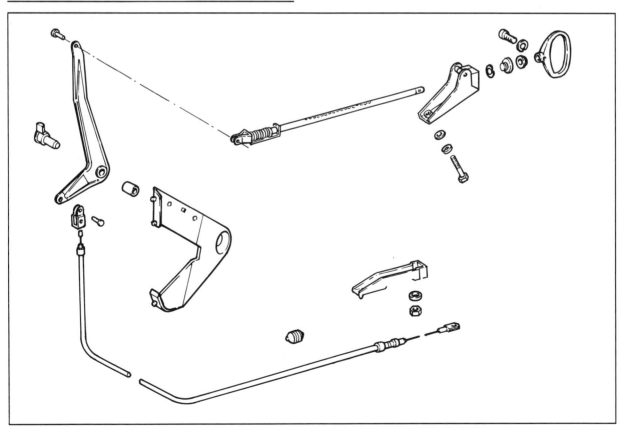

Exploded view of the handbrake lever and front cable assembly.

Brake cables - removal and refitting

Front cable - removal

- Put the vehicle on blocks, see page 244.

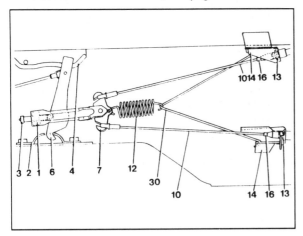

- In vehicles with a heat shield under the intermediate lever -6- support the rear exhaust system with jack and a wooden insert, unhook the rubber ring and lower the exhaust system a little at the back.

- Remove the heat shield.

- Unhook the return spring -12- with pliers from the wire -30-.

- Turn the adjusting screw -3- of the adjusting bracket -1- back totally. Unhook the intermediate lever -6- from the frame on the chassis floor -2- and remove it from the adjusting bracket.

- Loosen the hand brake cable assembly -17- from the intermediate lever -6-, by pulling the split pin out of the clevis pin. Other illustrated parts: 4 - support bracket of the intermediate lever, 7 -equalising lever, 10 - rear brake cable, 13 - spring clamp, 14 - bracket.

- Working inside the car, remove the trim panel of the dashboard to gain access to the cable.

- Disconnect the inner cable from the lever, then prise out the spring clip and disconnect the outer cable.

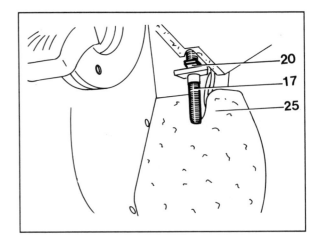

- Pull the brake cable assembly out of the bottom of the chassis floor.

Refitting

- Insert the brake cable assembly from the inside to the outside through the chassis floor and the rubber grommet. Check that the rubber grommet is secure.

- Attach the cable assembly into the clip of the lever and secure it with the spring clamp.

- Insert the cable assembly into the bracket and secure it with the spring clamp.

- Attach the front cable assembly to the intermediate lever.

- Insert the intermediate lever into the bracket and then hook it into the bearing on the chassis floor.

- Hook the return spring into the wire.

- Adjust the parking brake.

- If removed, refit the heat shield and rehook the rear exhaust system.

- Refit the dashboard cover, see page 198.

- Lower the vehicle, see page 244.

Hand brake rear cable - removal and refitting

Removal

- Put the vehicle on blocks, see page 244.
- Remove the hand brake shoes and expanders as described in the following section.

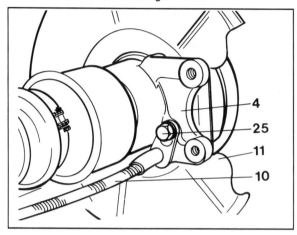

- Remove the screw -25- from the semi-trailing arm -4- and remove the brake cable.

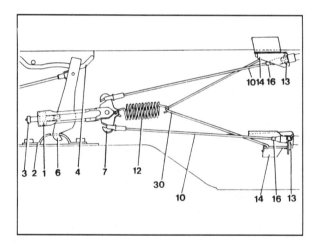

- In vehicles with a heat shield under the intermediate lever -6- support the rear exhaust system a little at the back.
- Remove the heat shield
- Unhook the return spring -12- with pliers from the wire.
- Turn the adjusting screw -3- of the adjusting bracket -1- back totally. Unhook the intermediate lever -6- from the frame on the chassis floor -2- and remove it from the adjusting bracket.
- Unhook the hand brake control cable -10- from the equalising lever -7-.
- Take out the spring clamp -13-, remove the brake control cable -10- from the bracket -14-Other illustrated parts: 4 - support bracket of intermediate lever, 7 - equalising lever.

Refitting

Caution:

Do not damage the rubber grommet of the control cable jacket, since dirt will otherwise get into the control cable.

- Fit the control cable in the same way as the previously fitted cable, checking that the rubber grommet is secure in the bracket of the semi-trailing arm.
- Secure the cable to the bracket with the spring clamp.
- Hook the cable into the equalising lever.
- Hook the return spring into the wire.
- Screw the control cable with the bracket to the semi-trailing arm.
- Refit the brake shoes.
- Adjust the parking brake.
- If removed, refit the heat shield and rehook the rear exhaust system.
- Lower the vehicle, see page 244.

Hand brake shoes - removal and refitting

Removal

- Remove the rear brake disc, see page 163.

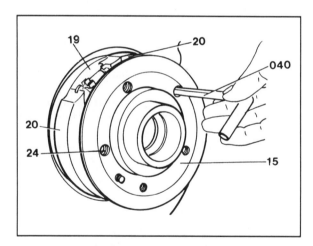

- Turn the rear axle flange -15- so that one threaded hole -24- is over the spring.
- Slightly compress the spring with a screwdriver -040-, turn it by about 90° and unhook the spring from the covering ring -19-. Other illustrated parts: 20 - brake shoes.
- Remove the other spring in the same way.

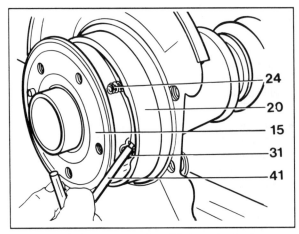

- Unhook the return spring -31- from the brake shoes.

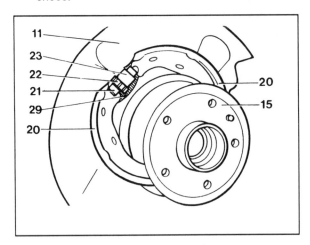

- Pull both brake shoes -20- apart at the bottom and remove them over the rear axle shaft flange -15-.
- Unhook the return spring -29- from the brake shoes and remove the adjusting device -21,22,23-.

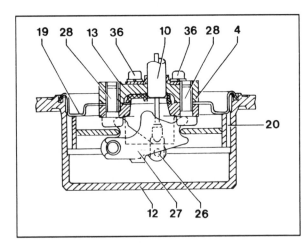

- Remove the bolt -26- out of the expander -27- and remove the brake control cable -10- from the expanding lock. Other illustrated parts: 4 -wheel carrier, 12 - brake disc, 13 - brake carrier, 19 - back plate, 20 - brake shoes, 28 - screw, 36 - screw with spring washer.

Refitting

- Lubricate all bearings and sliding surfaces of the expander with high temperature paste (e.g. Liqui Moly LM-36 or LM-508-ASC, Molycote-Paste-U, or G-Rapid).
- Attach the brake cable with the bolts to the expander. Now press the expander in the direction of the back plate -19-.
- Check that the two bolts of the brake bracket -13- are secure. Torque 50 N.m.

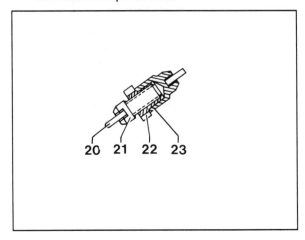

- Disassemble the adjusting device. Grease the thread of the pressure piece -21- and the cylindrical part of the adjusting wheel -22- with high temperature paste.
- Screw the pressure piece -21- into the adjusting wheel -22- and fit the pressure sleeve.
- Fit the adjusting device between the two brake shoes, so that the adjusting wheel -22- points torwards the front of the car.
- Hook the return spring into the brake shoes.
- Pull the bottom of the brake shoes apart, fitting them over the rear axle shaft flange and hooking it into the expander.
- Refit the spring with a tool through a threaded hole into the brake shoe, compress slightly, turn it by 90° thus hooking it into the backplate. Check the spring is correctly positioned.
- Hook in the spring of the other brake shoe.

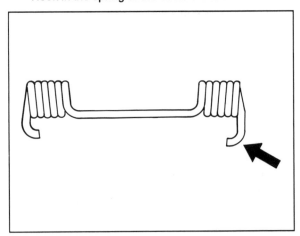

- Hook the return spring into the brake shoes by the small tang. Hook the large tang -arrow- into the other brake shoes with a screwdriver.
- Refit the rear brake disc.
- Adjust the handbrake.

Hand brake - adjustment

The hand brake must be adjusted if it requires applying by more than 5 notches to hold the vehicle.

- Unscrew one bolt of both back wheels.
- Put the back of the vehicle on blocks.
- If a cable control was refitted, unscrew the adjusting screw at the back of the chassis floor (brake equaliser), thus relaxing the brake cable control. If the parking brake is only to be adjusted, do not turn the adjusting screw.

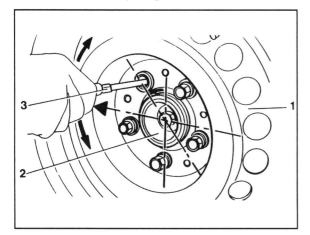

- Turn the wheel so that the bolt hole points about 45° to the rear top, see illustration.

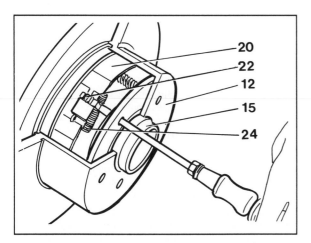

- Turn the adjusting wheel -22- of the adjusting device with a screwdriver, size 4,5mm, through the thread hole, until the wheel can no longer be turned by hand (with the handbrake loose). Always adjust the wheel by hand; the adjusting wheel of the adjusting device has 15 teeth.

Adjusting direction: Left wheel -from bottom to top; right wheel -from top to bottom.

- Now turn the adjuster back again by 2-3 teeth until the wheel can be turned without the brake shoes binding.
- Adjust the adjusting wheel -22- of the other wheel in the same way.
- When loose, turn the adjusting screw of the brake equaliser until the brake cables are tight.
  Caution: The lug of the adjusting screw must always be vertical.
- Apply the hand brake several times.
- Now check whether the back wheel is easy to turn when the hand brake is released. If the hand brake is now applied by one notch a slight brake action should be felt. If not, repeat the adjustment.

- Refit the wheel bolts, lower the vehicle and tighten the bolts to 110 N.m.

The ABS system

On option, the Mercedes can be fitted with an ABS (anti-lock braking system). Subsequent fitting of the ABS is not possible.

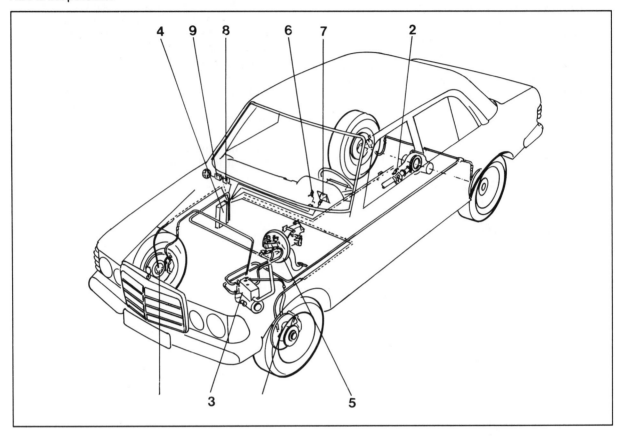

The anti-lock system consists of the following parts:
1 - Rotation speed sensor for the front wheels
2 - Rotation speed sensor for the rear axle
3 - Hydraulic unit
4 - Electronic control device
5 - Brake servo
6 - Steering lock
7 - ABS control lamp
8 - Excess voltage protector
9 - Relay

The anti-lock braking system (ABS) prevents the wheels from locking when braking sharply. This shortens the braking distance since the positive control between the wheels and road is better if the wheels still turn slightly. The vehicle also remains controllable during sharp braking.

The ABS is operative as soon as the ignition is switched on and a speed of 5 - 7km is reached. It regulates all brake processes in the locking range as soon as a speed of 12km has been exceeded.

The wheel speed is measured by the rotational speed sensors, two for the front wheels and one for the rear axle. By the signals of the various rotational speed sensors, the electronic control device calculates a mean speed, which is more or less in accordance with the vehicle speed. By comparing the wheel speed of a single wheel, and the average speed of all wheels, the control device recognises any skidding condition of each wheel, and can determine when a wheel is close to locking.

As soon as a wheel shows a tendency to lock and the brake fluid pressure in the brake caliper is then too high in relation to the road holding capacity of the wheels, the hydraulic system keeps the fluid pressure constant due to signals from the control system. This means the pressure in the brake caliper does not increase, even if the brake pedal is compressed more. If there is still a locking tendency, a release valve opens, lowering the fluid pressure until the wheel is once again accelerated slightly, at which point the pressure is again kept constant.

If the wheel speeds up beyond a certain value, the pressure is again increased by the hydraulic system, but not beyond the overall brake system pressure.

When braking sharply this process repeats itself until the brake pedal is lifted, or until shortly before the vehicle stops (5-7km/h).

A safety switch in the electronic control device ensures that the ABS switches itself off in case of a defect (e.g. fractured cable) or if the operating voltage (battery voltage below 10,5 volt) is too low. In this case the ABS control lamp lights up on the dashboard while driving. The original brake system remains operational. When braking the vehicle reacts as though an ABS was not fitted.

The hydraulic unit consists of the rear supply pump as well as 3 magnetic valves, one for each front wheel brake and one for the back wheel brakes.

Pressure build-up: The inlet valve in the magnetic valve is open. The fluid pressure in the brake caliper can rise to the value required by the master brake cylinder.

Maintaining constant pressure: The release and inlet valves in the magnetic valve are closed. The fluid pressure in the brake caliper does not change, even if the pressure between the master brake cylinder and the magnetic valve increases.

Pressure unloading: The release valve in the magnetic valve is open. Brake fluid flows into the rear supply pump via a storage unit, which pumps the fluid back into the master brake cylinder against the available pressure.

This is necessary so that the brake fluid can not be forced out of the master brake cylinder. The pump action is clearly noticeable by the pulsating of the brake pedal. The pump sounds are dampened by one damper for each brake circuit.

If the ABS control light lights up while driving, this indicates that the ABS has switched itself off.

- Switch off the engine and start it again.
- Check the battery voltage. If the voltage is below 10,5, recharge the battery.

Caution:

If the ABS control lamp lights up at the beginning of a trip then goes off a little later this means that the battery voltage was initially too low, but was increased by loading via the generator.

- Put the vehicle on blocks, remove the front wheels. Check the electrical leads for external damage (worn through).
- Further tests of the ABS should be carried through by a workshop.

Brake system maintenance

Brake fluid level/warning light testing

The reservoir -2- for the brake fluid is in the engine compartment. The cap -4- has a vent hole which must **not** be blocked.

The container is see-through, so that the brake fluid level can be checked at any time. The fluid level, with the cap closed, should not be above the "max." mark or below the "min." mark.

- Only refill with brake fluid according to DOT 4.

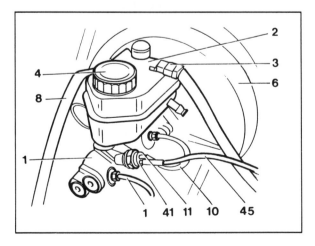

- Due to the wearing of the disc brake pads, the brake fluid level falls slightly. This is normal.
- If the brake fluid level falls rapidly in a short space of time, this indicates brake fluid loss.
- The leak must immediately be located. Normally it is caused by worn seals in the wheel brake cylinders. The testing of the system should be carried out by a workshop.

Warning lamp testing

- Switch on the ignition, release hand brake.
- Press the warning contact -arrow- down.
- A helper checks whether the warning lamp lights up. If not, test the electrical supply according to the current circuit diagram.
- The contact inserts cannot be removed. If necessary replace the reservoir.

Other illustrated parts:
1 - Master brake cylinder
3 - Plug of brake fluid level warning lamp
6 - Brake servo
8 - Vacuum line
10 - Brake line
11 - Brake line
41 - Switch for PDW*
42 - Pin
45 - Vacuum line of PDW*

* PDW = Pressure Difference Warning lamp. The PDW lights up if there is a pressure difference greater than 12,5 + 2,5 bar between the two brake circuits.

Disc pad thickness testing

If the **front** disc pads are worn out, a warning lamp lights up on the dashboard. In this case urgently replace the front disc pads.

- Loosen the wheel bolts.

- Put the vehicle on blocks, remove the wheels.

- Test the pad thickness with a vernier caliper -without the metal back plate.

Thickness	Front	Rear
Disc brake new	13mm	10,5mm
Wear limit	2mm	2mm
Metal back plate	4,5mm	5mm

If the wear is reached, replace the disc brake pads. Always replace all pads on one axle.

Caution:

If the disc pads have worn through to the back plate, this could lead to damage of the brake caliper, as the rib between the washer slot and dust cover brakes off and the brake caliper leaks.

Hint: As a rule of thumb 1mm disc brake pad equals at least 1000 km. This is under unfavorable conditions. Normally the pads last a lot longer. If the disc pad has a 4mm thickness (without the back plate), the disc brakes are good for at least another 2000 km.

Brake disc thickness testing

- Loosen the wheel nuts.

- Put the vehicle on blocks

- Remove the wheel.

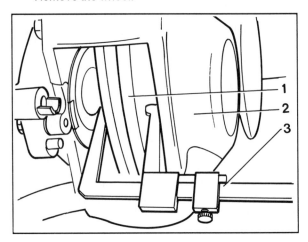

- Measure the brake disc thickness. Workshops use a special gauge -035-, because an edge forms when the disc is worn. The brake disc can be measured with a vernier caliper, but a 3mm pad must be inserted to both sides of the brake disc (or 2 coins). To get the correct thickness the 6mm must then be subtracted from the reading.

Thickness	Front	Rear
Disc brake new	12,6mm	10,0mm
Wear limit	11,1mm	8,6mm
Metal back plate	10,6mm	8,3mm

- If the minimum thickness is reached, new brake pads must be fitted.

- If the wear limit is reached, replace the brake disc.

- In case of large cracks or grooves,deeper than 0,5mm, replace the brake discs.

Visual checking of the brake lines

The brake lines should be checked every 20 000 km.

- Put the vehicle on blocks, see page 244.

- Clean the brake lines with a degreaser.

Caution:

The brake lines are covered with a plastic coating to prevent corrosion. If this coating is damaged, they could corrode. For this reason brake lines must not be cleaned with a wire brush, glass cloth or screwdriver.

- Check the brake lines from the master brake cylinder to the individual wheel brake cylinders. The brake master cylinder is in the engine compartment under the brake fluid reservoir.

- Brake lines may not be twisted, or squashed. No rust or scouring should be visible. If so, replace the line to the next joint.

- Brake hoses connect the brake lines to the wheel brake cylinders at the moveable parts of the vehicle. They consist of high pressure resistent material, but can become porous with time, distort or be cut by sharp objects. In such a case, they must be replaced immediately.

- Bend the brake lines from side to side to determine damage. The lines must not be twisted, take note of the coloured identification line!

- Turn the steering wheel totally to the right and left. The brake hoses must not touch any vehicle parts at any time.

- Check that the connections of the brake lines and hoses are not moist at any point.

Caution:

If the reservoir and seals are moist from leaking brake fluid, this does not necessarily indicate a defective master brake cylinder. The brake fluid would probably leak through the vent hole of the cap or the cap seal.

Brake fluid changing

The brake fluid absorbs moisture from the air through the pores of the brake hoses as well as the vent hole of the reservoir. Due to this the boiling point of the brake fluid is lowered with time. If the brake is taxed severely, steam bubbles could form in the brake lines, severely impairing the brake system.

The brake fluid should be renewed once a year, in spring if possible.

- Take note of the safety measures when dealing with brake fluid, see page 164.

- Suck brake fluid out of the brake fluid container with a syringe to a level of about 10mm.

Caution:

Do not totally empty the container or air will get into the brake system.

- Fill the storage container with **new** brake fluid to the "maximum" mark.

- Push a clean tube onto the bleed valve of the left rear brake caliper, put a suitable container underneath.

- Open the bleed valve, pumping out the old brake fluid by pumping the brake pedal about 10 times. Make sure that the bleed tube is always below the surface of the fluid.

- Close the bleed valve and fill the storage container with **new** brake fluid.

- Pump the old brake fluid out of the other brake calipers in the same way.

Caution:

The bleeding brake fluid must be clear and bubble free.

Parking brake testing

The hand brake acts on the rear wheels via two drum brakes.

- Put the back of the vehicle on blocks.

- Apply the hand brake to the 2nd notch. Turn both wheels by hand. A brake action should be felt on the back wheels.

- Pull the hand brake out 3-5 notches, the back wheels must now be locked.

- If not, adjust the parking brake.

- Lower the vehicle.

Brake fault diagnosis

Fault	Cause	Solution
No resistance of the brake pedal	Brake pads partially or totally worn.	Replace pads.
	One brake circuit has failed.	Check brake circuits for fluid loss.
Brake pedal can be compressed far and softly	Air in the brake system.	Bleed the system.
	Too little brake fluid in reservoir.	Fill up new brake fluid, bleed brakes.
	Disc pads badly worn, back plate touching spring.	Replace disc pads, using only original Mercedes pads.
	Steam bubble formation. Occurs after heavy stress, e.g. mountain driving.	Change brake fluid, bleed brakes.
Brake action decreases and brake pedal can be fully compressed	Leaking lines.	Tighten line connections or replace lines.
	Damaged piston in master brake cylinder.	Replace piston, if necessary replace master brake cylinder.
	Rubber seal damaged.	Repair brake caliper.
Bad brake action despite heavy foot pressure	Disc pads soiled. Unsuitable disc pad.	Replace disc pads.
	Brake servo defective, vacuum hose leaking.	Test brake servo.
	Leaking washers between servo and master brake cylinder.	Replace washers.
	Brake discs soiled, worn.	Clean brake discs, replace.
	Disc pads worn.	Replace pads.
Brakes pull to one side	Tyre pressure not according to regulation, irregular tyre wear.	Check and correct tyre pressure, Replace worn tyres.
	Disc pads soiled.	Replace disc pads.
	Different disc pads on one axle	Replace disc pads. Use only original Mercedes disc pads.
	Bad disc profile.	Change discs.
Brakes overheat when driving	Brake pistons tight.	Test pistons for ease of movement.
	Dirty brake caliper seats.	Clean seat and guide surfaces of brake calipers.
	Corrosion in the brake caliper cylinders	Replace brake caliper.
	Disc pads worn irregularly.	Replace pads (both wheels).
	Equalising bore in master brake cylinder blocked.	Clean master brake cylinder, have internal parts replaced.
	Brake pistons stuck, brake grinding.	Replace brake caliper.

Fault	Cause	Solution
Brakes rattling	Unsuitable disc pad.	Renew pads, using original Mercedes pads.
	Brake disc corroded in parts.	Meticulously straighten disc with grinding blocks.
	Brake disc has shimmy.	Recondition disc or replace.
	Brake caliper loose.	Tighten brake caliper using new screws.
Disc pads stuck to brake disc, wheels tight when turning by hand	Corrosion in brake caliper cylinders.	Recondition brake caliper.
Brake squeaking	Often to be found in atmospheric influences (humidity).	Do nothing, if vehicle squeaked after standing for long period in high humidity then stops after brakes applied a few times.
	Unsuitable disc pad.	Replace pads using original Mercedes pads.
	Brake disc not running parallel to brake caliper.	Check seating surfaces of brake caliper.
	Dirty shafts in brake caliper.	Clean brake caliper.
Irregular disc wear	Unsuitable disc pad.	Replace disc pad only using original Mercedes pads.
	Dirty brake caliper.	Clean brake caliper pistons.
	Piston stuck.	Test piston position.
	Brake system leaking.	Check seals of brake system.
Wedge shaped disc pad wear	Brake disc not running parallel to brake caliper.	Check seating faces of brake caliper.
	Corrosion in brake caliper.	Remove corrosion.
	Pistons not working properly.	Check piston position (piston ring).
Brake pulsates	ABS working.	Normal, no solution.
	Shimmy or brake disc too thick.	Check runout of disc and thickness, recondition or replace disc.
	Brake disc not running parallel to brake caliper.	Check seating face of brake caliper.
Brake pedal falls down slowly when applying	Master brake cylinder defective.	Repair or replace master brake cylinder.

WHEELS AND TYRES

The Mercedes model 123 can be fitted with various wheels and tyres. Only wheels with a disc depth of 30 mm at a rim diameter of 14 inches and 35 mm with 15 inch wheels are allowed. The disc depth is the measurement from the rim centre to the contact surface of the wheel bowl to the brake disc.

Wheel and tyre measurements

Variants	Type	Wheel	Summer tyres	Winter tyres
Sedan and Coupe Standard	200, 230 till 6.80 250 (129UP) till 8.79	5,5J x 14H2	175R 14 88 S	175R 14 88 QM+S
	250 (140UP) till 8.81		175R 14 88 H	
	230C 250 (140UP) since 9.81 280,280C 280E, 280CE	6J x 14H2	195/70R 14 90 H[1]	195/70R 14 90 QM+S[1] or 195/70R 14 90 TM+S
	200D, 220D 240D, 300D	5,5J x 14H2	175R 14 88 S	175R 14 88 QM+S
	200 since 7.80	5,5J x 14H2	175R14 88 S	175R 14 88 QM+S
	230E since 7.80		175R14 88 H	
	230CE	6J x 14H2	195/70R 14 90 H	195/70R 14 90 QM+S or 195/70R 14 90 TM+S
T-Model Standard allowed rear axle load 1150/1155kg or 1195/1200kg	200T 230T 240TD 300TD 300TD Turbo diesel	6J x 14H2	195/70R 14 90 S[2]	195/70R 14 90QM+S[2] or 195/70R 14 90TM+S
	230TE 250T 250TE		195/70R 14 90 H[2]	
T-Model with higher loading or stronger springs. Rear axle load up to 1295/1300kg	200T, 230T 230TE, 250T 240TD, 300TD 300TD Turbo diesel	5,5J x 15H2	185R 15 93 H	185R 15 93 QM+S
Special fittings	250 till 8.81 230E	6J x 14H2[3]	195/70R 14 90 H[1]	195/70R 14 90QM+S[1] or 195/70R 14 90TM+S
	200, 230 till 6.80 200 since 7.80 200D, 220D, 240D, 300D		195/70R 14 90 S[1]	

[1] Tyres until 1979 have the carrying capacity no 89.
[2] In vehicles with allowed rear axle load 1150/1155kg tyres with carrying capacity no. 89 also applies.
[3] The wheels series 5,5 x 14H2 may not be used.

Disc wheel descriptions

Example:

6 = Rim width in inches
J = Identification symbol for height and contour of rim flange
X = Identification of single part drop base rim
15 = Rim diameter in inches
H2 = Rim profile at inner and outer side with hump shoulder
ET30 = Disc depth 30mm

Tyre descriptions

Example:

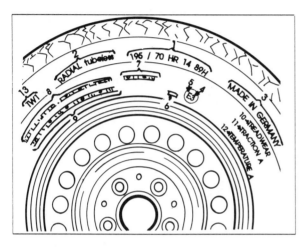

1 - Tyre description

195 = Tyre breadth in mm
/70 = Relationship height: breadth (the height of the tyre cross section equals 70% of the breadth).

If the cross section relationship is not indicated (e.g. 175 SR 14) then the height-breadth relationship is "normal". In radial tyres this is 82%.

H = Speed classification, H: up to 210 km/h, V: above 210 km/h (is not always indicated in new tyres, except in VR tyres).

R = Radial construction (=radial tyres).
14 = Rim diameter in inches.
89 = Carrying capacity identification number.
H = Identification for allowed maximum speed.

The speed identification number is normally found after the carrying capacity number.

Speed identification number

Identification letter	Allowed maximum speed
M	130 km/h
N	140 km/h
P	150 km/h
O	160 km/h
R	170 km/h
S	180 km/h
T	190 km/h
U	200 km/h
H	210 km/h
V	over 210 km/h

2 - Tyre auxiliary descriptions

RADIAL	=	radial tyres
tubeless	=	tubeless tyre
tube type	=	tube tyre

3 - Indication of the production country

4 - Country identification number
1 - Germany, 2 - France, 3 - Italy

5 - European identification number

E - Europe

6 - Date of production

Production date = 37. production week 1979

Caution:

The numbers 7 to 13 apply to identification specifications of tyres for the USA.

7 - Permission identification number

DOT = Department of Transportation (US Traffic Ministry)
XT = Manufacturer code
J9 = Tyre size
XNC = Tyre type

8 - Tyre substructure

9 - Maximum wheel load/maximum filling pressure

10 - Identification for profile wear

11 - Identification for skid resistance

12 - Identification for temperature stress

13 - TWI The tyre has a tread wear indicator (TWI). This consists of a 1,6mm high bumps on the base of the profile. When the wear limit is reached, they are seen as transverse lines in the tyre tread.

Changing the tyres

It is not desirable to change the rotation direction of the tyres when changing them.

A torque wrench should always be used to tighten the wheel bolts. This ensures that the wheel bolts are tightened equally.

- Before removing, mark the position of the wheel to the hub with chalk, so that it can be refitted in the same position.

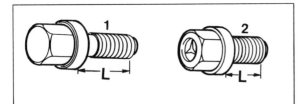

Caution:

Bolts -1- (length L = 29,5mm) only for alloy wheels, bolts -2- (length L = 21mm) only for steel wheels. The original bolts have a Mercedes star imprinted on the bolt head and these are the only bolts to use. If alloy rims are mounted later and a disc wheel is kept as a spare wheel the appropriate bolts should be kept in the toolbox.

- Alloy rims are protected against corrosion by a clear varnish coating. When changing a wheel take care not to damage this coating, touch up with clear varnish if this does happen.

- As protection against rust, grease the centering seat of the wheel at the front and back of the wheel hubs with roller bearing grease every time a wheel is changed.

- Clean dirty bolts. Replace bolts if the thread is damaged or the ball seat of the bolt head is corroded.

Caution:

The resting surface between the front wheel hub or the rear axle shaft flange as well as the wheel and bolt head must be carefully cleaned with a wire brush or a glass cloth.

- Check the thread of the front wheel hub or the rear axle shaft flange for ease of movement. If necessary carefully recut the thread.

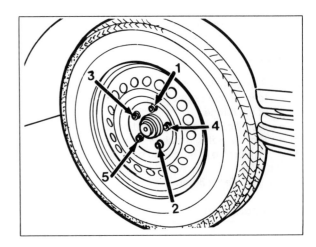

- Fit the wheel bolts **without** any lubricant (oil, grease) and tighten crosswise in several stages.

Caution:

By tightening the bolts on one side or to different torques, the wheel or the wheel hub could be distorted. **The tightening torque for all wheel bolts is 110 N.m.** In the case of new disc wheels, retighten the wheel bolts to the specified torque after driving 100 to 500 km.

Running in tyres

New tyres have a particularly smooth surface due to the production process, so new tyres must be worn in. During the wearing in phase the tyres become rougher through the wearing process.

For the first 300 km one should drive carefully with new tyres, particularly on wet surfaces.

Wheel storage

- Wheels should be stored in a cool, dark and draught-free place. They should not come into contact with grease or oil.

- Store tyres lying flat or hang then against a wall.

- Before removing wheels for storage, increase the prescribed tyre pressure by about 30 - 50 kPa (0,3 - 0,5 bar).

Balancing the wheels

The wheels are balanced in the factory. This is necessary to equalise differences in weight and material distribution.

Unbalanced wheels are noticed by fluttering and tramping characteristics. The steering wheel also starts to shake at higher speeds.

Generally this shaking only occurs at a certain speed then disappears again at a lower and higher speed.

These unbalanced characteristics can later lead to damage of the axle joints, steering gear and shock absorber.

Have the wheels balanced every 20 000 km and after repairs to the wheels, since wear and repairs change the weight and material distribution.

Tyre pressure in kPa (bar)

Model	Speeds up to 160 km/h		Speeds above 160 km/h	
	front	back	front	back
Sedan HL* to 1200kg	200(2,0) 250(2,5)	220(2,2) 300(3,0)	230(2,3) 250(2,5)	250(2,5) 300(3,0)
Long Sedan	220(2,2)	260(2,6)	220(2,2)	260(2,6)
T-Model				
Normal load	200(2,0)	220(2,2)	230(2,3)	250(2,5)
HL* to 1155kg	200(2,0)	250(2,5)	230(2,3)	280(2,8)
HL* to 1200kg	200(2,0)	270(2,7)	230(2,3)	300(3,0)
HL* to 1300kg	230(2,3)	320(3,2)	230(2,3)	320(3,2)

*) HL   =   Allowed rear axle load; indicated in the vehicle papers and on the type sign on the front transverse carrier.

- Tyre pressure for the **spare wheel** of the sedan:250kPa(2,5 bar). For the other models, fill the spare wheel to the maximum filling pressure of the back wheel tyres.

- All the inflation figures refer to cold wheels. The approximately 20 to 40 kPa (0,2 to 0,4 bar) higher inflation which occurs when warm (while driving) must not be reduced.

- For a sporty driving style it is recommended to increase the inflation of the back and front wheels by around 20 kPa (0,2bar).

Tyre maintenance

Tyre pressure - checking

- Only do this test on cold tyres.
- Check the tyre pressure once a month as well as when normal maintenance work is carried out.
- The pressure should be checked before longer highway trips, as this causes the most temperature stress for the tyres.

Tyre profile testing

The tyres of balanced wheels wear fairly evenly on all the running surfaces, if the correct tyre pressure, wheel adjustment and shock absorber function is maintained. No definite prediction can be made as to the duration of a tyre, since this depends on various factors:

- Road surface

- Tyre pressure

- Driving style

- Weather

In particular, sporty driving, fast acceleration and abrupt braking wear the tyres faster.

Caution:

The law requires that tyres may only be driven down to a profile depth of 1,6mm, this means across the entire tread of the tyre. It is however recommended that the tyres be replaced at a profile of 2mm.

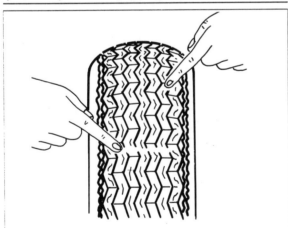

If the lawful minimum profile depth is nearly reached, this means, if the 1,6mm tread indicators around the tyre have no more profile, the tyres must be replaced.

Caution:

Inspect the tyres for cuts, determining their depth with a small screwdriver. If the cuts reach to the carcass, the steel belts will corrode from water entering. The tread could come apart from the carcass, the tyre will burst. So for safety reasons the tyres should be replaced.

Valve testing

- Unscrew the protection cap of the valve.

- Put a little saliva onto the valve. If a bubble forms, tighten the valve with the turned protection cap.

Caution:

To tighten the valve a metal protection cap must be used. These are available from service stations.

- Again test the valve. If a bubble forms again or the valve cannot be tightened any further, replace the valve.

- Always tighten the protection cap.

Faulty tyre wear

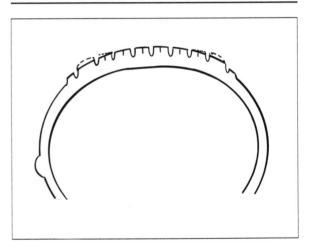

- On the front tyres it is normal for the wear to be higher at the tyre shoulders than the tread centre, but due to the road tendency, the wear of the tyre shoulder on the road centre side (right wheel: inside, left wheel: outside).

- Irregular tyre wear is normally the result of too little or too much tyre pressure, and can be traced back to faults in the wheel adjustment or balancing as well as defective shock absorbers or rims.

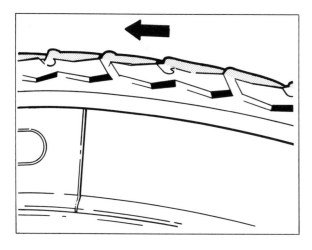

- Saw tooth shaped wear of the profile can generally be traced back to overloading of the vehicle.

- Test the pressure of the tyres at least every four weeks, making sure they have the correct pressure at all times.
- Test the tyre pressure in cold tyres only. The tyre pressure increases with increased temperature while driving, and it is incorrect to let air out of heated tires.

- If the tyre pressure is too high, the central tread is worn down more quickly, since the tyres are more rounded due to the high pressure.

- If the pressure is too low, the tread rests more on the tyre shoulders, while the centre caves in. So the tyre shoulders are worn more quickly.

- Incorrect wheel adjustment and unbalanced tyres cause very disctinctive wear patterns, which are pointed out in the fault diagnosis.

Fault diagnosis tyres

Wear	Cause
Increased tyre wear on both edges of the tread	Tyre pressure too low
Increased tyre wear in the centre of the tread over the whole circumference	Tyre pressure too high
Localised flattening of profile	Static and dynamic imbalance of the wheel. Possibly shimmy of rim too large, excess play in suspension
Localised flattening in the centre of the profile	Static imbalance of the wheel. Possibly due to excessive radial deviation
Increased wear in several parts in the centre of the tread	Brake lock tracks from locking the wheels
Scaly or saw tooth shaped wear of the profile. In severe cases, canvas cracks can be seen on the outside	Overloading of the vehicle. Check the inside of the tyres for canvas cracks
Rubber tongues on the sides of the profile. Tyre rubbing.	Incorrect wheel adjustment. Check the condition of the shock absorbers at the rear wheels
Burr formation on one profile side of the front wheel	Incorrect track alignment. Tyre rubbing. Frequent driving on bumpy roads. Taking curves too fast
Increased wear on the inner or outer side of the tyres	Too little or too much wheel toe-in or out
Blow cracks in the tyre casing. Can initially only be seen on the inside of the tyres	Driving over sharp stones, railway crossings and similar at high speeds
One sided worn tread	Check the camber adjustment

THE BODYWORK

The bodywork of the Mercedes is self-supporting. The platform unit with floor, side panels, roof and rear mudguards are welded together. Severe damage to the chassis can thus only be repaired by a specialist workshop.

The bonnet, boot, doors and the front mudguards are screwed on and are easily replaced.When refitting,the correct air gap measurements are to be observed, otherwise for example the door will rattle or increased wind noises could occur while driving.

The air gap must in any case be parallel, this means, that distance between the chassis parts must be equally large for the entire gap. Deviations of up to 0,5mm are allowed. The measurements in the illustration are given in millimeters, with a tolerance of 0,5mm.

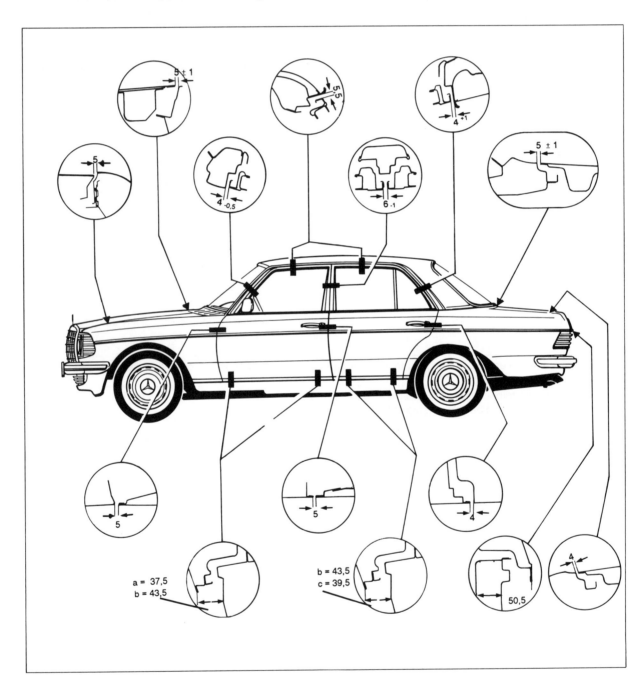

Front bumper removal and refitting

Removal

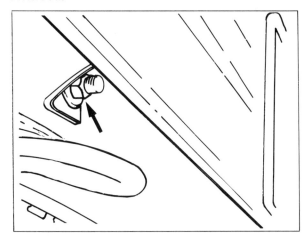

- Unscrew the nut -arrow- from the left and right side brackets.

- Pull the bumper and bracket out towards the front.

Refitting

- Cover the rubber side cover with soapy water, so that the cover glides more easily when refitting.

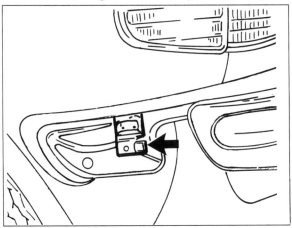

- Horizontally fit the bumper with a helper and push it sideways into the guide brackets of the mudguard.

- Refit the nuts of the bumper brackets and tighten.

Rubber cover - removal and refitting

Removal

- Remove the bumper.

- **Until 9/76:** Remove the headlights, see page 230. Remove the 3 screws from the headlight recess.

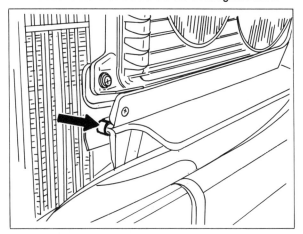

- **Since 10/76:** Unclip the securing clip -arrow- with a screwdriver and unscrew the 2 screws from underneath. The headlights need not be removed.

- Depending on the model, remove the screw below the headlight recess.

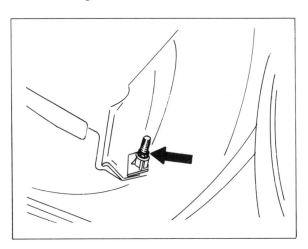

- Remove the securing nut -arrow- from inside the wheel arch.

- Remove the rubber cover forwards.

Refitting

- Refit the rubber cover and tighten.

- If removed, refit the tin clamp or the headlights, see page 230.

- Refit the bumper.

Rear bumper - removal and refitting

Removal

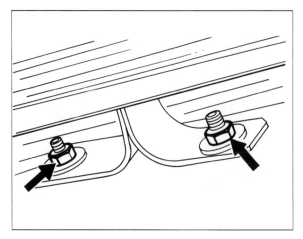

- Remove the securing nuts -arrows- from the left and right brackets.

- **T-Model:** Remove the lens of the reverse lights, by unscrewing the 2 phillips screws. Remove the reflectors out of the light housing, pull off the two electrical cables and put the reflectors aside.

- Remove the bumper and its bracket backwards.

Refitting

- Coat the rubber side covers with soapy water so that the cover glides more easily when refitting.

- Horizontally fit the bumper with a helper and push it sideways into the guide brackets of the mudguard.

- Refit the bumper bracket nuts and tighten them.

- **T-Model:** Connect the reverse lights and fog light, then refit them into the light housing. Tighten the reverse light lens.

Mudguards -removal and refitting

Caution:

Vehicles since 12/81 are fitted with plastic inner mudguards, which facilitates the removal and refitting. Until 11/81 the mudguards are sprayed with PVC protector. In this case the mudguards must be heated up with a blow drier at the joins, so that the protector softens and the mudguard can be loosened.

Removal

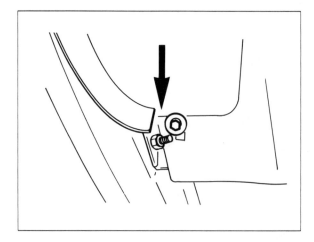

- Unscrew the screw -arrow- of the inner mudguard.

- Remove the front bumper.

- Remove the headlights, see page 230.

- Remove the rubber cover.

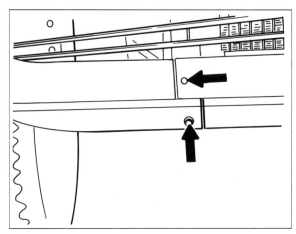

- Remove the 2 screws -arrows- from the bottom.

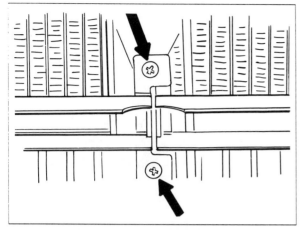

- Undo the 2 screws -arrows- of the air venting grate, swing the appropriate grate half downwards and remove it to the vehicle centre.

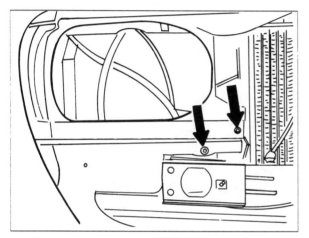

- Remove the 2 screws -arrows-.

- Remove one screw on the outer side of the headlight housing.

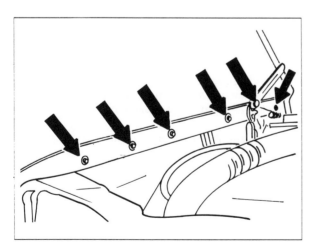

- Unscrew the 6 screws -arrow- on the mudguard. Remove the rubber stop of the bonnet.

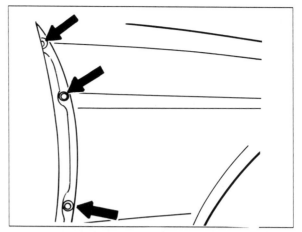

- Open the door and carefully unscrew the 3 screws -arrows- of the front panel wall with an allen key. Stick tape around the working area so as not to damage the paint.

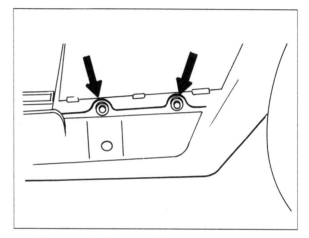

- Unscrew the 2 screws below at the side member.

- Loosen the mudguards from the side member with a plastic or wooden wedge.

Caution:

For vehicles up to 11/81, the following are also to be carried out:

- Remove the mud flap.

- Slightly heat the connecting surface of the mud guard to the headlight housing with a blow drier and loosen the mudguards in this area. **Caution:** If other devices such as a blow torch are used, the electrical leads in the engine block must be covered with an asbestos blanket.

- Slowly and evenly heat the entire rebate of the mudguard in the area of the screws.

- With a sharp knife, cut the softened PVC. The PVC must be cut through from the front corner of the rebate to the end of the layering.

- Lift off the mudguard, beginning at the front and pulling it out forwards.

Refitting

- Paint the inner part of the mudguard liberally with PVC protector.

- Check that the rubber seal of the inner mudguard is secure and without damage, replacing if necessary.

- Fit a new seal to the rebate of the wheel arch. Melt the screw holes out of the support with hot wire, since the support can otherwise turn when the screws are being refitted.

- Position and align the mudguard. The mudguards must be flush with the front door or jut out to a maximum of 1mm. Check the air gap between the mudguard and closed bonnet as well as the front door, see page 182.

- Refit all securing screws and tighten in stages.

- Again check the position of the mudguard.

- Spray the connecting points of the mudguard with PVC protector.

- Refit the headlights, see page 230.

- Adjust both buffers of the bonnet so that they are flush with the inner side of the mudguard.

- Refit the mud flap and seal it.

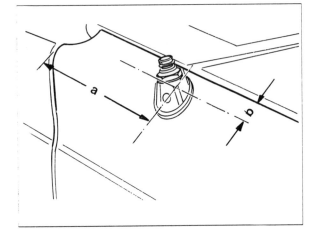

- Attach the radiator grill and tighten it with the 2 screws.

- Refit the rubber cover.

- Refit the front bumper.

- Have the headlights adjusted.

- If the aerial was fitted to the front wing, make a hole centred on the dimensions a - 138 mm b - 24 mm. When drilling the bodywork, take care not to damage the surrounding paintwork, see page 215.

Radiator grill removal and refitting

Removal

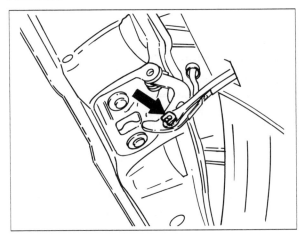

- Open the bonnet and remove the release handle by undoing the securing clip -arrow- with a screwdriver and removing the bolt.

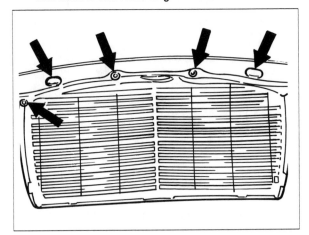

- Remove the 6 screws -arrows- and the radiator lining.

- Remove the 2 rubber stops.

- Undo the left and right securing clips of the radiator grill with a screwdriver. **Caution:** The clips are sprung and easily jump off.

- Unscrew the phillips screw from the bottom centre of the radiator lining.

- Push out the 2 securing clips from the front of the top centre of the radiator grill.

- Remove the grill downwards out of the radiator surround.

Refitting

- Refit the radiator grill into the radiator surround from the bottom, clicking it into the 2 clips.

- Tighten the screw in the bottom centre of the radiator grill.

- Refit the securing side clips. Tighten the 2 rubber buffers.

- Refit the radiator lining and tighten it. Check that the support is stuck to the bonnet.

- Position the release handle, insert the bolt and secure it with the clip.

Mercedes star - removal and refitting

Removal

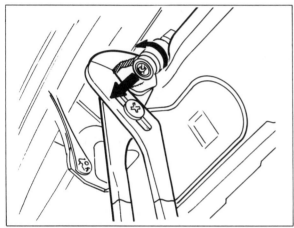

- Pull the spring retainer downwards with pipe grips, turn it to the left about 90°.

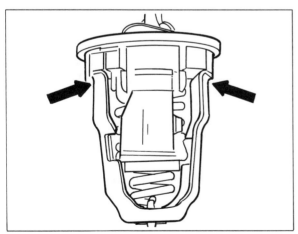

- Click the ends of the retainer into the provided slots -arrows-.

- Now remove the Mercedes star upwards out of the radiator grill.

Refitting

- Insert the Mercedes star from the top and turn the spring retainer to the right by 90°.

Bonnet cable - removal and refitting

Removal

- Remove the cover under the dashboard, see page 196.

- Remove the 2 screws for the handle of the bonnet release catch from the interior.

- Unhook the bonnet cable from the catch.

- Attach a piece of string to the bonnet cable, to facilitate refitting the new cable.

- Remove the cable from the retainer of the wheel arch and unclip it at the radiator bracket.

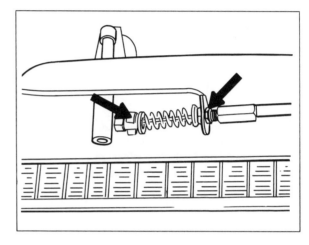

- Loosen the lock nut and press out the bolts from the bottom of the bonnet release catch.

- Pull the bonnet cable out forwards.

Refitting

- Hook the bonnet cable into the catch and tighten the lock nut to the bracket.

- Click the bonnet cable under the radiator bracket and pull it into the interior with the string through the retainer of the wheel arch.

- Hook the cable into the handle, tightening it with 2 screws.

- Refit the cover under the dashboard, see page 196.

Door removal and refitting

Caution:

In vehicles with central locking, electrical window lifter or side mirror adjuster, also remove the door lining, loosen the electrical leads and remove the vacuum pipes through the opening on the facing of the door.

Removal

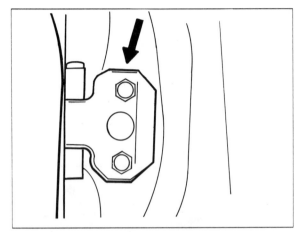

- Mark the position of the door hinges, by going around them with a thumb tack. In this way the old door need not be aligned when refitting.

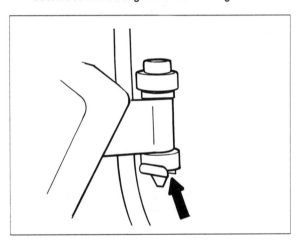

- Prise the lock spring clip off the bolt with a screwdriver, and remove the bolt.
- Support the door at the bottom.

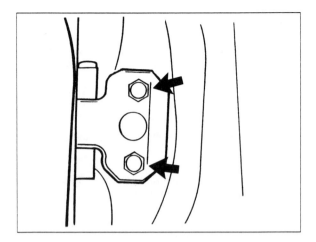

- Remove the 2 securing bolts -arrow- of each hinge and remove the door to the rear.

Refitting

- Position the door and slightly tighten the securing bolts.

- Position the door so that the hinges are aligned to the marks made.

- Tighten the securing bolts, then the bolts of the door retainer.

- If a new door is fitted, adjust it as follows:

Adjusting

- Only slightly tighten the securing bolts of the hinges. The bolts of the door retainers are removed.

- Close the door and position it so that the outer side of the door is flush with the contours of the mudguard. The door may be out by a maximum of 1mm.

- Position the door so that the correct air gap is maintained to all surrounding parts. The air gap must always run parallel. Air gap measurements, see page 182.

- Carefully open the door and tighten the securing bolts of the hinges.

- Check the adjustment of the back door. The surface must be flush with the rear mudguards.

- Adjust the retaining eye so that the outsides of the two doors and the rear mudguard are flush. The front door may stand out to a maximum of 1mm.

- Refit the bolts of the door retainer and secure it with the spring clip.

- Check the ease of movement of the door by opening and closing it several times.

Door handle removal and refitting

Removal

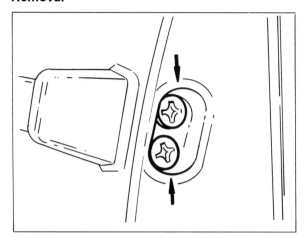

- Lift off the cover of the facing side of the door frame and unscrew the 2 phillips screws.

- Push the door handle forwards, to the front of the car.

- **Until 8/81:** Pull the handle retainers and remove the whole door handle.

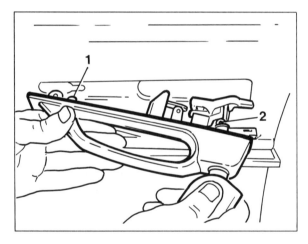

- **Since 9/81:** Put the door key into the lock, turn it about 50° and leave it in this position. Now pull out the door handle.

Caution:

If the door handle cannot be pushed forwards or removed, remove the door covering and sealing foil, then loosen or remove the screw-1-. Be careful not to drop the screw into the door frame. If the key cannot be turned, unscrew the door handle securing screws and pull the handle slightly out of the recess. Drive the pin -2- out of the rotating bar and remove the door handle.

Refitting

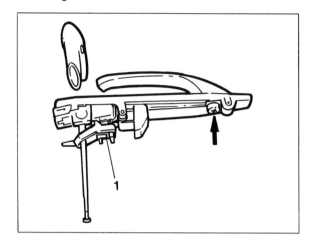

- Tighten the front securing screw -right arrow- slightly.

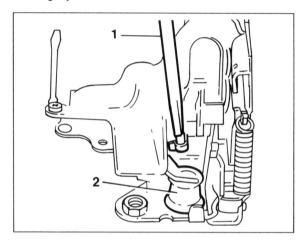

- Insert the door handle into the door recess, pull the handle retainer and fit the handle so that the rotating bar -1- grips the swivel nut. If necessary turn the key by 50° backwards.

- Push the door handle backwards. If this is not possible, remove the handle again and loosen the front securing screw a little.

- Tighten the door handle and check that the handle and lock are working. If necessary remove the Inner door covering and sealing foil and check the position of the retaining bolt.

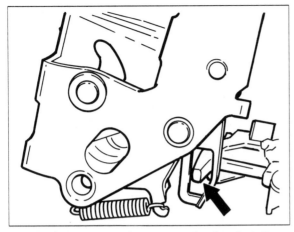

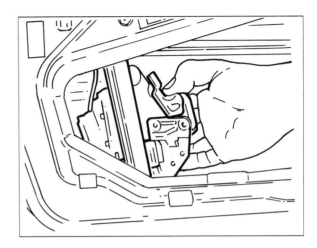

- The lever -arrow- must engage the door lock, the play between the lever and the slot of the lock should be about 1mm. If necessary, adjust the play by turning the hexagonal screw -1 in the illustration at the top of page 189.
- Press the cover into the opening on the facing side of the door.

Door lock removal and refitting

Removal

- Remove the door interior trim.
- Carefully pull off the sealing foil in the top region.
- Remove the pull rod of the inner door control from the securing clip. Unhook it from the door lock.
- Remove the door handle.

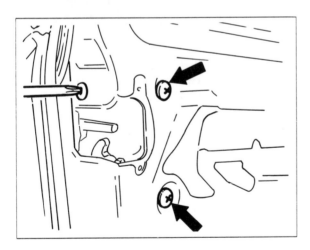

- Unscrew the 4 screws for the door lock.

- Lower the door lock, then swing it forwards past the rear window lifting track, and remove it through the lower opening in the inner door frame.

Refitting

- Refit the door lock with the locking rods.
- Tighten the door lock screws to 8 N.m. **Caution:** First tighten the two screws on the facing side.
- Refit the door handle.
- Rehook the pull rod of the inner door control to the door lock and clip it on with the retaining clip.
- Glue the sealing foil without creases, otherwise there could be draughts in the vehicle. Fix damaged foil with sticky tape.
- Refit the interior trim.

Interior door trim removal and refitting

Removal

- Unscrew the locking knob.
- Unscrew the two screws of the doorlock trim and remove it.
- Wind the window fully down.
- Remove the window winder. **Caution:** There are two different types.

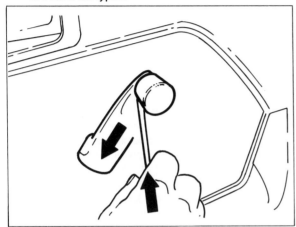

Type 1

- Press the securing clip of the insert in with a small screwdriver. Push the insert downwards in the direction of the arrow and remove it.

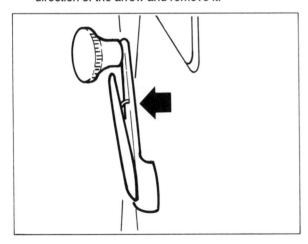

Type 2

- Prise the insert from the front of the window winder with a small screwdriver, pull it towards the knob and unhook it at the slot of the winder axle.
- Remove the window winder from the winder axle, then remove the spacing disc.

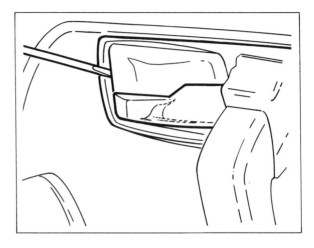

- Lever out the surround of the interior door handle with a small screwdriver.
- Pull the lever of the interior door handle and remove the screw from the surround.

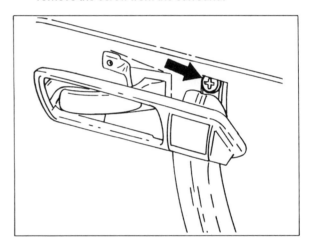

- Pull the surround away from the door and remove the screw -arrow- from the arm rest at the top.
- Remove the 2 screws under the arm rest then the arm rest with the surround.
- Pull the interior trim slightly away from the door frame, and unclip it.

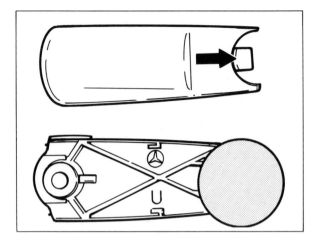

- Lift the door interior trim until the hook can be pulled out of the door frame -arrow-.
- Lift the trim over the locking rod and remove it.
- If necessary, carefully remove the sealing foil. **Caution:** The foil tears easily.

Refitting

Before refitting check the correct positioning of the sealing foil. Fix small tears in the foil with sticky tape; in case of large tears, replace the foil.

- Position the door inner trim over the locking rod, insert the hook into the door frame and carefully press the trim downwards.
- Clip the whole door trim into the door frame.
- Position the arm rest and secure with the 3 screws.
- Pull the door handle and tighten the handle surround. Refit the trim of the surround.
- Refit the spacing disc with its larger diameter facing the door trim.
- Push the window winder onto the winder axle. With the window open, the winder points to the front top.

- Push on the cover of the window winder from the back, making sure that the nose of the cover, rests in the slot of the winder axle. Push the cover forwards until the securing clip -arrow- clicks in. Refit the protective trim, pushing it into the slot until it clips in near the head.
- Wind up the window.
- Refit the trim of the door lock with the two screws.
- Screw in the locking knob.

Window opener - removal and refitting

Removal

- Remove the door trim.
- Carefully remove the sealing foil. **Caution:** The foil tears easily.

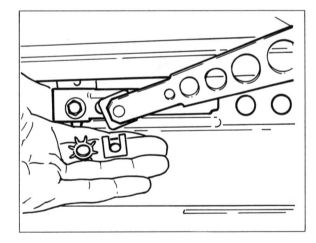

- With the window down, remove the front and back retainers from the opening arms.
- On electric windows, remove the earth cable from the battery.
- Unclip the cable of the electric moror.

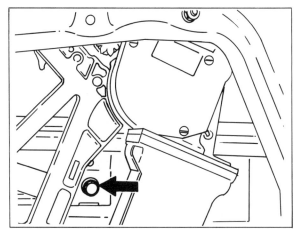

- Remove the screw -arrow- from the front of the window opener rail.

- Remove the back screw -arrow- from the window opener rail.
- Wind the window up or push it up, securing it with a plastic or wooden wedge, to prevent it from falling down.

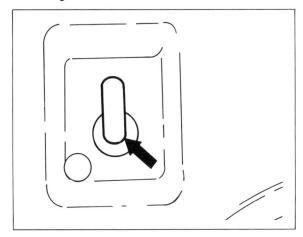

Caution:

Before removing the two back securing screws of the window opener, mark the position of the screws by going around them with a felt tipped pen. This facilitates the adjustment of the window when refitting.

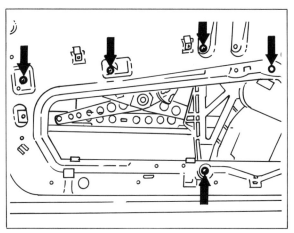

- Remove the 3 securing nuts -right arrows- from the front of the window opener and the 2 screws -left arrows- from the back of the window opener.

- **Manual window opener:** Remove the screws -arrow-.
- Pull the window opener from the guide rail and remove it downwards. Remove the electric window opener complete with the motor.

Refitting

- Refit the window opener into the door from the bottom and tighten all but the back screw.
- Carefully lower the window and insert it into the window opener rail with a sliding block.
- Screw the window opener arms into the opener rail, but do not tighten. The screws are only tightened after the window is adjusted.
- Refit the electrical wires - connect the same coloured wires together. Refit the battery earth cable.
- Adjust the door window.
- Glue on the sealing foil smoothly.

Caution:

The foil must not be damaged and must seal perfectly or there could be a draught in the vehicle.

- Refit the door trim.

Door window adjustment

- Remove the door trim.
- Carefully remove the lower section of the sealing foil. **Caution:** the foil tears very easily.

- Loosen the two screws -arrows- at the back of the window lifter, but do not remove them.
- Loosen one screw each at the back and front of the window lifter rail, but do not remove them.
- Fully wind down the window.
- Push the window lifting rail fully to the back, tightening the screws of the rail in this position.
- Wind up the window to about 5 cm from the top and push it backwards into the guide rail. **Caution:** with the window closed the back edge of the window must rest on the entire length of the guide rail.
- Push the back of the window downwards, tightening the back screw of the window lifter in this position. Now tighten the second screw of the window lifter.
- Wind the window up and down, checking it for ease of movement.
- Glue on the sealing foil smoothly.

Caution:

The foil must not be damaged and must seal properly, otherwise there could be a draught in the vehicle.

- Refit the door trim.

Door window - removal and refitting

Removal

- Remove the window lifter.
- Remove the inner window sealing rail by levering the securing clips and the sealing rail upwards out of the door frame with a plastic wedge.
- Remove the external rear view mirror from the driver door. Pull off the access plate from the inside of the passenger door then unscrew the triangular cover.

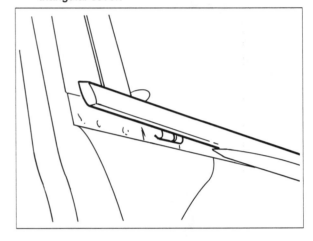

- Pull out the moulding by hand or with a plastic wedge.
- Remove the clips of the outer sealing rail upwards beginning at the back. Remove the sealing rail.
- Remove the front and back screws of the window lifter rail.
- Lift the back of the window, tilt it forwards, lift it upwards to remove it.

Refitting

- Fit the window pane into the guide rail.
- Drive the window lifting rail into the window supporting rail from below.
- Position the front sealing rails accurately and press them into the door frame with the securing clips.
- Clip in the moulding, by first separating the plug cap from the pins and pressing them into the holes. Now fit the moulding.
- Refit the external rear mirror and triangular cover.
- Refit the window lifter and adjust the door window.

Moulding - replacing

The mouldings are attached to the body by plastic
expanding clips.

Removal

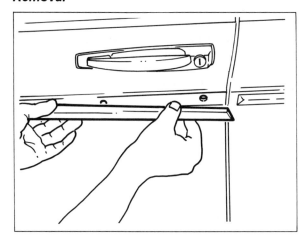

- Pull the mouldings off by hand or with a broad
  plastic wedge **Caution:** One or both ends could
  be screwed on from the inside.

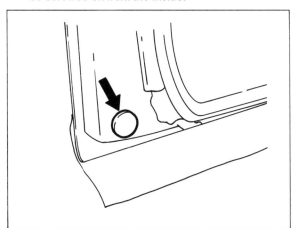

- Example bottom of drivers door: prise out the
  cover -arrow- from the inside of the door. Remove
  the plastic nut behind it.

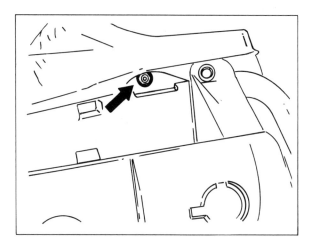

- Example left rear mudguard: Remove the
  securing screw -arrow- from inside the boot.

Refitting

- Generally the sleeves and expanding pins are
  removed together with the moulding, so first lift
  the sleeves from the pins and insert them into the
  corresponding holes of the body.
- Straighten bent mouldings before refitting.
- Now position the moulding with the expanding
  pins aligned to the corresponding hole and clip it
  in. If necessary, hit the expanding pins in by hand
- If removed, refit the securing screw.

External rear view mirror - removal and refitting

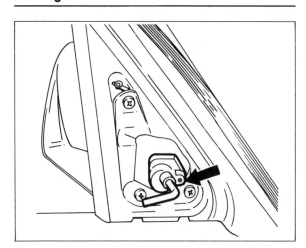

Caution:

If the mirror changes position, remove the lever and
cover, and tighten the screw -arrow- of the adjusting
part.

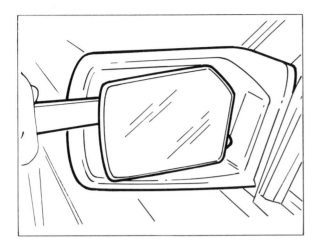

- If only the mirror glass is to be replaced, prise it off backwards with a plastic wedge and remove it towards the outside.
- If removed, hook the mirror glass into the adjusting lever on the left and push the ball head into the receptacle.

Removal

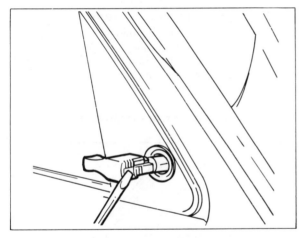

- Remove the handle of the mirror adjuster backwards. First push out the plastic retainer in the direction of the mirror -arrow- with your finger or a small screwdriver, and remove it.
- Pull the top of the cover away from the door frame with your fingers, unclip it, unhook it at the bottom and pull it out towards the top. **Caution:** If using a broad screwdriver, put a paper buffer under the blade, to prevent the paint from being damaged.
- Remove the 3 screws of the mirror foot. Hold the mirror while doing this, so that it does not drop.
- Remove the mirror.

Refitting

- Attach the mirror and tighten the screws.
- Refit the trim over the adjusting lever, hook it into the bottom and clip it into the top. **Caution:** first remove the thin spring leaf retainer from the pin of the triangle and press it into the hole of the door. Otherwise the triangle cannot be clipped in.
- Push on the handle, position the plastic retainer and insert it into the handle.

Under dashboard panel - removal and refitting

Removal

- **Up to 8/79:** Remove one screw each on the front panel and the bottom heater opening.
- Remove the panel downwards out of the control panel.
- **Since 9/79:** Lift off the 3 caps with a small screwdriver.

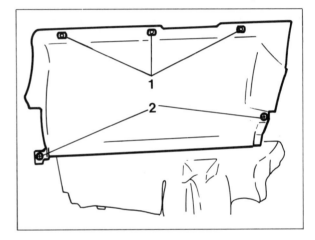

- Remove the 3 phillips screws -1-.
- Turn the plastic clips -2- by 90°, so loosening them, and remove them.
- Remove the panel.

Refitting

- Refit and tighten the panel.
- Refit the plastic clips, turn them by 90°, thus tightening them.
- Hook the panel in at the front, tightening it on the left and right.

Centre consol - removal and refitting

Removal

- Remove both foot mats with the foam rubber pieces.
- Remove the covers of the switches.

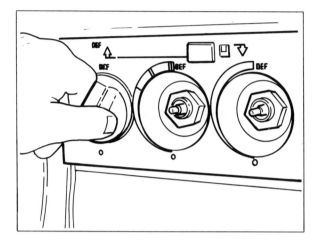

- Pull out the buttons of the fan and heater.

- Remove the 3 nuts, SW24.

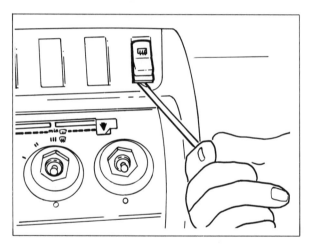

- Lift out the switch for the rear window heating with a small screwdriver.

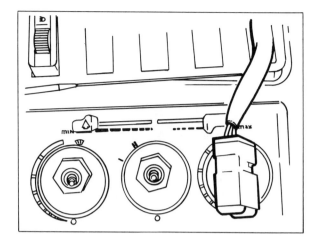

- Unscrew both screws to the left and right of the cover.

- Press the switch up and pull it outward from the bottom and unhook it.

- Unclip the bottom cover or remove the radio, see page 235.

- Remove the knobs of the ventilator control levers.

- Remove the cover of the heater controls. Remove the light wire cable from the back.

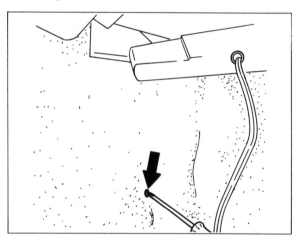

- Remove the screws -arrow- to the left and right of the tunnel.

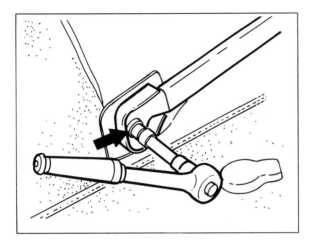

- Remove the bolts -arrow- to the left and right at the back of the seat rail.

- Remove the bolt from the storage compartment with the washer. First remove the insert if present.

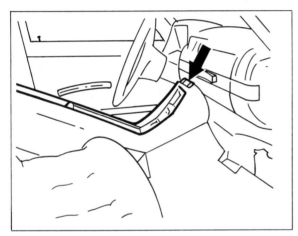

- Lift the centre consol at the back and pull it out of the dashboard, by spreading out the front of the consol.

Refitting

- Refit the consol from the back then tighten the left and right bolts at the front and back.

- Insert the bolt with the washer into the storage container and tighten it.

- Attach the cable to the back of the cover for the heating control and refit the cover.

- Refit the buttons of the ventilator control lever; the left arrow points upwards, the right arrow points downwards.

- Clip in the bottom cover or refit the radio, see page 235.

- Insert the switch cover at the top and press it in at the bottom.

- Remove both the bolts to the left and right of the cover.

- Connect the switch of the rear window heater to its plug and insert it into the cover.
- Tighten the heater switches with the 3 nuts SW 24.

- Refit the knobs of the fan and heater.

- Refit the cover of the gear shift lever.

- Put both foot mats with the foam rubber pieces into the foot space.

Gear shift lever cover - removal and refitting

Removal

- Open the ashtray fully, press down the retaining spring in the middle and remove the insert. Remove the 2 plugs at the back.

- Remove the screws -arrows- in the opening of the ashtray.

- Remove the 2 screws at the front of the cover.

- Unhook the retainer of the gear shift lever from the cover and push it to the top.

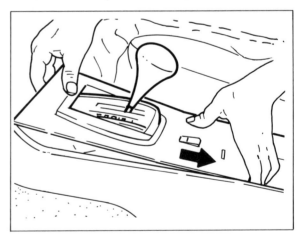

- Slightly lift the front of the cover and press out the hazard light switch from the bottom to the top. Remove the plug of the hazard light.

- Remove the cover backwards out of the centre consol.

Refitting

- Refit the cover so that the securing clips rest in the corresponding openings of the centre consol. Push the cover from the back to the front and click it in.

- Pull down the retainer of the gear shift lever and hook it into the cover.

- Tighten the front of the cover.

- Connect the plug of the hazard light and refit the switch into the cover.

- Refit the cover of the ashtray housing, insert the ashtray and click it into place. First connect the electrical leads.

- If removed, place the carpet into the storage compartment.

Front seat - removal and refitting

Removal

- Push the seat forwards fully and if present, adjust the height adjustment fully upwards.

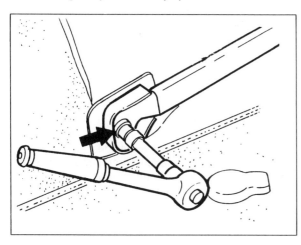

- Unbolt the guide rail and pull it backwards out of the seat fitting.

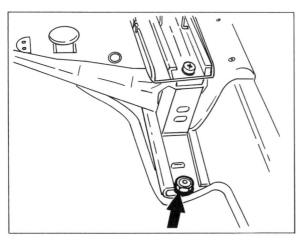

- Remove the 2 bolts -arrow- at the back.

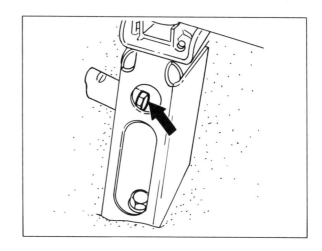

- If there is no height adjustment, remove the additional bolt -arrow-.

- Push the seat fully back and the height adjustment fully down.

- Remove the securing bolts at the front of both seat guide rails.

- Lift out the seat.

Refitting

- Position the seat at the front with the guide rail, and tighten it.

- Put the seat fully forwards and the height adjustment fully up. Tighten the seat at the back. If necessary bolt in the additional bolt -arrow-.

- Insert the guide rail from the back through the opening in the seat fitting, and tighten it at the back. Put the cap onto the bolt head.

Back seat - removal and refitting

Removal

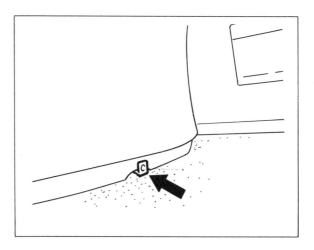

- Press the lock lever -arrow- at the left and right backwards, and lift the front of the back seat.

- Lift the back seat out.

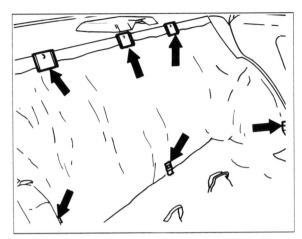

- Remove the securing screws -bottom arrows- from the bottom of the rear seat back rest.

- Pull out the centre arm rest, remove the screw behind it.

- Lift the back rest out of the securing clips -top arrows- and remove it.

Refitting

- Hook the rear seat back rest into the 3 securing clips, place the safety belts over the back rest.

- Tighten the bottom screws of the backrest. Refit the arm rest.

- Refit the rear seat, push it back to the stop and push it into the front locks. First placing the seat belts onto the seat.

The central locking

The Mercedes is available with central locking. This is a system which can be controlled through the locking cylinder or interlocking button of the driver's door. If the passenger door is unlocked, the other doors and the fuel cap remain locked.

Diagram of the central locking

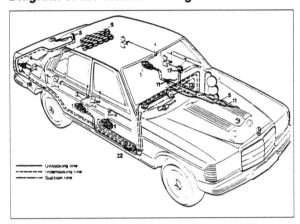

1	-	Vacuum element (driver's and rear doors)
2	-	Control rod (front passenger door)
3	-	Control rod (rear doors)
4	-	Vacuum element (flap for tank filler neck)
5	-	Vacuum element (trunk lid)
6	-	Vacuum supply tank
7	-	Vacuum switch
8	-	Check valve
11	-	Three-way distributor
13	-	Check valve
17	-	Connection
18	-	Compression spring
22	-	Four-way distributor

The central locking works through the vacuum created by a running engine. A vacuum storage tank ensures that the central locking can be used even after the engine has been switched off (about 8 to 10 times).

If the locking knob of the driver door is operated or is locked or unlocked from the outside with a key, the actuating valve in the vacuum switch moves as well. In this way one chamber is impinged the other one vented. According to the key position, the vacuum is transmitted to the various working elements via vacuum leads. The working elements each have a membrane and a control rod which rests in the locking mechanism or flap. Depending on which side of the membrane is under vacuum, the control rod is moved up or down thus locking or unlocking the door or flap. The diagram shows the central locking in locked position.

The various locks can be locked or unlocked mechanically at any time. This applies when the central locking is switched on as well as in cases of a lack of vacuum due to leaks.

BODYWORK MAINTENANCE

Bodywork parts - lubrication

The bonnet, door hinges and external rear mirror (up
to 12/83) must be lubricated every 20 000 km. Since
1/84 maintenance-free external rear mirrors are fitted
and can be recognised by the different positioning.

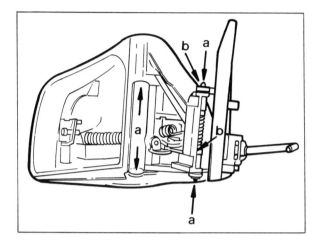

- Unhook the mirror by gently pushing it from the
  back to the front by hand.

- Oil the bearings of the stop bolts -b- and move the
  mirror to and fro several times.

- Grease the bracket and stop bolts at their
  bearings -a-.

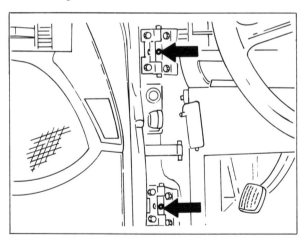

- Grease the door hinges -arrows- with multi
  purpose grease and a suitable lubricating gun.

- Grease the door locks at the locking spigot, lock
  eyes and contact surfaces of the rotating trap.

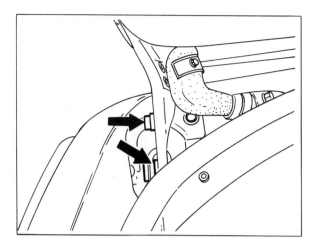

- **T-Model:** Lubricate the rear door and gas spring
  attachment of the rear door with engine oil.

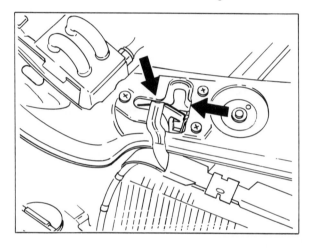

- Grease the bonnet lock with multi-purpose grease.

Oil the following parts with engine oil:

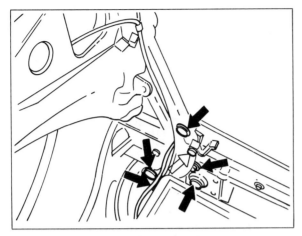

- The bonnet stay and hinge bearing.

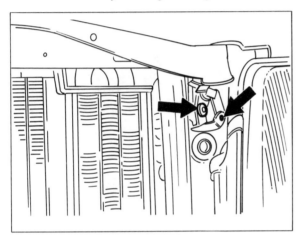

- The hinge at the securing hook of the bonnet.

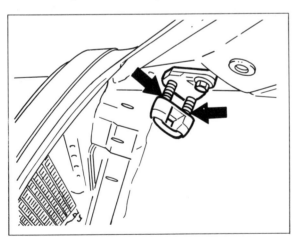

- The bonnet lock on the bonnet.
- The bowden cable.

Visual checking of the seat belt

Caution:

Noises made by the belt when it rolls up are normal. If the noises are irritating, the seat belt must be replaced. Never use oil or grease to stop the noises. The automatic roller must not be opened, since the tension spring will jump out.

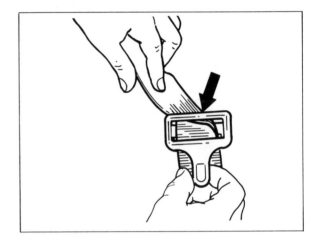

- Pull out the seat belt totally and check for tears in the material. Damage can be caused by jamming of the belt or cigarettes. In this case replace the belt.

- If there are rub marks without the threads being broken, the belt need not be replaced.

- If the belt will not move freely, check whether it is twisted. If necessary remove the trim of the central pillar.

- If the automatic roller does not work, replace the belt.

- Clean the belt only with soap and water, never use a solvent or chemical cleaner.

Water drains - cleaning

The water drains must be cleaned once a year.

- Blocked water drains are most easily cleaned with an old flexible speedometer cable. If necessary, fit the speedometer cable into an electric drill and drill out the drain at slow speed.

The water drains are found in the following places:

- The top of the fuel filling recess.

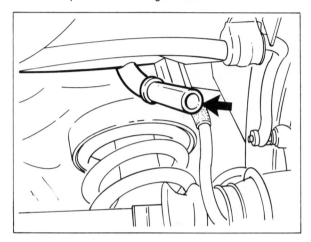

- The bottom of the fuel filling recess.

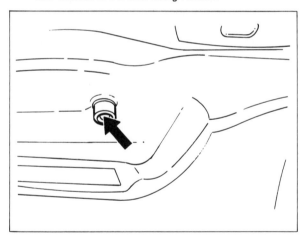

- On the rear mud guard.

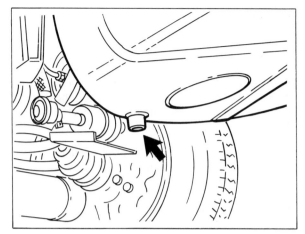

- At the bottom of the spare wheel recess.

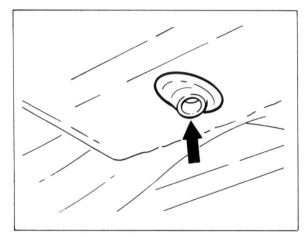

- On the side member.

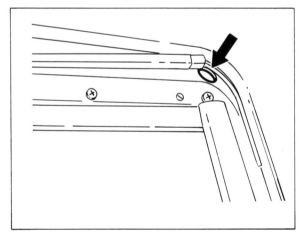

- At the front of the sliding roof.

PAINTWORK

For panel beating and paint jobs it is assumed that there is a basic knowledge of the equipment and its application. Such knowledge is generally only acquired after years of practice. For this reason only the repair of small chassis and paint damage will be discussed here.

To touch up the paint, the same paint colour is required since even the smallest differences in colour will immediately be obvious after completion of the job. The colour is indicated on a label glued to the inside of the chassis. The colour description and identification number is on this.

If there are still differences between the original paint and the touching up paint, this is because vehicle paint changes after a while due to ageing, exposure to ultra violet light, extreme temperature differences, weather conditions and chemical influences such as industrial fumes. Surface damage, colour changes and bleaching can also occur if unsuitable products were used to clean and polish the vehicle.

Metallic paint consists of two layers, a metallic base paint and a clear covering coat. When painting, the clear paint is sprayed onto the still wet base paint. The chance of colour differences is particularly high, since the difference in viscosity of the touch up paint compared to the original paint leads to colour differences. In practice it is thus almost impossible to achieve a satisfactory colour match with a spray can.

Stone damage touch up

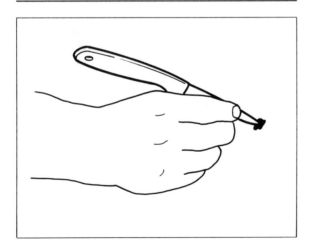

- Scratch out stone damage or small rust marks of the chassis with a "rust eraser", a knife or small screwdriver, until bare metal is visible. It is important that even the smallest rust marks are removed. A "rust eraser" is a small plastic sleeve which has small wire bristles to remove the rust with. Electrically driven grinders with interchangeable heads are also available.

- Apply a little primer to the metal spot with a brush. Since the primer is usually obtainable in spray cans, spray a little primer into the lid of the spray can.

Caution:

The bare patches must first be cleaned and be totally dry and free of grease.

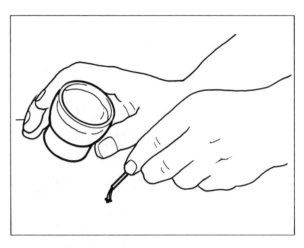

- After the primer is dry, touch up the patch with spot paint. The brush of the spot paint is integrated into the lid. If only spray cans of the particular colour are available, spray a little paint onto the lid and apply the paint with a normal water colour paint brush. Always apply only a thin layer of paint, so that it does not run. Let the paint dry completely. Repeat this process until the chip is totally filled and is even with the adjacent surfaces.

Bodywork touch up

Dent removal

To remove dents, a planishing hammer and suitable hand anvil are needed. After removing the dents, rust marks and old remains of paint should be carefully removed from the repaired area. Do this either with coarse wet & dry paper (120) placed over a sanding block, or with suitable sanding discs on the buffing disc or with a bodywork file.

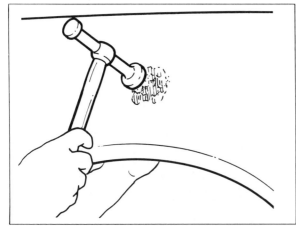

- Hit smaller dents back with a planishing hammer, while holding against the other side with a hand anvil. Do not hit too hard or the metal will stretch too much and a smooth finish will not be achieved. Starting from the edge work evenly towards the middle.
- Check the touched up area repeatedly by hand, until the desired shape is achieved. Smaller unevenness can later be smoothed out with body filler.
- Remove rust deposits and old paint remains in the touched up area with rough sand paper.

Rust damage touch up

The touching up of rust marks with a fibre glass mat is described here.

- Work at rusted areas on the chassis with a sanding disc, straighten the edges with shears and bend them slightly inward.
- Make a provisional support of wood or thick cardboard and push it against the back of the rusted hole. The shape of the support should be the same as that of the chassis. **Caution:** Without the support it is difficult to correctly shape the fibre glass mat.
- Since the support is to be removed again, it must be treated with a special stripping agent. It must not join to the polyester resin.
- Attach the fibre glass in three layers. The first layer should only slightly overlap with the metal edges, the third layer should overlap by about 3cm. Mix the polyester resin with the setting agent according to the instructions. Take care to stick to the mixing relationship exactly, or the prepared resin will dry too quickly or slowly. A plaster container is suitable for mixing. **Caution:** Do not mix too much resin at once or it will dry out in the container.

- First paint the support with polyester resin, position the first piece of fibre glass and dab on the resin with a brush.
- Carefully roll out any air bubbles (recognisable as light spots) with a roller before the next fibre layer is applied with and dabbed with resin.
- Allow the polyester resin to harden for about 24 hours then remove the support. Remove any protruding bits of fibre glass with a file.

Painting preparation

Body fillers

There are two types of body filler: a two part body filler and body putty. Two part body filler is mixed with hardening agent shortly before application. It hardens quickly so it must be used immediately. It is used to even out larger uneven areas on the metal. Body putty is a filler used for smaller uneven areas. It can be applied in several layers. Both fillers are available in tubes and cans.

- Apply two part body filler to the panel beaten or fibre glass repaired area and allow it dry.
- Once dry, smooth uneven areas with a sanding disc or independent sander. Wet & dry paper with a roughness of "180" should be used.

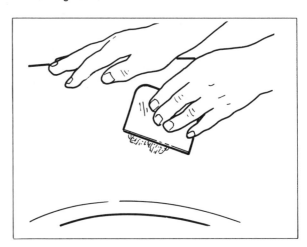

- With a broad elastic spatula, apply and let it harden for at least 2 hours.

Sanding

Wet & dry paper is available in various grit sizes. The smaller the number, the coarser the paper. Grit size 180 to 240 is recommended for sanding two part body filler; body putty and old paint is sanded with 320 to 360 grain, wet. For the final touch up of the paint, paper with a 600 grit is recommended.

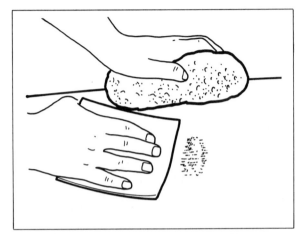

- Roughly sand the finished area with 180 paper, moistening with a sponge from time to time. For the following wet fine sanding, use special wet paper with a 320 grit. Sand the adjacent areas as well.

Cleaning

Before spraying, the sanded surface must be cleaned from grease and silicon particles. It is best to use a silicone remover for this.

- After sanding, carefully clean the repaired area and cover all adjacent areas with newspaper and masking tape. If painting the mud guards, also tape up the wheels and bumper.

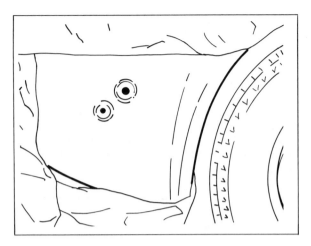

Caution:

Always tape up the repaired surface so that the sprayed surface reaches to the following joint or chassis segment, since a small edge will form on the edge of the taped area. If a flowing transition to the original paint is unavoidable, spray the entire repaired area as well as about 100mm width of the adjacent area during the first spraying. During the 2nd spraying, overlap by 200mm and the 3rd spraying, 300mm.

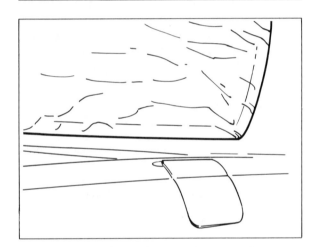

- When painting in the region of the windscreen or rear window, insert a 4 - 5 mm diameter nylon string under the rubber lip. Then tape up the window with the rubber lip so that the contact surface of the rubber lip to the chassis can also be painted. This instruction is not applicable to vehicles with glued windows.

- Wet the floor to avoid dust.

- Spray primer onto the repaired area to seal any hair cracks or pores which could have formed. Once dry, sand it with 600 paper. Repeatedly put the sponge into water and slowly wring out while sanding.

Painting

Three basic paints are used to paint vehicles: cellulose finish, imitation resin and acrylic paint. All three paints are differently made up and do not always mix together. Acrylic paint can for example dissolve old imitation resin paint.

To avoid problems when painting, the initially applied primer and the spray paint should be from the same manufacturer. The paint will then not form bubbles or shrink.

Caution:

It is recommended to first test the spray process on a suitable old piece of steel, eg an old mudguard.

- To paint, the particular surface must be dry and dust-free. If possible blow it with compressed air.

- Wet the floor to settle any dust.

- Before using, vigorously shake the spray can for at least 5 minutes, or paint ridges could form.

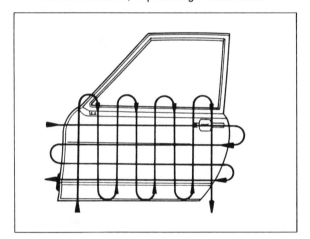

- Even surfaces, whether horizontal or vertical are painted in "cross form": begin outside the surface and spray across to the other outside, then spray back in the opposite direction.

- Move the spray can at the same speed and distance over the surface. The correct distance lies between 25 and 35 cm.

Caution:

If sprayed too closely or slowly or sprayed at different speeds, paint ridges will occur. This means that the paint will flow down in some areas where the paint is too thickly applied. This also happens if the changes of direction do not occur over the masked areas.

- To achieve sufficient colour with a spray can, several layers are necessary. The end of one layer is complete when the surface shines throughout and no single spots are recognisable.

Caution:

The spraying process is to be repeated at small intervals until the paint covers the area completely. When this is the case, clean the nozzle of the spray can by turning the can upside down and spraying until no more paint comes out.

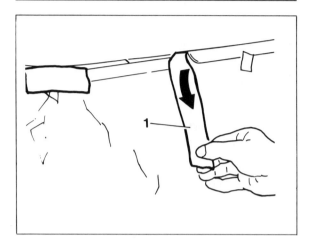

- When the spraying process is complete, pull the tape -1- away from the freshly painted area. In this way the wet paint can flow over the join.

- Allow the sprayed surface to dry. This process is hastened with the use of an electric heater or photo lamp. **Caution:** Do not use a blowing heat device, since dust particles will blow up onto the new paint.

- When the paint is hardened, after about 3 weeks, carefully remove the spray mist from the adjacent surfaces with polish and cotton wool.

HEATER

The fresh air for the heater is sucked in via the air intake grille under the windscreen and reaches the interior of the vehicle through the fan. The air flows through the heating box and is distributed to the various air vents by flaps. If the heater is switched to "warm" the heating valves open the flow to the heat exchanger in the engine. The heat exchanger is situated in the heater box and is heated by the hot coolant. The air flowing past is now heated by the hot segments of the heat exchanger and then reaches the vehicle interior.

The entering air is distributed more to the top or bottom a regulator above the 3 buttons. Since 8/80 there are only 2 regulators which direct the air.

The heating output is regulated separately for the left and right half of the vehicle.

To increase the heat output there is a three stage fan. To ensure that the fan runs at different speeds in the individual stages, resistances (2 x 0,8 Ohms) are preset. Depending on the switch position, the power flows via both resistances (total resistance 1,6 ohm), via one resistance or directly to the heater. By the preset resistance the power flow to the heater is reduced and the blower runs slower. For the highest speed (stage 3) the pre-resistances are switched off.

Air intake grille - removal and refitting

Removal

- If the left grille is to be removed, first remove the wiper blade arm, see page 238.

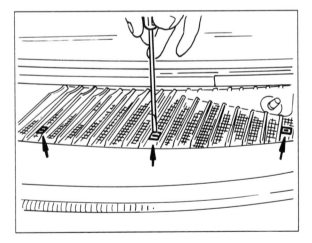

- Prise the pins of the 4 expanding clips -arrows- inwards with a small screwdriver.

- Now remove the expanding clips from the grille and pull the grille out to the front.

Refitting

- Position the grille and push the expanding clips into the openings.
- Drive the plastic pins with a screwdriver into the expanding clips.
- If removed, refit the wiper blade arm, see page 238.

Heater - removal and refitting

Removal

- Remove the cover under the dash board on the right hand side, see page 196.
- Remove the plug of the heater.

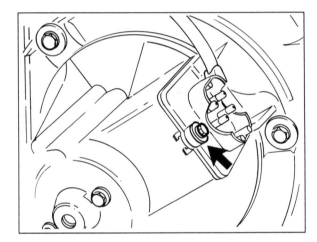

- Remove the screw -arrow- from the contact plate.

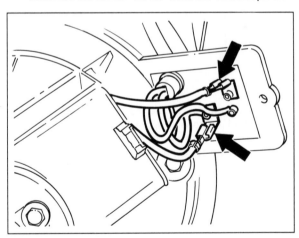

- Lift the contact plate and remove both connecting cables of the ballast resistor.

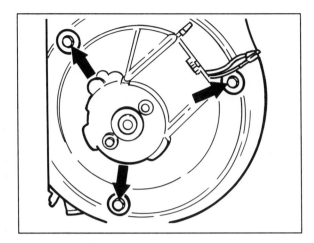

- Remove the screws -arrows- from the flange of the heater motor.

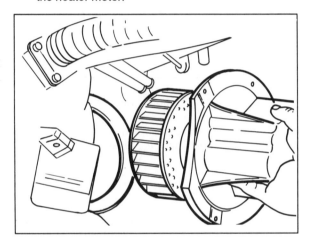

- Remove the heater motor from the housing.

Refitting

- Refit the heater motor and tighten the screws.

- Connect the ballast resistor, refit the contact plate and the plugs.

- Refit the cover under the dashboard, see page 196.

Heater cable - removal and refitting/adjusting

Caution:

The left rotary switch in the interior is connected to the right rotary valve of the tap in the engine bay and vice versa.

Removal

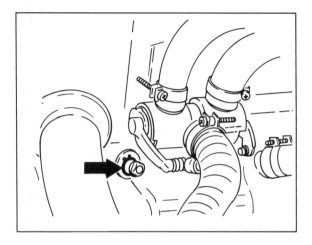

- Remove the securing washer -arrow- from the outer cable on the bulkhead in the engine and unhook the cable from the tap.

- Remove the cover under the scuttle board on the right hand side, see page 196.

- Remove the centre console, see page 197.

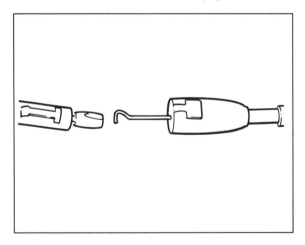

- Unhook the heater cable from the switch and remove it from the dash scuttle.

Refitting

- Insert the heater cable through the dash and hook it to the switch.

- Refit the centre console, see page 197.

- Refit the cover under the dash board, see page 196.

Adjusting

- Set the heater switch in the interior to "0".

- Close the rotary valve at the tap in the engine bay, i.e. press it backward.

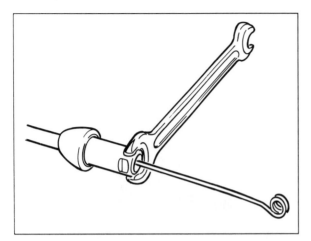

- Adjust the bowden cable with an open-end spanner so that the wire spiral can be hooked onto the rotary valve. By turning the square to the right, the wire is lengthened.

- Hook the heater wire to the valve, refit the circlip.

- Turn the heater switch from stop to stop and check that the tap changes accordingly.

Air conditioning compressor fanbelt -tensioning.

In the workshop the fanbelt tension is measured and adjusted with a special tool. If this tool is not available, tension the fanbelt so that it can be depressed by about 5 cm between the pulleys by hand.

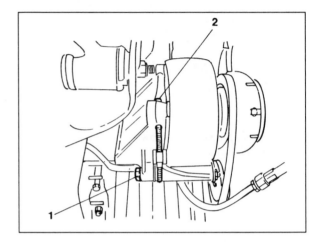

- Loosen the bolt -1-, but do not remove it.

- To tension the fanbelt, turn the tensioning bolt -2- accordingly. Check the tension with your thumb.

- Now tighten the bolt -1-.

- If the special tool is used, tension a new fanbelt to the value of 50, a used fanbelt to between 40 and 45. (see also page 224).

Fault diagnosis - heater

Fault	Cause	Solution
Heater fan not working	Fuse of fan motor defective	Check fuse according to wiring diagram, replace if necessary
	Fan switch defective	Check that ballast resistors have voltage. If not, remove fan motor and check.
	Fan motor defective	Check that there is voltage at plug of fan motor when ignition on and fan is switched on. if so, replace motor.
Heater does not work at one speed setting	Ballast resistor defective	Check ballast resistor.
Heater can not be switched off by rotary control	Rotary switch defective	Test rotary switch
	Bowden cables to heater valve damaged or maladjusted	Adjust Bowden cables
	Heater valve jammed	Free valve, replace if necessary
Heater performance inadequate	Coolant level too low.	Check coolant level and correct.
	Thermostat defective.	Check thermostat and replace if necessary.
	Heater valve does not open.	Check and free valve.
Noises in the area of the fan	Dirt or leaves present	Remove fan and clean. Blow out vanes with compressed air.
	Fan unbalanced Bearings defective.	Remove fan motor and check bearings.

ELECTRICAL SYSTEM

When checking the electrical system, the handyman will continually come across the terms voltage, amperage and resistance.

The voltage is measured in volts (V), the current in amperes (A) and the resistance in ohms. With reference to vehicles, the term voltage generally refers to the battery voltage. This means a voltage of about 12 volts. The battery voltage depends on the load on the battery and the surrounding air temperature. It can lie between 10 and 13 volts. On the other hand the system voltage is generated by the three-phase generator (alternator) and is about 14 volt at medium engine speed.

The term amperage only rarely appears in vehicle electronics. The amperage is, for example, indicated on the back of fuses and indicates the maximum current which can flow without the fuse blowing and so interrupting the circuit.

Where there is a current, resistance must bridge it. The resistance is, amongst others, dependant on the following factors: wire cross section, wire material, current absorption etc. If the resistance is too great, faults can occur. The resistance in ignition leads and ignition distributors, for example, may not be too high or a sufficiently strong spark will not be available at the spark plugs to ignite the fuel air mixture and thus start the engine.

Measuring devices

To measure electricity, measuring devices are available. They combine, in one device, a voltmeter, to measure the voltage, an ampere meter, to measure the amperage and an ohmmeter, to measure the resistance. With a switch, the required measurement can be selected.

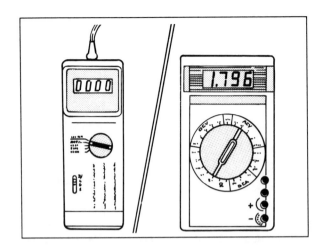

For the home handyman there are multi purpose testers which are specifically adapted for test jobs on vehicles. With such a device the engine speed and the ignition dwell can be measured. as well as voltages up to 20 Volts. In measuring resistance, the device is generally limited to 1 - 1000 k Ohm. If it allows ampere measurements, then this is only in the region of the starter amperage.

In addition, there are measuring devices for testing electrical and electronic components. In these devices the measuring capacity for the engine speed and ignition dwell is naturally lacking. Such a device has an advantage, since it allows a comprehensive measurement of small resistances through to large resistances; Voltages can be measured accurately at all levels.

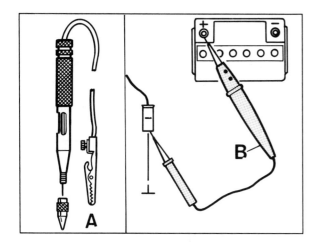

If the test is only to indicate whether there is voltage, a simple test lamp -A- will suffice. This only applies to circuits which have no electronic components, since electronic control devices are extremely sensitive to high currents. Electronic components can be destroyed by the attachment of a test lamp. For vehicles with electronic components such as the transistorized ignition or the electronically driven injection system, a special high ohm voltmeter -B- is required. It has practically the same functions as the test lamp without damaging the electronic components.

Measuring techniques

Voltage measurement

Voltage can be detected with a simple test lamp or a voltage tester. This does, however, only indicate whether there is voltage. To measure voltages, a voltmeter must be attached. The voltmeter is always integrated in a multi purpose measuring device.

Firstly the scale has to be adjusted within which the voltage to be measured probably lies. Voltages in vehicles are generally not higher than 14 volts. An exception is the ignition system in which the voltage could reach up to 30 000 volt. This can only be measured with a special measuring device or an oscilloscope.

While the voltmeter need only be switched on in measuring devices specially designed for vehicles, a number of decisions must first be taken when using a general multi purpose measuring device. Firstly the selector switch must be set to DC as opposed to AC. Then the scale must be selected. Since there is no higher voltage than 14 volt in a vehicle, except for the ignition system, the upper limit of the adjustable measuring region should be a little higher (around 15 to 20 volt). If it is certain that the measured voltage is substantially lower, for example in the region of 2 volt, the measuring region can be switched lower, to achieve a more exact reading. If there is a higher voltage than can be read on the scale, the measuring device could be destroyed.

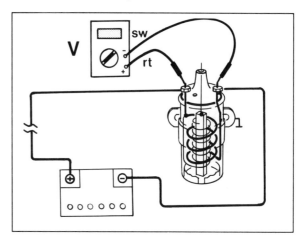

Attach the cables of the measuring device according to the illustration, parallel to the component. The red cable is attached to the lead coming from the positive pole, the black cable to the earth lead or the vehicle earth, such as the engine block.

Test example: If the engine will not start properly because the starter turns too slowly, it is useful to test the battery voltage while the starter is applied. To do this attach the red cable (+) of the voltmeter to the positive pole of the battery and the black cable (-) to the vehicle earth. Now let a helper apply the starter and read off the voltage value. If the voltage lies below about 7 volt, the battery must be tested and possibly charged before starting again.

Amperage measurement

It is relatively rare to measure the amperage of a vehicle. An ammeter is required for this, which is also integrated into a multi purpose measuring device.

As in the voltmeter, the scale in which the probable amperage lies is to be selected before measuring. If this is not known, select the highest scale and if there is no reading, switch down to the next scale.

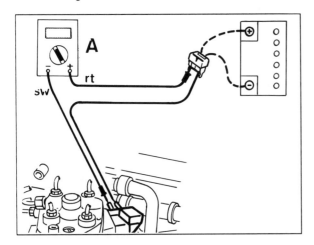

To measure the amperage, the circuit must be broken, as shown in the illustration and the measuring device (ammeter) switched inbetween. The plug is removed for this and the red cable (+) of the ammeter is attached to the current lead (terminal 30, terminal 15). The black cable (-) is placed against the contact to which the interrupted lead is normally attached. The earth contacts between the consumer and plug must be connected to an auxiliary cable.

Example: "Battery discharges itself", see page 216.

Caution:

Never measure the amperage in the lead to the starter (about 150 A) or to the starter plugs in a diesel engine (about 60 A) with a normal ammeter. The high currents can destroy the measuring device. A workshop uses an ammeter with direct current tongs, which is clamped to the insulated current cable and measures the current value by induction.

Resistance measurement

Before testing the resistance make sure that there is no voltage at the contacts which are to be connected to the ohmmeter. So always first remove the plugs, switch off the ignition, remove the lead or unit or disconnect the battery. Otherwise the measuring device could be damaged.

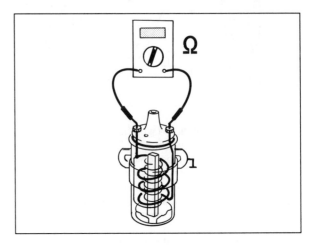

The ohmmeter is connected to the 2 connections of a component or the 2 ends of an electrical lead. It does not matter which cable (+/-) of the measuring device is attached to which contact.

The resistance measurement in a vehicle is mainly in two areas:

1. The control of a resistance in the circuit with a constant or variable value. **Example:** Testing the resistance of the temperature gauge, by removing the plug from the temperature gauge and connecting the ohmmeter between the plug and gauge. Switch the ohmmeter to the scale within which the value probably lies, and compare the indicated value with the specified value in the table.

2. "Continuity" test of an electrical lead, a switch or a heater filament.This tests whether an electrical lead in the vehicle is broken and the connected electrical device thus cannot work. The ohmmeter is attached to both ends of the particular electrical lead. If the resistance is 0 ohm, then there is "continuity", this means the electrical lead is fine. If the lead is broken, the measuring device shows infinite ohm.

Fitting of accessories

When drilling holes in the bodywork, the edges of the holes must subsequently be rounded off and varnished. The burrs which cannot be avoided when drilling, must be totally removed from the chassis.

In all fitting jobs concerning the electrical system the earth cable should be removed from the vehicle battery and placed to one side, to avoid short circuits in the wiring.

If cables are to be added to the existing cables when fitting accessories, these should, where possible, be placed along the fitted cable clips and rubber funnels.

If necessary, the newly fitted cables should additionally be secured with insulation tape, plastic putty, cable tape and such like, to avoid noise when driving and the cables rubbing. Particular care should be taken that there is a gap of 10mm between the brake lines and the laid cables, and a minimum gap of 25mm between the brake lines and the cables which move with the engine and other parts of the vehicle.

If additional electrical items are fitted, check that the higher load can still be carried by the existing alternator. If necessary, an alternator with a larger output should be provided.

Battery removal and refitting

The battery is on the right side in the engine compartment.

Removal

- Open the bonnet, see page 13.

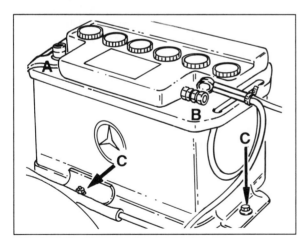

- Remove the battery cables, first the earth cable -A- then the positive cable -B-.

- Unscrew both brackets at the battery base -C- and remove them.

- Lift out the battery.

Refitting

- Position the battery.
- Refit the brackets and tighten them.
- Attach the positive cable (red) to the positive pole (+), then the earth cable (black) to the negative cable (-). **Caution:** A wrongly connected battery can cause considerable damage to the alternator and electrical system.
- Close the bonnet, see page 13.

Battery charging

- Never short circuit the battery as it heats up and can explode. Never hold a naked flame to the battery. Battery acid is corrosive and may not come into contact with the skin or eyes, if necessary rinse thoroughly with water.
- Remove the positive and earth cables from the battery, earth cable first.
- Before charging, check the electrolyte level, refilling with distilled water if necessary.
- Defrost a frozen battery before charging. A charged battery freezes at around -65° C, a half charged one at around -35° C and a discharged one at around -12° C.
- Unscrew the caps of the battery and lightly rest them on the openings. This prevents acid spots on the paint while the gases, formed when charging, escape.
- Charge the battery only in a well ventilated room. If charging a fitted battery, have the bonnet open.
- The charging rate of a normally charged battery is around 10% of the capacity (in a 45-Ah battery, thus about 4,5 A).
- Connect the positive pole of the battery with the positive pole, the negative pole of the battery to the negative pole of the charger.
- While charging the acid temperature may not exceed 55° C; interrupt the charging or lower the charging rate if necessary.
- Charge until gas escapes all the cells and specific gravity of the acid and the voltage has not increased during 3 measurements at one hour intervals.
- The battery may also be charged with a fast charger.

Caution:

Only use the fast charger for emergencies. Do not fast charge batteries which have been unused for long periods or new batteries.

- Check the electrolyte level after charging, filling up with distilled water if necessary.
- Check the specific gravity. If the value of one cell is noticeably below the others (e.g five cells show 1,26 and 1 cell 1,18), replace the battery.
- Allow the battery to stand for about 20 minutes, then screw on the lids.

Warning:

The engine should not run with the battery disconnected as the electrical system will be damaged.

Battery discharges itself

If there is a suspicion of slow discharge, test the electric wiring in the following way:

- Use a charged battery for the test.

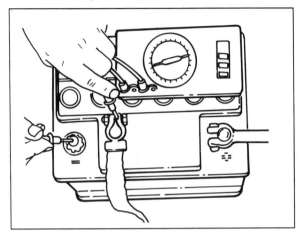

- Set the ammeter to its highest scale (from 0-5 mA to 0-5 A). Remove the earth cable from the battery. Place the ammeter between the battery negative pole and the earth cable. The ammeter positive connection to the earth cable and the ammeter negative connection to the battery negative pole.

Caution:

The test can also be carried out with a test lamp. If the test lamp does not light up between the earth strip and the negative pole, an ammeter will still have to be used.

- Switch off all electrical consumers, disconnect the clock and close the doors.

- Switch back to the milli-ampere scale from the ampere scale until a reading results. (1-3 mA is allowed).

- By removing the fuses one after the other, interrupt the various circuits. If the reading goes back to zero at one of the interrupted circuits, the fault is to be found there. The faults could be: corroded and dirty contacts, leads rubbed through, internal shorting of the units.

- If no flow is found in the circuit, then the connections to the uninsulated components must be removed: they are the starter, alternator and ignition.

- Reconnect the battery.

Battery maintenance

Battery checking

Electrolyte level checking

Caution:

Do not look into the battery using a naked flame. Danger of explosion!

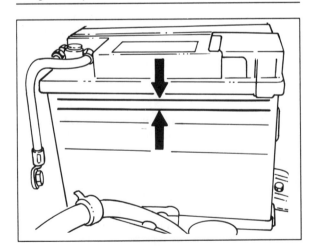

- The electrolyte level must lie between the minimum and maximum mark -arrows-.

- If the electrolyte level cannot be determined from the outside, unscrew the lids of the various cells. The electrolyte level must lie about 6 mm above the plates including the separators. If there is an electrolyte level mark, the electrolyte level should be adjusted accordingly.

- If necessary top up the electrolyte level to the specified level.

Warning:

Only use distilled water for topping up.

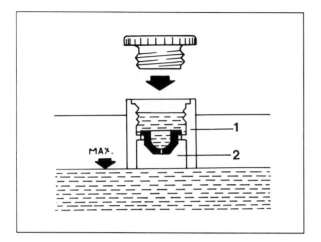

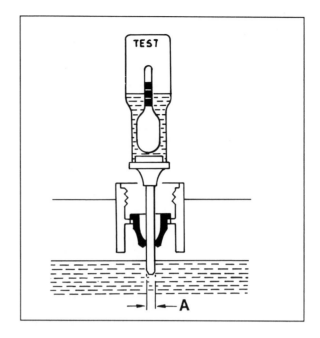

- If the electrolite level or the separators in the various cells are not visible when the lids are removed, top up with distilled water up to the level shown. 1-discharge air duct, 2-air cushion.

- Batteries which have excessive electrolite levels can boil over when charged too much (on hot days). Insufficient acid decreases the life of the battery.

Acid strength checking

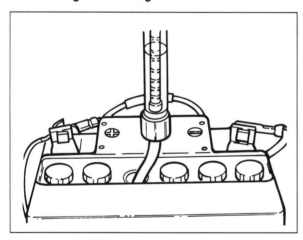

- The acid strength together with the voltage measurement give an exact indication of the charging condition of the battery. For testing, a reasonably priced hydrometer is available. The higher the specific value (acid strength) of the battery acid, the more the floater bobs up. The acid strength can be read from the scale in either specific weight or Baume degrees ($+°$Be). The following weights must be reached:

Charging	Norm. climatic condition zones		Tropics	
	°Be	g/ml	° Be	g/ml
Discharged	16	1,12	11	1,08
Half discharged	24	1,20	18	1,16
Well charged	32	1,28	27	1,23

Caution:

In battries with over flow acid fillers put the hydrometer through the 3-piece membrane and draw off the electrolyte.

Battery terminal cleaning

Part of the general maintenance of the vehicle includes cleaning the battery terminals and connectors, then applying an acid protection grease, such as vaseline.

Battery conservation

An unused battery eventually discharges itself. If the vehicle is to be left standing for some time, the following measures should be taken:

- Check the charging condition of the battery, charge the battery if necessary.
- Remove the earth cable from the battery so that it is not discharged by constant consumers, e.g. the clock.
- After 3 months, recharge the battery. **Caution:** depending on the age of the battery, check the charging condition of the battery at shorter intervals. Do not leave the battery discharged, since permanent damage can occur to the plates.

Fault diagnosis

Fault	Cause	Solution
Acid level too low	Over charging (particularly in summer)	Top up with distilled water to prescribed level (in charged battery)
Acid escapes from the caps	Charging voltage too high	Test regulator, replace
	Acid level too high	Suck out excess acid with hydrometer
Acid strength too low	Acid strength lower in one cell	Short circuit in one cell. Replace battery
	Acid strength lower in two neighbouring cells	Dividing wall leaking, causing wire connection between cells, thus discharging cells. Replace battery.
	Battery discharged	Charge Battery
	Faulty alternator	Check alternator, repair or replace as necessary
	Short circuit in wire	Check electrical system
	Acid too diluted with water	Equalise acid
Output too low voltage drops too much	Battery discharged	Charge battery
	Charging voltage too low	Test regulator, replace if necessary
	Connecting clamps loose or oxydised	Clean connecting clamps and grease particularly under side with acid protection grease. Tighten screws
	Earth connection battery engine-chassis is bad	Check earth connection, if necessary reconnect metallic connections or tighten screw connections
	Battery discharges too much due to dirt in battery acid	Replace battery
	Battery possibly sulfurised (grey-white deposit on positive and negative plates)	Charge battery with low voltage to slowly decrease deposit. If still too low after repeated charging and discharging, replace battery
Not charging sufficiently	Fault in alternator, regulator or wire connections	Test alternator and regulator correct fault or replace; secure wires properly
	Fanbelt loose	Tension or replace fanbelt
	Too many consumers connected	Fit larger battery, if necessary also larger alternator
Always over charged	Fault in regulator possibly also in alternator	Replace regulator or test alternator

Fuses - changing

To prevent short circuit and overloading damage to the leads and consumers of the electrical system, the circuits are protected by fuses.

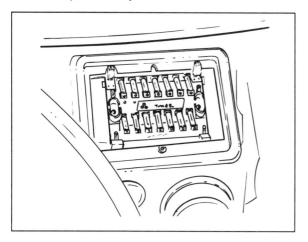

The fuses are mainly housed in a fuse box which is located in the back right hand side of the engine bay, on the bulkhead.

- Before changing a fuse, always first switch off the relevant consumer.
- Remove the cover of the fuse box by unscrewing both screws.
- A burned out fuse is recognisable by the melted metal strip.
- Carefully remove the defective fuse from the holder by slightly bending down the lower spring contacts.
- Insert the new fuse with the **same fuse strength** with the metal strip pointing upwards, between the spring contacts. Do not press onto the metal strip or bend the spring contact.

Caution:

The fuse must be secure in the holder, if necessary slightly bend the contacts. The contacts must not be corroded at the points of contact.

- If a newly fitted fuse burns through after a short time, the relevant circuit must be tested.
- Never substitute a fuse with wire or other items, since these can causes serious damage to the electrical system.
- It is recommended to always keep a few spare fuses in the vehicle. To store these there are suitable holders in the side of the fuse box.
- Refit the cover of the fuse box and tighten the screws.

Fuse layout

The fuse layout depends on the equipment and the year of manufacture of the vehicle. The relevant layout of the fuses is inside the cover of the fusebox.

No.	Amp	Consumer
1	8	Right parking light, right rear lamp, headlight cleaning system*
2	16	Interior light, boot light, clock, aerial*
3	8	Left parking light, left rear lamp
4	8	Glovebox light, cigarette lighter, electrical window lifter*, radio* (has an additional inline fuse of 2A)
5	8	Auxiliary fan *
6	16	Windscreen wiper
7	8	Right high beam
8	8	Rear window heater
9	8	Left high beam, high beam warning light
10	16	Heater
11	8	Right lower beam
12	8	Brake light, control light, air conditioner*
13	8	Left lower beam
14	8	Horn, reverse lights, automatic choke, thermal time switch, idle switch-off valve
a	16	Electrical window lifter*
b	16	Electrical window lifter*
c	16	Electrical auxiliary ventilator*
d	16	Electrical sliding roof*

* Special equipment

Relay testing

The best way of testing the function of a relay is by
exchanging it for a new one. This is how it is generally
done in a workshop. Since the handyman does not
often have a spare relay on hand, the following
process is recommended for testing relays, such as
those used for switching of fog and main headlamps.

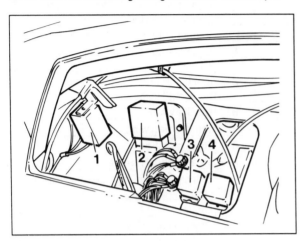

The relays are mainly located behind the switch board
fitting or in an auxiliary relay box on the right side in
the engine bay. 1 - timing relay for rear window heater,
2 - relay for windscreen automatic interval, 3 + 4 -
relay for automatic window lifter. Since 9/81 the hazard
light relay is no longer at the hazard light switch, but
under the switch lever cover between the ashtray and
switch lever.

- Remove the relay from the bracket.
- First determine with a voltage tester whether there
  is any voltage at pin 30, by connecting the voltage
  tester to earth and inserting the other contact
  point into pin 30. If the light of the voltage tester
  lights up, there is voltage. If there is no voltage,
  track down the interruption between the positive
  battery terminal and pin 30 using the wiring
  diagram.
- Make a wire bridge from a piece of insulated wire,
  the ends must be stripped.
- Connect pin 30 in the relay bracket (battery +,
  always has voltage) to the exit of the relay pin 87
  with this bridge. Where the pins are to be found in
  the relay bracket, is indicated on the relay or on
  the plug contact.
- If, for example, the high beam comes on when the
  bridge is in place, it can be assumed that the relay
  is defective.
- If the high beam does not come on, trace the
  interruption in the wire from pin 87 to the high
  beam with the aid of the wiring diagram, and
  rectify.
- If necessary, replace the relay.

The alternator

The Mercedes is fitted with a three-phase alternator. Depending on the model and equipment, a alternator with a performance between 35A and 80A could be fitted.

The alternator is driven by the crankshaft via the fanbelt, while the rotor turns with the generating winding within the stationary stator winding at about double the engine speed.

The generating voltage flows through the generating winding via carbon brushes and slip rings which creates a magnetic field. The position of the magnetic field in relation to the stator winding changes constantly according to the rotation of the rotor. This creates a three-phase current in the stator winding.

Since the battery can only be charged with a continucus current, the three-phase current is converted to a continuous current by rectifiers in the diode plate. The regulator converts the charging current by switching the generating current on and off, depending on the charging condition of the battery. At the same time the regulator keeps the working voltage constant at around 14 volt, irrespective of the engine speed.

Caution:

As opposed to a generator, the three-phase alternator must never be operated without the battery. Never let the engine run without the battery.

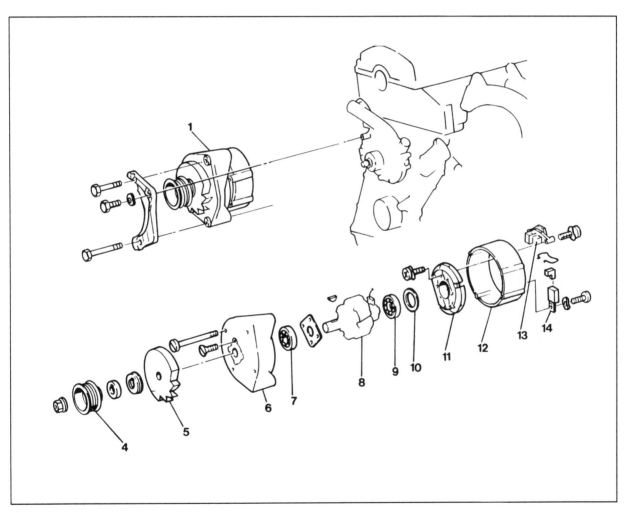

1	-	Alternator	9 -	Rear bearing
4	-	Pulley	10 -	Washer
5	-	Fan	11 -	Diode plate
6	-	Front bracket	12 -	Rear bracket
7	-	Drive bearing	13 -	Regulator
8	-	Rotor	14 -	Suppressor condenser

Alternator removal and refitting

Removal

- Remove the battery earth cable.
- Remove the multistage plug from the back of the alternator. First unclip the wire clamp with a screwdriver and put it to one side.
- Slacken the fanbelt and remove it.

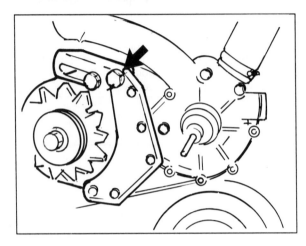

- Unscrew the bracket of the alternator at the 2 bolts -1- and -top arrow- and remove it.

Caution:

If the top securing bolt -arrow- is stuck, remove the alternator with the bracket -2-.

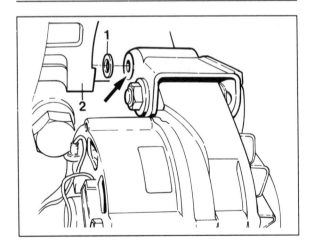

Caution:

Between the bracket and cylinder head -2- there could be a spacer -1- of 0,85 thickness. When removing, do not lose the spacer. When refitting, the spacer must rest in the recess -arrow- of the bracket.

Refitting

- Refit the alternator and tighten it with the 2 bolts. Tighten the top bolt -arrow- to the cylinder head to 45 N.m.
- Position the fanbelt and tension it.
- Refit the multistage plug and secure it with the wire clamp.
- Connect the earth cable to the battery.

Alternator fanbelt - removal and refitting

Removal

- Slacken the fanbelt and remove it. Depending on the vehicle model, first remove the fanbelts for the other auxiliary devices such as the air conditioning compressor.

Engine 102

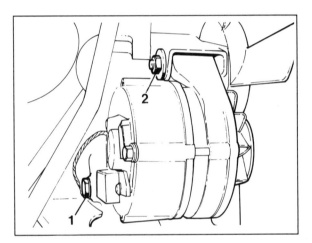

- Loosen the nuts -1- and -2-.

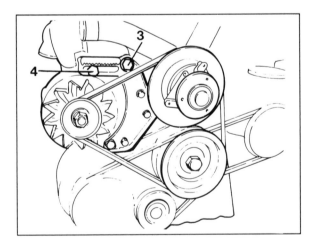

- Loosen the bolt -3-. Turn the tensioning bolt -4- to the left, thus tilting the alternator in relation to the engine and relaxing the fanbelt.

Engine 123

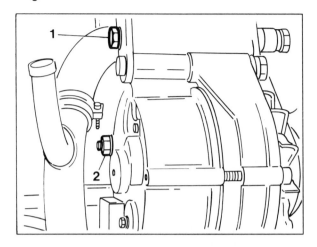

- Loosen the bolt -1- and nut -2- from the back of the alternator.

- Turn the tensioning bolt on the front of the alternator to the left and slacken the fanbelt.

Engine 110 with 55-A alternator

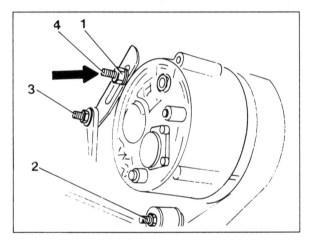

- Loosen nuts -1,2,3-.

- Turn the tensioning bolt at the front of the alternator to the left and slacken the fanbelt.
  Caution: In engines with air conditioning, turn the tensioning bolt -4- by the 6mm square -arrow- to the right (seen from behind).

Engine 110 with 80-A alternator

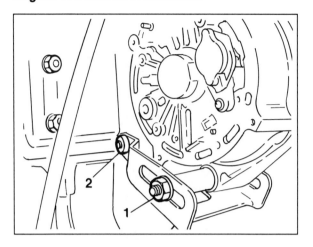

- Loosen nut -1-, since 7/84 loosen the bolt -2- from the back of the alternator.

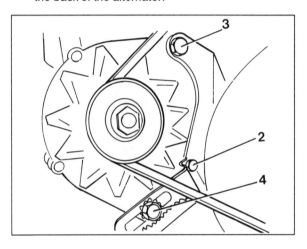

- Loosen the bolt -3-. Up to 7/84 loosen the bolt-2- from the bottom of the engine, by putting the vehicle on blocks if necessary, see page 244.

- Turn the tensioning bolt -4- to the left, thus slackening the fanbelt.

Petrol engine 115 and diesel engine 615, 616, 617

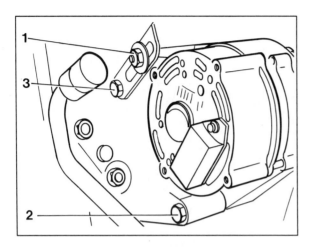

- Loosen the nut -1- and bolts -2,3-.

- Loosen the nut -5-, thus slackening the fanbelt.
- Remove the fanbelt.

Refitting

- Before refitting, check the fanbelt. If the flanks are frayed, or if there are tears and cracks, replace the fanbelt. In vehicles with dual belt transmission (300 Turbodiesel), always replace both fanbelts. Only fit two belts of the same make.
- Position the fanbelt.

Tensioning

- By turning the tensioning bolt to the right, swing the alternator away from the engine, thus tensioning the fanbelt.

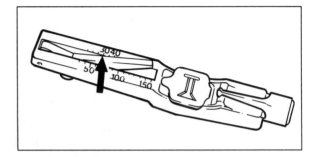

- A workshop will test the fanbelt tension with a special tool. A new belt is tensioned to the value of 30, while a used fanbelt should reach 20 to 25. **Caution:** in the diesel engine since 2.79 (except the Turbodiesel) the tensioning value for a new belt is 50, for a used belt 40 to 45.
- If this tool is not available, compress the fanbelt with your thumbs between the pulleys. The belt should be compressible by about 5mm, or the tension must be corrected. In the diesel engine turn the tensioning bolt another 90° to180° further. Subsequently have the tension checked with a measuring device as soon as possible.
- Tighten the securing bolts and nuts.

Carbon brushes of alternator / regulator : replacing/checking

The carbon brushes should be checked every 60 000 km.

Removal

- The removal is possible without removal of the alternator.
- Remove the battery earth cable.

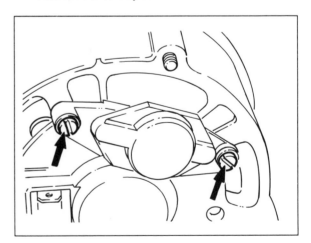

- Unscrew the regulator from the back of the alternator and carefully remove it.

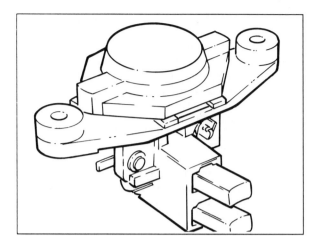

- Replace the carbon brushes if the length is 5mm or less, by soldering out the connecting wires.

Refitting

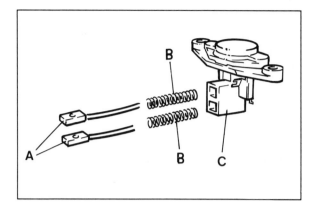

- Fit the new carbon brushes -A- and springs -B- into the brush housing -C- and solder the connections.
- To prevent any solder from rising through the wire, hold the connecting wire of the brushes with straight pliers. **Caution:** Rising solder would stiffen the strands, thus making the carbon brush unusable.
- The insulating tube above the strands must be clamped with the existing eye next to the soldered area.
- Check the ease of movement of the new carbon brushes in the brush housings after fitting.
- Refit the regulator and tighten the screws.
- Connect the battery earth cable.

Alternator fault diagnosis

Fault	Cause	Solution
Charge indicator light not burning with ignition switched on	Lamp burned out	Replace
	Earth strap of alternator loose or corroded	Check earth strap for good contact, tighten screw
	Battery discharged	Charge battery
	Interruption in the lead between alternator, ignition lock and control light	Investigate with voltmeter according to wiring diagram
	Plug connection between relay plate and alternator not connected	Check, replace plug if necessary
	Carbon brushes not in position on slip ring	Check ease of movement of the carbon brushes and minimum length of 5mm
	Generating winding in alternator burned through	Replace rotor
Charge indicator light does not go off with rising engine speed	Indicator defective	Check indicator, replace
	Lead between three-phase alternator and indicator light has earth connection	Replace wire
Charge indicator light burns with ignition off	Short circuit in positive diode	Check diodes, replace diode plate

The starter

To start the engine, a small electrical motor, the starter, is necessary. For the engine to start, the starter must accelerate it to an engine speed of at least 300 rpm. This only happens if the starter is working properly and the battery is sufficiently charged.

The starter consists of a drive, armature and end cover. In the brush housing are carbon brushes, which slowly but steadily become worn down. If the carbon brushes are badly worn, the starter can no longer work properly. The pinion drive is in the drive housing.

When the starter receives voltage via the ignition switch, the pinion, on a coarse pitch thread, is pushed into the toothed rim of the flywheel via the solenoid on the starter housing. As soon as the pinion has run to the front of the flywheel, it is connected to the flywheel by positive control. The starter now turns and brings the engine to the required starting engine speed. When the engine has started, the pinion is accelerated by the engine, so for a short time it runs faster than the starter, which breaks the connection to the engine.

Since the starting of the combustion engine requires a high current consumption all cable connections should be checked during servicing. Clean corroded connections and paint them with protective grease.

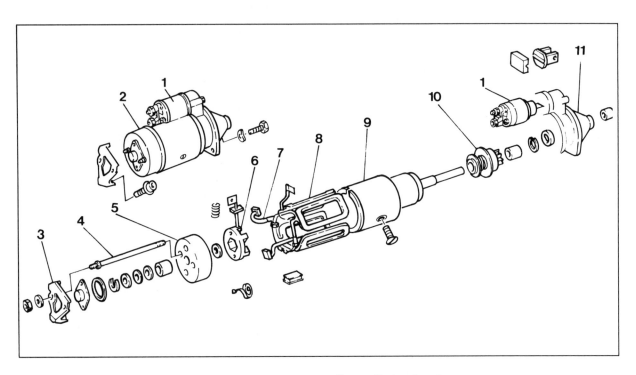

1	-	Solenoid	7	-	Carbon brush
2	-	Starter	8	-	Field coils
3	-	Retainer	9	-	Yoke
4	-	Through bolt	10	-	Pinion
5	-	End cover	11	-	Drive housing
6	-	Brush housing			

Starter - removal and refitting

Removal

- Remove the earth cable from the battery.
- Remove the air filter, see page 105.

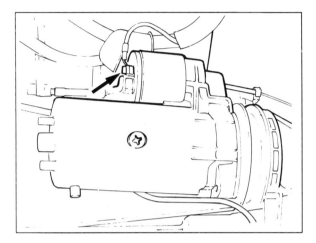

- Lift the plastic cover from the solenoid of the starter and remove the electrical leads -arrow-. In the **230E** remove the electrical wires of the starter from the battery and the wire connector. Unscrew the induction manifold bracket at the top and bottom.
- Put the vehicle on blocks.

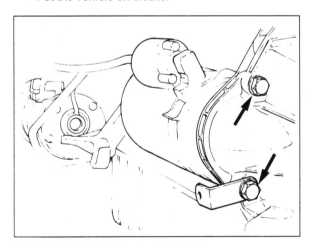

- Unscrew the fixing bolts -arrows- of the starter from below.
- Remove the starter from the gearbox and lift it out.
- **230E:** Unscrew the bracket of the starter from the engine block, swing the starter towards the engine block and lower it with the cables connected. First turn the steering hard to the right. Remove the electrical wires from the starter.

Engine 115

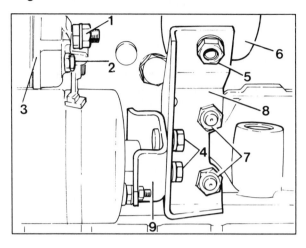

- Unscrew the nuts -5,7- and bolts -4- and remove the bracket -8-.
- Remove the bolts from the starter flange and pull the starter out until the bracket -9- can be unbolted.
- Turn the front wheels to the right and remove the starter between the idler arm and the front axle bracket. Other illustrated parts: 1 - terminal 30, 2 - pin 50, 3 - solenoid.

Refitting

- Insert the starter from the top, fit it into the gearbox and tighten from below. **230E:** Connect the electrical wires to the starter, insert the starter from below and tighten it.
- **Engine 115:** Tighten the bracket -9-, by tightening the nuts only slightly.
- Refit the starter. Refit the bracket -8- and slightly tighten the bolts and nuts. Make sure the grub bolts -7- each with a washer of 4mm are fitted.
- Tighten all nuts and bolts equally.
- Lower the vehicle.
- Connect the electrical wires to the starter. Refit the cover. **230E:** Connect the wires to the battery and the wire connector. Tighten the induction manifold bracket.
- Refit the air filter, see page 105.
- Refit the earth cable to the battery.

Starter fault diagnosis

If the starter does not turn, first check whether the required voltage of 8 volt is present at terminal 50 of the solenoid. If the voltage is below this value, the wires of the starter circuit must be tested according to the wiring diagram. Whether the starter retracts at full battery voltage, can be checked in the following way:

- Do not engage any gear, switch on the ignition.
- With a thick wire (cross section at least 4mm^2) bridge terminals 30 and 50 of the starter, see also circuit diagram.

If the starter engages properly, the fault lies in the wire to the starter. If the starter does not engage, it must be removed and tested.

Testing condition: The wire connections must be secure and not oxidised.

Fault	Cause	Solution
Starter does not turn starter:	Battery discharged Bridge terminals 30 and 50 of starter. starter then turns. Wire 50 to ignition switch or ignition switch defective	Charge Battery Fix break, replace defective parts Check battery cable and connections. Measure voltage, charge if necessary
	Cable or earth connection interrupted, battery flat	Clean battery terminals and clamps. Check and clean secure connection between battery, starter and earth
	Insufficient voltage flow due to loose or oxidised connections	Replace solenoid
	Measure voltage at connection for winding solenoid. No voltage at pin 50 (magnetic pin)	Wire broken. Ignition switch defective
Starter turns too slowly to start engine	Battery flat No winter oil or multi-grade oil in engine	Charge battery Fill up with multi-grade oil
	Insufficient voltage flow due to loose or oxidised connections	Clean battery terminals and clamps and connections of starter, tighten connections
	Carbon brushes loose, jammed in guides, worn, broken,	Check carbon brushes, clean or replace. Check guides oil-logged, dirty
	Insufficient space between carbon brushes and commutator	Replace carbon brushes and clean guides of carbon brushes
	Commutator ridged or burned and dirty	Clean commutator or replace armature
	Not sufficient voltage at terminal 50 (at least 8 volt)	Check ignition switch or solenoid
	Bearing worn	Check bearing, replace if necessary
	Solenoid defective	Replace solenoid
Starter engages and turns, engine does not turn or jerks	Pinion drive defective	Replace pinion drive
	Pinion dirty	Clean pinion
	Ring gear of flywheel defective	Repair ring gear, if necessary replace
Pinion drive does not disengage	Pinion drive or coarse pitch thread dirty or damaged	Clean pinion drive, replace if necessary
	Solenoid defective	Replace solenoid
	Release spring weak or broken	Replace release spring
Starter runs on when ignition key is released	Solenoid jammed, does not switch off	Switch off ignition immediately, replace solenoid
	Ignition switch does not switch off	Immediately disconnect battery, replace ignition switch

LIGHTING SYSTEM

The lighting system consists of the main head lights, fog lights, tail lights, brake lights, reversing lights, number plate lights, indicator lights, interior light and instrument lighting.

Before changing a bulb, switch off the relevant consumer.

Warning:

do not touch the glass bulb with bare hands.

Replace a bulb only with one of the same make. Remove any accidental finger marks with a clean cloth and alcohol or spirits.

Bulb changing

Headlights

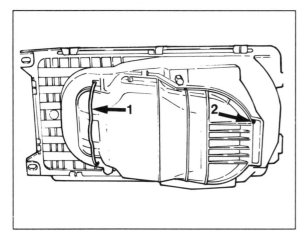

- Unhook the wire clip -1-, open the plastic cover and unhook it on the other side -2-.

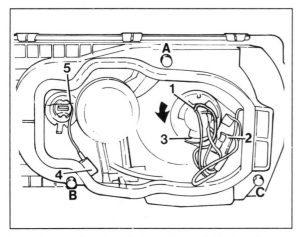

- Remove the plug -1- from the H4 bulb, turn the retaining ring -2- in the direction of the arrow and remove the bulb.
- Fit the bulb so that the nose fits into the relevant recesses in the housing. Refit the retaining ring, turn to the right until it is in position.

Parking light

- Pull out the socket, turn the bulb slightly to the left and remove it from the socket.
- Place the bulb into the socket, turn right slightly until it is secure. Refit the socket into the opening.

Fog light

- Remove the plug -4-, Press the wire clips -5-first to the head light, then press together and push it away. Remove the H3 bulb.
- Fit the bulb, pull over the wire retainer and secure it in the retaining hook. Connect the plug.
- Refit the plastic cover and secure it with the 2 wire clips. **Caution:** first check the seal for porosity or damage, replace if necessary.

Indicator light

- Remove the indicator light.
- Remove the plug.
- Turn the light socket about 60° to the left and remove it.
- Push the bulb slightly in, turn it to the left and remove it.
- Press the bulb into the socket, turn it to the right and secure it.
- Refit the socket into the indicator light, turn it totally to the right. Reconnect the plug.
- Refit the indicator light.

Tail light

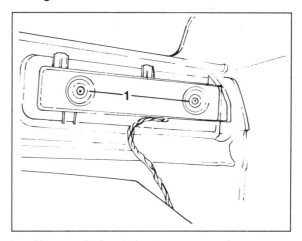

- Unscrew the knurled nuts -arrows- and remove the light housing -1-.
- Press the defective bulb in, turn it to the left and remove it.

Number plate light

- Unscrew the 2 screws of the number plate light and remove it.
- Pull the bulb from the socket.
- Fit a new bulb into the socket.
- Check the seal for porosity or damage, replacing if necessary.
- Refit the number plate light and tighten the 2 screws, checking that the seal is in position.

Head light / indicator light - removal and refitting

Caution:

In replacement headlights the inner, upper retaining clip can be a little closer to the vehicle centre than the original head light. In this case relocate the retaining clip so that it is in the same position as the removed head light, or the paint in the area of the clip could be damaged.

Removal

- Open the bonnet.

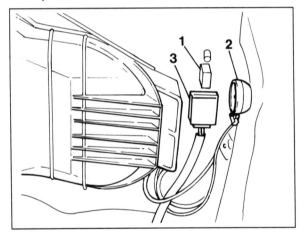

- Unscrew the knurled nut -2- of the indicator light, press the indicator light forwards and remove it.
- Remove the multi-plug of the indicator light.
- Remove the electrical leads -3- of the head lights and vacuum lead -1- of the height adjustment.

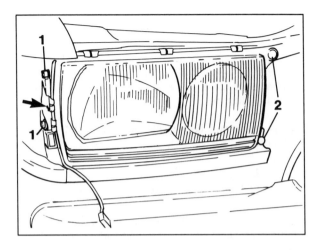

- Unscrew the 2 screws -1-.
- If present, unscrew the 2 additional screws -2.
- Unhook the locating pivot -arrow- of the head light at the mudguard and remove the head light.

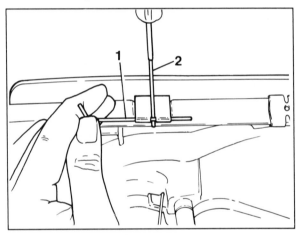

- If the head light glass is to be removed, undo the securing clips, by inserting a wire of 1,5mm diameter into the clip and prising it off with a small screwdriver.
- Remove the rubber gasket.

Refitting

- If removed, position the headlight glass to the housing, press it on evenly and secure it with the securing clips. First check the gasket for porosity, replace if necessary.
- Reconnect the plug and vacuum lead to the head light.
- Refit the head lamp from the vehicle centre towards the outside and fit the screws.
- Position the head lights according to the bodywork and tighten the screws.

- Connect the plug of the head light.
- Connect plug of the indicator light.
- Press the indicator light into the opening from the front and tighten it with the knurled nut. Both locators of the indicator light must fit into the guide of the head light.

Head light adjustment

The correct adjustment of the headlight is very important for road safety. The exact adjustment of the head lights is only possible with a special adjusting device, so it is only shown how the head lights are to be adjusted and which conditions are necessary for correct adjustment of the headlights.

- The tyres must have the correct tyre pressure.
- The empty vehicle must be loaded with 75 kg (one person) on the driver seat.
- Fill the fuel tank.
- The vehicle must stand on a flat surface.
- Press the front of the vehicle downwards several times so that the springs of the front suspension settles.
- Set the light distance regulator to "0", start the engine and let it run for a short while, while accelerating several times to build up sufficient vacuum. Switch the engine off.
- With the car positioned square to and 5 m from a screen and the headlights on main beam, the light pattern should not be higher than the centres of the lights marked on the screen.

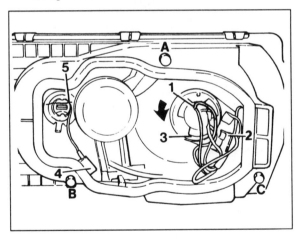

- The adjusting screws are reached from the engine bay. A - adjusting headlights up and down; B - adjusting head lights left or right; C -adjusting fog lights up or down.

Tail light - removal and refitting

Removal

- Remove the plug from the light housing.
- Remove the knurled nuts and the housing.

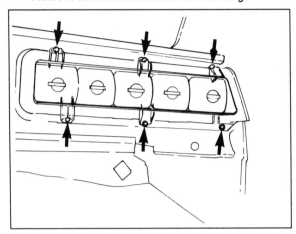

- Unscrew the 6 securing nuts -arrows-.
- Remove the reflectors to the inside and the glass of the tail light with the gasket to the outside.

Refitting

- Check the gasket for porosity or damage, replace if necessary.
- Refit the glass of the tail light with the gasket from the outside into the body.
- Press on the reflectors and tighten evenly with the 6 securing nuts.
- Position the light housing and tighten it with the knurled nuts.
- Connect the plug.

THE INSTRUMENTS

In the Mercedes 123 the instruments are combined in an instrument panel. After the instrument panel is removed, the instruments or bulbs can be removed.

Instrument panel - removal and refitting

Removal

● Disconnect the battery earth cable.

● Remove the lower cover, see page 196.

● Unscrew the union nut of the speedometer cable from underneath, behind the instrument panel. Remove the speedometer.

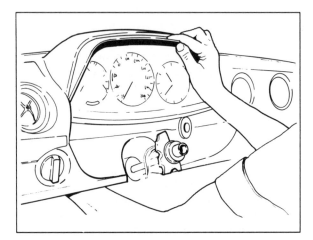

● Press the instrument panel out from behind, while slightly lifting the instrument panel. The instrument panel is held in position by the vacuum action of a molded rubber part.

● Unscrew the capillary lead of the oil pressure indicator, holding from behind with a flat spanner. Wipe the connections with a clean rag.

● Remove the 15 stage plug as well as, if present, the electrical leads of the clock and pre glow control, then remove the instrument panel.

Lay-out of the 15 stage plug on the instrument panel

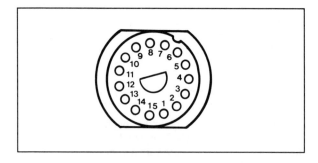

No.	Description
1	High beam indicator lamp
2	Coolant temperature gauge
3	Fuel indicator transmitter
4	Fuel reserve indicator transmitter
5	Fuse 12, pin 15
6	Pin 15 not secured
7	Charge indicator pin 61
8	Control light of brake lining wear indicator
9	Light warning buzzer
10	Brake fluid control, control light for parking brake
11	Instrument light pin K
12	Pin 58d
13	Indicator control right
14	Indicator control left
15	Earth

Refitting

● Pull the speedometer cable out slightly, fit it to the speedometer and tighten it with the union nut.

● Fit and tighten the oil pressure pipe, connect the 15 stage plug. Connect the electrical leads of the clock (and pre-glow control, if fitted).

● Fit the instrument panel into the opening and press it in evenly.

● Connect the battery earth cable.

Speedometer / instrument panel gauges - removal and refitting

Removal

- Remove the instrument panel

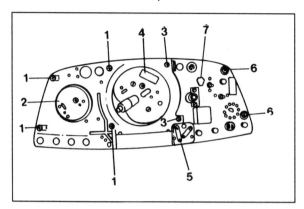

- Unscrew the screws -1- and remove the clock -2-.
- Unscrew the screws -3-, turn the speedometer -4- slightly to the left and remove it.
- Pull out the potentiometer -5-.
- Unscrew the screws -6- and remove the cluster gauge -7- with the indicator light to the right.

Refitting

- Refit the cluster gauge and tighten it. Refit the right indicator light and clip in the cable.
- Refit the potentiometer.

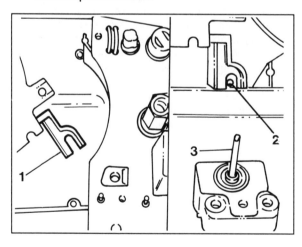

- Refit the speedometer so that the reset lever -1- is positioned so its slot -2- of the tripmileage shaft -3- goes over the potentiometer.
- Refit the clock and tighten with the speedometer.
- Refit the instrument panel.

Indicator- /wiper switch - removal and refitting / return checking

Caution:

To remove the indicator / wiper switch, the steering wheel need not be removed. In the illustration, the steering wheel is omitted to show the parts more clearly.

Removal

- Remove the rubber collar.

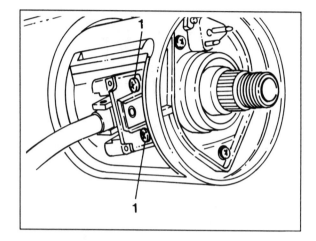

- Unscrew the securing screws -1- and pull the switch slightly out.

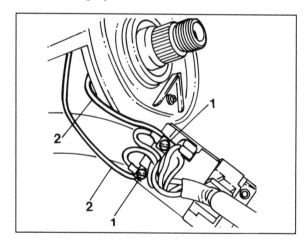

- Loosen the screws -1- and remove the cables -2- of the carbon brushes of the horn.
- Remove the cover under the instrument panel, see page 196.
- Remove the 14 pin plug and then the indicator switch.

Return - testing

This test is only necessary if the indicator switch does not always return automatically.

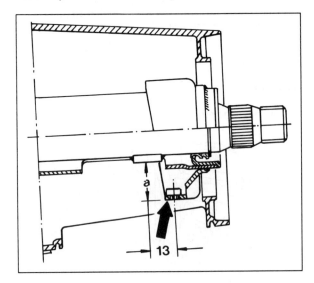

- With a depth gauge, measure the measurement "a" to a distance of 13mm from the centre of the threaded bore. Specified value:
  a = 20,2 + 0,4/ - 0,2 mm.
- If the specified value is not reached, remove the steering wheel, see page 150.
- Unscrew the 2 screws of the plastic trim and remove it to the back.
- Clean the contact surface -arrow- of the combi-switch to the steering column tube of paint traces. Carefully work at the contact surface with a file, until the required distance is reached, if necessary, remove the ridge.
- Check the return tongue of the switch. If there are marks of wearing, round off the edges of the return cam with a file (diameter about 6mm) until a radius of about 0,8mm is reached.
- Tighten the steering shaft trim with the 2 screws.

Refitting

- Connect the cable of the carbon brushes to the indicator switch.
- Set the indicator switch to its central position and tighten it to the steering column tube.
- Press in the rubber trim.
- Connect the 14 pin plug and refit the lower cover.
- If removed, refit the steering wheel.
- Check that the indicator-/wiper switch is working.

Brake light switch - checking / adjusting

The brake light switch is mounted on the bearing bracket of the brake pedal.

- Remove the bottom cover, see page 196.

Checking

- Hold a rule against the brake pedal in the direction of the front floor panel.
- Press the brake pedal forwards, after 5 - 15mm the brake lights must come on. The control button has then come out 6 - 8mm.

Adjustment

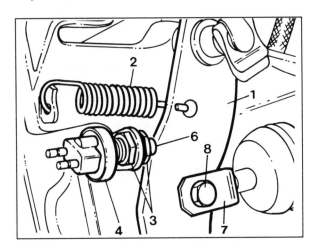

- Loosen the nuts -3- of the switch -4-. Slightly move the switch in the bracket and tighten the nuts. If the brake light lights up too late, move the switch backwards, if it lights up too early, move the switch forwards. Carry out the test again, correcting the position of the switch again if necessary. Other illustrated parts: 1 -brake pedal, 2 - return spring, 6 - control button, 7 - connecting rod master cylinder, 8 - clevis bolt.
- Refit the bottom cover.

Radio - removal and refitting

Some radios are fitted with a push-in bracket which allows easy fitting and removal of the radio. This is, however only possible with a special tool, which is included in the purchase of the radio, or can be bought separately. A radio with a push-in bracket is normally recognised by the 2 or 4 holes in the front panel. In removing a radio with a push-in bracket, the ashtray need not be removed.

Removal

* Remove the battery earth cable.
* Open the ashtray, push down the expanding spring in the centre and remove the ashtray.
* Remove the multi-pin plug from the ashtray.

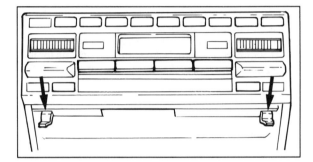

* Through the opening, take hold of the back of the radio and push it out forwards. **Caution:** Radios are secured differently depending on the make. If necessary, remove the operating buttons and unscrew the trim.

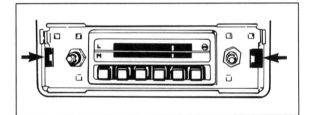

* If there are securing springs, press these to the centre with a small screwdriver, thus releasing them. In another case, unscrew one tensioning screw each on the left and right, thus loosening the two securing brackets, similar to an electric socket.

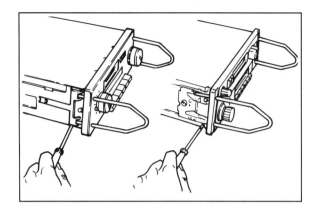

* For a radio with push-in bracket, insert the removing tool into the holes. Pull the radio out evenly by pushing the removing tool to the outside, thus undoing the securing clips. To release the removing tool, carefully press the securing clips together with a small screwdriver.
* Mark the cable at the back of the radio with tape and disconnect it.

Refitting

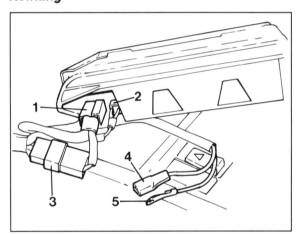

* In subsequently installing a radio, the electrical connection is made by an auxiliary lead via the cigarette lighter. 1 - Plug for cigarette lighter. 2 -lighting, 3 - connecting plug of radio lead, 4 - connector (positive) for radio, 5 - earth connector for radio.
* In certain models there is no aerial cable or control lead for the electric aerial, and if needed, this must be fitted.
* Connect the plug at the back of the radio according to the taped mark or the manufacturer's instructions.
* Press the radio into the opening of the console and clip in or tighten the securing screws.
* If removed, tighten the trim and refit the control buttons.
* Connect the multi-pin plug of the ashtray and refit the ashtray.

- Connect the battery earth cable.

- Adjust the radio to the aerial by choosing a weak MW station and adjusting the best reception by the aerial tuning screw (under the front of the radio trim) with a small screwdriver.

Aerial - removal and refitting

The aerial is built either into the front right mudguard or the left rear mudguard, depending on the model. The removal of the aerial on the rear mudguard is described here. For the measurements of the aerial holes of the front mudguard, see page 186.

Removal

- Open the boot, unclip the left side trim and remove it.

- Disconnect the aerial cable and, if present, the electrical control lead from the aerial.

- Unscrew the earth strip.

- Unscrew the aerial down at the bracket and remove it towards the inside.

Refitting

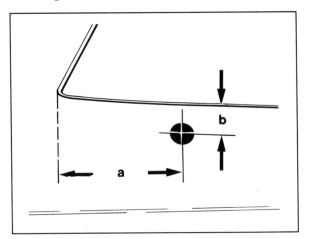

- If fitting an aerial, drill the aerial hole on the left rear mudguard according to the supplied measurements. Aerial hole 22mm diameter, a = 140mm, b = 40mm. Follow the instructions for the subsequent fitting of accessories, see page 215.

- If the same aerial is to be refitted, check the rubber funnel for porosity or damage, replace if necessary.

- Fit the rubber funnel into the aerial bore.

- Insert the aerial from the bottom, fitting the ball head of the aerial into the funnel.

- Tighten the aerial to the bracket.

- Tighten the earth strip.

- Connect the aerial cable.

- Connect the electrical control lead to the aerial motor.

- Position the left side trim and clip it in.

WINDSCREEN WIPERS

Windscreen wiper rubber - replacing

Removal

- Lift up the wiper blade.

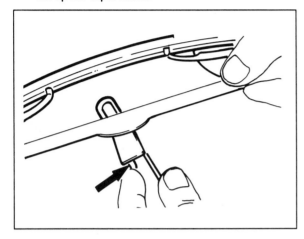

- Push down the spring retainer and push the wiper blade downward out of the hook of the wiper arm.

- Push the wiper blade upward and remove it from the hook of the wiper arm.

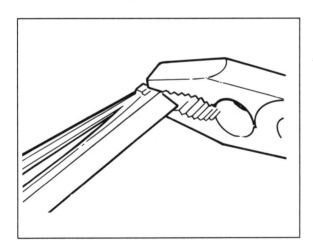

- Press both steel rails together on the closed side of the wiper rubber with pliers, remove it sideways out of the top retainer and pull the rubber together with the rails from the remaining retainers of the wiper blade.

Refitting

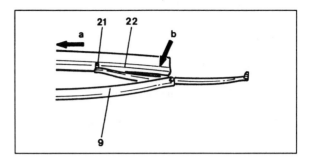

- Loosely place the new wiper rubber -21- without the retaining rails into one retainer of the wiper blade.

- Insert both rails -22- into the wiper rubber so that the notches of the rails point to the rubber and fit into the groove.

- Press both steel rails and the rubber together and insert it into the other retainer, so that the retainer fits into the securing slots of the wiper rubber on both sides -arrow B-

- Push the wiper blade onto the wiper arm and clip the spring retainer into the hooks of the wiper arm.

- Place the wiper arm back against the window and check that the rubber is in contact with the glass along the whole length.

Windscreen wiper nozzle - removal and refitting / adjusting

Removal

- Open the bonnet.

- Remove the feed tube of the nozzle.

- Press out the nozzle and remove it upwards.

Refitting

- Press the nozzle in from the top until it is secure.

- Connect the tube.

Adjusting

- The spraying direction of the jet can be adjusted with a pin.

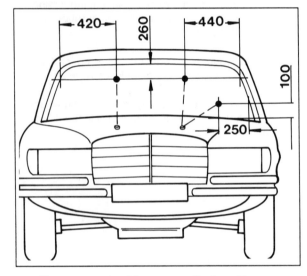

- Measurements of the spray adjustment in mm.

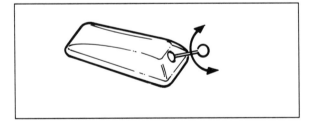

- The nozzle can be cleaned with compressed air and adjusted with a pin.

Head light wiper - adjusting

As soon as the windscreen wiper is switched on with the headlights on, the wipers of the headlights also work. At the same time the headlight wiper pump sprays against the headlight glass.

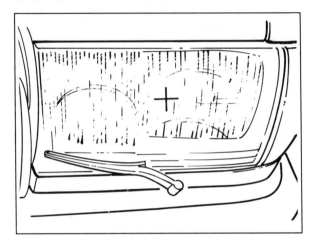

- Adjust the nozzle of each wiper arm so that the spray jet hits the marked spot -cross- on the headlights. Do this by carefully inserting a needle into the nozzle and adjusting it to the correct position.

Wiper motor - removal and refitting

Removal

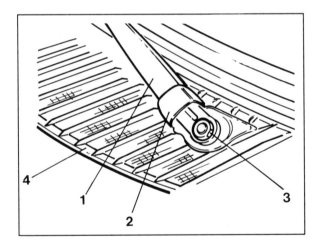

- Swing the wiper arm away from the windscreen thus loosening the lock of the plastic cover -2-. Slightly lift the cover, swing the wiper arm back again and lift the cover up totally.

- Unscrew the securing nut -3- and pull the wiper arm from the spindle.

- Open the bonnet, setting it vertically, see page 13.

- Disconnect the battery earth cable.

- Lift the cover on the left wiper spindle with a screwdriver and remove the nut underneath it.

- Remove the grille -4-, see page 208.

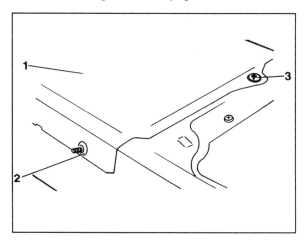

- Remove the centre trim -1- by pushing out the clip centre pins -2-. Remove the phillips screws -3- each on the left and right.

- Remove the drain tube from the right spindle.

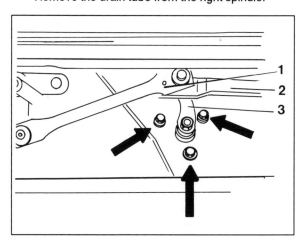

- Remove the connecting rods right -1- and left -2- from the motor crank.

- Disconnect the multi-pin plug from within the engine compartment. Unclip the wiring plug.

- Unbolt the wiper motor mounting bolts -arrows-and remove the wiper motor to the side.

- If the crank rod -3- is to be removed, first mark its position relative to the motor spindle with a marker.

Refitting

- Refit the wiper motor and tighten it.

- Refit the plug connection.

- Refit the connecting rods.

- Temporarily refit the wiper arms to check that the wiper system is working. Connect the battery earth cable for this. Now remove the wiper arm again.

- Refit the drain tube to the right spindle.

- Refit the centre trim and secure it with the 4 expanding rivets, and tighten screws.

- Refit the grille and tighten it to the wiper spindle with a nut on the left side.

- Close the bonnet, see page 13.

- Refit the wiper arms to the wiper spindles and tighten with one nut each.

- Swing down the cover of the wiper arm, by lifting the wiper arm slightly, if necessary.

Windscreen wiper - fault diagnosis

Wiping pattern	Cause	Solution
Streaky	Wiper rubber dirty	Clean rubber with a hard nylon brush and cleaning solution or spirits
	Frayed wiper lip, rubber torn or worn	Replace rubber
	Aged wiper rubber, torn surface	Replace rubber
Water remains in wiper field, forming as pearls	Windscreen dirty from remains oil or diesel.	Clean windscreen with clean cloth and a polish, grease-oil-silicone remover
Wiper blade wipes well on one side - other side badly,	Wiper rubber distorted	Replace wiper rubber
	Wiper arm distorted, blade is skew on screen	Carefully turn wiper blade, until correct vertical position is achieved
Areas not wiped	Wiper rubber pulled out of retainer Wiper blade no longer rests evenly on screen, spring rails or metal could be bent	Carefully refit rubber into retainer Replace wiper blade. This fault often happens if new blade not fitted according to instructions
	Pressure of wiper blade to windscreen too low	Lightly oil wiper arm joints and spring or fit new arm

• Wiping pattern of perfect wiper blades.

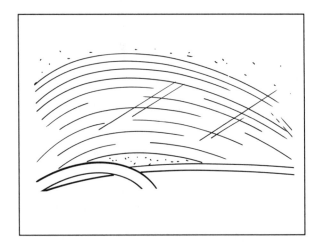

• Wiping pattern of worn rubber or dirty windscreen.

GENERAL VEHICLE CARE

Washing vehicle

- Wash a dirty vehicle as soon as possible.
- Use plenty of water.
- Use a soft sponge or very soft brush connected to the hose.
- Do not spray the paint with a strong jet, rather shower it down and let the dirt soak off.
- Wash off the soaked dirt from the top to the bottom with plenty of water.
- Rinse the sponge often.
- To dry, use a clean chamois.
- Use only good brand cleaners (if at all). Rinse the vehicle thoroughly to remove any remains of the cleaner.
- If cleaning solutions are often used, conserve more often.
- Never wash or dry the vehicle in the sun, as water marks are unavoidable.
- All interior rebates, flanges and joints of the doors, boot and bonnet should be cleaned thoroughly with a sponge, then rinsed and dried after each wash - even after automatic wash -.

Washing alone does not always remove tar or oil marks, insect and other dirt. Such dirt must be removed immediately or it could leave lasting marks on the paint.

Paint care

Wax / polish

The washed and dried paint should be treated with a wax as often as possible, to protect the surface from the weather by a pore sealing and water resistant wax layer.

The waxing must be repeated when the water no longer beads off the paint, but runs over larger surfaces. Regular waxing results in maintaining the original shine of the paint for a long time.

Another possibility of waxing is the wash/wax. A measuring cup of this is added to the washing water (after the worst dirt was first removed from the vehicle with clear water). Subsequently the bodywork need only be dried with a chamois. Wash/wax is only effective, however, if it is used with **every** wash, and the time between washes never exceeds two to three weeks.After the use of detergents (foam wash) the subsequent treatment with a wax is recommended (follow the instructions).

Caution:

Do not wax directly in the sun.

Polishing

Polishing the paint is only necessary if the paint does not look good due to the effects of dust, industrial fumes, sun and rain, and if a treatment with wax no longer brings out a shine.

Do not use strong chemical polishes, even if the first use of these achieves good results.

Before polishing, the vehicle must be thoroughly cleaned and dried. Then the instructions of the particular polish are to be followed exactly. The treatment should be carried out on small areas, to prevent the polish from drying out. After the use of some polishes, the vehicle must subsequently still be waxed. Do not polish in the direct sun! Matt painted areas must not be treated with polish or wax agents.

Light metal parts of the body need not be treated.

Tar stains

Tar stains eat into the paint in a short space of time, and can then not be removed again totally. Fresh tar stains can be removed with a cloth soaked with benzine. Normal fuel, petroleum or turpentine can also be used if necessary. A wax also does a good job in cleaning tar stains. When using this, there is no need to subsequently wash the area.

Insect marks

Insect remains have substances which can damage the paint if they are not removed soon. Once stuck, they cannot be removed with water or a sponge, but must be removed with a weak lukewarm soap or detergent solution. Special insect removers are also available.

Cement, lime and other building material splashes

Wash splashes of any building materials with a luke warm solution of neutral detergent. Rub only lightly or the paint will be scratched, then rinse thoroughly with clear water.

Conservation

To prevent corrosion on the vehicle front (e.g. side panels, side member or finishing metal) and the driving unit, the engine compartment including the parts of the brake system, front axle elements and steering, should be sprayed with a high quality conservation wax, specially after the vehicle was washed. **Caution:** Before washing the engine, cover the generator and brake fluid container with plastic covers. The bearings of the generator are water protected, but there is a danger, for example when cleaning with steam, that the bearings are drained by oil dissolving agents. The result could be bearing noises or faults due to defective bearings.

When using the vehicle, there could be odours, since the wax burns on the hot parts. After the wax application, lubricate all joints (fuel system) and hinges with a Molybdenum Sulphide paste.

Underfloor protection/cavity conservation

The complete floor system including the rear wheel housings are coated with PVC underfloor protection. The particularly endangered areas in the front mudguards are partly protected against stones by plastic covers. All cavities of the Mercedes are sprayed with a special wax. Before the cold season, the underfloor protection should be checked and restored. After the cold season an underfloor wash is recommended to remove any dirt particles.

Many of the cavities in which moisture (rain water, evaporating water) can collect are equipped with ventilation and water drain holes, so that the cavities can dry out. In the region of the vehicle chassis these holes are exposed to the road dirt and could clog up. This means that water collected in the cavities cannot drain or dry out. If the dirt is not totally removed there is a danger that these areas also cannot dry out. This could lead to rust formation from the inside out, which in time cannot be totally avoided by the corrosion protection.

Cleaning plastic parts

If normal washing is not enough, these parts should only be cleaned with special detergents and cleaning agents for plastic.

Window cleaning

Clean the windows with a clean, soft cloth. If the windows are very dirty, use spirits or liquid ammonia and luke warm water. When cleaning the windscreen, lift up the windscreen wipers.

There are silicones in some paint cleaning agents. If some of this gets onto the windscreen, smudge marks will form on the windscreen when it rains, thus impairing vision. These can be removed by a window cleaner with silicone remover. Pastes are normally more effective if there is a lot of silicone on the windows, in preference to liquid agents which are added to the windscreen wiper water.

When cleaning the windscreen, also clean the wiper blades.

Caution:

When using silicone containing agents to clean the paint, use separate cloths, brushes and sponges for the windows. When spraying the paint with cleaning agents containing silicone, cover the windows with cardboard or other covers.

Rubber gasket care

All rubber gaskets should be powdered with talcum from time to time, to preserve the flexibility and ease of movement of the window seals.

Squeaking or rattling noises developing at the gaskets can be removed by powdering the sealing and mating surfaces with talcum or painting with glycerine. Soft soap will also help.

Upholstery care

Textile upholstery

Vacuum the upholstery or brush it down with a fairly hard brush.

Treat oil or grease marks with stain remover mixed into water. Do not pour the stain remover straight onto the upholstery, as this will make marks. Work at the stain from the outside in.

Other stains can normally be removed with luke warm soapy water.

Patent leather upholstery

Patent leather upholstery has a dirt resistant surface. Special detergents are not needed. For removing normal dirt, the following cleaning methods will suffice:

- Soapy suds, made with water and a normal cleaning agent.
- Cleaning solution, made with water and a patent leather cleaner.

A soft brush facilitates the removal of the dirt from patterned surfaces.

The worst dirt should be removed immediately; with suitable cleaning agents, refer to the table below. Note that cleaning agents, particularly cleaners naphtha, spirits and thinners must not be poured on, but are to be applied with a damp cloth. This avoids the agent getting into the seams or upholstery. Do not allow the cleaning agent to soak into the surface, as this will damage the dirt resistant surface.

After each cleaning, the patent leather, and in particular the seams, must be dried properly.

Stain	Removal	
	Fresh stains	**Older stains**
Oil or grease	Remove with dry, soft cloth; turn cloth often. Do not make stain larger by moving back and forth. Remove remaining shiny patches with cloth soaked in cleaners naphtha. Dry properly with dry clean cloth.	Slightly dampen with benzine or spirits. Clean then dry with clean, soft cloth. Turn cloth often to avoid smudging of stain.
Shoe polish	Same as with oil or grease.	Turpentine can also be used in place of cleaners naphtha or spirits.
Imitation resin, nitro cellulose or grease.	Remove with soft, clean cloth as in oil	Rub with soft moist cloth soaked in turpentine Rub remaining stains with dampor fuel. Dry thoroughly. Nitro thinner for imitation resin and nitro paint, turpentine or fuel for oil paint.
Blood	Dab with cloth moistened with cold or luke warm water, without enlarging the stain by rubbing back and forth.	
Rust	Dab with soft cloth moistened with acidified water (1 part hydrochloric acid to 9 parts water). The acidified water must not get into gaps, corners or seams, as this will cause rust. After the treatment thoroughly wash area with water soaked cloth, to remove remains of acidified water. The used cloths should be destroyed.	

Putting vehicle on blocks

For many repair and maintenance jobs, the vehicle must be put on blocks. In a workshop the vehicle is generally lifted on a floor jack, it can however also be lifted with the vehicle jack or workshop jack. The vehicle must only be lifted on the jacking points.

For jobs under the vehicle it must, if not standing on a floor jack, be put onto four strong blocks. **Never carry out jobs under the vehicle if it is not properly secured.**

- Tools to lift the vehicle may only be attached to the following parts, since permanent marks to the vehicle can otherwise result.

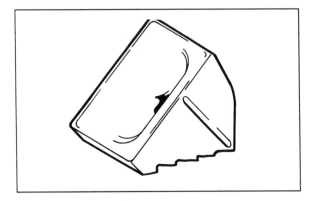

- Secure the wheels, which remain on the ground, from rolling with wedges. Do not depend on the hand brake, as this must be loosened for some repair jobs.

- Only put the vehicle on blocks on a flat, even surface.

Caution:

If the vehicle is to be put on blocks on a soft surface, additional broad planks must be placed under the trestle and jacks to distribute the weight onto a larger area.

- Damage to the chassis can be avoided by inserting a suitable piece of rubber or wood when lifting the vehicle.

- Support the vehicle with the trestles so that one leg stands out in each case.

- The vehicle may only be lifted when unladen.

Caution:

The vehicle must never be lifted or supported by engine or gearbox parts.

Lifting and blocking up points

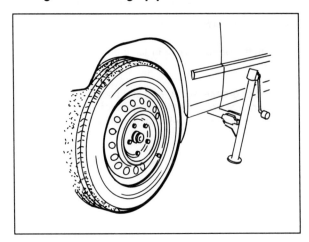

Vehicle jack

- Remove the rubber stopper from the appropriate jacking tube.

- Completely insert the spiggot of the jack into the jacking tube.

- Position the jack perpendicularly - even on a slope.

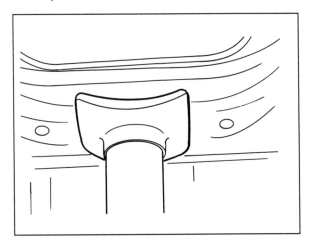

Workshop jack

- Lift on the chassis cross member of the front axle.

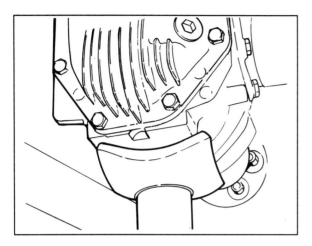

- Lift the vehicle at the back by the rear axle centre piece.

Caution:

Do not lift the vehicle by the semi-trailing arm.

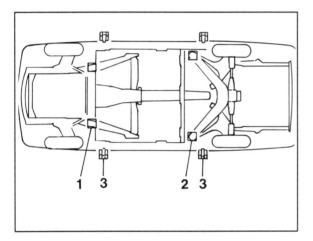

Floor jack

- The receptacles in the front -1- at the inner side members.

- The receptacles at the back -2- at the front bearings of the rear axle bracket. **Caution:** Do not load the centre of the support panels.

- The receptacles back and front -3- are under the jacking tubes of the vehicle jack.

SPECIAL TOOLS

The range of tools depends on the type of jobs one wants to carry out on the Mercedes. Besides the basic tools a torque wrench is definitely recommended.

Good quality tools are offered by Hazet. The table shows the tools with the Hazet part number. These tools are freely available in the trade.

Special tools

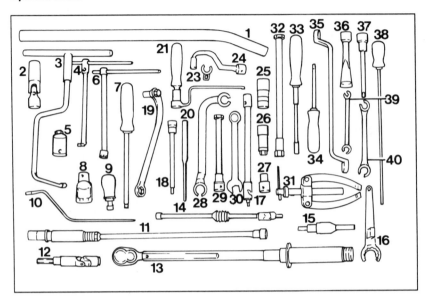

No.ILLTool	Special tools	Hazet No.
1	Straightening tool set	
2	Allen spanner socket set	2756
3	Angle spanner	
4	Spanner SW13 for preheating flange	4514
5	Spanner SW17 for idle shut-off valve (engine 102)	4512
6	Jointed stillson wrench	
7	Bolt remover	
8	Valve play adjusting spanner	2768-1
9	Punch for securing caps	4520
10	Valve play adjusting spanner	2769
11	Spark plug spanner	767 ACT-20
12	Hexagonal joint spanner	2755
13	Torque wrench 20-200 N.m.	6122-1CT
14	Double joint socket to tighten oil sump	2722
15	Inner remover 14,5-18,5mm	788-18
16	Supporting spanner for valve spring plate	2769-3
17	Hexagonal joint socket	2739
18	Hexagonal spanner SW10	986 Lg-10
19	Oil service spanner	2760
20	Pin driver	748 Lgb-4
21	Valve play adjusting spanner	2767

No.ILLTool	Special tools	Hazet No.
23	Open ring spanner	
24	Valve adjusting spanner 240D, 300D	329-2
25	Spark plug socket	880.MgT
26	Spark plug socket	900 MgT
27	Dual hexagonal socket900 Z-12	
28	Open dual ring spanner	
29	Screwdriver socket	
30	Ring open-end spanner	603-15
31	Puller	788-1437
32	Spark plug spanner	
33	Flexible hexagonal spanner for coolant pipe clips	426-7
34	Screwdriver for fuel injection system	837-T30
35	Dual ring spanner	630-21x23
36	Spanner for injection leads (Diesel)	4550-1
37	Multi-toothed spanner for cylinder head bolts	990 SLg-12
38	Screwdriver for CO adjustment (carburetor engine)	4517
39	Open ring spanner for brake lines	612 S-10x11
40	Open ring spanner for clutch cylinder	62-12x14

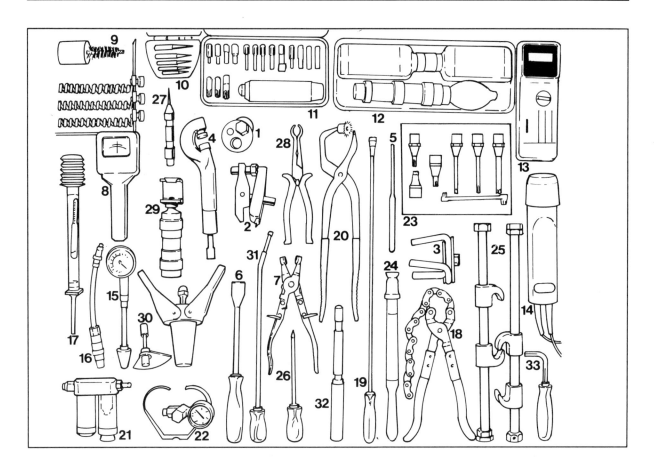

No.ILLTool	Special tools	Hazet No.
1	Stud remover	845
2	Ball joint remover	779
3	Oil filter key (not for W123)	–
4	Hydraulic nut breaker	846-22
5	Pin driver for securing pins	748 Lgb-4
6	Scraper to remove sealant remains from cylinder head and carburetor seals	824
7	Special pliers for spring strap clips	789-4
8	Battery tester	802-53
9	Terminal and clamp brush	802-4
10	Screw remover set	840/8
11	Impact driver	2272
12	Cylinder head seal testing device	801/3
13	Pocket engine tester	Bosch
14	Ignition timing stroboscope	Bosch
15	Compression pressure tester	–
16	Compressed air adaptor to Valve shaft seals	3428
17	Hydrometer	802-1
18	Chain exhaust pipe cutter	2182
19	Magnetic probe	1976

No.ILLTool	Special tools	Hazet No.
20	Brake spring pliers	797
21	Testing device for detecting leaks between combustion chamber and cooling system	809
22	Device for testing cooling system	808
23	Socket for hexagonal and other bolts	3090
24	Valve grinding tool	795
25	Spring tensioner	–
26	Remover for securing caps of carburetor	4518
27	Self impact punch	747
28	Spark plug pliers	1849
29	Impact removing device for windscreen wiper arms	1966-5
–	Impact removing device for disc brake pads	1966-1
30	Angle measuring device for throttle control adjustment of K-Jetronic	4502
31	Angled punch for exhaust dowels	4519-1
32	Clutch mandrel	–
33	Allen key, 7 mm	2110-7

Notes

SERVICE SCHEDULE W123

Lubrication

The lubrication service should be carried out every 10 000 km, or at least once a year.
In difficult driving conditions such as mainly city and cold starting, traffic, frequent mountain driving, trailer towing and dusty road conditions, carry out the service every 5 000 km.

- Engine: oil and filter change.
- Accelerator rods: lubricate, check for ease of movement and wear.

Carry out once yearly (preferably in spring):

- Brake fluid: renew.
- Bodywork: clean water outlets, check Bodywork for paint damage, touch up if necessary.
- Frame and loadbearing bodywork parts: check for damage and corrosion.
- Footwell and side boot recesses: check for water leakage and corrosion.
- Sliding window: clean and lightly lubricate the slide rails and slide jaws.
- Brake: check brake pad thickness.

Maintenance

Maintenance is to be carried out every 20 000 km or at least once every 2 years.

Engine and clutch

- Engine: change the oil. Replace full flow oil filter.
- Valves: test the play, adjust.
- Air filter: replace filter insert.
- Fanbelt: check tension and condition.
- Spark plugs: Replace.
- Cooling and heating system: check fluid level, check the concentration of frost protection. Visual checking for leaks and outer blockages of the radiator.
- Idle and CO content: check in warm engine.
- Accelerator rods: lubricate, check for ease of movement and wear.
- Exhaust system: check for damage.
- Engine: visual checking for oil leaks.
- Clutch: check hoses, leads and connections for leaks. Check brake fluid level.
- Carburetor: check float level.

Transmission, axle drive

- Rubber boots: check for leaks and damage.
- Transmission and rear axle: visual checking for leaks, check oil level.
- Level control: check fluid level, if necessary refill with hydraulic fluid.
- Automatic transmission: check fluid level, if necessary fill up with ATF.

Front axle and steering

- Tie rod ends: check play and secureness, check dust covers.
- Axle joint: check dust covers.
- Steering: check play, check bellow for leaks and damage. Tighten securing screws to correct torque.
- Power and mechanical steering: check fluid level, fill up with hydraulic fluid if necessary.

Body

- Door hinges, door locks: oil.
- External rear mirror: grease.
- Bonnet hinges, boot lock: grease with multi-purpose oil.
- Under floor protection and cavity wax: check.
- Safety belts: check for damage.

Brakes, tyres, wheels

- Brake system: lines, hoses and connections: check for leaks and damage.
- Disc brake: check the pad thickness of front and back brake pads.
- Hand brake: adjust.
- Tyres: check profile and tyre pressure; check tyres for wear and damage (including spare tyre).
- Wheels: tighten, check condition of rims (also inside), clean wheels and tighten to prescribed torque.

Electrical system

- All voltage consumers: check function.

- Lighting system: check, adjust headlights if necessary.

- Horn: check.

- Windscreen wipers: check wiper rubbers for wear.

- Windscreen wiper system: check function, check jet adjustment, fill up liquid, check headlight wiper system.

- Battery: check voltage and acid level.

Additionally every 60 000 km

- Fuel filter: replace.

- Automatic transmission: oil and filter change.

- Clutch disc: check wear.

- Hand brake: check brake cables for ease of movement, grease.

- Compression: check.

Every 3 years:

- Coolant: change.

WIRING DIAGRAMS

How to use the wiring diagram

The wiring diagram clearly shows the wiring in a vehicle. With it, it is easy to see the path of the current within a circuit.

All electrical wires are represented in the wiring diagram. The connecting wires go from the positive pole of the battery to the earth connection of the various consumers including the wiring parts in between.

The various wiring parts and consumers are indicated by numbers in the wiring diagram. In the index next to each wiring diagram, the corresponding descriptions of the electrical components are listed.

For components whose housing has direct contact to the earth, i.e. where there is no specific earth connection, these are indicated by a line on the wiring diagram, which ends with a short cross line.

The numbers at the connection points of the wires to the consumers, switches etc. correspond to the numbers of these components in the vehicle. The larger numbers indicate the pin description of the various circuits. The principal circuits are:

31 - Earth connection. The cables in the vehicle are generally brown.

30 - Wires always carry current, even when the ignition is off. The cables are normally red or red with a different coloured stripe.

15 - Wires only carry current when the ignition is on. The cables are usually green or black with coloured stripes.

Wire identification

Colours of the wires

bl = blue

br = brown

el = ivory

ge = yellow

gn = green

gr = grey

nf = natural colour

rs = pink

rt = red

sw = black

vi = violet

ws = white

Example:

Wire description 1,5 gr/rt	=	grey/red
Wire cross section 1,5	=	1,5 mm^2
Basic colour	=	grey
Identification colour rt	=	red

Wiring diagram Mercedes 200/230
Wiring diagram Mercedes 250/280
Wiring diagram Mercedes 200 since 7/80
Wiring diagram Mercedes 230E since 7/80

Due to a cost factor it is not possible to include the wiring diagrams of all the year models or types. Since the changes generally only occur in small detail areas, one can orientate oneself with the following wiring diagrams, even if the vehicle is from a different year.

Notes

1 Headlight unit, left:
  a High beam
  b Low beam
  c Standing/parking light
  d Fog light
  e Turn signal light
2 Brake fluid indicator light switch
3 Contact sensor, brake pads, front, left
4 Contact sensor, brake pads, front, right
5 Instrument cluster
  a Turn signal indicator light left
  b High beam indicator light
  c Coolant temperature gauge
  d Fuel gauge
  e Fuel reserve warning light
  f Charge indicator
  g Brake pad wear indicator light
  h Brake fluid and parking brake indicator light
  i Instrument lights
  j Rheostat, instrument lights
  k Warning buzzer
  l Turn signal indicator light right
  m Electronic clock
6 Cigarette lighter with ashtray illumination
7 Radio*
8 Headlight unit, right
  a High beam
  b Low beam
  c Standing/parking light
  d Fog light
  e Turn signal light
9 Heater coil, automatic choke
10 Idle fuel cut-out valve
11 Automatic antenna*
12 Parking brake indicator light switch
13 Temperature sensor, coolant
14 Warning buzzer contact
15 Front dome light with switch
16 Door contact switch, front, left
17 Door contact switch, front right
18 Horn
19 Warning flasher switch
20 Glove compartment light switch
21 Glove compartment light
22 Fusebox
23 Thermal time switch, pull-down

24 Idle fuel cut-out valve
25 Relay I, electric windows*
26 Relay II, electric windows*
27 Door contact switch, electric windows*
28 Combination switch
  a Turn signal switch
  b Headlight flasher switch
  c Dip switch
  d Washer switch
  e Switch for wipe speed
  I Wipe delay
  II Slow wipe
  III Fast wipe
29 Horn switch
30 Wiper motor
31 Timer delay wipe
32 Ignition starter switch
33 Rotary light switch
34 Sliding roof motor*
35 Switch, electrically operated sliding roof*
36 Solenoid valve, automatic transmission*
37 Kick-down switch*
38 Starter-lockout and back-up light switch
39 Relay, air conditioner II*
40 Relay, air conditioner I*
41 Blower switch with light
42 Brake light switch
43 Washer pump
44 Wiper motor, headlight, left*
45 Wiper motor, headlight, right*
46 Relay headlight cleaning system*
47 Washer pump, headlights*
48 Distributor*
49 Spark plugs
50 Ignition coil
51 Illumination
  a Air deflector control
  b Heater switch
  c Switch
52 Temperature switch 62° C dehydrator, air conditioner*
53 Temperature switch 100° C
54 Auxiliary fan*
55 Relay auxiliary fan
56 Pressure switch, refrigerant compressor*
57 Solenoid clutch, refrigerant compressor*

58 Temperature control with lighting air conditioner*
59 Pre-resistance, blower motor
60 Blower motor
61 Electric windows motor, back left*
62 Switch, window, back left*
63 Switch cluster, electric windows*
  a Switch, window, rear left
  b Safety switch
  c Switch, window, front left
  d Switch, window, front right
  e Switch, window, rear right
64 Electric window motor, front left*
65 Pre-resistance 1,8 ohm
66 Time-lag relay, heated rear window
67 Switch, heated rear window
68 Starter
69 Battery
70 Alternator with regulator
71 Door contact switch, rear left*
72 Rear dome light switch*
73 Door contact switch, rear left*
74 Rear dome light*
75 Plug connection, cable to rear components
76 Boot light
77 TDC transmitter
78 Electric windows motor, rear right*
79 Diagnosis plug socket
80 Fuel gauge sending unit
81 Electric window motor, rear right*
82 Switch, window, rear, right*
83 Tail light unit, left:
  a Turn signal light
  b Tail/parking light
  c Reversing light
  d Brake light
  e fog tail light
84 Number plate light
85 Heated rear window*
86 Lighting, shift gate*
87 Tail light unit, right
  a Turn signal light
  b Tail/parking light
  c Reversing light
  d Brake light

* Special equipment

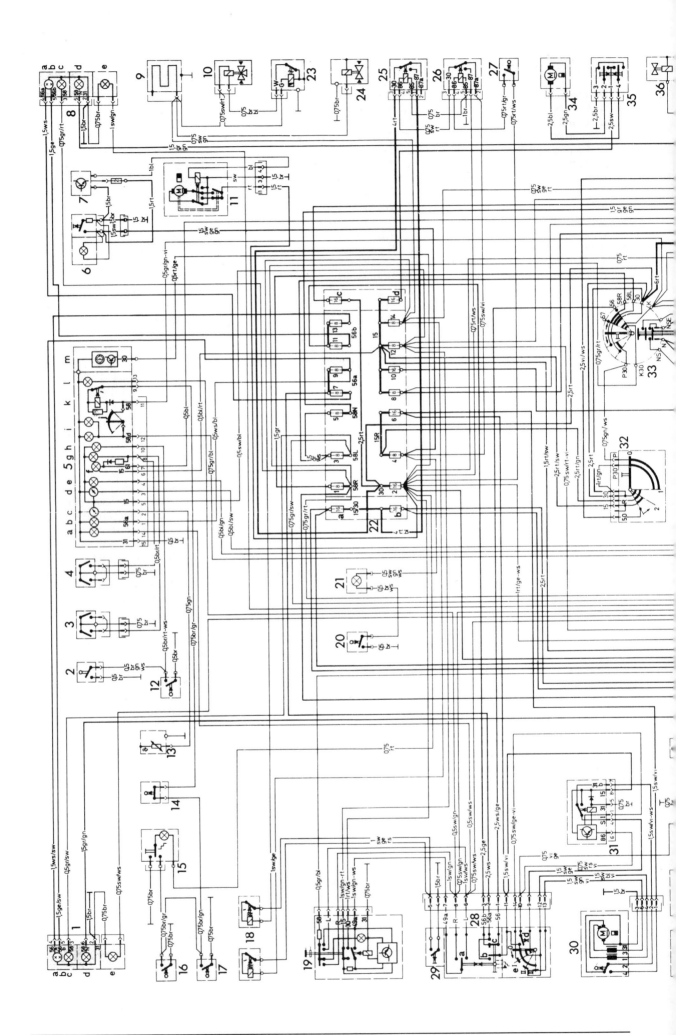

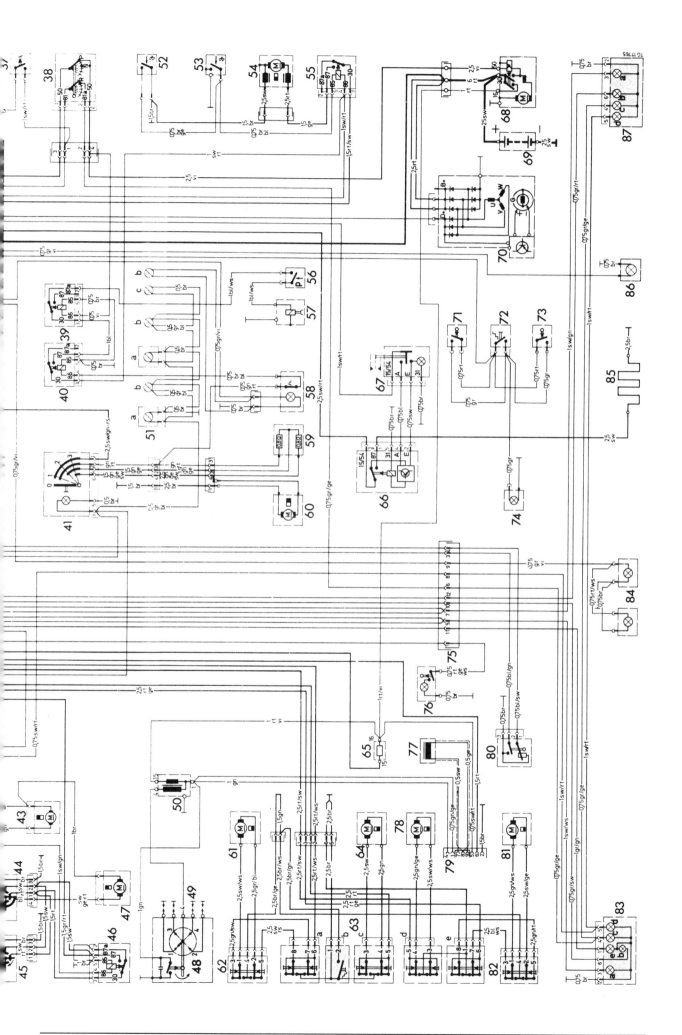

Notes

1 Headlight unit, left:
  a High beam
  b Low beam
  c Standing/parking light
  d Fog light
  e Turn signal light
2 Brake fluid indicator light switch
3 Contact sensor, brake pads, front, left
4 Contact sensor, brake pads, front, right
5 Instrument cluster
  a Turn signal indicator light left
  b High beam indicator light
  c Coolant temperature gauge
  d Fuel gauge
  e Fuel reserve warning light
  f Charge indicator
  g Brake pad wear indicator light
  h Brake fluid and parking brake indicator light
  i Instrument lights
  j Rheostat, instrument lights
  k Warning buzzer
  l Turn signal indicator light right
  m Electronic clock
6 Cigarette lighter with ashtray illumination
7 Radio*
8 Headlight unit, right
  a High beam
  b Low beam
  c Standing/parking light
  d Fog light
  e Turn signal light
9 Heater coil, automatic choke
10 Idle fuel cut-out valve
11 Automatic antenna*
12 Parking brake indicator light switch
13 Temperature sensor, coolant
14 Warning buzzer contact
15 Front dome light with switch
16 Door contact switch, front, left
17 Door contact switch, front right
18 Horn
19 Sensor cruise control*
20 Amplifier, cruise control*
21 Throttle actuator*
22 Warning flasher switch
23 Glove compartment light switch
24 Glove compartment light
25 Fusebox
26 Idle fuel cut-out valve I
27 Float chamber vent
28 Relay I, electric windows*
29 Relay II, electric windows*
30 Door contact switch, electric windows*

31 Switch, cruise control*
  A Off
  V Decel/set
  SP Resume
  B Accel/set
32 Combination switch
  a Turn signal switch
  b Headlight flasher switch
  c Dip switch
  d Washer switch
  e Switch for wiper speed
  I Wipe delay
  II Slow wipe
  III Fast wipe
33 Switch, horn
34 Wiper motor
35 Timer delay wipe
36 Ignition starter switch
37 Rotary light switch
38 Sliding roof motor*
39 Switch, electrically operated sliding roof*
40 Solenoid, automatic transmission*
41 Kick-down switch*
42 Starter-lockout and back-up light switch
43 Relay, air conditioner II*
44 Relay, air conditioner I*
45 Blower switch with light
46 Brake light switch
47 Washer pump*
48 Wiper motor, headlight, left*
49 Wiper motor, headlight, right*
50 Relay headlight cleaning system*
51 Washer pump, headlights*
52 Switching device, transistor ignition
53 Ignition distributor, breakerless
54 Spark plugs
55 Ignition coil
56 Illumination
  a Air deflector control
  b Heater switch
  c Switch
57 Cable connector (only 280,280C)
58 Temperature switch 60° C
59 Temperature switch 100° C
60 Auxiliary fan*
61 Relay auxiliary fan*
62 Solenoid clutch, refrigerant compressor*
63 Solenoid clutch, refrigerant
64 Temperature control with lighting, air conditioner*
65 Pre-resistance, blower motor
66 Blower motor
67 Pre-resistance 0,6 ohm
68 Electric window motor, rear left*
69 Switch, window, rear left*

70 Switch cluster, electric windows*
  a Switch, window, rear left
  b Safety switch
  c Switch, window, front left
  d Switch, window, front right
  e Switch window, rear right
71 Electric window motor, front left*
72 Pre-resistance 0,4 ohm
73 Time-lag relay, heated rear window*
74 Switch, heated rear window*
75 Starter
76 Battery
77 Alternator with regulator*
78 Door contact switch, rear right*
79 Rear dome light switch*
80 Door contact switch, rear left*
81 Rear dome light*
82 Plug connection, cable to rear components
83 Boot light
84 TDC transmitter
85 Fuel gauge sending unit
86 Electric window motor, front right*
87 Diagnostic plug socket
88 Electric window motor, rear right*
89 Switch, window, rear right*
90 Tail light unit, left:
  a Turn signal light
  b Tail/parking light
  c Reversing light
  d Brake light
  e Rear fog light
91 Number plate light
92 Heated rear window*
93 Illumination shift gate
94 Tail light unit, right
  a Turn signal light
  b Tail/parking light
  c Reversing light
  d Brake light

* Special equipment

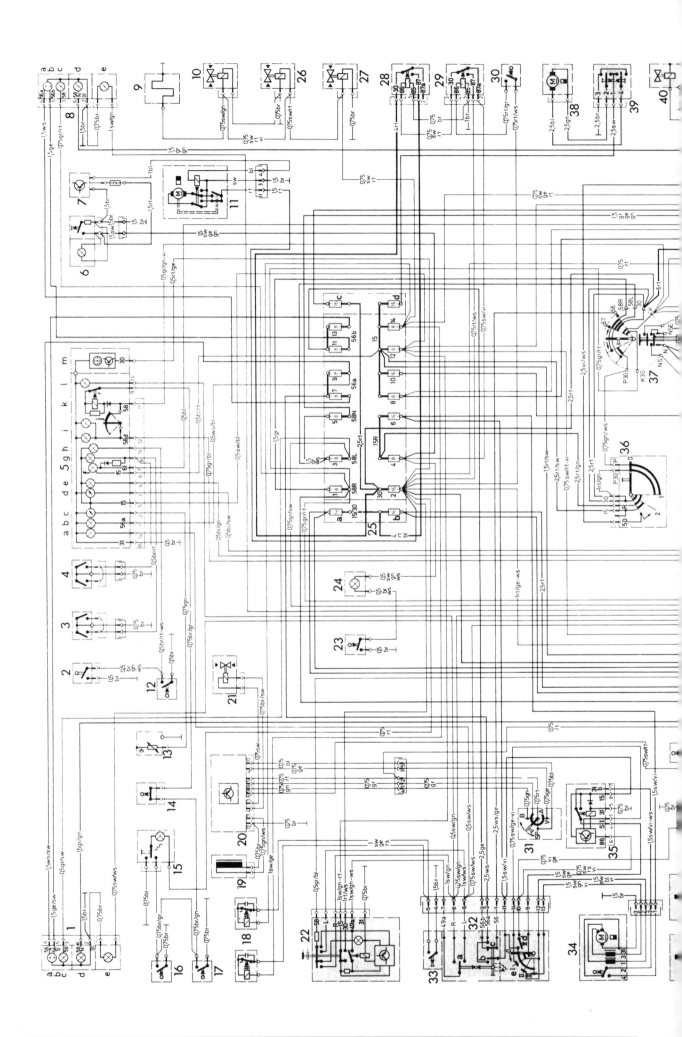

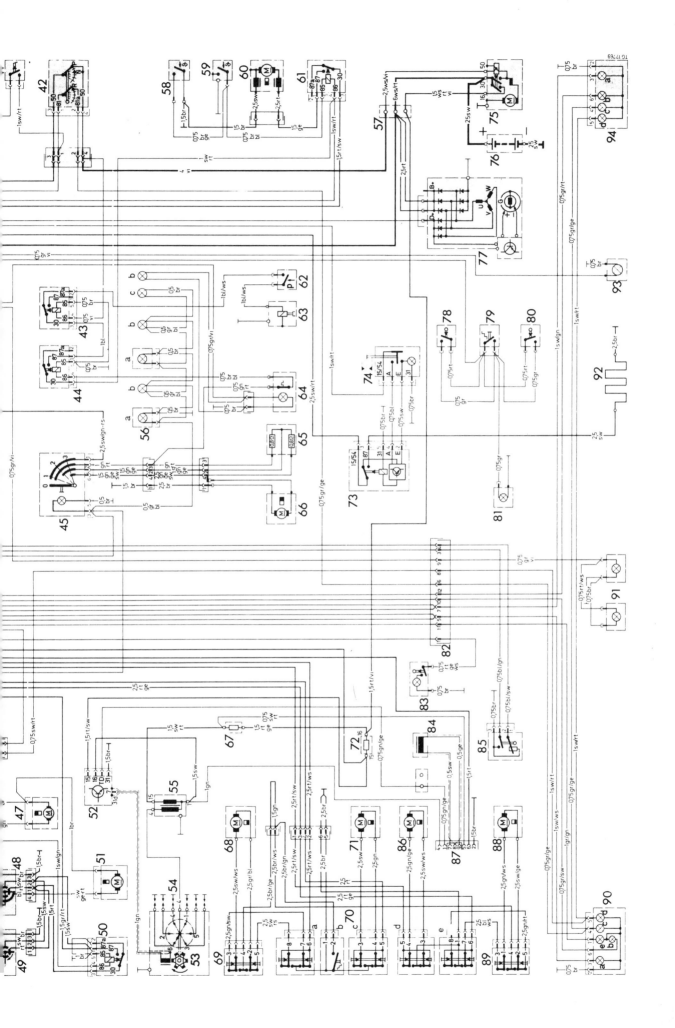

Notes

1 Headlight unit, left:
  a High beam
  c Standing/parking light
  d Fog light
  e Turn signal light
2 Brake fluid indicator light switch
3 Contact sensor, brake pads, front, left
4 Contact sensor, brake pads, front, right
5 Instrument cluster
  a Turn signal indicator light left
  b High beam indicator light
  c Coolant temperature gauge
  d Fuel gauge
  e Fuel reserve warning light
  f Charge indicator
  g Brake pad wear indicator light
  h Brake fluid and parking brake indicator light
  i Instrument lights
  j Rheostat, instrument lights
  k Warning buzzer
  l Turn signal indicator light right
  m Electronic clock
6 Cigarette lighter with ashtray illumination
7 Radio*
8 Headlight unit, right, front
  a High beam
  b Low beam
  c Standing/parking light
  d Fog light
  e Turn signal light
10 Switch, parking brake control
11 Temperature sensor, coolant
12 Warning buzzer contact
13 Front dome light with switch
14 Door contact switch, front left
15 Door contact switch, front right
16 Timing device cruise control*
17 Transmitter cruise control*
18 Switch, cruise control*
  A Off
  V Decel/set
  SP Resume
  B Accel/set
19 Amplifier, cruise control
20 Glove compartment light switch
21 Glove compartment light
22 Induction manifold heaterd
23 Heater coil warm-up control
24 Relay induction manifold
25 Temperature switch 40° C
26 Fusebox, induction manifold heater
27 Idle fuel cut-out valve
28 Relay, idle fuel cut-out valve engine speed limit
29 Relay I, electric windows
30 Relay II, electric windows

31 Fusebox
32 Brake light switch
33 Horn
34 Relay, turn signal and warning flasher
35 Warning flasher switch
36 Switch, horn
37 Combination switch:
  a Turn signal switch
  b Headlight flasher switch
  c Dip switch
  d Washer switch
  e Switch for wiper speed:
    I Wipe delay
    II Slow wipe
    III Fast wipe
38 Wiper motor
39 Timer delay wipe
40 Ignition starter switch
41 Rotary light switch
42 Door contact switch, electric wind.*
43 Sliding roof motor*
44 Switch, electrically operated sliding roof*
45 Solenoid valve, automatic transmission*
46 Kick-down switch*
47 Starter lockout and back-up light switch*
48 Cross-over valve, fresh air/ circulating air*
49 Temperature sensor, air conditioner*
50 Temperature control, air conditioner*
51 Blower switch with light
52 Transistor ignition switching device
53 Washer pump
54 Wiper motor, headlight, left*
55 Wiper motor, headlight, right*
56 Relay, headlight cleaning system*
57 Washer pump, headlights*
58 Switch, window, rear left*
59 Electric window motor, rear left*
60 Distributor, breakerless
61 Spark plugs
62 Ignition coil
63 Cable connector, pin 58d*
64 Illumination:
  a Air deflector control
  b Heater control
  c Switch
  Temperature control, air conditioner*
65 Relay, air conditioner
66 Temperature switch 52° C dehydrator*
67 Temperature switch 100° C
68 Auxiliary fan*
69 Solenoid clutch, motor fan*
70 Pressure switch refrigerant compressor in 2,6 bar, out 2,0 bar
71 Solenoid clutch, refrigerant compressor*
72 Cross-over valve engine speed stabilisation*

73 Pre-resistance, blower motor
74 Blower motor
75 Automatic antenna*
76 Switch cluster, electric windows*
  a Switch, window, rear left
  b Safety switch
  c Switch, window, front left
  d Switch, window, front right
  e Switch, window, rear right
77 Electric window motor, front left*
78 Electric window motor, front right*
79 Diagnostic plug socket
80 TDC transmitter
81 Plug connection to rear
82 Time-lag relay, heated rear window
83 Switch, heated rear window
84 Dual contact relay, auxiliary fan/ Solenoid clutch motor fan*
85 Starter
86 Battery
87 Alternator with regulator
88 Door contact switch rear right*
89 Rear dome light switch*
90 Door contact switch, rear right*
91 Rear dome light*
92 Fuel gauge sending unit
93 Boot light
94 Electric window motor, rear right*
95 Switch, window, rear right*
96 Tail light unit, left:
  a Turn signal light
  b Tail/parking light
  c Reversing light
  d Brake light
  e Rear fog light
97 Heated rear window
98 Number plate light
99 Illumination shif gate*
100 Tail light unit, right
  a Tail signal light
  b Tail/parking light
  c Reversing light
  d Brake light

Special equipment

Earth connections
M1 Main earth (behind instrument cluster)
M2 Earth front right (near headlamp unit)

M3 Earth wheelhouse, front, left

M4 Earth dome lamp, front
M5 Earth engine
M6 Earth trunk, wheelhouse, left
M7 Earth trunk, wheelhouse, right

Example:
M1 (60)
M1 = Earth connection
(60)= Position number of component

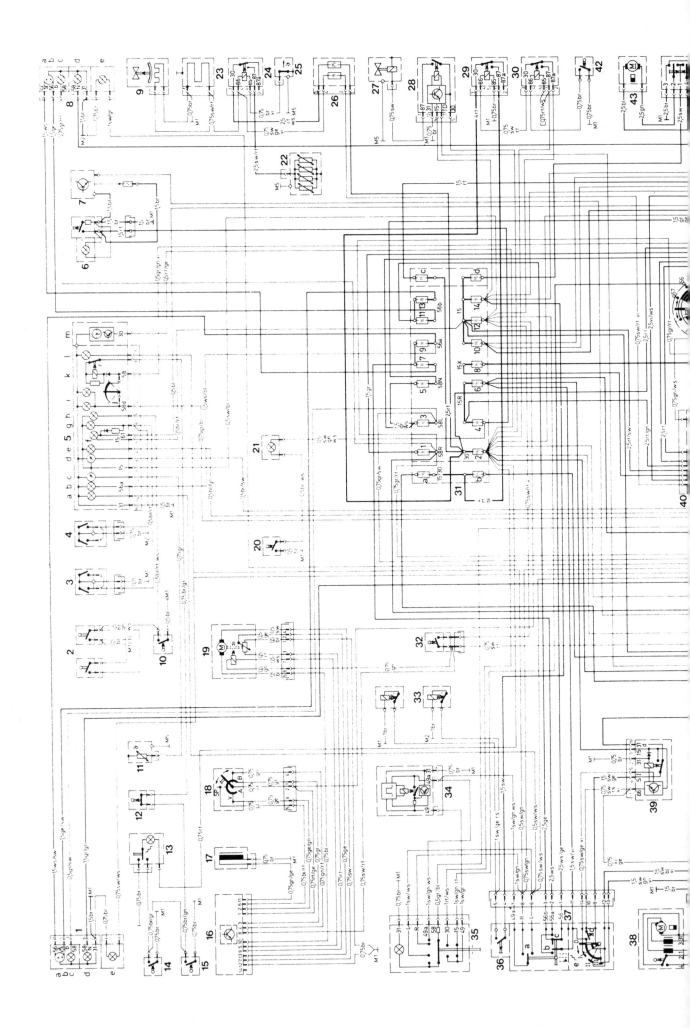

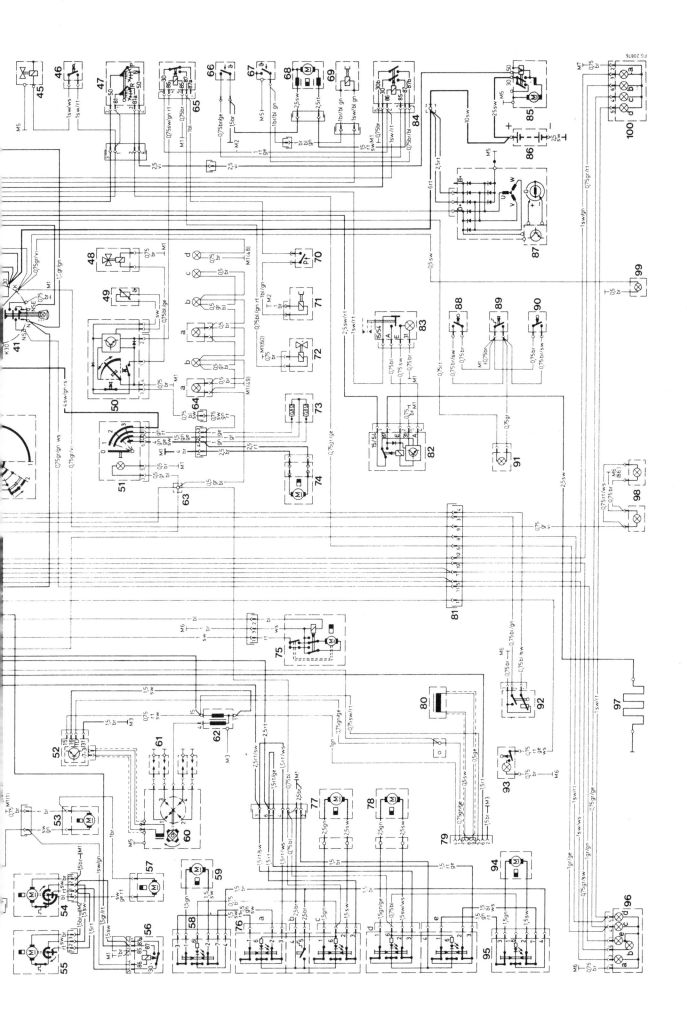

Notes

1 Headlight unit, left:
  a High beam
  b Low beam
  c Standing/parking light
  d Fog light
  e Turn signal light
2 Horn
3 Brake fluid indicator light switch
4 Contact sensor, brake pads, front left
5 Contact sensor, brake pads, front right
6 Instrument cluster
  a Turn signal indicator light, left
  b High beam indicator light
  c Coolant temperature guage
  d Fuel guage
  e Fuel reserve warning light
  f Charge indicator
  g Brake pad wear indicator light
  h Brake fluid and parking brake indicator light
  i Instrument lights
  j Rheostat, instrument lights
  k Warning buzzer
  l Turn signal indicator light right
  m Electronic clock

7 Relay cross-over valve engine speed stabilising*
  (only in automatic transmission and air conditioner)

8 Cigarette lighter with ashtray illumination
9 Radio
10 Headlight unit, right, front
  a High beam
  b Low beam
  c Standing/parking light
  d Fog light
  e Turn signal light
11 Thermo time switch
12 Starter valve
13 Switch, parking brake control
14 Temperature sensor, coolant
15 Warning buzzer contact
16 Front dome lamp switch
17 Door contact switch, front left
18 Door contact switch, front right
19 Timing device, Tempomat*
20 Amplifier, cruise control
21 Switch cruise control
  A Off
  V Decel/set
  SP Resume
  B Accel/set
22 Adjustment cruise control
23 Glove compartment light switch
24 Heater coil, warm-up control
25 Glove compartment light
27 Cross-over thrust cut-out
28 Micro-switch thrust cut-out
29 Relay, fuel pump with electronic engine speed limit/thermo regulator

30 Fuel pump
31 Relay I window lift*
32 Relay II, window lift*
33 Fusebox
34 Brake light switch
35 Relay, turn signal/warning flasher
36 Warning flasher light switch
37 Switch, horn
38 Combination switch
  a Turn signal light switch
  b Passing light switch
  c Dimmer switch
  d Washer switch
  e Switch for wiper speed:
    I Wipe delay
    II Slow wipe
    III Fast wipe
39 Wiper motor
40 Timer delay wipe
41 Ignition starter switch
42 Rotary light switch
43 Door contact switch, window lifts*
44 Sliding roof motor*
45 Switch, electrical sliding roof*
46 Solenoid valve, automatic transmission *
47 Kick-down switch*
48 Starter lockout/back-up back-up light switch
49 Cross-over valve, main air flap
50 Temperature sensor, air conditioner*
52 Blower switch with light
53 Transistor ignition, switching device
54 Washer pumpeRear fog light
55 Wiper motor, headlight, left*
56 Wiper motor, headlight, right*
57 Relay, headlight cleaning system*
58 Washer pump, headlights*
59 Distributor, no contact
60 Spark plugs
61 Ignition coil
62 Cable connector, terminal 58d
63 Illumination:
  a Air deflector control*
  b Heater control*
  c Switch*
  d Temperature control, air air conditioner*
64 Relay, air conditioner*
65 Temperature switch 52°C dehydrator
66 Temperature switch 100° C
67 Auxiliary fan*
68 Solenoid clutch, motor fan
69 Pressure switch, refrigerant compressor*, in 2,6 bar, out 2,0 bar
70 Solenoid clutch, refrigerant compressor*
71 Cross-over valve, engine speed stabilisation*
72 Pre-resistance, blower motor
73 Blower motor
74 Automatic antenna*
75 Window lift motor, rear left*
76 Switch, window, rear left*
77 Switch cluster, window lifts

77 Switch cluster, window lifts*
  a Switch, window, rear left
  b Switch, window, front left
  c Switch, window, front left
  d Switch, window, front right
  e Switch, window, rear right
78 Window lift motor, front left*
79 Window lift motor, front right*
80 Diagnostic plug socket
81 Cable connector, retainer TD
82 TDC transmitter
83 Plug connection to rear
84 Time-lag relay, heated rear window
85 Switch, heated rear window
86 Dual contact relay, air conditioner*
87 Starter
88 Battery
89 Alternator with electric regulator
90 Door contact switch, rear left[1])
91 Rear dome light switch*
92 Door contact switch, rear right[1])
93 Rear dome light*
94 Fuel guage sending unit
95 Boot light
96 Window lift motor, rear right*
97 Switch, window, rear right[&]

98 Tail light unit, left:
  a Turn signal light
  b Tail/parking light
  c Reversing light
  d Brake light

99 Number plate light
100 Heated rear window
101 Illumination shift gate*
102 Tail light unit, right
  a Tail sign light
  b Tail/parking light
  c Reversing light
  d Brake light

Special equipment
[1]) Not in coupe

Earth connections

M1 Main earth (behind instrument cluster
M2 Earth, front right (near headlamp unit)
M3 Earth, wheelhouse, front left (ignition coil)
M4 Earth, dome lamp, front
M5 Earth, engine
M6 Earth, trunk, wheelhouse, left
M7 Earth, trunk, wheelhouse, right

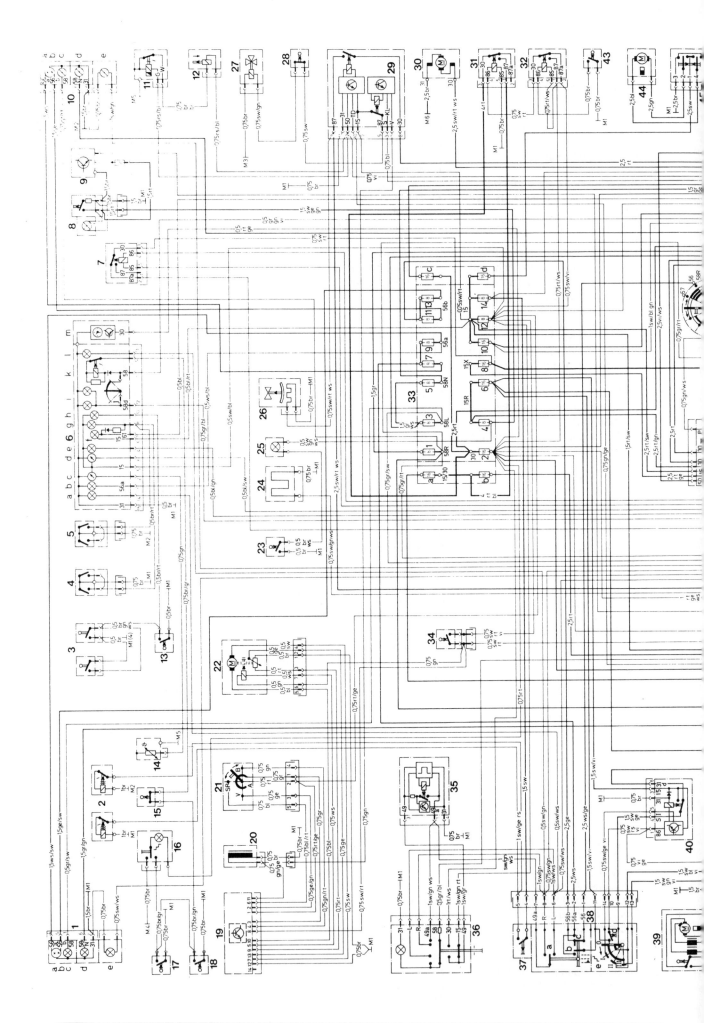

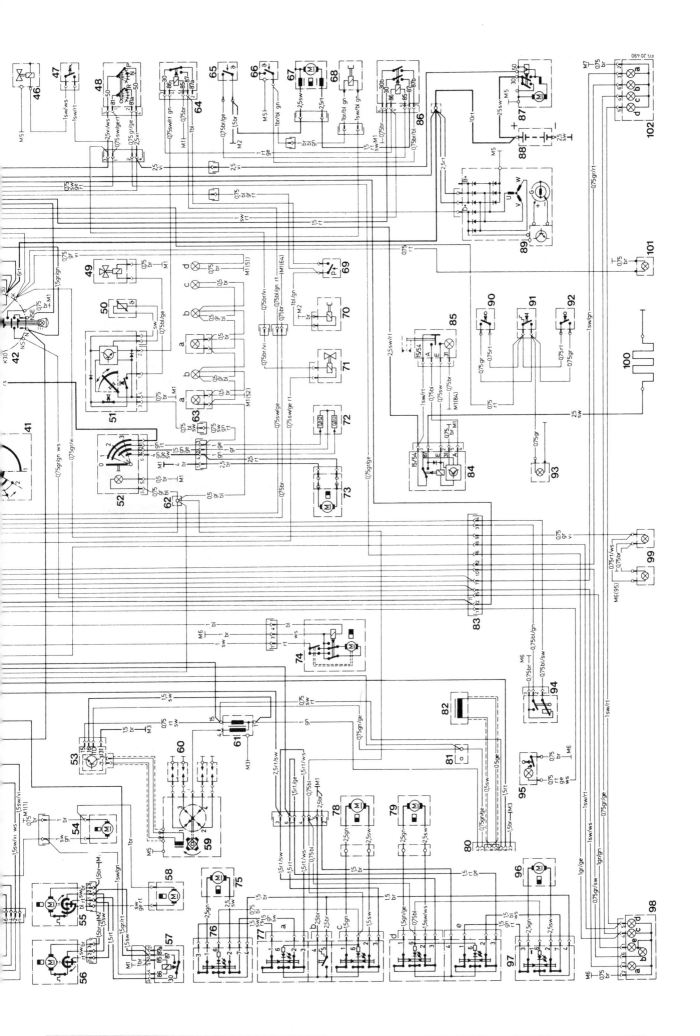

Further reading on
MERCEDES-BENZ

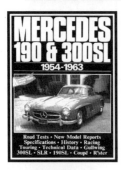

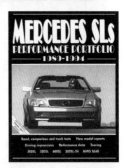

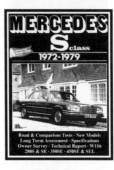

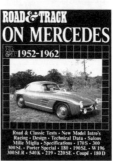

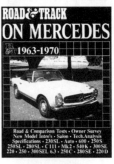

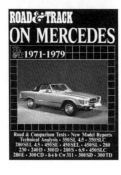

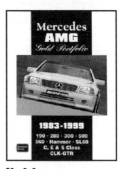

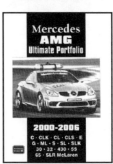

Also Available:

Owners Workshop Manual Mercedes-Benz 190 & 200 1959-1968	Owners Workshop Manual Mercedes-Benz 230 1963-1968	Owners Workshop Manual Mercedes-Benz 250 1968-1972	Owners Workshop Manual Mercedes-Benz Sprinter 2000-2006	Owners Workshop Manual Mercedes-Benz W124 1985-1995

www.brooklands-books.com

**From specialist booksellers or, in case of difficulty,
direct from the distributors:**

Brooklands Books Ltd., P.O. Box 146, Cobham, Surrey, KT11 1LG, England. Phone: 01932 865051
E-mail us at info@brooklands-books.com or visit our website www.brooklands-books.com
Brooklands Books Australia, 3/37-39 Green Street, Banksmeadow, NSW 2019, Australia. Phone: 2 9695 7055
CarTech, 39966 Grand Avenue, North Branch, MN 55056, USA. Phone: 800 551 4754 & 651 277 1200
Motorbooks International, P.O. Box 1, Osceola, Wisconsin 54020, USA. Phone: 800 826 6600 & 715 294 3345